Robert Ashton was born in Chester in 1924. He served in the Royal Air Force during the war and is a graduate of London University where he took a first in 1949 and a doctorate in 1953. He worked as a postgraduate under the late Professor R. H. Tawney and was a contributor to the *Festschrift* for Tawney which was published in 1961, as well as to the *Festschrift* for another of his mentors, F. J. Fisher, published in 1976. He taught Economic History at Nottingham University from 1952 to 1962. In 1962–3 he taught History at the University of California, Berkeley, and since 1963 he has been Professor of English History at the University of East Anglia. In 1973–4 he was a Visiting Fellow of All Souls College, Oxford, and in May 1982 was James Ford Special Lecturer at Oxford.

His publications include a great many articles and the following books: *The Crown and the Money Market 1603–1640* (1960); *James I by His Contemporaries* (1969); *The English Civil War: Conservatism and Revolution 1603–1649* (1978) and *The City and the Court 1603–1643* (1979). He is at present working on a detailed history of the Second Civil War and the developments leading up to it.

ROBERT ASHTON

Reformation and Revolution 1558–1660

Granada Publishing

Paladin Books
Granada Publishing Ltd
8 Grafton Street, London W1X 3LA

Published by Paladin Books 1985

First published in Great Britain by
Granada Publishing 1984

ISBN 0-586-08449-5

Reproduced, printed and bound in Great Britain by
Hazell Watson & Viney Limited,
Aylesbury, Bucks

THE PALADIN HISTORY OF ENGLAND

General Editor: Lord Blake
Advisory Editor: Cameron Hazlehurst

Other titles in this series will include:

The Formation of England 550–1042 *by* H P R Finberg
Peace, Print and Protestantism 1450–1558 *by* C S L Davies
England Transformed 1760–1865 *by* Charles Stuart
The Crisis of Imperialism 1865–1915 *by* Richard Shannon
The Decline of Power 1915–1964 *by* Robert Blake

To my wife

FOREWORD

by Robert Blake

History does not consist of a body of received opinion handed down by authority from the historiographical equivalent of the heights of Mount Sinai. It is a subject full of vigour, controversy, life – and sometimes strife. One of the purposes of the Paladin History of England is to convey not only what the authors believe to have happened but also why; to discuss evidence as well as facts; to give an idea and an evaluation of the controversies which surround so many episodes and interpretations of the past.

The last twenty years have seen important changes in the approach to history and to historical questions. There has also been much painstaking research which throws new light on old problems and brings new problems into the field of discussion. Little of all this has so far got through to the general reader because it has been, naturally, confined to specialist journals and monographs. A real need exists for a series of volumes to inform the wide public interested in the history of England, and this is what the Paladin volumes are intended to meet.

All history is in one sense contemporary history. These volumes inevitably and rightly reflect to some extent the outlook of those who, whatever their own age, are writing in the 1970s. But there are in any decade a wide variety of attitudes and schools of thought. The authors of this series are not chosen to represent a particular body of doctrine; conservative, liberal, Marxist – or whatever. They are scholars who are deeply involved in the historical questions of their particular fields, and who believe that it is possible to put across something of the challenges, puzzles and excitements of their theme to a large audience in a form which is readable, intelligible and concise.

All historical writing must in some measure be arbitrary as to dates and selective as to area. The dates chosen in this series do not depart far from convention but perhaps just enough to encourage both author and reader to take a fresh view. The decision to make this a history of England, rather than Britain, is quite deliberate. It does not mean omission of the important repercussions of events in Scotland, Ireland, Wales or the countries which later constituted the Empire and the Commonwealth; rather a recognition that, whether for good or ill, the English have been the dominant nation in what Tennyson called 'our rough island-story', and that a widening of the scope would lead to diffuseness and confusion.

Historical writing also has to be selective as to themes. Each author uses his own judgment here, but, although politics, ideas, art and literature must always be central features in any work of general history, economic background, social structure, demography, scientific and technical developments are no less important and must be given proper weight.

All sorts of reasons can be given for reading history, but the best of them has always seemed to me sheer pleasure. It is my hope as editor of this series that this enjoyment will be communicated to a large number of people who might otherwise perhaps have never experienced it.

CONTENTS

ACKNOWLEDGEMENTS

I must first express my deep gratitude to the General Editor of the Paladin History, Lord Blake, both for his encouragement and for his patience. It is only necessary to recall that the volume written by my former colleague Richard Shannon was published in 1974 to appreciate the need for editorial forbearance over this book. The delays in producing it were partly due to my over-optimism about deadlines, and the prior need to complete two other books for which I had earlier contracted; no less responsible were the great difficulties which I experienced in compressing a history of what is one of the most written about and hotly disputed periods of English history into the required length. The first drafts of each chapter had to be subjected to drastic revision and – more agonizingly – ruthless reduction, and my greatest problem has been not what to put in but what to leave out. In this process of production my main debts are three. The first is to my much-enduring secretary Mrs Vera Durell, who has by now become all too well acquainted with my crabbed hand and tendency to produce a succession of heavily amended drafts without prior warning and at the most inconvenient times. Her quiet efficiency and willingness has, as with my earlier books, been a factor which it is all too easy to take for granted. Secondly I owe an enormous debt to the encouragement and forbearance which I have as always received from my wife, and of which the dedication of this book is a totally inadequate recognition. Finally, for valuable criticism of and suggestions about a number of my early draft chapters I am deeply indebted to my colleagues Professor J. R. Jones, Dr A. Hassell Smith and Mr Roger Thompson. For the defects of this final version I alone am responsible.

R.A.

INTRODUCTION

The vertical fragmentation of historical studies which is one of the most characteristic features of twentieth century historiography has undeniably been responsible for many spectacular advances in historical knowledge. But the concentration of different sorts of historian on different sorts of history – most of them with their appropriate analytical tools derived from the appropriate social science – carries with it a corresponding danger that, in their concern with economic, social, constitutional, religious, cultural, military, or any one of the numerous other sub-disciplines into which historical studies have become divided, history seen as a whole will take a back seat. My original intention was that this book should be an essay, however imperfect, in integrated history and that I would strive to bring together some of these disparate historical strands. While not abandoning this plan, I have, however, yielded to the extent of including two introductory chapters dealing with economic and social themes which did not fit easily into the chronological (rather than topical or analytical) framework which I saw as the best means of achieving some degree of integration in the main body of the book. Here I have deliberately avoided devoting separate analytical chapters to the exclusive treatment of the constitutional, political, social, economic or other aspects of the period, and, while not running these together, have endeavoured to stress the connection between them. Thus the first of these chapters on the

Elizabethan settlement argues that what was settled in the opening years of this period was in fact a great deal more than the re-establishment of a Protestant church, within which terms the settlement is normally construed; that the settlement as a whole can be characterized as a massive conservative reconstruction, even if this description fits its religious aspect less comfortably than it does its social and economic. Much of the rest of the book could be described as a study of the strains and pressures to which this settlement was subjected, leading to its ultimate breakdown and the search for something permanent with which to replace it, culminating in the Restoration of 1660.

But in seeking to avoid the dangers arising from vertically fragmented history, it is, of course, all too easy to fall into the opposite error of neglecting the very spectacular advances which have been made on these separate historical fronts and the fundamental revisions which have been the products of recent research. Some of the most spectacular and earliest of these examples have been made in the field of economic and social history, where most of the historiographical certainties which characterized even the early 1950s have been subjected to serious revision, and some have disappeared almost without trace. Increasingly, for example, the great price inflation of the period is seen against a background of expanding population rather than of expanding money supply. Virtually no-one these days believes in the so-called 'early industrial revolution' which held the field for two decades between the mid 1930s and the early 1950s. Features such as family history, the history of the professions and the growth of educational provision have come into their own. Even the fires of the controversy in the 1950s over the rise of the gentry, stoked as they were by the rival theses of two of the most exciting historians of our time, have died down, and the attention of agrarian historians has shifted from fielden to forest communities, or at least to a new and sharper emphasis on the differences between the two, and – peculiarly relevant to our theme of integrated history – the implications of these differences in the field of general, and more especially religious and political history. Urban history has enjoyed a renaissance, some of the impetus of which has derived from the careful and historical use of the work of urban sociologists. Similarly, and even more momentous in its consequences for integrated history, is the use of anthropological insights in the study of phenomena such as magic and witchcraft. This has helped to transform what were formerly very peripheral topics, widely regarded as the exclusive concern of cranks and antiquarians, into centrally important phenomena. The work of Mr Keith Thomas, in particular, has radically altered the way in which many historians regard central issues such as the religious Reformation, the Price Revolution, enclosures, poverty and the structure of rural society. Such topics will never be quite the same again. The wizard, the wise woman, the cunning man and the soothsayer have taken their place beside the priest and the minister of the church as figures in the forefront of the popular imagination; and historians of religion have been made aware of the complicated and inextricable connection between popular religion and magic.

Similarly, in the last decade or so there have been crucial reinterpretations of the political history of the period. The author of the previous volume in this series stressed his determination to escape from the shadow cast by the Elizabethan period on especially the latter part of the period covered by his book. Much recent work on the political history of the reign of James I and the first decade of that of his successor has been done with the laudable object of freeing that period from the shadow cast upon it by the great civil war and the Interregnum, the so-called English Revolution. Nor has this baleful shadow confined itself to the early Stuart period. In a very real sense the work of the late Sir John Neale on Elizabethan parliaments sought to place the origins of seventeenth century conflicts firmly in this earlier period; and since these conflicts were inevitably interpreted exclusively in terms of the lead-up to the Civil War, Elizabethan parliamentary history was seen as foreshadowing those conflicts over which men were to shed not only one another's blood but also that of their king. Recent research on early Stuart parliamentary history before 1629, and more especially that associated with the name of Professor Conrad Russell, has striven to think away the Civil War, the search for whose origins, it is argued, has bedevilled our understanding of the issues which were important to contemporaries who themselves could not, in the nature of things, be aware of the horrifying events which were to take place in the 1640s. There is an important point of contact here with the emphasis laid by the historian of Tudor England, Professor G. R. Elton, on consensus rather than conflict, and on the fact that the major concerns of contemporary MPs – which it should be the concern of the historian to recapture – related mainly to very different matters from those emphasized by historians who have been dazzled by the conflagration of the 1640s, a sight of which was denied to the political nation in the 1620s. Of course, it is the business of historians to seek the origins of great events and, in doing so, perforce to reason from effect to cause. It may be that these revisionist tendencies, while offering a salutary caution to hasty and ill-considered judgments, are exerting too strong an influence in the direction of inhibiting such inquiries.[1] Be this as it may, the recent stress on consensus rather than conflict, even if it has been somewhat overdone, has had a profound and, on balance, beneficial effect not only on the historiography of the period before the Civil War but on that of the Civil War itself. To cite but one example, both the reformers and the revolutionaries whose activities have given this book its title – though it is concerned with much else besides – were people who looked to the past for much of their political inspiration: whether, in the case of some of the more radical Puritan reformers, it was to an imagined primitive non-episcopal church of the days of the apostles; or, in that of some of the more cautious and conservative critics of the Caroline court, it was to the mists of remotest antiquity whence England derived her immemorial common law and constitution; or, in that of radical political revolutionaries like the Diggers and Levellers in the 1640s, it was to the imagined freedoms and equality of the happy days before the Norman Conquest; or, in that of Cavaliers after 1649, it was to the imagined golden days of King Charles I, which they earnestly sought and ultimately succeeded in recapturing in their own revolution. Like the disappointed hopes of all these other aspirants this was to be the revolution of a wheel come full circle. For, *mutatis mutandis*, all these aspirants had in common the desire to return to imagined ancient ways. All would have agreed with John Pym's observation, in a speech made in parliament in 1628, arguing in favour of that Petition of Right which he saw as 'demanding . . . ancient and due liberties, not suing for any new'. Pym observed that

> . . . those commonwealths have been most durable and perpetual which have often reformed and recomposed themselves according to their first institution and ordinance, for by this means they repair the breaches and counterwork the ordinary and natural effects of time . . .

Revolution itself to be beneficial must, it was argued, be restorative. Such recurrent recapturing of past conditions was necessary in a sub-lunar world in which change and mutability were associated with decay and degeneration. To expect otherwise was to expect to transcend the limits of earthly existence.

> Then gin I thinke on that which Nature sayd,
> Of that same time when no more *Change* shall be,
> But stedfast rest of all things firmely stayd
> Upon the pillours of Eternity,
> That is contrayr to *Mutabilitie*;
> For, all that moueth, doth in Change delight:

But thenceforth all shall rest eternally,
With Him that is the God of Sabbaoth Light,
O that great Sabbaoth God, graunt me that Sabbaoths sight.[2]

NOTES TO INTRODUCTION

(1) For some criticisms of the 'revisionist' histories, see J. H. Hexter, 'Power struggle, Parliament and liberty in early Stuart England', *Journ. of Mod. Hist.* l (1978), 1–50; C. Hill, 'Parliament and people in seventeenth-century England', *Past & Present* xcii (1981), 100–24; D. Hirst and T. K. Rabb, 'Revisionism Revised: Two Perspectives on Early Stuart Parliamentary History', *ibid*, 55–99; M. Fulbrook, 'The English Revolution and the revisionist revolt', *Social History* vii (1982), 249–64.

(2) Spenser, *The Faerie Queene*, canto viii, 2.

Chapter One

THE SOCIAL AND ECONOMIC FRAMEWORK

THE CHARACTER OF THE ECONOMY

(i)

Although roughly the same period of time separates them, the England of Elizabeth II differs far more fundamentally from the England of the early years of the reign of George III than does the latter from the England of Elizabeth I. For England in both 1558 and 1760 had still to undergo the transforming experience of industrialization which, more than any other process in its long history, was to alter the character of the country and the way of life of its inhabitants. At both dates England was still, to use a modern term, an underdeveloped economy, which exhibited many of the central features of the economies of the so-called Third World today. It is not surprising that among the most perceptive students of Tudor and Stuart society are those who, observing these points of similarity, have made skilful and imaginative use of tools of economic, sociological and anthropological analysis which have been devised to shed light on the underdeveloped economies of our own time.

But it is important not to overstress the similarity. Unlike the modern Third World nations, Tudor England did not have constantly before its eyes the demonstration effect exerted by richer and more advanced and industrialized national economies, fundamentally different in kind from its own. This is not, of course, to say that there were no significant differences between Tudor and Stuart England

and other national economies at that time. At the beginning of our period, while England led the world as a producer of fine quality (though mostly unfinished) woollen textiles, her other industries, her technology and her commercial and financial organization and techniques, lagged far behind those of the northern and southern Netherlands, south Germany, the Hanseatic towns such as Riga, Hamburg, Danzig and especially Lübeck, and, perhaps most of all, the towns of northern and central Italy, such as Venice, Genoa, Florence and Lucca. On the other hand, England's economy was relatively advanced compared with that of the neighbouring realm of Scotland, or of Norway, or Poland, although the difference between the two extremes – between (say) the southern Netherlands on the one hand and Scotland on the other – was, unlike that between the modern industrialized and the Third World nations, a difference of degree rather than of kind.

(ii)

Within England itself there were marked regional differences, of which the broadest was that between the richer and more economically advanced south and east and the more backward north and west.[1] The distinction corresponds roughly with what historical geographers describe as the lowland and highland zones, the former characterized by a drier climate, more sun and richer soil, the latter by heavier rainfall, less sun and poorer soil. These facts dictated the greater concentration on animal than on arable production in the highland zone, where sheep and cattle were reared for wool, dairy produce or meat, as well as other livestock such as horses and pigs. Conversely, in the more richly endowed lowland zone, grain production was of much greater importance, though most farming was basically mixed, a fact which in itself afforded scope for variation in land use in response to changing market trends. Thus in the early sixteenth century, parts of lowland zone counties such as Leicestershire and Northamptonshire had responded to the increased demand for wool from the expanding textile industry and had become one of the most important areas of pasture farming and animal husbandry in the country. But this development of highland zone type economy within the lowland zone carried with it very different social effects from those associated with pasture farming in the more sparsely populated north and west, since it took place in areas where – at least from the third decade of the sixteenth century onwards – land was in distinctly short supply relative to population. The result was the rural depopulation traditionally associated with enclosure for pasture, but in actual fact associated with it only in these rather special circumstances.

Such cases serve only to emphasize that the geographical contrast between highland and lowland zone economies is no more than an approximation to which exceptions are legion. Quite apart from areas which had recently been enclosed and converted to pasture, there were areas such as the wood-pasture region of central Suffolk, which had long found its economic mainstay in highland zone type cattle rearing and dairying – Suffolk cheese was in great demand in London, for instance – and drew some of its other food requirements from elsewhere in East Anglia. Similarly, in the eastern marshlands of Lincolnshire, Essex and Kent, animal rearing, and in particular cattle fattening, was as dominant a feature as anywhere in the highland zone. Conversely, within the geographical limits of the highland zone there were areas such as parts of Herefordshire, Devon and Somerset and the coastal districts of Durham and Cumberland, which were given over to the sort of stock and grain farming which is normally connected with the lowland zone.

But even when these important exceptions have been made, the distinction (rough though it is) between the nature of the highland zone economy of the north and west and the lowland zone economy of the south and east does go far to explain the main contrast between relatively backward and poor and relatively advanced and rich parts of the realm. It is a contrast reflected not only in land use, settlement patterns, inheritance customs and field systems, but also, as many historians argue, in the state of public order and the relative influence and power of central and local government. For the more sparsely populated lands of the north and west tended to be areas where the king's writ ran less surely and more sporadically. Many of them – notably the six northern and, most of all, the border counties – were lands where the old loyalties to the great magnates and the old church were less rapidly eroded than in the lowland zone. Others – notably those pockets of highland zone type production within regions predominantly concerned with classic lowland zone mixed farming – were the more conspicuous in being the exceptions to the regional rule of tightly-knit social organization and in their relative freedom from the all-seeing eye of the lord of the manor. In these circumstances it is hardly surprising that, in the eyes of their contemporaries in the stock-and-grain-production areas, the men of hillside, moorland and forest and woodland were a type set apart. Here, it is often argued, was one of the notable breeding grounds of that third world of Tudor and Stuart England which, until it recently became a fashionable subject of inquiry, had almost completely escaped the attention of historians. Another such breeding ground was the suburbs of London and the so-called 'liberties' within the City, over which significantly the City had no jurisdiction, and where lawlessness and crime abounded. In such dark places, both rural and urban, there seem to have flourished not only outlandish religious sects which had little or nothing in common with mainstream Protestantism, but also men and women with no religious beliefs at all, either because they had left them behind when they had migrated from fielden villages or because they had never known them.

It has been suggested that highland areas on the continent provided the original setting for witch beliefs and witch hunts,[2] but there is no evidence that the same was true in England. Indeed, while persons were convicted of, and executed for, witchcraft in all parts of the country, it is arguable that the most likely environment for the classic role of the witch as social outcast is to be found in the more tightly-knit, strongly conformist setting of lowland fielden villages with their necessarily strong traditions of community action and their characteristic subjection of almost every aspect of the lives of the individual members of the community to public scrutiny. But it is in fact the process whereby the traditional communal ethos of mutual help, so characteristic of lowland fielden communities, was being eroded by economic developments such as inflation and population pressure, that provided the most potent force making for the increase in witchcraft accusations over the period covered by this book. Such factors were making the old and the poor a greater burden to their communities, which many of their neighbours were finding it increasingly difficult to sustain. In these circumstances the temptation to kick the beggar at one's door and send him packing was enormously strengthened. And if he or she (more especially she, for there were more dependent and indigent females than males in most communities, just as there were also more female than male witches) departed muttering imprecations which in turn were followed by disasters to one's own already precarious economy – a cow refusing to give milk or an indispensable member of the household falling suddenly sick, for example – what more natural than to place the blame on the curses of the disreputable cadger whose pleas for neighbourly assistance had been turned down! Indeed there is every reason to believe that desperately indigent persons exploited fears of being bewitched as a means of extracting from neighbours who were often only marginally better off than themselves charitable assistance which worsening economic conditions were making it an almost impossible burden to provide. In these circumstances belief in witchcraft performed a conservative social function in helping to preserve traditional modes of behaviour and obligations which were threatened by economic changes. Or to put it in another way, economic changes were forcing many indigent and helpless people into witchcraft or, at the very least, to simulate the role of witches, as a means of gouging out of their neighbours what in better times they had given as a matter of neighbourly duty. But the previous argument also suggests that witchcraft beliefs could also serve a diametrically opposite function by acting as a powerful solvent of the traditional communal ethos of mutual aid via the process whereby guilt about the withholding of charity was transferred from the refuser to the refused. By relating the phenomenon of witchcraft firmly to the social and economic pressures of the age, Mr Keith Thomas and Mr A. Macfarlane have succeeded in assigning a central significance to a factor which had formerly stood on the periphery of the historian's concern.[3]

(iii)

Areas of highland zone type farming – whether or not they were within the geographical boundaries of the highland zone – were particularly suited to a variety of forms of industrial production. Here the typical employee – and this often applied to mining and metallurgical industry no less than to a cottage domestic industry such as textile production – was engaged only part of the time in industrial production, and part of the time in agricultural pursuits. Sometimes, especially in the case of cloth weaving, he owned the simple and relatively inexpensive instruments of production on which he worked even when he had no property in the materials put out to him and therefore in the end-product he created. The latter belonged to his employer, for so we must term entrepreneurs such as the clothier in the textile industry who sometimes controlled the many stages of production from the sorting of wool to the finishing of the cloth and sometimes bought intermediary products, such as spun yarn, from a petty capitalist such as the master-spinner. The above description does no more than hint at the bewildering variety of economic relations between employer and employee which was a feature of the organization of England's most important manufacture. Some clothiers – certainly the vast majority in less highly capitalized areas such as the West Riding of Yorkshire, the Lake District and north and central Wales, and probably a majority even in the more highly developed industries of the southwest, East Anglia and Kent – were small men, hardly distinguishable from weavers and often employing no more than their own families. Others put out materials to hundreds of spinners, weavers and finishers – though some of the latter worked on commission – spread over a large number of villages. Some very exceptional clothiers even operated a rudimentary factory system, though, unlike the modern factory, this form of organization was not dictated by the nature of the technical process, the instruments of production being no more elaborate than those which other workers used in their own cottages. In such circumstances the sole advantage of the manufactory as a form of organization of production was that it allowed for stricter supervision to prevent the embezzlement of materials which, rather than withdrawal of labour, was the characteristic weapon of labour when industry was organized on a domestic basis. For geographical dispersion was a formidable barrier to collective action by artisans. In the case of the mining and metallurgical industries, though not necessarily in the manufacture of metal wares, the elaborate and expensive machinery, such as winding and pumping gear in the larger and deeper mines, and blast furnaces in the larger ore-smelting enterprises, made a factory form of production essential.

The conditions favouring industrial byemployment in a highland zone environment were many and mixed in proportions varying with different economic situations.[4] They include the proximity of raw materials, which was, however, not always a necessary condition. While obviously applicable to the exploitation of minerals such as coal and metals, it was by no means essential in the matter of woollen-cloth production. Areas of wool production, and notably the newly enclosed lands of counties such as Northamptonshire, Leicestershire and Buckinghamshire, were often far removed from many of the chief areas of textile production, and even when the two were relatively close, the quality of wool produced was not always suitable for the type of cloth manufactured. Another factor which frequently encouraged industrial byemployment was partible inheritance (the parcellation of holdings among coheirs as opposed to impartible inheritance by the eldest male), though such parcellation was by no means unknown in the lowland zone either. The continued process of partible inheritance was obviously likely to make the holdings of many occupiers too small to yield them even a bare subsistence. Something like this seems to have occurred in some of the west Yorkshire dales, where the inhabitants made up for the inadequacy of their progressively diminishing holdings of land by such occupations as the knitting of coarse stockings.

In contrast to the classic arable mixed farming regions of the lowland zone with their more continuous need for labour, pastoral farming of one sort or another gave its practitioners ample time to spread their energies between farming and industrial employment. It was, for example, not only the presence of mineral resources but also the ready availability of part-time labour which made mining and metallurgy important in the highland zone and in parts of the lowland zone, such as the Kent and Sussex Weald, where pastoral rather than arable farming predominated, and where the woollen textile industry was an even more important source of industrial byemployment. Similarly, the rearing of cattle, sheep, horses and geese in the Lincolnshire fens was accompanied and complemented by the weaving of flax, hemp and woollen cloth. A somewhat different case is the concentration on the production of cheese and butter rather than grain in the northwest and southwest corner of Wiltshire and in the wood-pasture region of central and southern Suffolk, which provided a reservoir of underemployed labour for the cloth industry. The same availability of labour, in conjunction with the slaughtering of young beasts which is associated with dairying, fostered the growth of the manufacture of leather from calf-skins (as distinct from hides) in Suffolk, a speciality which also characterized the dairying area of west Cheshire and east Shropshire.

Sometimes the situation described above was reversed in that it was industrial activity which provided the mainstay, and agriculture the byemployment. On occasion the process of sub-parcellation had gone so far, or the land was so barren, or both, that a high proportion of the inhabitants came near to being full-time manufacturers. The preamble to the Halifax Act of 1555, allowing the wool-dealer to operate in the enormous parish of Halifax on account of the prevalence of very small-scale clothiers who could not afford to go far afield for their wool, describes just such a situation. The parish, states the statute, was

> planted in the great wastes and moors where the fertility of ground is not apt to bring forth any corn nor good grass, but in rare places and by exceeding and great industry of the inhabitants; and the same inhabitants altogether do live by clothmaking.

A similar state of affairs is described by some Somerset JPs in the reign of James I as applying to some of the forest and woodland parts of that county. Similarly, in Derbyshire by the 1620s, while many families carried out mining or metallurgy in tandem with agriculture, there were many others who were solely occupied in the former activity.

Nevertheless, throughout our period the English economy retained its overwhelmingly agrarian character, despite the importance of the manufacture of woollen textiles in areas of the highland zone such as the Cotswolds,

Wiltshire, Somerset and Devon, and its growth in the West Riding, the Lake District and northern and central Wales, and despite the expansion of mining and metallurgical activity in the same zone, as most spectacularly manifested in the production of coal and the development of coal-burning industries such as the manufacture of glass and, on the banks of the Tyne and the Wear, the evaporation of seawater to produce salt. But it was in the south, the Midlands and the east that the most notable advances were made on the agricultural front. Of vital importance here was the pull of urban markets, and especially the metropolitan London market, a potent factor fostering the growth of specialization of many areas in the farming products which they were best fitted by nature to produce.[5]

(iv)

Among the other central characteristics of underdeveloped economies are the preponderant importance of labour and the relative unimportance of capital as factors of production. The most notable manifestation of these twin features is to be found in the relatively low level of technology and productivity. In agriculture this finds its most familiar expression in the prevalence not only of 'champion' over 'severalty', that is of open-field over enclosed farming in large parts of the country, but also, within the context of open-field farming, of two- over three-course rotations of crops in some areas. However, it is as easy to underrate the adaptability of open-field farming as to exaggerate the extent to which improvement was made difficult by the obstacles imposed to enclosure by the tenacity of customary rights and traditional ways of doing things in which progress was limited to the pace of the slowest member of the community. Nevertheless, there is no doubt that enclosure and economic consolidation was carried out on quite an extensive scale by the wealthier peasants as well as by landowners; and that during this period, unlike the early sixteenth century, there was increasing emphasis on enclosure for increased food, as distinct from wool, production.

An economy in which the level of productivity and technology is low is also, by definition, an economy in which devices substituting capital for labour are conspicuous if not by their absence, at least by their comparative rarity. It is true that in the woollen textile industry the fulling mill had been in use since the thirteenth century, and there was still a great deal of scope for its extension in Tudor England. A fifteenth-century innovation, the gig-mill, which used water power to mechanize the raising of the nap of woollen cloth, continued to be employed even though its use was forbidden by statute. In the coalmining industry, especially on the Tyne and the Wear, the use of railed ways for surface transport of coal was extended, and more elaborate pumping and draining devices employed, while in the smelting of iron the blast furnace was rapidly replacing the bloomery forge. But labour-curtailing devices were relatively few and far between, and their rarity was at least as much a function of the abundance of labour as of the shortage of capital. The growth of population which is a feature of the Elizabethan, or at least the late Elizabethan, period was modest by modern standards but enough to produce alarm in government circles and an abundance of complaints that England was becoming, in Sir Humphrey Gilbert's colourful phrase, 'pestered with inhabitants'. In a period in which the supply of labour was plentiful and its price therefore cheap – according to one estimate real wages reached an all-time low in the 1590s – the need to abridge labour by capital was less strongly felt than would have been the case if it had been scarce and expensive. It was this disparity between wages and the prices of manufactured goods which was remarked by Professor Earl Hamilton, who saw the resultant profit-inflationary situation as providing the stimulus to investment by gentlemen entrepreneurs whose surplus cash would in other circumstances have gone into one form or other of conspicuous consumption.[6]

Indeed it might be argued that it was these spectacular opportunities of profit which afforded to Elizabethan landowners such as Sir Francis Willoughby of Wollaton or the formidable Bess of Hardwick, countess of Shrewsbury, the opportunity of consuming more conspicuously than would otherwise have been possible. Wollaton Hall and Hardwick Hall, those spectacular Elizabethan prodigy houses, were both built to no small extent on the profits of such industrial enterprise.

Among the objections which have been raised to this thesis are some which, whether fully justified or not, point up sharply one of the most formidable limitations on economic growth during the period. If, argued Professor J. U. Nef, inflated industrial profits were in fact the product of squeezing the real wages of industrial workers, an inevitable corollary of this situation would surely be a constriction of mass purchasing power to an extent incompatible with large-scale industrial growth; the more so since the many industries for which such growth has been claimed were almost completely dependent upon domestic demand, unlike the woollen textile industry, where foreign demand was of crucial importance.[7] Against this view it could be argued that in an economy which was preponderantly agrarian rather than industrial in character, and in which the main market for manufactured goods was certainly not to be found among those actually engaged in manufacture, this constriction of industrial real wages would impose a far less serious obstacle to industrial growth than would be the case in a modern industrialized economy. But the mass constriction of real income was not confined to the industrial field. Expanding rural population exerted both an upward pressure on rents and food prices and a downward pressure on real agricultural wages. Those affected would have to spend more on the necessities of life, products for which their demand was relatively inelastic, and so would have less to spend on other commodities. In Elizabethan England what counted as the necessities of life – food, and especially carbohydrate foodstuffs, and the most rudimentary forms of shelter – covered a far narrower range of satisfactions than is the case today. With due allowance for differences in climatic conditions the necessities of the indigent Tudor peasant and labourer relate them more closely to the modern Indian peasant or the dweller in Calcutta or Bombay than to their British counterparts.

It may at first sight seem paradoxical to speak of the prevalence of high preferences for leisure over work in a situation in which population was pressing on employment. Yet the reluctance of the working population to increase work effort, which is characteristic of most underdeveloped economies, is also a feature of Tudor and Stuart England; at least when it comes to gainful work for employers, as distinct from a variety of spare-time, self-employed activities. These high leisure preferences are yet another reason why chronic underemployment was endemic, and are of course closely related to the absence of large amounts of cheap mass-produced products, the abundance of which might have had the effect of rendering increased work effort worthwhile. On the other hand, if the real incomes of most Englishmen were decreasing, then obviously there was little or no incentive for entrepreneurs to cater for this sort of market. The Tudor and Stuart economy was in fact caught in the vicious circle which has to be broken through by any underdeveloped economy if it is to undergo the process of industrial transformation, which was not in fact experienced in England before the classic industrial revolution of the eighteenth and nineteenth centuries.[8]

For all these very great obstacles, the period did see some very real, if relatively modest, industrial progress. The familiar contrast between the operations of English and French manufacturers in the sixteenth and seventeenth century – the former concentrating on objects for which there was a widespread demand, such as cheap window-glass, and the latter on luxury products such as goblets and mirrors – has perhaps been overdone by some historians, but is not entirely without foundation. At the very least, it suggests a limited growth of mass effective demand in England, despite the population pressures which were raising rents and food prices and reducing wages. And from where was such demand to come in contemporary society if not from what was quantitatively the overwhelmingly preponderant agrarian sector? For the economic history of the Elizabethan and early Stuart peasantry is by no means entirely a tale of increasing and undifferentiated misery. While some peasants indeed suffered what to the modern western mind are barely imaginable hardships, others prospered. The rise in the economic fortunes of the yeomanry, the substantial peasants who were secure through their tenure from eviction and rack-renting and were enjoying a rise in the prices of the agricultural produce they marketed, is one of the characteristic and most important features of the period. Effective demand is, of course, the product of two distinct elements: purchasing power and propensity to consume. While it is normal today to regard the former as being preceded by the latter – the idea of a pre-existing demand being made effective by the acquisition of purchasing power – it seems distinctly probable that in the case of the Elizabethan yeomen the process was reversed. Studies of their economic behaviour which have been made in recent years support the conclusion that, while initially they showed a tendency (parallel to that of the classic entrepreneur in the great Industrial Revolution of the eighteenth century) to eschew personal expenditure and self-indulgence, choosing instead to plough back their profits into their fields, many of them came sooner or later – but the example once given was contagious – to ape their betters, the gentry, many of whom were filling England with the manor houses which are among its most striking and delightful features. In general in this period what has been described by some historians as 'the great rebuilding' and by others as a 'housing revolution' was a lowland rather than a highland zone phenomenon. Some yeomen farmers were building new houses, while others were inserting upper floors into their old houses, glazing their windows and buying better and more elaborate furniture. This by no means insignificant element in the growth of effective demand may have afforded an important stimulus to manufacturing industry.

(v)

In the foregoing analysis stress was laid on the under-employment of the bulk of the working population during this period. Other factors which contributed to this were seasonal fluctuations in employment and the serious defects of internal communications which had the effect of confining many producers to local markets too small to afford them full-time employment. The appalling state of overland routes in fact put a heavy premium on waterways, most particularly in cases where the value of commodities was low in relation to their bulk. Thus it was that wheat, whose price relative to that of other grains was high, was less dependent than barley on the availability of navigable waterways linking areas of production with areas of demand, a fact which helps to explain the importance of barley production in west Norfolk, with its ready access not only to deep-penetrating rivers but also to the sea. Similarly, the coal industry of the Tyne and the Wear area, linked by the sea with the most important domestic and industrial market for fuel in London, and, though less important, to the relatively heavily populated and prosperous region of East Anglia, enjoyed the most spectacular expansion of all English coalfields at this time. By contrast, there were coalfields which were neither in close proximity to markets for fuel – whether for domestic consumption or by industries in which fuel represented a significantly high proportion of total costs – nor linked with such sources of demand by navigable waterways. Such were what have since become great centres of coal production in Lancashire, Yorkshire and parts of the Midlands. In this period these were restricted to sale by land over a few miles, beyond which the difference between the price of coal at the pithead and at the place of sale became prohibitively high. Since the scale of industrial operations is necessarily limited by the size of the market, production in such places remained minuscule, and their potential was unrealized until the Industrial Revolution. Somewhere between the two extremes were the mines on the southern extremity of the Nottinghamshire coalfield, where the proximity of the Trent made possible cheap transportation to a wider than local market, and fired the most important of the local pitowners, the Willoughbys of Wollaton near Nottingham, with the grandiose, but never realized, notion of transhipping coal on the Humber for shipment to London in competition with the coalowners of the Tyne and Wear region. Similarly, proximity to the Severn provided the coalowners of Coalbrookdale in Shropshire with access to a much wider market than they could have reached via overland sales.

(vi)

Economies in which labour is plentiful and cheap are often economies in which capital is scarce and dear, both in the sense that they consume a relatively high proportion of the wealth they create and in that such capital as is available for investment does not readily flow into the sort of productive investment which yields an increase in the wealth of the country. To some extent this is the product of the lack of an organized capital market with a highly institutionalized credit structure which serves to canalize available funds into one form or another of productive enterprise. But it also reflects some fundamental features of contemporary social aspirations, government and institutions. The decision of fifteenth- and early sixteenth-century manufacturers (like Thomas Spring of Lavenham) or landowners to invest surplus capital in perpendicular churches rather than in improved industrial technology, industrial organization or estate management may be ascribed to consciousness of the need to build up a treasury of merit on which to draw in the hereafter; or to motives of social emulation; or even simply to the relative scarcity of alternative investment opportunities. Very likely all of these considerations played a part. There was no longer a place for treasuries of merit in the Protestant scheme of things in Elizabethan and early Stuart England, and it is certainly no coincidence that the Elizabethan age was a period in which church building and church repairs – and indeed religious benefaction in general – occupied a lower place in most men's scale of priorities than at any previous, and perhaps even at any subsequent, time. Indeed the partial – and it was only partial – revival of such religious benefactions under the early Stuarts was probably due at least as much to the need to tackle the obvious dangers resulting from decades of Elizabethan neglect as to a notable revival of enthusiasm for religious forms of giving.[9]

But to postulate a measure of secularization of the uses to which surplus funds were put is emphatically not to postulate a diversion of such funds from churchbuilding or almsgiving to one form or another of productive investment, least of all to investment in manufacturing industry. There were any number of competing uses for such funds, not least one form or another of conspicuous consumption, whether in building large and elaborate houses or in riotous living. This is not to deny, of course, that building and riotous living have important economic effects via the transfer of incomes generated by such expenditure. But the prevalence of such decisions to spend rather than to invest will obviously materially affect the nature of the economy.

As far as productive investment itself is concerned, given a situation in which the prices of agricultural products and raw materials rose faster than those of manufactured goods, landowners as an economic group tended to be in a stronger position than manufacturers, unless, as was sometimes the case, considerations of tenant-right – or social obligation – imposed obstacles in the way of their making the most of their estates. Was this an important factor encouraging the diversion of capital away from manufacture into land, where a better return was to be had? Certainly, as a chorus of contemporary social comment, much of it hostile, suggests, the flow of capital from business into land was a notable feature of the period, and an important factor making for discontinuity of business enterprise. But just as many landowners found more congenial, if less economically productive, uses for their wealth than investing in estate improvements which were often very expensive and sometimes yielded a return which was enjoyed by their heirs rather than themselves, so was it probably other than economic considerations which weighed most in encouraging the diversion of capital from trade and manufacture into land. For while such purchasers of landed estates might well have an eye to their economic possibilities, in the majority of cases it was, one suspects, social rather than economic considerations which loomed largest. If this is true, these same factors would impose serious limitations upon the alleged tendency, celebrated in so many history textbooks, for business purchasers of land to import those methods and attitudes of mind which had brought success in business, or in professions such as the law, into the very different sphere of landownership. Such was the strength of traditional notions about the virtues of old-fashioned, hospitality-dispensing, paternalistic landowners who dwelt on their estates and cared for their tenants and other dependants, that to engage in depopulation, large-scale eviction, rack-renting or enclosure of common land was to court a measure of social disapprobation even for the long-established landowner. How much more so for the parvenu, struggling to find social acceptance!

The purchase of land in pursuit of the seductive vision of the bourgeois turned gentleman was an important but by no means the only diversionary channel for capital which might otherwise have been employed in productive business investment. Seeking the most profitable outlet for their capital, some of the biggest businessmen found it not in more ordinary lines of business but in the exploitation of government concessions. Some of these concessions arose out of the need of the government, which intervened actively in the economic life of the country but lacked a civil service to implement its policies, to make use of the services of private enterprise to perform what today would be regarded as functions of public control. Similar to these uses and often connected with them was the practice, which became a feature of the war years during the 1590s and continued to operate under the first two Stuart kings, whereby a government short of cash but rich in the concessions in its gift paid many of its officers of state, courtiers and others whom the prince delighted to honour, partly and sometimes wholly in economic concessions such as monopolistic privileges, export and other licences and economic controls of one form or another. These were sublet by the grantees of first instance to City businessmen who exploited them directly for profit. And the profits were often very great indeed. These developments helped to create what a French historian has described, referring to similar tendencies in France, as a haemorrhage of capital away from productive investment. A further significance of this tendency was that it helped to create, or at least to cement, an alliance based on a real community of interest between the court and big business interests in the City of London. Nor was it simply because it diverted capital from more productive investment that the phenomenon is of interest to the historian of economic growth. Too often, as in the obvious case of patents of monopoly, by restricting the scope and increasing the cost of enterprise, its effect was not merely to divert capital from investment which would foster economic growth but also to act as a factor making directly for economic retardation.

THE URBAN MINORITY

(i)

Among English towns in the period between the accession of Elizabeth I and the Industrial Revolution, London stood alone, dominating England as never before nor since. Vital statistics for this period are notoriously approximate, but it has been suggested that the population of the capital had reached about 70,000 by the middle of the sixteenth century, topped the 200,000 mark by the beginning of the Stuart period, and had reached about 320,000 immediately before the great plague of 1625 and about 400,000 by 1650. To claim that the relative importance of a capital city whose population was so tiny by modern standards was at least as great then as it is now might seem to be inviting ridicule. But these figures have to be set off against a total English population of probably around 3½ million in 1558 and 4 million in 1603, and a situation in which the population of no other town, except possibly Norwich, which may have topped the 20,000 mark in the 1630s, approached 20,000 at any time during the period.[10] Bristol, the next town after Norwich, and the one that was to replace it in second place during the early eighteenth century, had to wait until the end of the seventeenth century before approaching this figure. Norwich indeed was, by contemporary standards, an important city in many senses: the capital of a large, populous and economically advanced region, a cathedral city and an important textile centre whose prosperity was given a notable fillip by the immigration of alien craftsmen from the Low Countries in the reign of Elizabeth I, as were those of lesser centres such as Colchester, Maidstone, Sandwich and Canterbury. All of those functions were also performed by Exeter, whose population may have reached 9,000 by the end of the sixteenth century. Newcastle-upon-Tyne, whose population quadrupled between the end of the sixteenth and the end of the seventeenth century, when it probably exceeded 16,000, was another regional capital and important provincial port, though its industrial base rested on coal and coal-burning industries rather than textiles. Worcester, like Norwich and Exeter, was both a cathedral city and a textile centre, though in no sense a regional as distinct from a county capital; it probably had between 4,000 and 5,000 inhabitants in the 1560s and may have topped 8,000 by the 1640s.[11] York, while the days of its medieval glory as a textile centre had now passed, was a cathedral city, the seat of the archbishop of the northern ecclesiastical province, and a regional capital *par excellence* with a population of about 12,000 in the mid-seventeenth century. The most important factor in its size and prosperity was probably that it was the seat of the Council of the North, which not only generated a vast amount of administrative business, but also heightened its importance as a social centre. The abolition of the Council of the North by the Long Parliament arrested York's spectacular development, and though Charles I's migration to York at the beginning of 1642 produced a temporary influx of fashionable supporters and future Cavaliers, the effect was short-lived and its population was much the same at the end as it had been in the middle of the seventeenth century.

Just as London was an exceptional phenomenon, so would it be misleading to regard the larger provincial towns mentioned above as in any way typical of English towns in this period. Indeed, the vast majority of the market towns, of which there were some 800 in England by the middle of the seventeenth century, were much smaller and, though distinguishable from villages, merged imperceptibly with the adjacent countryside. For the rural neighbourhood, the town marketplace with its surrounding inns and taverns provided a real focal point, a function which can still be sensed today in small market towns such as Aylsham in Norfolk or Shipston-on-Stour in the Warwickshire Cotswolds. Even in the largest market town the open fields were virtually on the doorstep. Indeed of a city as large as Exeter, perhaps the fifth largest in England, Dr Hoskins informs us that the area enclosed by the city walls, whose circuit was only a mile and a half, was a mere 93 acres, with an additional minimal suburban ribbon development stretching a few hundred yards along each of the roads outside the city gates. While the economic function of most market towns was as centres of distribution for the immediate countryside, a few served as regional and national markets in some at least of the commodities in which they dealt. Doncaster, for instance, was the great market where many of the clothiers of Yorkshire and elsewhere in the north and north Midlands obtained their wool. Oswestry in Shropshire was the place at which Welsh cloth was bought for sale all over England as well as in France. Maidstone and Canterbury were national markets for Kentish hops, and Northampton for horses.

(ii)

London, however, was unique. If one had to single out one factor to account, more than any other, for the difference between the quality of life in the metropolis and in the provinces, one would probably settle for the presence of the court for the greater part of each year. Besides being the magnet which drew ambitious gentlemen in search of office and preferment, projectors seeking influential backing for their schemes, and domestic servants seeking employment, the court was also, then as now, a major tourist attraction, while around and connected with it there proliferated a host of luxury trades and crafts. Professor Fisher has shown how, between about 1590 and 1620, there developed something akin to the phenomenon of the fashionable season in London, which in turn led to a growth in the number of gentlemen who possessed town houses, and, in order to accommodate those who did not, an expansion both of the hotel industry and of the practice of furnished letting.[12]

Some of the facilities afforded by London were, of course, unique – the tombs at Westminster, the lions in the Tower, the playhouses, Paris Garden, to mention but a few. Others put to shame anything offered in the provinces. No doubt the élite of the shires, who were increasingly fond of congregating in the larger county towns and regional capitals such as Norwich, Exeter and York and even sometimes had town houses there, knew something of the conviviality of a sort of urban club-life, but in this respect no provincial town could hold a candle to London. The baiting of bulls and bears and visits by travelling players were not unknown in the provinces, but the range of entertainment and the number of places where it could be enjoyed both on Bankside and north of the river were peculiar to London. From the closing years of the sixteenth century the Curtain, the Red Bull and perhaps the Fortune in the north seem to have catered increasingly, though never exclusively, for citizens and apprentices, while south of the river the old- fashioned ring-theatres of Bankside such as the Rose, the Swan, the Hope and, above all, the Globe presented a marked contrast to the completely roofed 'private' and other playhouses such as the Salisbury Court and Blackfriars theatres north of the Thames, where the clientele was more socially exclusive and the minimum price of admission much higher. Not all of these theatres were functioning at one and the same time, and deserted and converted playhouses were among the more dismal landmarks of seventeenth-century London, comparable with the erstwhile cinemas of our own time whose great age ended with the television boom after the Second World War. The contemporary equivalent of the modern conversion of cinemas into Bingo halls was the conversion of playhouses such as the Curtain, the Swan and the Hope into centres for gladiatorial displays by fencers, prizefighters, bear baiters and acrobats. Theatregoing indeed was only one of the manifold attractions of Bankside, which drew multitudes of sightseers from north of the Thames to sample the bearbaiting and other diversions of Paris Garden and elsewhere, not to mention the pleasures of the most notorious and extensive of the many red-light districts of contemporary London.

Similarly, the largest provincial towns had their great public occasions which attracted visitors from all around, among them the opening of quarter sessions and assizes, and the very occasional visits of royalty and, more frequently, of regional notabilities. But what were these when set beside such splendid metropolitan occasions as royal coronations, funerals and weddings, the weddings of fashionable courtiers, state openings of parliament, and the Lord Mayor's annual show? Curiosity, sadism, or just the need for relief from the boredom of everyday life might draw provincial crowds to savour the sanguinary delights of exemplary public punishments and, above all, executions. But to an age which savoured such theatrical occasions to the full, these provincial displays were hardly comparable with the metropolitan opportunities to observe the violent ending of the careers of once powerful persons such as the duke of Norfolk in 1572, the earl of Essex in 1601, Sir Walter Raleigh in 1618, the earl of Strafford in 1641, the archbishop of Canterbury in 1645, and, most spectacular of all, the king himself in 1649, and his murderers in 1660. In addition, the stories of sex and scandal which increasingly circulated around life at court heightened enormously the interest in the court and helped to make it more and more a focus of provincial attention, at least before 1642, as after 1660. The shocked reception of the newsletters which carried such information down to the country does not betoken any lack of eagerness to devour their accounts of an intriguingly different world, as fascinating to many country squires, and perhaps still more to their wives, as was the celluloid dream-world of Hollywood to the shopgirls of the 1930s. Many country gentlemen might shake their heads at the accumulating evidence of metropolitan and courtly wickedness, but an increasing number of them – often, no doubt, yielding to continued pressure from wives and daughters – determined to go and see for themselves.

Business as well as pleasure took many countrymen to London in connection with such matters as the sale of the produce of their demesnes, the search for loans and the ordering of their investments. Legal business bulked especially large, whether in the form of the prosecution of lawsuits or the need to consult expert advice about complicated matters such as marriage settlements, conveyancing problems and the making of wills with a view to burdening estates as little as possible with wardship or other charges. For London was the undisputed centre of that legal world with which many country gentlemen had formed an initial, if very fleeting, acquaintance in their youth as residents at one or other of the Inns of Court. While a recent study of these institutions has been justifiably sceptical about the value of this experience in acquainting gentlemen with the rudiments of a legal education which would stand them in good stead in later life in their twin roles as estate owners and local magistrates,[13] the fact that it afforded them an unparalleled opportunity to sample the cultural, intellectual and general educational, as well as many of the less respectable, delights of metropolitan life is hardly in doubt. These were tastes which some of them never lost and which visits in later life on business or pleasure or perhaps as representatives of shires or boroughs in parliament offered further opportunities of indulging.

The increasing influx of fashionable persons to the capital was affecting both the occupational structure and the residential geography of the metropolis. First there was the growth of luxury crafts and trades associated with this development. Secondly, by the turn of the sixteenth and seventeenth centuries there had already begun that westward movement of the world of fashion away from the City towards Westminster, with the growth of building and the creation of residential areas such as St Martin's Lane, Long Acre, Covent Garden, Drury Lane and Great Queen Street, the latter named after Henrietta Maria. The most prestigious of all the fashionable streets of Elizabethan and – despite the above important developments – early Stuart London, remained the ancient thoroughfare of the Strand, especially on the south side, which boasted a series of magnificent aristocratic town houses with splendid gardens to the rear sloping gently down to the Thames. Among the occupants of such houses were Lords Bedford, Essex, Burghley and Arundel and, in the 1620s, the royal favourite, the duke of Buckingham. Burghley's second son and successor in royal office, Robert Cecil, the later earl of Salisbury, built himself a second Strand house in 1605, while the earls of Bedford owned a second house on the north side, behind which the fourth earl constructed during the 1630s with the aid of the great Inigo Jones, the most imaginative exercise in town-planning of the period, the famous Covent Garden piazza, the last remains of which were to disappear as the result of municipal vandalism three centuries later.

An inevitable product of the expansion of the West End as the most fashionable quarter of London was the growth of a number of shops west of Temple Bar, and more especially of establishments selling luxury and semi-luxury products. While a silkman of high repute such as the celebrated Sir Baptist Hicks, who was also a moneylender to the world of fashion and himself ended his days as a peer of the realm, would never lack customers at his shop in the City, there was a notable growth of similar establishments, as well as of high class tailors' shops, further west. Similarly, no amount of pressure from the crown, horrified at the dilapidated state of the once universally admired Goldsmiths' Row in Cheapside, or from the City government, for whom reasons of civic aggrandizement were at least as powerful as those of civic pride, could avail to secure the return of adequate numbers of those City goldsmiths who had found life more congenial and profitable in Westminster. Although the campaign to re-people Goldsmiths' Row and Lombard Street with goldsmiths was stepped up in the 1620s and 1630s, as late as January 1638, forty-eight shops, in places in the City specifically reserved for goldsmiths were still occupied by lesser breeds. But the fears of City interests that they were bound to suffer from the increasingly westward orientation of the courtly world of fashion and establishments catering for it probably find their most striking expression in the protests from the shopkeepers of the Royal Exchange within the City at the earl of Salisbury's project of 1608 to erect a fashionable shopping centre, the so-called New Exchange, on the site of the former stables of Durham House in the Strand.

Despite the westward drift of the metropolitan world of fashion, not everyone connected with the court moved to the West End. For example, there was a number of fashionable Elizabethan and Jacobean houses along Holborn which continued to be occupied. One such house belonging to the earl of Southampton was demolished in 1638 to make room for eighty small dwellings. Other residents were Sir Christopher Hatton, Elizabeth I's lord chancellor, and another notable Elizabethan, Fulke Greville, later Lord Brooke, who was murdered at his Holborn house in 1628. Moreover, some courtly residents continued to dwell within the confines of the City of London, and more especially in the so-called 'liberties', which, though lying within the City boundaries, were yet exempt from its jurisdiction. Nevertheless the westward movement of the courtly world inevitably meant that the City was acquiring a more distinctively bourgeois and business character as it lost so many of its courtly residents. But in case this gives too modern an impression, one important difference needs to be noticed between the City then and now. In contrast with the situation today, when only a tiny minority of those whose business is conducted in the City actually resides there, in Elizabethan and early Stuart times all but a handful of citizens lived in close proximity to, and often at, their places of work. The citizens who dwelt outside London during their business careers, as distinct from those who set the seal on their social respectability by purchasing country estates on or immediately before retirement, were very exceptional indeed. The city houses of the greater merchants were, however, often very impressive. Indeed some of the great city houses once occupied by noblemen were purchased by wealthy citizens, such as the great Elizabethan magnate, Sir John Hart, who was occupying one of the earl of Oxford's town houses at the end of the reign. But there were also many opulent houses several storeys high – with consequently horrifying fire risks – which were built specifically for the greater London merchants. It was only in the larger provincial towns such as Norwich, York, Bristol and Exeter that more than a tiny handful of such houses were to be found. In Leicester, for example, two storeys was the norm for the better sort of house, supplemented very occasionally by gloomy unlit attics.[14]

Some of the former aristocratic houses in the City found a civic use as halls of Livery Companies. Others became inns, taverns, gaming establishments and tenement-houses. Coldharbour near the river, the former town house of the earls of Shrewsbury, was the most notorious example of a great house becoming slum tenements which housed at least 125 persons in 1637 – a cold harbour indeed for the indigent. Such cases of chronic overcrowding serve to remind us that it was not simply country gentlemen and aspirant courtiers who thronged to London from the provinces. The growth of the intimate economic connections with provincial England consequent upon London's increased need for food and fuel and its importance as a centre through which manufactured goods – and especially woollen cloth – passed on their way to overseas markets meant that ever-increasing numbers of travelling hucksters, wagoners and dealers were available to spread the news of the unique opportunities and wonders of the metropolis to groups of admiring yokels in alehouses in the Home Counties and even further afield. Many a young man must have owed his decision to go to London to just such an occasion as this. Most of the immigrants probably came from nearby counties, although some certainly came from further afield. There is, for example, abundant evidence of immigrant vagrants being dispatched by the municipal authorities to places of origin which were often in remote parts of the realm. With regard to those immigrants who served apprenticeships in the City, as opposed to those who swelled the pool of unskilled and often casual labour, Professor Stone's investigation of the records of the Fishmongers' and Carpenters' companies has revealed that forty per cent of these apprentices hailed from the highland zones in the north and southwest of England – a rather startling discovery, though it would be unwise to make too much of evidence drawn from such a narrow base.[15]

In drawing many immigrants from foreign lands, London was certainly not unique, except perhaps in terms of the occupational heterogeneity of the alien population. A number of provincial towns such as Norwich, Colchester, Canterbury, Maidstone and Southampton owed much to the Elizabethan influx of refugees from Roman Catholic persecution in the southern Netherlands, often bringing with them new skills, and more particularly the manufacture of new speciality fabrics, which were, especially in the seventeenth century, to contribute strikingly to the diversification of English textile production and the exploitation of southern European markets on a hitherto unprecedented scale (see pp. 355–60). It was more particularly to the suburbs that immigrants to London, both English and alien, flocked, for here they were outside the jurisdiction both of the municipality and of the City gilds and companies, so that it was much easier for unapprenticed workmen to find employment. This factor is also of no small importance in the development of rural industry in general and, more particularly, of the woollen textile industry. In addition, accommodation of a sort was more readily available and rents cheaper in the suburbs, not least because the regulations relating to the subdivision of houses and the harbouring of inmates were less strictly enforced. The suburbs were expanding at what, to many citizens and to both the municipal and national government, seemed a very alarming rate: eastwards along the Thames through Wapping, a district reclaimed from mudflats in the early years of this period, and increasingly inhabited by seafaring men and, especially after the construction of the East India Company's dockyard at Blackwall in 1614, by shipyard workers; eastwards also via Ratcliffe Highway beyond

Shadwell, and from Aldgate East to beyond Whitechapel Church. South of the Thames, Bermondsey, Newington and Lambeth were in process of being linked by a chain of buildings with the borough of Southwark and London Bridge. To the north metropolitan expansion was severely restricted by the lie and nature of the land, but to the west, the area of expansion of the world of fashion *par excellence*, the increased population of Westminster was by no means limited to courtly residents and their domestics. Some of London's most notorious slums were in process of being created in the seventeenth century in the parish of St Giles-in-the-Fields, which lay athwart the northernmost point of linkage between the cities of London and Westminster. Quite apart from early seventeenth-century districts of high fashion, such as St Martin's Lane and Covent Garden, there was another notable growth of building which extended the southwestern limit of the metropolis well beyond Westminster Abbey, much of it, despite the proximity of the court, slum property.

While slum districts were growing in metropolitan London, slum buildings were almost ubiquitous, and directly off many well-kept and fashionable streets there lurked sordid alleys crammed with filthy tenements. Nowhere was this incongruous mixture of squalor and opulence more prevalent than in the City of London itself. The parish of St Michael, Cornhill, for example, contained a large number of splendid merchant houses, but in some of the alleys off the streets, such as Harp Alley, where six rooms were inhabited by sixty-four persons in 1637, very different conditions prevailed. There were many fine houses occupied by residents of quality in the precincts of Whitefriars and St Bartholomew the Great, Smithfield. Yet Whitefriars also contained Alsatia, the notorious haunt of thieves and other criminals, while in 1636 a correspondent of the earl of Middlesex, one of the residents of St Bartholomew's, characterized its slums as 'the commodity the parish hath gotten by the Earl of Holland's building'.

The census of new buildings, divided houses and inmates which was made in 1637 provides details of misery and squalor in depressing abundance: one small room occupied by a couple, five children and a lodger; another, in the same building in Portsoken ward, by a man and two widows; twenty-four families occupying one house in the riverside parish of St Martin's Vintry; people dwelling in converted stables, slaughterhouses, barns, haylofts, bakehouses, tallowhouses and coalhouses in many parts of the City. Conditions were almost certainly far worse in the suburbs, where the City authorities claimed that the prevailing administrative inefficiency fostered slum conditions and precipitated swarms of beggars into the City. In September 1595, for example, the lord mayor complained about the hordes of beggars from the parts of Southwark lying outside City control, and more particularly from the number of crowded tenements erected by covetous landlords for their private gain. The continued flow of rural immigrants to London in search of work provided golden opportunities both for such landlords and for speculative builders.

It was more or less inevitable when the pros of metropolitan growth came to be weighed against the cons that London should receive a great deal more blame than praise. The provincial ports complained that their lifeblood was being drained away by the growth of the metropolitan stranglehold on overseas trade exercised through the medium of great chartered companies dominated by Londoners. In addition, there were many who deplored the increasingly attractive force exercised by the metropolis over landowners, causing them to neglect both to maintain their traditional functions of 'hospitality' in the countryside and to carry out the duties of local magistracy. No one disapproved of this tendency more strongly than King James I. In a celebrated speech in the Star Chamber in June 1616 the king argued that London was a corrupting influence and that, as in the case of the first sin, the process of corruption operated via female agency:

> One of the greatest causes of all Gentlemens desire, that have no calling or errand, to dwell in *London*, is apparently the pride of the women: for if they be wives, then their husbands, and if they be maids, then their fathers, must bring them up to *London*: because the new fashion is to be had no where but in *London*: and here, if they be unmarried, they mar their marriages, and if they be married, they lose their reputations, and rob their husbands purses. It is the fashion of *Italy* . . . that all the Gentry dwell in the principal Towns, and so the whole country is empty. Even so now in *England*, all the country is gotten into *London*, so as with time, *England* will only be *London*, and the whole country be left waste . . .

John Chamberlain, that purveyor of court gossip *par excellence*, was decidedly of the opinion that it was the women who were particularly infuriated by the Stuart proclamations which ordered country gentlemen with no business in London to return to the country. A steady stream of such proclamations issued from May 1603 onwards, but particularly galling must have been those of 22 December 1622 and 26 May 1623, which commanded that even those gentlemen with legitimate excuse for visiting London should leave their wives and families behind.

The emphasis which has been laid in this chapter on the attractive force of London to all social classes lays it open to the obvious criticism that it emphasizes the exceptional at the expense of the typical Englishman. Professor Everitt is right to remind us that it is fatally easy to overestimate the impact of London on the country gentry as a whole, some of whom hardly ever crossed even the borderlines of their native counties, while others, like the Kentish gentleman, Henry Oxinden, were horrified by what they found on their only visit to the metropolis. Nevertheless, writing of London's influence in the century after 1650, Dr Wrigley has suggested that something approaching one-sixth of the whole population of England may have had direct experience of life in London, for there was an outflow of persons from, as well as an influx to, London.[16] Although the proportion would probably be lower, there is every reason to believe that it was considerable in the earlier period. Whatever it was, its precise influence on English society as a whole can only be conjectured. It may well be, as Wrigley suggests, that life in London put a premium on literacy, and moreover that the greater volume of cheap goods available there was an important factor in breaking down those preferences for leisure over work which were stressed earlier as a characteristic of labour in any pre-industrial society. Whatever the nature of London's influence, the man who returned to provincial life after several years of residence in London was a very different creature from the provincial who had no such experience of metropolitan life. Whether he became part of that leaven which was ultimately to transform the pre-industrial lump or whether his desire to abandon metropolitan life and to seek employment or purchase land and obtain social acceptance in the provinces acted as a significant counterweight to the lessons of his London experience obviously varied from one individual case to another. We know all too little about the attitudes of returning members of the poorer classes, whether skilled or unskilled workers or vagrants who were whipped and returned to their places of origin and settlement. Of merchants and tradesmen who bought up land, much – admittedly biased – contemporary comment suggests that despite their ambition to find social acceptance, there all too often continued to cling to their persons the faint but inextinguishable odour of the counting-house. The carefully cultivated habits and values which made for a successful business career were not easily divested overnight.

Chapter Two

THE SOCIAL AND POLITICAL ORDER

DEGREE AND PATERNALISM

It must be clear from the preceding chapter that 'class' relationships, arising out of the differing economic position of different groups in relation to the ownership and exploitation of the means of material production and embodied more particularly in the relationship between employer and employee, were an important feature of Elizabethan and early Stuart society. But it has been argued with some force that a more characteristic form of social stratification was provided by hierarchical relationships conceived in terms of degree and order, and organized, in the words of the French historian Professor Roland Mousnier, 'not according to the wealth of . . . members . . . nor yet by their role in the process of production of material goods, but according to the esteem, honour and rank that society attributes to social functions that can have no connection at all with the production of material goods.'[1]

This can be illustrated by reference to the tendency mentioned in the last chapter for capital to be diverted from industry and commerce into land. When entrepreneurs invested the profits of a working lifetime in the purchase of land, they were not normally doing so because land was a better economic investment, in the sense of affording a higher yield, than was provided by their former occupations. First and foremost they were demonstrating that their business careers had come to be a means to the higher end of acquiring a superior status which bore no relation to their role in the organization of economic production, and which was unattainable without the ownership of land. It is, of course, true that many business magnates today are by no means unaffected by similar considerations, though with the significant difference that it is now possible for them to have their cake and eat it – simultaneously to be both entrepreneurial giants and to occupy an elevated position in the social order – though no one would deny that in the highest reaches of British society, whatever the title of honour held, social prestige remains proportional to the antiquity of riches. In Tudor and Stuart, as in modern, times, English society was distinguished from that of other monarchical countries such as Spain and France by the relative ease by which wealth was transmuted into status. But in the earlier period the gulf between the two modes of living was enormously wider than today, and while it could be bridged far more easily than in Spain or France, it was normal, though not quite invariable, for those making the social crossing to sever their links with the other side.

Even more significant perhaps was the contemporary tendency for the relationships between employers and employees to be subsumed under a form of social categorization which was essentially one of degree and order rather than of social class, a relationship basically authoritarian, but in a very particular sort of way. The employer, like the great landowner, the teacher, the university don, and everyone else exercising authority, stood *in loco parentis* to his dependants. This was the common feature between all levels of authority and subordination, from the purely paternal authority exercised by the fathers of individual families to that of the monarch himself at the apex of society. When James I outlined his views on his royal authority to parliament in 1610, he made use of three significant analogies, or correspondences as he termed them. The power of kings in their realms was likened unto that of God in the universe; of corporeal heads over the other limbs of the human body; and of fathers over their families. 'The state of monarchy,' he averred, 'is the supremest thing upon earth; for kings are not only God's lieutenants upon earth and sit upon God's throne, but even by God himself they are called gods.' The greatest strength of monarchy rested in the simple fact that royal authority was reflected in every other form of authority, whose exercise was inextricably connected with the power of kings, and therefore, following James I's analogy, with divine authority itself. Whether a man was an employer, teacher, local magistrate or village constable, the power which he exercised was at once connected with royal and paternal power. ''Twas the great Interest and strength of Monarchy,' wrote an English republican in 1651, 'to set up in its Image a petty Monarchy in every considerable Association of men,' adding that to prevent the return of monarchy, it would be necessary 'to pull down these great Idols'.[2] Obedience was to be accorded by kings to God, subjects to kings, men to masters, wives to husbands, children to fathers, and this in turn was reflected in innumerable outward and visible signs of deference, differing from rank to rank, but all indispensable aspects of a society in which everyone ought to know his place, which such ubiquitous social constraints were designed to afford him no opportunity of forgetting.

To this rule the relationship between employer and employee was no exception, the neo-paternalistic aspect being reckoned as at least as significant as that arising out of the position of each in respect of ownership of the means of production. Farm employees, many of whom lived on their employers' premises, and domestic industrial workers were in every respect analogous to subordinate members of families, and their employer stood in the same paternalistic relation towards them as did the great estate-owner towards his tenants and other dependants. A government memorandum drawn up in the 1570s probably for the guidance of magistrates who had to enforce the apprenticeship clauses of the Statute of Artificers of 1563 justified the statutory insistence on a seven-year apprenticeship not only on the grounds of the desirability of a thorough technical training, but also because 'young men should work to sustain the aged who were their bringers-up'. Moreover, a young man who emerged from apprenticeship at the age of twenty-four would be 'of a more riper or better judgment to guide or rule himself'. Until such time it was more appropriate for him 'to remain under government as a servant and learner, than to become a ruler, as a master or instructor'. Indeed even on conclusion of their training, most apprentices would simply pass from one form of neo-paternal subordination to another. For although there were significant economic differences between the status of journeyman and apprentice, in social terms both fell within the paternalistic frame of reference. Thus our memorandum emphasizes that it was the duty of young men to cherish the masters who had brought them up, and not to bring them to ruin by cut-throat competition, just as it was the duty of grown-up sons and daughters to cherish and sustain their aged and infirm parents. Conversely, rather than get rid of reluctant or difficult employees, masters should treat them like difficult children who 'if they were corrected . . . and forced to continue in service, divers would be reclaimed and brought to honest conversation that continue stubborn and grow from evil to evil, from naught to worse'. In a society which viewed order as indivisible, an employer of labour had a double interest in monarchical authority, for both as employer and as paterfamilias his authority was linked with that of the monarch as *pater patriae*.

THE ROYAL PREROGATIVE AND THE CONSTITUTION

While some of those who heard King James's famous speech to parliament in 1610 affected to be shocked by the familiar use which the king made of the deity, the idea that there was a divinity which hedged kings was not seriously questioned. The awesome ceremony of coronation, the anointing of the sovereign with holy oil, the royal powers of magical healing whose efficacy was amply borne out by the spectacular cures for scrofula apparently brought about by the royal touch, a phenomenon which the modern sceptic can ascribe to psychosomatic considerations, all testified to that. Nevertheless it was by no means impossible that the Jacobean argument from correspondences might be employed to the end of enhancing royal power so as to eclipse all else. For if the power of kings within their realms really corresponded with that of God in the universe, it must surely be absolute and uncontrollable.

However, at the point at which our period begins there were notable obstacles in the way of the acceptance of such a complete correspondence between royal and divine power. For with the restoration of Roman Catholicism by Mary Tudor, the Henrician notion of England as an 'empire' – that is an autonomous entity in which the monarch's power was supreme and in no way subject to external authority or jurisdiction – was replaced by the older notion of the existence within the community of the realm of a church which, however much subject to royal interference in actual practice, was nevertheless an organization which transcended national boundaries and whose head was a foreign potentate, the bishop of Rome or pope. The papal claim of the right to interfere in the affairs of any realm whose ruler was contravening divine law made the pope and not the monarch in question the only human ruler whose power corresponded strictly with that of God. The most striking claims for the exercise of *plenitudo potestatis*, the fullness of power, had, after all, come from popes and not from kings. As Mary's archbishop of Canterbury, Cardinal Reginald Pole, had emphasized long before: 'inasmuch as there are interests beyond the temporal, so there is a jurisdiction beyond the king's'.

Nor was this the only obstacle to the absolute power of the monarch. In the first place, not all writers who used the analogy between kings and God confined the correspondence to kings. The immensely influential early Elizabethan handbook *A Mirror for Magistrates* (1559) was at pains to emphasize that it was not simply kings but 'all officers under them' whom God called by his own name: 'Ye be all Gods, as many as have in your charge any ministration of justice.' Moreover there was a long-established body of doctrine stemming from Sir John Fortescue in the fifteenth century, which claimed that far from being an absolute monarchy (*dominium regale*), England was a limited or mixed monarchy (*dominium politicum et regale*), that is, a form of government in which the characteristic virtues of monarchy, aristocracy and democracy were judiciously combined, and their characteristic vices of tyranny, faction and tumultuous disorder kept in strict control. Under this theory certain powers were assigned to the king acting alone (*Rex Solus*), and these constituted the so-called prerogative powers, which were completely beyond the scope of the subject to discuss except by invitation from the monarch.

'Queen Elizabeth,' declared a pamphleteer in 1643, 'spake little of her *Prerogative*, but never had a Prince a Prerogative at more length and more freedom.' The author was drawing attention to what he regarded as the inflated claims for the royal prerogative which were made by Elizabeth's Stuart successors. But while Elizabeth I never claimed that the royal prerogative existed above, or irrespective of, the law, one thing that no Tudor monarch would ever tolerate was the idea that its exercise should be continually subjected to judgments in the lawcourts. What precisely were these miscellaneous powers which went to make up the royal prerogative? To attempt to define them is to run immediately into the problems which were to make the subject a central constitutional issue in the period. First there was the legal uniqueness of the position of the monarch, the fact that he could do no wrong and therefore could not be held liable for his actions. Of course, the ministers of the crown could be sued or (after 1621 when the process of parliamentary impeachment was revived) impeached, but in matters of policies pursued or recommended they could frequently extricate themselves by pleading the royal command as the occasion of their actions, and if their plea was corroborated by the monarch, the matter ended there. Then there was the royal right to commit to prison without showing cause other than by special mandate of the monarch, a right tested and confirmed in 1627 in the case of the five knights imprisoned for their opposition to a forced loan, when no reason for their detention was given and the royal warrant was declared sufficient cause. This was only one of a number of powers exercised by the monarch alone and in no way controlled by parliament, which itself was summoned, adjourned, prorogued and dissolved entirely at the royal will and pleasure, at least down to 1641. With the monarch alone rested the conduct of foreign affairs, including the right to declare war or establish peace. Connected with this in an age when royal children were pawns in the game of international diplomacy was the monarch's right – both as paterfamilias and *pater patriae* – to marry his children to whomsoever he chose.

If the right of *Rex Solus* (or *Regina Sola*) to deal with all the above matters was beyond question, there were other areas where the monarch's right to act alone was from time to time questioned. At bottom, no one would dispute the royal responsibility for the defence of the realm, but the question of militia training became an issue in which prerogative powers were questioned by early Stuart parliaments. 'It was an indisputable part of the Crown's prerogative,' declares one modern authority, 'that it could regulate external trade in what it claimed to be the national interest.'[3] Yet one of the main media of such regulations, the vesting of branches of overseas trade in chartered companies with monopoly control, gave rise to bitter controversy in both mercantile and parliamentary circles; while another, the levying of impositions or customs duties not voted by parliament, was one of the most contentious constitutional issues of the early Stuart period. The same is true of the internal monopolies over which Queen Elizabeth experienced a great deal of trouble in the last parliament of her reign, and her successors in those of 1621, 1624 and 1640. Religion was another area where there was by no means complete agreement about the exact scope of the prerogative. While both Elizabeth I and her two Stuart successors insisted on treating religion as a matter for the monarch alone, this was not the view taken by all of their subjects, and the foundation documents of the Elizabethan settlement afforded some grounds for those who strove to make it a parliamentary matter.

In a celebrated speech in the debate on Monopolies in the House of Commons in 1601 Francis Bacon distinguished between the 'Inlarging and Restraining Liberty' of the royal prerogative. The former, the royal power to dispense with the operation of statute in particular cases, was not the least important and potentially one of the most contentious areas of the prerogative. Given the fact that parliament met rarely, the power to enlarge (viz. relax) the operation of statutes in particular cases according to varying circumstances, in matters such as, for example, the prohibited export of certain foodstuffs or unfinished cloth, clearly falls within the prerogative exercised in the public interest, though some such licences to disregard parliamentary statutes were issued fairly regularly and not just in abnormal years. By 'restraining' power Bacon meant the royal power to restrict activities which would otherwise be free to all – free, that is, by common rather than by statute law – so that the monopolies of manufacture and commerce which were the most notable products of the exercise of this power appeared as obnoxious to many common lawyers as they did to the producers or traders who were excluded from these benefits and to the consumers who had to pay monopoly prices.

Not all of the prerogative powers of *Rex Solus* have been dealt with here. One omission is the powers exercised by the monarch as apex of the 'feudal' pyramid. These matters were by now mainly of fiscal significance. Among them were the purveyance of supplies for the royal household at undervalues – or the various forms of composition in lieu of the exercise of this right – and the right of wardship exercised over minors who had inherited lands held by feudal military tenure. But for the moment enough has been said to demonstrate that, while many of these prerogative powers were essential to the exercise of efficient and responsive government, their indiscriminate use might threaten the constitutional balance. Indeed the reader at this point might well question whether a monarchy equipped with such formidable powers could be regarded as in any sense 'mixed', and whether in fact any notable rights were left to the subject. But great though the monarch's power undoubtedly was, it was recognized to be greater in parliament than it was out of parliament, a doctrine which finds its clearest expression in the supremacy of statute, since statutes can be made only by the king (or queen) in parliament.

However, the frequent recourse to use both of the royal dispensing power and of royal proclamations issued independently of parliament might on occasions appear to be undermining seriously the force of statute, so that in the latter case for example the House of Commons in 1610 expressed the fear that 'proclamations will by degrees grow up and increase to the strength and nature of laws'. Similarly, while the royal levying of impositions might be justified on the grounds of the royal prerogative right and duty to foster national commerce, there can be little doubt that the crown's real motive for impositions was to be found in their fiscal, rather than their protectionist, significance. Since, as James Whitelock argued in the great debate on impositions in parliament in 1610, 'the power of imposing and power of making laws are *convertibilia* and *coincidentia* and whatsoever can do the one can do the other', it was by no means impossible that impositions, like other prerogative revenues, might help to fashion a situation in which the crown might be able to dispense altogether with parliament.

Such considerations go far towards explaining what might otherwise be regarded as the obsessive concern of the House of Commons with what might be described as the thin ends of prerogative wedges. The trouble lay partly in the fact that, especially under the Stuarts, the royal prerogative, far from simply representing, in John Selden's phrase, 'the law as it concerns the King', became bound up with theories of royal divine right and the monarch's God-given authority, which, corresponding within the confines of his realm to the authority of God in the universe, was conceived by some as putting him above the law. But even if this extreme view was not generally held, it is undeniable that the idea of England as a mixed monarchy, with a nice balance maintained between royal and parliamentary power, did not marry very happily with the idea of the prerogative as something divinely ordained rather than legally prescribed. For who is to question a divinely ordained prerogative if it is pushed to its limits? And if it is pushed to its limits, it is undeniable that not much remains of the balanced concept of mixed monarchy. Indeed it has been argued that the concept fell into disuse in the course of this period, only to be revived by the advisers of Charles I when they were anxious to refurbish his image as a law-abiding constitutional monarch on the eve of the Civil War. During the intervening period more extreme and uncompromising notions of the scope of royal power were in the ascendancy.[4]

OBEDIENCE AND REBELLION

Order and obedience were indivisible. And just as order was the principle by which God's will was manifest, so were disobedience and rebellion the manifestation of disorder and defiance of God's will. But, what if the powers that be, far from being godly princes, were evil men, tyrants who defied God's word, or at least were deceived into doing so by evil advisers? Might not the godly son disobey the commands of his wicked father or the godly subject those of a tyrannical godless king? There were, of course, those who claimed that it was a contradiction in terms for rightful kings, who were by definition God's analogues, also to be tyrants. However, it was more usual for even passionate upholders of the duty of obedience and the evils of revolt in any conceivable circumstance to admit the possibility of kings becoming tyrants, while ruling out the right of revolt even against such rulers. For although the rule of tyrants created disorder through their defiance of God's word, to seek to overthrow them was to compound rather than to remove that disorder. Moreover, oppressed subjects must never overlook the possibility that tyrants could be sent either as the scourge of God against notorious sinners or to test the Christian submissiveness and obedience of good men, as God had tested Job. Thus the Edwardian Homily of Obedience of 1547, ordered to be read from the pulpits to emphasize the duty of Christian submissiveness, ruled out the possibility of revolt even against the most abominable tyrant. Disobedience was allowed, indeed might well be a duty, but not revolt:

> Yet let us believe undoubtedly, good Christian people, that we may not obey kings, magistrates or any other (though they be our own fathers) if they would command us to do anything contrary to God's commandments. In such a case . . . we must rather obey God than man. But nevertheless in that case we may not in any wise resist violently or rebel against . . . the anointed of the Lord or any of his approved officers.

This was, in essence, the doctrine of passive obedience, which allowed limited scope for individual disobedience while rendering it politically innocuous. It was the duty of the Christian subject both to disobey the tyrant who commanded him to perform unrighteous acts, and to submit uncomplainingly to the frightful consequences of such disobedience. In this somewhat tenuous way the claims of conscience and order were reconciled.

But while rebellion was always wicked, it could still be

used by God as a means of bringing evil kings to book. However wicked the act of rebellion, the fear of revolt was constantly before the eyes of potential tyrants, urging them to toe the line. In this view the people who took part in such rebellions were seen as an almost blind force, as God's terrible instrument who were themselves destroyed doing God's work. But according to the succinct and impressive account of seditions and troubles in Francis Bacon's essay of that name, although 'the rebellions of the belly are the worst . . . common people are of slow motion if they be not excited by the greater sort; and the greater sort are of small strength except the multitude be apt and ready to move of themselves'. The real danger came when well-born malcontents made use of plebeian unrest for their own ends. And indeed while some peasant revolts in Tudor and Stuart England, like the Norfolk revolt of 1549 and the anti-enclosure disturbances in the Midlands in 1607, were in a real sense class revolts by the victims against the perpetrators of economic oppression, others, such as the Pilgrimage of Grace and the Lincolnshire revolt of 1536 and the northern revolt of 1569, came near to Bacon's idea of a junction of high- and low-born malcontents, that is, to Professor Mousnier's concept of a 'revolt of the orders'.

The pattern differs, of course, from one revolt to another. Sometimes, as in Lincolnshire in 1536, the revolt started far below the level of the political nation, but received the often tacit and sometimes explicit support of notables who hoped to use it to impress upon the crown the need to bring about fundamental changes, such as scrapping its evil advisers. Such movements had, it could be argued, an important function to perform as unmistakable warning signs to governments that they were going off the rails.[5] But in other cases, of which the great Civil War is the outstanding example, the idea of an enraged peasantry as the blind instrument of God's retribution against tyranny was obviously inapplicable. In the first type of situation most of the dissident well-born rebels were normally able to get out in time and to shuffle off the blame for the sin of revolt on to the common people, while hoping to derive certain advantages from the fact of the revolt and using it to press home lessons about what they deemed to be the proper conduct and ordering of government. In the second type, since revolt was initiated by the well-born and influential, it could not be passed off as a lower-order aberration from which the monarch, while punishing the rebels severely, ought yet to learn some lessons. A way had to be found of justifying revolt itself while at the same time imposing clear limitations on who could initiate it. A similar sort of sanction had existed in the feudal *diffidatio*, by which feudal magnates formally defied their king, and the sixteenth century – notably in the revolt of the Huguenots in the French wars of religion, of the Scots against Mary Stuart, and of the Dutch against their overlord, the king of Spain – was to provide parallels adapted to the needs of differently organized societies. These were to find an English expression in the Civil War. For the Huguenots in France, the Dutch rebels in the Netherlands, the Calvinists in Scotland and the Puritans in England were unwilling to trust to the people at large the right of deciding whether revolt against their kings was justified. They were at great pains to limit the social implications of an already frightening enough insistence on the right to revolt by carefully confining the right to what came to be described as the inferior magistrates; inferior that is to the supreme magistrate, the monarch. This was an attempt, successful in the case of France, Scotland and the Netherlands, but less so in that of the English Civil War, to reap the advantage of a limited right of revolt without threatening the foundations of the deferential society and opening the floodgates of democracy.

STATUS AND DEFERENCE

(i)

It is now time to look more closely at the social order of which deference and authority were the keynote; the deference accorded by men and women to their social superiors, and the authority which the latter, by virtue of their rank, exercised over the former. The most fundamental of all divisions within society was that between gentlemen and the rest. But while this was true, and was to remain a characteristic feature of the social order for centuries, there were also finely adjusted gradations of rank amongst the superior orders who were accounted gentlemen, although needless to say these nice distinctions did not completely dispose of the problem of status confusion among the upper orders of society. This is demonstrated, for example, by the disputes after 1611 as to whether the newly created order of baronets had precedence, not over barons – there was no doubt about the superiority of the latter – but over the younger sons of barons. It is in fact arguable that disputes over precedence and status were the fiercer in direct proportion as precedence was *not* clearly indicated by titles of honour, and notably within a single rank of society. The importance of such matters can be seen, for example, in the jostling of justices of the peace to be named above their local rivals on the Commission of the Peace; and, higher up the social scale, in the mutual jealousy between the earls of Essex and of Nottingham in the 1590s. Since both noblemen were earls, the issue came to turn on the precedence in terms of the offices of state held by each, a distinction which exacerbated the factional rivalries and scramble for office in the closing years of Elizabeth's reign.

Elizabethan England saw what seems to have been an attempt to restore social equilibrium by reasserting the value of titles of honour, following the inflation of honours in the reigns of Henry VIII and Edward VI. In the queen's view the best way to enhance and restore the value of titles of honour, and the force of considerations of social hierarchy, was to be sparing in their bestowal. Thus during the forty-five years of her reign Elizabeth created eighteen peerages, as opposed to the forty-seven created in the only slightly shorter period of the reigns of her father and half-brother. Moreover her parsimony became even more marked as time went on. She created only two new peerages and promoted only one peer in the last thirty years of her reign, and at her death there were two fewer peers in England than there had been at her accession. It is true that the less exalted ranks of the English gentry were not subject to such stringent controls. Two thousand grants of arms conferring gentility were made between 1560 and 1589 alone, while the title of esquire, traditionally confined to the younger sons of peers, the heirs male of knights and a strictly limited number of carefully defined office-holders, was now being used more indiscriminately. In neither case did the crown exercise direct control. This lay with the College of Heralds, in whose interest it was to inflate the titles to gentility which provided them with an income from fees. In these circumstances it is hardly surprising that the controls exercised by the heralds were confined to periodic visitations and inspections of titles to arms, carried out primarily with the aim of ensuring that as little as possible slipped through their net, and so maximizing their returns from the lucrative process of converting grubs into butterflies. Nor was it the queen's fault that the number of gentlemen boasting the title of knight was as large as it was. Indeed by about 1580 the number of knights in England had roughly halved from its level at her accession. The fact that at her death, out of the total of about 550 knights, there were only some fifty fewer than at her accession, was primarily due to the generosity of her military commanders in the 1540s, and especially of the earl of Essex. It has been reckoned by Professor Lawrence Stone, to whose work on the peerage and titles of honour all historians of the period are deeply indebted, that more than a quarter of the knights in England in 1603 were Essex's creations.[6]

Elizabeth's fury at this prodigality serves to underline the significance of considerations of title and rank as points of social reference in Tudor England. Not only had Essex's precipitate flood of creations debased an important title of honour; it also militated against that stability of social relationships which the very notion of titles of honour was designed to serve. For those knighted were frequently men of lesser, more obscure families than many gentlemen over whom, by virtue of their new titles, they now took precedence. The result was to augment social confusion and jealousy by creating status anomalies and uncertainty. But if this was the consequence of the later Elizabethan inflation of the knightage, it was nothing to what happened during the next reign, when the social floodgates were opened. During the first four months of the new reign no less than 906 persons were knighted. In the thirty-eight years which bridge the accession of James I and 1641, between three and four times as many men were knighted as during the forty-five years of Elizabeth's reign, even though the latter included those knighted not by the queen but by her military commanders. There was a similar inflation of the number of baronets, the new title created in 1611. Originally for sale at £1,095, baronetcies seem at first to have been a moderately attractive proposition in view of the debasement of the knightage consequent on the inflation of its numbers and of the royal undertaking to keep down the numbers of baronets. But that undertaking was soon disregarded; moreover, unlike Elizabeth, the Stuarts did not restrict the flow of honours to levels below the nobility. It is true that Elizabeth's parsimony in the matter of the creation of new peers had been overdone, and there was some need for relaxation in this respect. But relaxation such as occurred at the beginning of the reign of James I was one thing; the shameless selling of peerages, which after 1615 were added to knighthoods and baronetcies as commodities marketed for cash, was quite another, and a simple indication of the declining worth of once coveted titles was the progressive decline of the price they fetched. The main beneficiary of the peddling of honours was the royal favourite George Villiers, successively viscount, earl, marquis and duke of Buckingham, after whose assassination in 1628 the flow of new creations was halted. But between 1615 and 1628 there was a rise of about fifty-six per cent (eighty-one to 126) in the number of peerages, including, most striking of all, a rise of 141 per cent (twenty-seven to sixty-five) in the number of peers of the quite senior rank of earl. 'The peers under Charles I,' writes Professor Stone, 'were a more upstart group than at any time in the previous 200 years – far more so than at the present day, when the pattern more closely resembles that of 1558.'

The effects of the inflation and debasement of titles of honour were those which have been already described in the case of Essex's creation of knights, only writ exceedingly large. It enormously exacerbated status uncertainty, or, in the words of one of the charges brought against the duke of Buckingham at his impeachment in 1626, it 'introduceth a strange confusion, mingling the meaner with the more pure and refined metal'. When a barber and an ex-convict could be knighted; when the inflation of the baronetage revealed anomalies, such as that some of those holding this highest of all titles below the peerage had previously not even been of gentle birth; and when merchants and moneylenders rushed to buy peerages, contemporaries might be excused for believing that the traditional social values of the deferential, hierarchical society were indeed in jeopardy. And if it is true that the carefully defined gradations of social position, as expressed in titles of honour, drew their force from the institution of monarchy, so is it arguable that monarchy itself was endangered by the erosion of these distinctions.

(ii)

But for all these uncertainties, precedence and deference continued to express themselves in countless ways right through society. 'The key symbols of Tudor and early Stuart society,' writes Professor Stone, 'were the hat and the whip. The former was ever being doffed and donned to emphasize the complex hierarchy of ranks and authorities'; similarly: 'while corporal punishment was endured by children and adolescents of the upper and lower orders alike', the contrast between gentlemen, who became exempt from it on coming of age, and adult servants who were thrashed by order of their masters or vagrants who were whipped till their backs became bloody is among the most eloquent testimonies to the difference between the gentry and the rest of society.

Another striking manifestation of the importance of rank and precedence is to be found in the sumptuary legislation which the Tudors had inherited from the Middle Ages, and which was augmented and stiffened both in the early sixteenth century and in the great period of conservative reconstruction in the first decade of the reign of Elizabeth I. As well as forbidding the wearing of some articles, for example double ruffs and 'excessive long cloaks', to all and sundry and reserving the wearing of certain luxury fabrics such as silk and velvets to the gentry and upwards, the sumptuary regulations reflected in considerable measure the more complex hierarchical gradations which so obsessed contemporaries, extending not only to the fabrics themselves but also to their colours. Purple silk, for example, was restricted to members of the royal family by an act of 1533; and scarlet and blue silk and velvet to persons of the degree of Knight of the Garter and above and the children of upper peers above the rank of earl. The repeal of this legislation in the reign of James I did not betoken disapproval of its purpose, but the impossibility of enforcing it.[7]

An equally eloquent, if somewhat less elaborate and complicated example of regulations designed to emphasize the importance of social precedence and deference appears in the seating arrangements which obtained in many churches. For instance, the churchwardens of St Ebbe's in Oxford were actively conscious of the social dangers arising out of the no doubt quite innocent behaviour of a humble member of the congregation, an ale-bearer, who occupied a seat in too exalted a section of the church. Special places were appropriate for different social groups in this rigid form of congregational social apartheid, and the churchwardens considered it outrageous for such inferior persons 'in show of the world [to] . . . sit above their betters'.[8] It is true that the significance of such regulations is not entirely exhausted by reference to considerations of social precedence. Like the sumptuary laws, which were not unrelated to the economic desirability of restricting demand for luxury imports and increasing that for home products (silks and velvets were imported goods, and one law on the statute book between 1571 and 1597 insisted on all below the gentry wearing woollen caps on Sundays and holy days), the reservation of pews for the social élite of a parish often had an economic as well as a social purpose, connected with the importance of pew-rents as an item of parish income. In both cases motives of economic advantage and social differentiation were in a real sense complementary. But there can be little doubt that the latter counted for far more than the former.

Similar considerations apply to the sartorial and academic privileges connected with social rank at the universities and Inns of Court. The introduction at some Oxford and Cambridge colleges of the status of fellow-commoner or its equivalent in the later sixteenth century is a case in point. Fellow-commoners were, by definition, gentlemen, and as such marked off from undergraduates of lower social degree and allowed a number of privileges, including the right to dine at high table. They also paid higher fees, the economic advantages to the college complementing social considerations in much the same way as was previously noticed in the case of pew rents in some churches. Although an important feature of the social history of the period was the growing attractiveness of a university education to young men of good family, not least because it was increasingly regarded as a useful grounding for public service, there was, as Professor Stone has demonstrated, no question of the greater number of well-born entrants – many of whom did not take degrees and occupied themselves in extracurricular pursuits reducing the educational opportunities for young men of less exalted status. For the growth of colleges carried with it an expansion of the number of places, while the admission of greater numbers of gentlemen undergraduates also involved a corresponding need to admit poor scholars who could work their way through college by performing menial tasks as sizars and servitors. But, needless to say, while this development tended to widen (or at least not to narrow) the scope of educational opportunity, it also made the social stratification of academic and social life at the university more striking than before.

(iii)

Counterpointing this ubiquitous sort of deference based upon social distinction was another sort based upon professional standing, and both sorts of distinction existed side by side in the universities and the Inns of Court. Something has already been said about the variety of privileges available to undergraduates of superior social status, but the fact that among the privileges accorded to fellow-commoners, for example, was the right to sit at high table, itself points to the existence of a different kind of distinction – one which operated within a professional, as distinct from a social hierarchy, but like the latter was reflected in forms of address, seating arrangements, distinctive garments and a number of other things marking the distinction between undergraduates, bachelors, masters, fellows and heads of houses at the universities, and benchers, barristers and students at the Inns of Court. At the universities there was emphatically an increase in the importance of distinction between academic ranks, connected with the rise in the significance of the colleges and their heads. Oxford and Cambridge were becoming ordered, disciplined places in the later sixteenth century, with more of their undergraduates living in college under a heightened discipline, in marked contrast to their late medieval predecessors and their continental contemporaries dwelling more freely and promiscuously in inns and taverns. The new statutes of 1570 for Cambridge and the reforms under the chancellorship of Archbishop Laud in the 1630s for Oxford set the formal constitutional seal on these developments.

In urban as in university government there was a clear movement towards creating a more structured and socially differentiated magistracy, what Professor Stone has described as 'a deliberate effort to destroy those remnants of democratic government in local affairs that had survived from the Middle Ages'. The granting of new urban charters was normally accompanied by noteworthy restrictions on the size of the body which elected the municipal rulers. While individual parishes in both town and country were assuming an increasing importance in the sixteenth century as units of local administration in civil as well as ecclesiastical matters, there was a growing tendency to exclude the majority of parishioners from any effective say in parish affairs via the emergence of select vestries as parochial governing bodies. In Kirkham, Lancashire, for example, parish affairs were ordered by a select vestry known as the 'Thirty Men', who held office for life or until they chose to resign. When vacancies on the select vestry occurred, they were filled by nominees of the existing vestrymen.[9]

Similar methods of indirect election fostering the growth of oligarchy were to be found among the urban gilds. These, of course, had never been egalitarian and had always been the institutional expression of the subordination of journeymen and apprentices to masters and of the latter to the master and wardens of the gild. What they also reflected, however, had been a large measure of equality of economic opportunity, since, given the relatively unelaborate nature of the fixed capital required to set up independently, every journeyman had more than an outside chance of himself becoming a master, and might reasonably regard his period of service and subordination as a time to accumulate capital with this end in view. To accept subordination and to pay appropriate deference is less irksome if there is a reasonable chance that ultimately it will be accorded to oneself. But in the larger towns, and especially in London, by the middle of the sixteenth century this state of affairs had long since ceased to obtain. Certainly in London the old craft gild had been replaced by the livery company, a far grander institution with its splendid hall and with its livery, the outward and visible signs of power and authority, confined to relatively few persons. In the process of becoming a livery company the gild had been divided into two parts, the livery and the yeomanry (sometimes called by other names), often reflecting a distinction between those who traded in the products of a craft and those who made them. This distinction was not, however, an absolute one. In many of the smaller London companies, for example, the liverymen were master craftsmen rather than traders, even if they also traded from their workshops, while in some of the larger companies a minority of members of the yeomanry or lower sector of the gild might be younger tradesmen rather than craftsmen.

But it was not simply in this division of gilds and companies into upper and lower sections that the growth of social differentiation within the gild consisted. Especially within the larger London companies there were highly significant splits within the 'clothing' or livery itself, expressed in the insulation of the governing bodies – the masters, wardens and the select bodies usually though not always known as Courts of Assistants – from the rest of the company and indeed even from the remainder of the livery. The executive heads of the companies, the master and wardens, were frequently selected simply by the Court of Assistants, and occasionally even by their retiring predecessors. The Court of Assistants itself was often dominated by former masters and wardens, if not always in sheer numbers, frequently in terms of the influence which they brought to bear in decision making. A good example of these oligarchic arrangements was the new charter obtained by the London Drapers' Company in 1607, whereby the former direct election of the master and wardens was replaced not by election by the Livery or even by the Court of Assistants, but by such members of that court as had already served either as master or as one of the wardens.

This increasing tendency towards widening the social gulf between different members of institutions such as gilds had parallels in many other areas of society, not least in the royal court itself, more especially during the reign of Charles I, when there is a good deal of evidence to suggest that protocol was becoming stricter and social differentiation more strongly marked. In these circumstances it is perhaps surprising to find the crown offering enthusiastic support under the early Stuarts to movements for the new incorporation of groups of dissident craftsmen seeking to dissociate themselves from parent organizations increasingly dominated by mercantile elements. In supporting the attempts of the London Glovers to free themselves from the Leathersellers, the Feltmakers from the Haberdashers, the Apothecaries from the Grocers and (ultimately) the Distillers from the Apothecaries, the crown no doubt saw itself as performing its paternalistic function of protecting humble craftsmen from commercial exploitation, but in so doing it trod on the toes of the municipal élite of London, all of whom saw such royal policies as derogatory both to their own authority and to authority in general, since they gave 'the government to the inferior sort to the great danger and prejudice of the government of this City'.

A HIERARCHY OF OCCUPATIONS

While 'professional' distinction counterpointed social distinction within a single occupation, different occupations were distinguished from each other in terms of their social respectability. It has already been remarked that the distinction between gentlefolk and the rest was the most fundamental point of cleavage in Tudor and Stuart society. Of all occupations, that of landowner was the most respectable and the most appropriate vocation for a gentleman. However, one of the main points of controversy in the debate on the fortunes of the Elizabethan and early Stuart landowning classes, on which so much ink was spilt in the 1940s and 1950s, was the precise importance which ought to be attached to sources of income other than those derived from the land in the economies of individual gentlemen. One school of thought argued that it was impossible for a 'mere gentleman' – one whose income was derived entirely from land – ever notably to improve his economic fortunes, on account of what he must spend in order to maintain his 'port' – the style of life deemed appropriate to his station. In the celebrated words of the Hampshire gentleman Sir John Oglander, 'he must have some other vocation with his inheritance'. What was the nature of such extra-agricultural vocations and how did they rank in terms of social respectability?

According to Professor Stone, in the sixteenth and seventeenth centuries, 'the ranking of the professions was only slightly higher than that of a tradesman'. While this may be true of such professional people as doctors, surgeons, university dons and some of the lower reaches of the legal profession such as country attorneys, it is certainly not applicable to the legal profession as a whole, at least not to common lawyers, as distinct from the civil lawyers who practised chiefly in the ecclesiastical courts. Above all it does not apply to office-holding, except perhaps in its lowest manifestations. The expansion of the machinery of government, which is one of the principal features of Tudor history, created many new governmental posts, and, far from these being below the dignity of a gentleman to occupy, a central theme of Tudor conservative propaganda was the danger of their falling into the hands of men of low birth. It was not only the right but the duty of nobles and gentlemen to serve their prince and to equip themselves to do so by acquiring the necessary skills, which in turn helps to explain the invasion of the universities by well-born undergraduates in the period.

Office was complementary to landowning and a proper pursuit for gentlemen, providing an additional source of income that helped them to cut an appropriate figure in an age in which nothing more surely denoted the social importance of a man than the amount of money he spent and the way he spent it. Nor was the economic value of office measured by official salaries, which were dwarfed by the less tangible, but very substantial, profits from such things as fees exacted from the public, the right to present the inferior offices in one's gift, and a variety of other perquisites in kind as well as in cash, revenue farms, licences, monopolies and a host of other juicy pickings. For example, the lord treasurership, which carried a fee of a mere £366 per annum, was reckoned to be worth £4,000 per annum during the earl of Salisbury's tenure of the office between 1608 and 1612 and £7,000 by the mid-1630s.

On the other hand office-holding might carry with it considerable additional expenditure. The argument that landowners needed additional extra-agricultural sources of income if they were to maintain their port needs to be treated with some caution, for the 'port' of a great office-holder was after all a very different thing from that of a 'mere' gentleman, and might consume part and perhaps all of the concomitant extra-agricultural source of income in order to maintain the more lavish style of life deemed appropriate to the great office. Such arguments are perhaps less applicable to great aristocrats for whom a high style of life was *de rigueur* whether or not they were office-holders. While the early Stuart inflation of the numbers of the nobility was bound to create some disequilibrium between noble claimants to office and the number of such offices available, Dr Aylmer's researches have demonstrated that roughly one in four of the Caroline peers held high office at some time or other during the reign, a higher proportion than that of any other social group.[10] Below the peerage the proportion of office-holders within each social rank tends to decline as we descend the social scale, though there was a higher proportion of knights than baronets who held office, probably because, then as now, knighthoods were a standard reward for government officials of a middling to upper order. Whatever else they prove, Aylmer's calculations clearly demonstrate that the peerage, at least under Charles I, was by far the most important social group of office-holders relative to their numbers. Moreover, viewed qualitatively, it was the most prestigious offices – not all of which, however, were the most lucrative – which they occupied both in the court and in the administration of royal government; and the higher their rank within the peerage the greater the likelihood of their obtaining such office.

While the social importance and prestige attaching to office-holding is not in doubt, some long-established notions about the declining attractiveness and prestige of a career in the church have recently been challenged. There may be some truth in the contention that, just as the entry of so many well-born undergraduates elevated the status and social importance of a university education, the university-trained parson would partake of some of these advantages. This in turn was likely to be reflected to some extent in the status of his profession, for, despite the almost unbelievable ignorance of some parochial clergymen, there can be no doubt that, since the abolition of the monastic orders, there had been far more scope for the admission to the universities of young men studying to be parsons. Such considerations need to be set against the fact that, from the later Elizabethan period onwards, the supply of graduate clerics seems greatly to have exceeded the demand for their services, though a recent article by Dr Ian Green suggests that historians have seriously underestimated both the size of the pool of ordinands in the market for livings and the variety of opportunities open to them.[11]

It was probably at the top end of the clerical scale that the decline in the status of churchmen was most apparent. 'The bishops,' writes Dr Hill, 'were being transformed from feudal potentates, powerful in their own right as landowners, to hangers-on of the court, making what they could of their office while they held it.' The reasons for the social decline were primarily economic. As so often the great Richard Hooker puts it in a nutshell. 'Where wealth,' he wrote, 'is held in so great admiration, as generally in this golden age it is . . . surely to make bishops poorer than they are were to make them of less account and estimation than they should be.'

If the wealth and prestige of the church and churchmen was decreasing relative to other orders, the fault lay partly in the orgy of secular plunder of the church, of which the dissolution of the monasteries was only the first stage; and partly in the improvident and selfish behaviour of some of the principal churchmen themselves. The temptation of great ecclesiastical landholders, who unlike their lay counterparts had no hereditary interest in their benefices, to make hay while the sun shone and to screw the most out of their lands in their own lifetime was very strong and not always resisted. Hence the sacrifices of future rental income in return for large capital sums in the form of fines payable by tenants for admission to their tenancies was a not uncommon procedure. Episcopal lands were, moreover, shamelessly used by the crown as a form of courtly out-relief. New bishops were often not appointed until they had promised Queen Elizabeth that they would comply with her wishes in the matter of beneficial leases to courtiers. Sometimes benefices were kept vacant for scandalously long periods, the most shocking example being the bishopric of Ely, which Elizabeth left empty for eighteen years. A main beneficiary of this was the courtier and later lord chancellor, Sir Christopher Hatton, who occupied the bishop's splendid town house, Ely Place in Holborn, and whose widow offered stubborn and protracted resistance to the attempts of subsequent bishops to dislodge her.

Another notoriously bad bargain for the episcopate was Elizabeth's compulsory exchange of scattered former monastic revenues such as tithes, whose revenues were often consumed in the charges of their collection, in return for compact blocks of episcopal land. Moreover, the secularization of state offices consequent upon the growth of an educated laity meant that high office in the church was no longer a road to the acquisition of high secular office. Not the least important consequence of the Reformation was the spectacular reduction of the practice of using bishops and other ecclesiastical dignitaries in the highest secular offices, of which the lord chancellorship is a good example. It might, of course, be argued that the consequent economic loss to churchmen was offset by the spiritual gain resulting from the forcible diversion of their concern from secular affairs to matters more appropriate to their calling. But if the balance had been tilted too far in the one direction before the Reformation, it swung too far in the other afterwards. Certainly the tendency for high ecclesiastical office to be filled by men of relatively obscure social origins – men such as Archbishop Whitgift, the son of a Grimsby merchant, Archbishop Laud, the son of a Reading clothworker, Archbishop Neile, the son of a London tallow-chandler, and Bishop Pierce of Bath and Wells, son of a hatter – was bound to affect the standing of churchmen in that acutely status-conscious age. That the radicalism of that titled anti-episcopalian, Robert Greville, the second Lord Brooke, did not extend from religious to social considerations is indicated by his scornful description of the Caroline bishops as '*ex faece plebis, humi serpenti*, of the lowest of the people'.

At the bottom of the hierarchy of occupations which were compatible, if only just, with gentility was one form or another of merchandizing or entrepreneurial activity. It was a nobleman, and moreover a nobleman of ancient lineage, the ninth earl of Shrewsbury, to whom Bacon makes reference in his essay *Of Riches* as having 'the greatest audits of any man in my time, a grazier, a great timber-man, and so of iron and of the like points of husbandry'. Nor was Shrewsbury a solitary example. But it is significant that Bacon, himself the grandson of a Suffolk sheep-reeve, speaks of such noblemen as *stooping* to husbandry. For, as he was at pains to emphasize, 'the ways to enrich are many . . . and most of them foul'. Certainly undue concern with entrepreneurial activities, whether in the form of marketing the agricultural produce of their demesnes or exploiting the metalliferous resources of their estates, could divert the attention of estate-owners from the essential functions of a gentleman, which, in Sir Thomas Smythe's famous phrase, were to 'live idly and without manual labour and . . . bear the port, charge and countenance of a gentleman'. A gentleman, in short, was one who lived like a gentleman, discharged his paternalistic duties and shrank from oppressing his tenants – a man of whom it might be said, as Ben Jonson puts it of the Sidneys at Penshurst:

> And though thy walls be of the country stone
> They're built with no man's ruin, no man's groan,
> There's none that dwell about them wish them down.

Such ideals, if carried out, imposed severe limits on exploiting the resources and economic potential of one's estate. But quite apart from this it was better if the estate-owner kept a safe distance from sordid and character-soiling concerns, however much his ability to continue to bear the 'port' appropriate to his station depended on the proceeds of such things. Referring to criticism of his concern with the minute details of management of the Dorset alum mines in the 1560s, Lord Mountjoy admitted that 'some say I vary from my vocation far to become a miner.'[12]

It is nevertheless true that gentlemen did quite often apprentice their younger sons to trade, a practice which points an important difference in terms of social fluidity between contemporary English and French practice.

However, for these purposes some forms of trade were right outside the pale. Within the mercantile community itself there was a great gulf fixed between the 'mere merchant', who engaged exclusively in wholesale trade, whether in the sphere of foreign or domestic trade, and the retailer, who was very much an inferior type to be excluded as far as possible from engagement in these superior forms of commercial activity. Hence while it increasingly came to be regarded as not derogatory to the dignity of a gentleman to apprentice his sons to wholesale trade, the undignified and petty business of retail was altogether a different matter. Indeed it is important not to lose sight of the fact that even the more dignified and prestigious forms of wholesaling occupied the lowest place in the hierarchy of socially respectable occupations for the younger sons of gentlemen. Its place on the very edge – and in some views over the edge – of social respectability is evidenced by the taunt of 'vulgar merchant' levelled at the erstwhile Merchant Adventurer, Lionel Cranfield, earl of Middlesex, by the earl of Bristol in the 1620s. Certainly none would think of attaching the adjective in question to the profession of lawyer or cleric.

CLIENTAGE

If the social position of a man was denoted by how he spent his money as well as by his formal designation in terms of title, at the very top level of society a man's power, standing and influence was related to the size of his following, his clients. Patronage, or clientage as it is sometimes called, according to whether it is the dispenser or the recipient of favours whose role is stressed, is an institution of prime importance in contemporary society. 'In a world of dependence,' writes Sir John Neale, 'independence was a quixotic luxury. The smaller man found friendship, patronage and protection in the system. The great man gained reputation and power; he made manifest his greatness by the number of gentlemen whom he could on occasions summon to follow him.'[13] Francis Bacon might jib in his essay *Of Followers and Friends* at the expense of maintaining what he called 'costly followers . . . lest while a man maketh his train longer, he make his wings shorter'. But costly or not, the magnate who aspired to political leadership must both sustain and find employment for a large following if he were not to lose face and sink into obscurity. This was impossible to do without retaining the favour of the greatest patron of all, the crown itself, out of whose munificence a costly following might – at least in part – be maintained. As the court grew more magnificent and the apparatus of government more complex, the wider range of offices at the disposal of a sagacious monarch provided a means of keeping her greatest subjects sweet and preventing some of them from becoming over-mighty.

For a gentleman, client dependence on a great patron might afford the means to cut a greater figure in county society, perhaps to be placed in a higher position on the Commission of the Peace or the local militia or to become a deputy lieutenant. In an acutely status-conscious society such things mattered a great deal. Professor Stone has demonstrated how while the ancient practice of gentlemen putting out their sons to serve as retainers in the households of local noblemen survived even into the 1630s, when it found spectacular exemplification in the earl of Worcester's household at Raglan Castle, it was on the way out even in the reign of Elizabeth. It was increasingly being replaced by the centralization of patronage on great figures at court such as the earls of Leicester and Essex, Lord Burghley and his son Sir Robert Cecil. Even the apparent survival of locally orientated patronage through the county lieutenancy was less exclusively local than might appear at first sight, for the lieutenancy was also one of the centralizing agencies *par excellence* of the period.

Patronal efforts on behalf of clients might operate via use of influence with the monarch to place them in the important state offices which were in the crown's gift. However, there were also many medium and lower-ranking offices which were in the gift of great office-holders themselves. In general the boundaries between private and public service were indistinct, and the ease with which individuals could move from one to the other is illustrated by the case of Laurence Squibb who, from being receiver of the private revenues of Lord Cottington in the reign of Charles I, became a teller of the Exchequer, for Cottington was also chancellor of the Exchequer. As the title of Dr Aylmer's study of the Caroline administration suggests, great officers of state were 'the King's servants', and those holding office under them the servants of the king's servants. Analogies between the position of such people and that of modern civil servants can only be misleading.[14]

Another important source of patronage operated via magnate control of seats in the House of Commons. The most prestigious seats were the county constituencies, but it was not these but parliamentary boroughs which offered special scope for the exercise of patronage. As the researches of Sir John Neale have demonstrated, sixty-two such boroughs were either newly created or restored in the Tudor period, thirty-one of them in the reign of Elizabeth I. Many of these boroughs owed their newly acquired or restored status to the efforts of magnates, to whom they stood in a very real sense as clients to patrons. Some indeed were formally owned by such magnates; others, though nominally independent, could not afford to despise the good will and offices of a Leicester, a Hatton or a Burghley. When they had charters to revise or private bills to promote, such support might be invaluable and operate via pressure exerted by both the patrons at court and their MPs in parliament. There was therefore absolutely no reason why a newly enfranchised or restored borough – or older boroughs for that matter – should regard as demeaning the patronage of a great man, even to the extent of his nominating one, or even both, of their MPs. From the client's point of view it might be objected that a seat in the House of Commons was by no means the same thing as a potentially lucrative office, and the argument has some force. Nevertheless, the growing significance of parliament in the national consciousness, beginning with the Reformation Parliament in the 1530s, undoubtedly made the role of MPs much less of a burden and more of a privilege to be eagerly sought after. To some it offered the opportunity of serving a useful political apprenticeship and of making a name for themselves. To the genuinely public-spirited it could be the means of furthering their ideals in matters such as religion. Indeed, quite apart from the need to find places for their clients, it was becoming important for patrons to place them in parliament as well as in other strategic positions in which their influence might be brought to bear in the service of their interests.[15]

Magnate patronage was also of crucial importance in the sphere of religion, but in this field the institution extended down to less exalted reaches of society. Lay patronage, in the form of the right of laymen to present parsons to benefices, had of course existed before the Reformation, but as a result of the dissolution of the monasteries something like one-third of the existing advowsons, or rights of presentation to benefices, had passed into the hands of the laity, and the Elizabethan and Jacobean periods were to see further movements in this direction. Unless a parson thus nominated was guilty of manifest scandals in terms of personal conduct or manifestly incapable of administering the cure of souls, the nominee in question was bound to be accepted by the bishop, whose objections, if any, could be tested at common law by obtaining a writ of *Quare impedit?*; and on the whole the common law looked on the advowson as a property right whose exercise was contestable only in extreme cases. In such circumstances it was natural enough for the churchmanship of the local parson to echo that of his patron, great or small, and for the deference he owed to impose serious limitations on the parson's freedom to reprove his patron for acts of personal immorality, including acts of economic oppression such as rack-renting and depopulation. In his famous treatise on the country parson written in the early 1630s, George Herbert, while recommending a different sort of parsonical rebuke as appropriate to well-born parishioners from that used to ordinary men and women, was nevertheless emphatic about the value of 'a bold and impartial reproof even of the best in the Parish: for this may produce hatred in those that are reproved, but never contempt'. But relatively few parsons were able to draw upon the reserves of strength provided by Herbert's unquestioned gentility of birth and aristocratic family connections. More typical probably are complaints such as that of Robert Burton of patrons presenting low-born parsons 'fitter for the pig-sty than the altar', who fawn on them and 'subscribe to any opinions and tenets contrary to the word of God, only so as not to offend their patrons'. Nor were all lay patrons immune to the temptations of simony. 'He that hath the biggest purse to pay largely, not he that hath the best gift to preach learnedly,' complained Archbishop Whitgift in 1584, was far too often the man appointed. If no such candidate were available, some patrons were not averse to putting in ministers on a temporary basis until better bargains were in prospect.[16]

Although lay patrons were to be found in every order of society from gentlemen upwards, there was some degree of concentration of patronage rights. The most important dispensers of religious patronage were the monarch, ecclesiastical institutions and colleges at the universities, the latter being afforded thereby an opportunity to place some of their graduates in benefices. The monarchy was the largest advowson holder of all, much of its ecclesiastical patronage being exercised by the lord keeper or lord chancellor, who held in his personal gift all crown livings of below £20 annual value as well as the right to present to many other livings. Elizabeth's first lord keeper, Sir Nicholas Bacon, presented on average to 113 benefices in every year.[17] There was also a number of magnates whose extensive multiple patronage made them key figures. The more radical Puritan brand of Protestantism in the Elizabethan period owed a great deal to the support of aristocratic patrons such as the earls of Bedford and Huntingdon, and above all to the Dudley brothers, the earls of Warwick and Leicester. The numerous advowsons held by Robert Rich, the Caroline earl of Warwick – chiefly, though not exclusively, in the area of his territorial power in Essex – were perhaps the most important factor making that county the most solidly Puritan in England. On a smaller but by no means insignificant scale was the patronage exercised by Puritan squires such as Sir Nathaniel Bacon and Sir Richard Knightley in Norfolk and Northamptonshire respectively.

The religious patronage of magnates might express itself in many other ways than simply that of presentation to livings in their gift. Professor Collinson has argued persuasively for the crucial importance of influential noblemen such as Leicester, Bedford and Warwick in the appointment of divines of a more radically Protestant persuasion than suited the queen to some of the vacant Elizabethan bishoprics.[18] Another such service might be exerting influence to obtain preaching licences for one's clients or to get their books and pamphlets past the censor. The last of these functions was a particularly useful prerogative of Leicester, the greatest of Elizabethan aristocratic Puritan sympathizers, since he was chancellor of Oxford University. As such he also used his influence to secure the election of Puritan fellows, and even heads of colleges. Finally, and certainly by no means least important, was the protection against persecution which great men could afford to religious dissidents, whether by pulling strings to get them released from imprisonment, as Leicester did for the Puritan John Field in 1572, or by putting them out of harm's way by taking them on as chaplains in their households or finding lucrative and safe posts for them, as Leicester did for the arch-Presbyterian Thomas Cartwright in 1586, when he made him master of his hospital at Warwick. It was beyond doubt of inestimable value to have as patron a magnate to whom one's potential persecutors were hardly less beholden than oneself. Such a persecutor, Thomas Cooper, bishop of Lincoln between 1570 and 1584, was almost certainly the person to whom Leicester addressed an undated letter urging him to cease molesting the Puritan Arthur Wake, 'as you intend to have me favourable in any of your requests hereafter, and as you will give me cause to continue your friend and think well of you'.[19]

If anything, fugitive Roman Catholic priests were even more dependent on the protection of magnate co-religionists such as Lord Arundel and Lady Vaux, Sir Thomas Tresham in Northamptonshire and the Cornwallis and Bedingfield families in East Anglia, all of whom from time to time offered succour to fugitive Catholic missionaries. But in examining the religious manifestations of patronage, whose importance in other spheres and notably in that of artistic production will be considered elsewhere, this chapter has necessarily to some extent anticipated some of the conclusions of those which follow. For the England inherited by Elizabeth I was a realm in which the religious fugitives were not Catholics but Protestants. It is now time to turn to the settlement of the problems which faced the new queen in 1558, within the context of which the developments which have been described in this chapter took place.

Chapter Three

THE ELIZABETHAN SETTLEMENT, *c.* 1558–71

> *S*[r] Thomas Cornwalleys sonne of *S*[r] John Cornwalleys was of Queen Mary her Prevy Councell and Tresurer of Caleys [Calais] after Comptroller of her Houshold in Speciall Grace and Trvst of His *M*[rs] who vntimely losing her life retired him selfe home to this towne where he spent the rest of his own privately and loyally all the rayne of Queen Elizabeth her sister and died heer the second year of King James the 26 of December 1604 in the 86 yeer of his age.
>
> (Inscription on the tomb of Sir Thomas Cornwallis, in the parish church of Brome, Suffolk)

The above epitaph serves to remind us that it was not simply the ignorant priests and Roman Catholic prelates of the Protestant-Whig version of Tudor history who viewed the accession of Elizabeth Tudor less than enthusiastically. The notion of a groundswell of national relief at the death of Mary and the end of religious persecution and expensive foreign entanglements does scant justice to the widespread uncertainties about what the new regime would do to tackle the many fearsome problems which confronted it in 1558. The purpose of this chapter is to examine the nature of these problems and the solutions devised for them – solutions constituting *in toto* what may be called the Elizabethan Settlement, which comprises a great deal more than the settlement of religion, in which terms it is usually comprehended.

THE NEW PRIVY COUNCIL

Just how new was the Elizabethan regime in terms of its personnel, leaving aside for the moment the matter of the churchmen, which is dealt with in the next section? Considering that Mary had reigned for only five years, it would have been perfectly possible for her successor to institute a complete turnover in the personnel of her Privy Council without having to have recourse to men who lacked experience at the highest level of government. But there was in fact no such complete turnover. Of the eighteen members of the Elizabethan Privy Council in the spring of 1559, ten had served on Mary's and eight on Edward VI's.[1] Those councillors who had served her half-sister and were retained by Elizabeth were men whose loyalty to the Tudor dynasty was more powerful than their dislike of Protestantism, which in view of Elizabeth's position as the daughter of Anne Boleyn was bound to be, to a greater or lesser degree, a feature of the new settlement. Such men were William Paulet, marquis of Winchester, Mary's lord treasurer, who was to continue in that office for a further fourteen years; Lord Clinton, the lord admiral; Sir John Mason, the treasurer of the Chamber; the earl of Arundel; the earls of Derby and Shrewsbury with their vast territorial influence in the north, and, in Shrewsbury's case, also in the north Midlands; and, although the Herberts were a more newly arrived family than the Stanleys or the Talbots, the earl of Pembroke, with his rapidly accumulating territorial holdings in Wiltshire and in Wales. Nevertheless, the new queen retained less than a third of the Marian councillors of 1558, though it needs to be remembered that the size of her council was reduced by exactly that proportion and that not all of the Marian councillors who lost their seats on the council did so because their loyalty was suspect. By far the most notable omission was that of Lord Paget, who – perhaps like Sir Thomas Cornwallis – was a suitable scapegoat, among other things, for the loss of Calais to the French.

Despite Elizabeth's retention of some of Mary's councillors, there can be no doubt that removing the majority of them, reducing the size of the Council, and appointing new councillors did produce a very notable alteration in the character of the regime. It was not that the government took a violent lurch to the left. This was the last thing that the new queen wanted, and among her new councillors only Francis Russell, the second earl of Bedford, Sir Francis Knollys, a relative of the queen, and perhaps William Parr, marquis of Northampton and brother of Henry VIII's sixth queen, could be described as Protestant zealots of the sort which would soon be distinguished by the name of Puritan. But the new regime was to take its essential character less from such people than from moderate reformers such as the new secretary of state, Sir William Cecil, subsequently to be the most important and influential of all Elizabeth's ministers; his relative, Sir Nicholas Bacon, who succeeded Archbishop Heath of York (who however remained on the Council for the remainder of 1558) as lord keeper of the Great Seal; and Sir Thomas Parry, who replaced the Marian master of the Court of Wards, Sir Francis Englefield. A more ominous portent for the future was perhaps the bestowal of offices on the two Dudley brothers, sons of that duke of Northumberland whose abortive *coup d'état* of 1553 had cost him his head, and grandsons of that Edmund Dudley who had also been executed for treason in 1509. Ambrose, later to be earl of Warwick, displaced the former Marian privy councillor, Sir Richard Southwell, as master of the Ordinance, while Robert, the future earl of Leicester and favourite of the queen, became master of the Horse. Robert became a member of the Privy Council in 1562, and both brothers were later to be among the most notable aristocratic patrons of those Puritans who sought to push the Elizabethan religious settlement in a more decisively Protestant direction. It is the nature of that settlement to which we must now turn.

THE RELIGIOUS SETTLEMENT

The central feature of what has been since 1950 the standard account of the Elizabethan religious settlement is the notion that the religious preferences of the new queen were almost certainly of an essentially conservative kind; at least within the limits set by the need to restore the reformed religion outside of which her own hereditary claim to the throne, and indeed her very legitimacy, were in serious doubt. She sought, in fact, the restoration of the royal ecclesiastical supremacy with the minimum of doctrinal innovation compatible with this. So much, as Sir John Neale argued,[2] is made clear by the fact that the first bill presented to parliament re-establishing the royal supremacy in the church also contained a provision which had nothing whatever to do with the issue of supremacy, namely that communion should be administered to the laity in both kinds – that is that communicants should receive both bread and wine. The inclusion of such a doctrinal matter in a bill relating to the problem of ecclesiastical supremacy suggests that, for the time being at least, the supremacy bill was not to be followed by a uniformity bill (the obvious place for such a provision) and that the introduction of communion in both kinds represented the doctrinal limits of Elizabethan Protestantism, beyond which the queen was unwilling to go.

Some doubt has recently been cast on this emphasis on the queen's doctrinal conservatism and her sole responsibility for the attempt to limit the doctrinal changes to the allowance of communion in both kinds. Arguing that 'there were several important men in parliament who, no matter how they felt about the mass, were willing to profit from the return of the supremacy to the Crown', Dr Norman L. Jones has drawn attention to the fact that, in terms of the time devoted to measures in parliament in 1559, religion took second place to more material issues. These neglected activities whose importance he stresses relate especially to the attempt of powerful secular interests to recover the episcopal lands which the Protestant supplanters of Marian Catholic bishops had granted to Edward VI and he to private individuals, but which Mary had restored to the original Catholic bishops when they regained their sees from the usurpers during the Catholic reaction of her reign. The restoration of the royal supremacy was obviously in the interest of those seeking – mostly successfully – to lay their hands on their Edwardian episcopal spoils again. On the other hand radical doctrinal settlement was of no significance in this respect and might even run counter to their wishes and inclinations.[3] Nevertheless, however much importance is attached to their and other people's conservative doctrinal inclinations – as distinct from the views of the queen on such matters – the ultimate religious settlement was far more decisively Protestant than was desired by such conservative interests, and the Supremacy Act of 1559 was in fact followed by an Act of Uniformity. Before discussing how and why this came about, it will be appropriate to explore the main differences between the Elizabethan and the Henrician ecclesiastical supremacy.

The Henrician supremacy had been personal rather than parliamentary in character, and the purpose of the Henrician statute of that name had been to establish pains and penalties to be imposed on those who denied it. Technically, as far as the supremacy itself was concerned, the act was regarded as purely declaratory and as Professor Elton neatly puts it, parliament's official role 'was to provide for the enforcement of a power in the making of which it had no share'. But while, to employ contemporary constitutional terminology, the Henrician supremacy was exercised by *Rex Solus*, it is certainly arguable that the foundation documents of the Elizabethan religious settlement provided grounds for those who were to claim that the queen's ecclesiastical supremacy was parliamentary not personal in character. Clause eight of the Elizabethan Act of Supremacy of 1559 enacted that the ecclesiastical supremacy and its associated powers 'shall for ever *by authority of this present Parliament* be united and annexed to the imperial crown of this realm'. Even more strikingly, clause twenty assigned to parliament functions in the matter of definition of doctrine which serve to reinforce the notion of the supremacy as something exercised by *Regina in Parliamento* rather than *Regina Sola*. For in laying down very specific limits to the matters which might be adjudged to be heresy by any persons appointed by the queen in her capacity as Supreme Governor of the Church, it restricted these to beliefs which had been so adjudged by the canonical scriptures or by any of the first four general councils of the church, and – an astonishing addition – whatever might hereafter be 'determined to be heresy by the High Court of Parliament of this realm with the assent of the clergy in their Convocation'.

How is this change in the powers of the monarch as head or governor of the church to be explained? It had been one thing for Henry VIII and his son to claim that their ecclesiastical supremacy had centuries of history behind it. But the fact that the situation of which the Henrician Act of Supremacy claimed to be declaratory was in reality, though not in theory, new, had necessitated a statute laying down pains and penalties for its contravention. Just as these had required a Henrician statute to establish, so did they require a Marian statute to annul, along with the royal supremacy itself. In these circumstances it was impossible for the Elizabethan Act of Supremacy to take quite the same line as its Henrician predecessor. It was no longer sufficient to denounce and repudiate centuries of papal usurpation. Acts of parliament, even of a Marian parliament, could not be dismissed so lightly. What parliament had done, only parliament could undo.

While these facts provide an explanation of the difference between the Henrician (and Edwardian) and the Elizabethan ecclesiastical supremacy, they do not explain why it was that the Elizabethan religious settlement was of so decisively Protestant a nature. What seems to have happened was that the opposition of the episcopate which Elizabeth had inherited from Mary even to a relatively conservative religious settlement played into the hands of the more radical Protestants and pushed the doctrinal aspects of the settlement in a strongly Protestant direction.

At first sight this is perhaps surprising, for among those who were to boggle at accepting the Elizabethan supremacy were bishops, such as Nicholas Heath, the archbishop of York, Cuthbert Tunstall, bishop of Durham, and Edmund Bonner, the much-hated persecuting bishop of London, all of whom had accepted the Henrician supremacy apparently without demur. For while Henry VIII's theological conservatism had made it relatively easy for all, save men such as More and Fisher – men of great percipience, unwavering logical capacity and with the stuff of martyrs in them – to turn a blind eye to some of the radical implications of the royal supremacy as remote and unlikely contingencies, the events of the next reign had forced such considerations upon their attention. In these circumstances the Marian restoration of papal supremacy must have been viewed with relief by men like Heath, Bonner and Tunstall. Their inability to stomach the Elizabethan supremacy may also have owed something to their objections to a woman being head of the church – or even supreme governor, this last a concession made in the third and final supremacy bill put before parliament with the object of placating both conservatives and the advanced Protestants who recognized no head of the church save Christ. But it is undoubtedly explicable chiefly in terms of the experience of the decade following the death of Henry VIII, in which must be included not only the English, and especially the Edwardian, experience, but also the consciousness of that stiffening of the temper of international Catholicism commonly known as the Counter-Reformation and finding expression in the decrees of the General Council meeting at Trent.

The refusal of the Marian bishops to accept the royal

supremacy put paid to any hopes of a conservative Henrician (or at the very least early Edwardian) type of settlement. The royal supremacy bill had passed through the upper house with some difficulty in the face of the opposition of the bishops. On the other hand, it had been supported by most of the lay peers, many of whom, however, opposed major changes in the direction of Protestant worship, at least beyond the introduction of communion in both kinds. The uniformity bill, based on the 1552 Prayer Book, had therefore to wait until after the Easter recess, and passed in the Upper House only by three votes. Even this narrow margin was obtained only as the result of the imprisonment of some of the more intransigent Marian bishops and the absence from the House of some of the others.

So far, it looks rather as if the Elizabethan religious settlement can be represented as a triumph for the Protestant radicals, and arguably the greatest radical triumph of the reign. But that this triumph was less than complete is clear from the fact that, by even the most conservative of those returning Protestant exiles who exercised such an enormous influence on the temper of Elizabethan Protestant aspirations – the exiles returning from centres such as Frankfurt and Strasburg rather than from Calvinist Geneva and Zwinglian Zürich – the second Edwardian Prayer Book was viewed as no more than a step in the right direction, and certainly not as setting the limits of doctrinal innovation. By contrast, the queen refused to go even so far as the position which had been reached in 1552 and insisted on a number of points which emphasized that her settlement stopped short of this position. Thus the so-called Black Rubric of 1552, which declared that kneeling at the sacrament must not be held to imply the adoration of the elements of bread and wine and therefore the corporeal presence of Christ in them, was omitted as inimical to the comprehensiveness which Elizabeth had hoped that her church would achieve. Also omitted was the reference in the second Edwardian Prayer

Book to the bishop of Rome and all his detestable enormities. As Neale pointed out, the juxtaposition of two apparently contradictory formulae, both present in the Anglican communion service to this day, allowing of interpretations of the sacrament both in terms of the real presence and in a purely commemorative Zwinglian sense, as in the 1552 Prayer Book, is eloquent testimony of Elizabeth's desire for her church to be all things to almost all men. The same is true of the celebrated Ornamental Rubric retaining the vestments of the old church, which were later to be such an important source of contention, and which had been abandoned even by Richard Cox and his allies at the most conservative of all the communities of Marian Protestant exiles at Frankfurt, along with the giving of the ring in marriage and kneeling at the communion. Even to such very moderate reformers the retention of kneeling at the communion, along with the refusal to reinstate the Black Rubric, which explicitly repudiated its conceivably Catholic implications, must have come as a shock.

There can be no doubt that the above modifications in the settlement insisted upon by the queen, along with such things as her strongly expressed antipathy to clerical marriage, and her use of candles and crucifix in her own chapel despite her failure to persuade the clergy to retain them in churches, were as much designed to placate foreign Roman Catholic princes as to win over English Catholics. She was no doubt delighted by a report from her ambassador in Paris, Sir Nicholas Throckmorton, that impeccably Catholic adherents of the Guises in France had been suitably impressed by reports of these practices in the chapel royal. However, before proceeding to examine the way in which the new regime tackled the problems of foreign relations which confronted it in 1558, it will be useful to turn to a particular issue with which foreign affairs were intimately connected: the queen's own title to the throne and the problem of the succession.

THE SUCCESSION AND FOREIGN AFFAIRS

(i)

Elizabeth was twenty-five on her accession to the throne and was to reign for nearly forty-five years, but, given the expectation of life in the sixteenth century, her subjects could certainly not count on a long reign. From the outset, therefore, the succession was a matter of the utmost significance, as contemporaries were to be forcibly reminded when she hovered between life and death from the smallpox during 1562. If strict hereditary succession were to be observed, there was only one candidate for the position of heir presumptive, Mary Stuart, queen of Scotland, the descendant of Henry VII's eldest daughter, Margaret.* But there were two arguments against Mary's claim which were commonly advanced by Protestants fearful of the prospect of another Catholic queen, and more especially of a queen closely allied with, and at the beginning of the reign married into, the French royal family. The first was that, as an alien, she was excluded by the common law. The second was that Henry VIII's will had placed the descendants of his elder sister Margaret lower in the order of succession than those of his younger sister Mary by her second husband the duke of Suffolk (she had previously been married without issue to the aged Louis XII of France). If neither of these objections applied – and both were very shaky in law – then Mary Stuart was obviously the heir presumptive. If the first applied but not the second, then the strongest claim was that of the eldest living descendant of Margaret by her second marriage to an Englishman, the earl of Lennox. This was Margaret, countess of Lennox, whose son, Lord Darnley, was later to be the means of uniting the two claims of the descendants of Margaret in the person of the issue of his marriage to Mary Stuart, the later James VI of Scotland and James I of England. If however the second or both of the

* What follows is illustrated by the genealogical table on p. 439.

two above objections to Mary Stuart as heir presumptive applied, then the prime claimant was the grand-daughter of Henry VIII's younger sister Mary, Lady Catherine Grey, the younger sister of the Lady Jane Grey who had lost her head in the previous reign – a not very inspiring choice, not least on account of her secret marriage with the earl of Hertford, the son of the discredited and decapitated Protector Somerset. At least, however, this marriage by producing a son, was to demonstrate the advantages of an assured male succession.

But all these possibilities ranging from the distasteful and dangerous to the uninspired could be ruled out by the queen's own marriage and production of an heir. The problem was to whom? For, in terms of the avoidance of internal turmoil, independence from foreign domination and the preservation of the Protestant religion, there were few foreign princely candidates for whom the pros might seem to outweigh the cons. As to the queen's own subjects, the one person whom Elizabeth might be expected to prefer, if personal feelings were the only consideration, was ruled out. Not only was Robert Dudley, whose close relations with the queen were becoming a matter of widespread comment, the scion of an upstart and treason-tainted house – both his father and grandfather had died on the scaffold – and as such, anathema to the conservative members of the older aristocracy. He was also married, at least down to 1560, and when in that year his sick wife fell downstairs and broke her neck, there were not wanting scandalous rumours about his personal responsibility for her death, rumours which would certainly have been heightened if this event were seen to have left him free to marry the queen.

But if Dudley, the later earl of Leicester, was inadmissible as royal consort, he might still be capable of throwing his great influence as royal favourite against the queen's marriage to anyone else. For any such marriage would most likely result in his losing his influence over the queen, since no spirited consort would be likely to tolerate the existence of a male favourite with its inevitable sexual undertones. Indeed, as Professor MacCaffrey has pointed out, there is another significance to the quest for a foreign husband for the queen than that of a simple attempt to secure the succession and safeguard the Elizabethan settlement. A foreign marriage also tended to become one of the main weapons in the armoury of Dudley's enemies at court. If no such marriage were made, and the rules of strict hereditary succession were observed, then Mary Stuart's claim was unchallengeable, and it was only the uncertainty about Henry VIII's will which made Mary so anxious to obtain a ratification of her claim by Elizabeth and so unwilling to renounce the right to use the royal arms of England, since this might be regarded as tantamount to her relinquishing her claim.[4]

(ii)

While the succession was a foreign policy issue of first-rate importance, the most urgent and immediate problem facing the new regime in the sphere of foreign relations was how to extricate England from the disastrous war with France into which it had been drawn as a result of the Habsburg marriage of Elizabeth's predecessor. Mary's reign had ended disastrously with the loss of Calais, the last remnant of the once enormous possessions of the English crown in France. Although, as will be seen, Elizabeth was by no means reconciled to the permanent loss of Calais, there was no question of prolonging the war in order to regain it, not least because the widowed husband of Mary Tudor, Philip II of Spain, wanted to bring the war to an end, and peace was no less essential to the English regime. Accordingly a face-saving solution was devised, whereby Calais was ceded to the French crown on condition that 500,000 crowns were to be paid to England if it was not restored after eight years.

But this problem was no sooner settled than another arose. It is true that the worst English fears that the French might insist on the confirmation of Mary Stuart's position as

Elizabeth's heir presumptive as the price of peace, or perhaps even prolong the war as a means of supplanting Elizabeth by Mary, were not realized. But this disposed of only the worst of a number of frightening possibilities. Mary, of course, was married to the French dauphin and was soon herself to become queen consort of France in addition to her existing title of queen of Scotland. The dangers of the revival of the old Franco-Scottish alliance, cemented by this marriage, were looming very large again. Indeed it could be argued that, given doubts about the legitimacy of Henry VIII's divorce of Katherine of Aragon, and therefore of Elizabeth herself, Mary had a claim to the English throne – as distinct from her claim to be Elizabeth's successor – which was a great deal more respectable than the claims of Edward III, Henry V or Henry VIII to the French throne had been. Nor did the peace concluded between England, Spain and France in 1559 dispose of these dangers, for the former Habsburg and Valois antagonists now displayed an alarming propensity to fraternize. There thus arose the awful possibility of a Franco-Spanish Roman Catholic alliance, of which the Guises, the family of Mary Stuart's mother, the regent of Scotland, were for long to be the principal French proponents; an alliance which might be directed against Protestant England with the idea of restoring Roman Catholicism and replacing Elizabeth by Mary Stuart. In actual fact this danger was more apparent than real. For one thing, Philip II had at this stage his own designs on Elizabeth; for another he had his own reasons to fear the increase in French power which would result from Mary's combining in her person the titles of queen consort of France and queen regnant of both Scotland and England. Philip's Habsburg dynasticism was, at this point at least, a more powerful motive than his concern for international Catholicism.

Nevertheless, the spring and summer of 1559 saw two events which emphasized the danger that the new English regime might be toppled almost before it had been established. The first was the revolt of the Protestant Lords of the Congregation against the rule of the French queen regent of Scotland, Mary of Guise; the second was the death of the French king Henry II, and the succession of Francis II, the husband of the young queen of Scotland. The fact that the French royal couple flaunted the arms of England gave additional point to the danger that the dispatch of a French expeditionary force to aid the regent of Scotland against the rebels might turn out to be only the first step in a process which might end with Mary on Elizabeth's throne. If England did not take resolute action to forestall this alarming possibility, the Elizabethan settlement might indeed be stillborn. This was the view strongly urged by Cecil and his allies on the council, and which lay behind their advocacy of English intervention by land and sea to secure the expulsion of the French force from Scotland. The queen and some other councillors were not so sure. For one thing, the proposed course of action involved aiding and encouraging rebellion, something which Elizabeth viewed with extreme distaste. Moreover, it was feared that English support for the Scottish rebels might revive the danger of an international Catholic alliance between France and Spain as a response to this obvious manifestation of international heretical action. Last and not least was the expense of the operation to a government wishing to pursue a policy of financial and economic retrenchment. But ultimately the queen yielded, the English intervened, the French withdrew from Scotland, and the treaty of Edinburgh of 1560 seemed to lay the foundations of Anglo-Scottish amity on the basis of mutual interest and common religion. Scotland's young queen (Mary of Guise, the regent, had died in the meantime) might be both Frenchified and papist, but she had renounced any claim to the English throne (though not, of course, to the succession) and her right to display the arms of England. Notwithstanding her private religious observances, papal jurisdiction had been abolished in Scotland, where the pro-English Protestant party was in control.

Moreover, by the end of the year Mary was a widow, and no longer queen consort of France. For the time being the Elizabethan settlement seemed safe from danger from without.

Elizabeth had hoped to include the restoration of Calais as one of the conditions imposed on the vanquished French in the treaty of Edinburgh, but fortunately – for the French would never have agreed – the treaty had been concluded before her instructions to this effect reached Scotland. But with the French menace in Scotland checked for the moment, and the French state distracted by the renewal of strife between Catholic and Huguenot in 1562, it was tempting to try to do something to regain an English presence on the Continent. Accordingly Elizabeth yielded to the interventionist policy advocated by her favourite, Lord Robert Dudley, with an eagerness she had never displayed towards Cecil's much sounder and more fruitful policy of intervention in Scotland. She consented to the dispatch to France of an expeditionary force led by Dudley's brother, Warwick. As Professor Wernham has pointed out, there were persuasive, if misleading, parallels which could be drawn between English intervention in Scotland in 1559–60 and in France two years later. Was it too much to hope that the end-products of English intervention in France might be not only the return of Calais in exchange for Newhaven (Le Havre), held by the English invaders, but also the establishment of a friendly Protestant ascendancy in France, as in Scotland? Here begins that advocacy of a militantly Protestant foreign policy of which Dudley was to be the principal proponent for the rest of his career. But his expectations were pitched far too high, and the treaty of Troyes in 1564 testifies as much to the failure of English intervention in France as the treaty of Edinburgh had done to its success in Scotland. However, the worst possible consequences of the failure were avoided as a result of the assassination of the aggressively Catholic and pro-Marian duke of Guise in the previous year, and the regaining of power by the queen dowager, Catherine de Medici, whose studied friendliness towards Elizabeth and accommodating attitude to the Huguenots removed, however temporarily, the conditions which had prompted this ill-conceived and expensive English intervention.

But the government had other reasons for bringing the English involvement in France to an end. In that the war was fought with economic as well as military weapons there were more parties to it than the two governments directly concerned. For it was England's commitment in France and the expense of her military operations – necessitating heavy royal borrowing on the Antwerp capital market – which prompted Margaret of Parma, the regent of the king of Spain in the Netherlands, to attempt to strike a deadly blow to the very heart of the English economy. By placing an embargo on the imports of English cloth into the Netherlands she probably hoped to create widespread distress and discontent in England which might lead to the overthrow of the government and the restoration of Roman Catholicism, or at the very least to the institution of a regime and policies more favourable to the English Catholics as a condition of renewed cooperation from the government of the Spanish king in the Netherlands.

There was a Flemish saying that even if Englishmen were hanged at Antwerp's gates, their sons would creep between their legs to get into that city. For not only was the English crown, like so many others, dependent upon the Antwerp capital market for its large-scale borrowings, but in addition the English cloth export economy was totally dependent on the outlet afforded by the great Antwerp entrepôt, and the regent seems to have believed that she could bring England to its knees by placing an embargo on this trade. It is true that her action in December 1563 was not entirely unprovoked, since the economy of the Netherlands had undoubtedly suffered from a number of acts of English economic nationalism. In 1560 Low Countries merchants had protested to Philip II against, among other things, the new customs duties imposed on them in England in contravention of the Anglo-Burgundian treaty of 1496. In 1563 an act of parliament 'for the avoiding of divers foreign wares' forbade the importation of a wide variety of foreign goods to England. This prompted a retaliatory proclamation from Philip against English trade in the Netherlands, which, however, specifically exempted wool and cloth from its provisions. But the regent's embargo on the imports of English woollens in December on the pretext of the plague which was currently raging in England, turned a major irritant into a potential economic catastrophe. Choosing a moment of singular English vulnerability, with expensive military operations in France involving Sir Thomas Gresham, the royal financial agent at Antwerp, in complicated and difficult fund-raising and loan-prolonging operations, the regent was trying, in Dr G. D. Ramsay's words, 'to exploit the virtual stranglehold of Antwerp upon the traffic of London for purposes that reached far into the spheres of politics and religion'. That she failed was due to the fact that Elizabeth perceived the danger and pulled out of France, thus reducing her financial entanglement at Antwerp. Indeed 1564 sees important steps taken both to free the crown from financial, and the English export economy from commercial, dependence on Antwerp.[5]

The second of these developments was made possible by the offer of the conveniently Protestant ruler of East Friesland to make the German port of Emden available as the new staple town for the great English cloth-exporting agency, the Merchant Adventurers Company. The English government acceded to that company's request that, in return for its undertaking this venture into the economic unknown, all trade from England with the Netherlands should in fact be conducted via Emden, a provision which, by cutting out all direct Anglo-Netherlands commerce, would favour the company at the expense of foreign merchants trading between London and Antwerp. At the last moment in 1564 Margaret of Parma, who had been made forcibly aware that economic warfare was hurting Antwerp's economy at least as much as England's, had declared herself willing to withdraw her embargo in return for reciprocal concessions by the English queen. Far from the diminution of economic nationalism which acceptance of her new terms would have involved, the move from Antwerp to Emden involved its increase. This was the price paid for freeing England from financial and commercial dependence on the Low Countries. Although the royal debt at Antwerp was not fully liquidated until 1574, and the Merchant Adventurers were to make a temporary return there after the failure of the Emden experiment, in each case 1564 marks a real turning-point, whose full significance will be more apparent as a result of examining the economic aspects of the Elizabethan settlement.

ECONOMIC AND SOCIAL SETTLEMENT

(i)

Ranking first among the economic problems to be tackled by the new regime was that of inflation and monetary disorder. In recent years the attitude of historians to the Tudor inflation has undergone some significant modification, not least on account of their own first-hand experience of the phenomenon. Indeed the inflation experienced by our sixteenth-century ancestors has been described by Professor J. D. Gould as 'a tame affair by present day standards'. But in many ways it is misleading to dwell on this point, for an appreciation of the nature of the hardships endured and the problems created by the fact that the prices of agricultural produce had about doubled between the 1520s and 1550s (prices of manufactured goods rose far less) is not really helped by such cross-century comparisons. For, by contrast with modern times when prices respond fairly smoothly to inflationary (and deflationary) stimuli, the sixteenth century was a time when their response was a great deal stickier.

Sixteenth-century prices were more rigid, institutionalized and resistant to change than is nowadays the case, and their very failure to adjust smoothly to inflationary pressures was in itself a cause of very serious economic dislocation and social hardship.[6]

What was the nature of these inflationary pressures? Until fairly recently economic historians confidently stressed the primacy of monetary factors, that is of increases in monetary supply: in the early sixteenth century, the expanded output of central European mines (which, of course, raises significant and unanswered questions about the media through which these supplies reached England); in the 1540s, the debasement of the currency by the governments of Henry VIII and Edward VI; and, during the second half of the century, following the cessation of currency manipulation under Mary and the restoration of the coinage by Elizabeth, the increased output of Spanish-American mines (which again raises questions about the mechanism by which England was affected). Over the century as a whole it was also tentatively conceded that both the quickening rate of economic change and the heavy fiscal demands of governments may have induced some dehoarding which would add to the existing stock of money, and that some part may also have been played by changes in the velocity at which coins circulated.

Such purely monetary explanations formerly went almost unquestioned. However, in the work done on Tudor price history since the last war, attention has increasingly been focused on real, that is non-monetary, stimuli. It has been observed, for instance, that there was a much greater divergence between the prices of different commodities than might be expected if monetary factors had been the main long-term influence on prices. This divergence is illustrated by the following table which shows decennial average price rises expressed in terms of an index in which the average prices of 1450/99 are represented as 100.[7]

TABLE I

Decade	*Grain prices*	*Prices of other arable crops*	*Livestock prices*	*Prices of animal products*	*Timber prices*	*Prices of industrial products*
1520–9	154	132	138	105	98	110
1530–9	161	128	143	127	100	110
1540–9	187	145	185	159	115	127
1550–9	348	261	259	213	174	186
1560–9	316	294	281	236	178	218
1570–9	370	288	336	257	206	223
1580–9	454	328	352	295	247	230
1590–9	590	428	414	372	289	238

Before examining the implications of these figures a word of warning will be salutary. It needs to be borne in mind that in this period, data for price history, as for all other matters which cry out for quantification, are extremely shaky. Quite apart from the absence of consecutive price series over long periods, there were in many cases wide regional variations between the prices of the same commodities, while – an added and unwelcome complication – some weights and measures differed as between different regions. All that can be said is that Dr Bowden, the compiler of these statistics, was fully conscious of these evidential deficiencies, and took them fully into account, attempting, where possible, to devise adequate correctives. In these circumstances one can be confident that they are as proximate as possible to the complex reality they are designed to illuminate.

As already remarked, the most striking feature of these figures is the divergence between agricultural and other prices, which is especially notable in the case of grain and other arable produce, except perhaps in the third quarter of the century. The divergence is particularly notable in the 1540s, the period of the great debasement, though one thing which the use of decennial averages conceals is the fact that the rise in prices did not become spectacular until the end of that decade. The divergence is also notable in the 1590s, of which more will be said later.

It is this striking divergence between the prices of different commodities which has impelled some price historians to look for factors of a general, but non-monetary, nature, and more especially those operating not uniformly but diversely on different sorts of commodity. Given also that the inflation was indeed a long-term phenomenon, attention has tended to switch to the similarly long-term factor of population expansion as a possible cause. Insofar as statistics are concerned, figures for demographic growth are, if anything, even harder to come by than figures of monetary supply. A recent estimate suggests that population may have climbed to approximately 2.8 million by 1545 from a figure of about 2.3 million in 1522–5, rising further and more spectacularly to about 3.75 million in 1603, though the author of these findings would be the first to stress their very approximate nature.[8] They are, however, entirely compatible with the thesis that population was the main factor in contemporary price determination. For it is undeniable that an increase in prices which is far greater for agricultural than for manufactured products fits better a thesis which assigns a crucial importance to demographic rather than to monetary factors. As was argued in the opening chapter, given sixteenth-century conditions, the goods whose prices will rise are necessities of life such as foodstuffs, and, more especially, cereal foodstuffs. Now, if consumers have to spend more on cereal foodstuffs, they will have less to spend on other things, in so far as their incomes are not proportionately increased. And there are a number of factors suggesting that they were not. An upward movement in population would put pressure on the level of rents, even though many rents were fixed by custom and others were inelastic over long periods. It also would probably produce a larger labour force, and there is some evidence to suggest that a growing proportion of the population was becoming dependent upon wages in Tudor England. This increased labour force, moreover, may well have been competing for a diminished amount of employment, consequent – at least during the first half of the century – on the conversion of so much land from labour-intensive arable to labour-economical pasture farming as well as on the creation of more economical units of production via the engrossment of farms. All these factors combined to produce what was probably a continuing process of reducing the real incomes of people near the bottom of the agrarian heap, culminating in the mid-1590s, a period of disastrous harvests, in what has been described as an all-time low in the standard of living of the English labouring classes.

So much for the long-term causes of Tudor inflation, which are still the subject of disagreement and debate among economic historians of the period. It is perhaps difficult to see how a problem whose solution consistently eludes modern governments, with all the administrative means and specialized knowledge at their disposal, was susceptible of solution or settlement by the Elizabethan government. Nevertheless, it must be emphasized that, more than at any other time, it can confidently be asserted that monetary factors had played a crucial (though certainly not an exclusive) part in the inflation of the middle decades of the Tudor century; monetary factors, moreover, which had been set in motion by royal action, and were capable of being reversed by royal action; in a word, the manipulation of the currency. For all the formidable difficulties of the evidence, the heroic researches of Dr C. E. Challis have established beyond reasonable doubt the central importance of debasement as a cause of the mid-Tudor inflation, operating chiefly via the consequent increase in monetary supply rather than via the no less consequent fall of the foreign exchange value of sterling, making imports dearer and exports cheaper.[9] For, in contrast to our own times, the range and volume of commodities entering into foreign trade was very small and the consequent impact of changes in import prices upon the domestic price level correspondingly minor.

Inflation was unquestionably one of the most urgent problems facing the new regime. It was reducing the purchasing power of people who were already near the margin of subsistence, a matter of real moment to the government, partly for genuinely paternalistic reasons and partly because of the potential threat which it presented to public order. Nor were these the only considerations prompting the government to tackle inflation by undertaking the reform of the currency. It needed, in fact, to look no further than its own financial benefit; to the way in which inflation had eroded the real landed income derived from its largely unmodernized estates and unreconstructed tenures. Moreover, there was another reason why the monetary reform which was the basic deflationary instrument lying to hand was in the crown's own interest. The existence of a large foreign debt maturing at Antwerp made it desirable to keep the foreign exchange rate as favourable as possible, at least if large repayment operations and the use of the exchanges rather than the shipment of specie were envisaged. However, since the exigencies of foreign policy made it necessary for Elizabeth to borrow heavily abroad at the beginning of the reign, so that the amount of English royal debt owing at Antwerp was about £279,000 in 1560, it might be better for the crown to defer monetary reform for a time, since as a borrower a low exchange rate was in its interest. It was only when extensive repayment operations were envisaged that the higher rate which would be a product of English currency reform would be desirable, a fact which might go some way towards explaining the two years' delay before such reform was undertaken.[10]

One method of currency reform which had been recommended by the anonymous author of the influential treatise, *A Discourse of the Common Weal*, in 1549 was that, after a certain date, debased coins should cease to be current and be left to find their value as bullion, and that only coins of pre-debasement fineness, whether actually issued before the debasement or newly issued at the ancient sterling fineness, should be allowed to circulate at their face value. The Elizabethan currency reform plan instituted by a proclamation of 27 September 1560 worked somewhat differently. The values of all the base coins in circulation were called down, that of the more debased coins more drastically than that of the less, and arrangements were made for distinctive stamping of coins so as to distinguish the more from the less debased coins of the same denomination. Moreover, from 3 January 1561 no debased coins were to be current even at their revised valuation, so that thereafter they would be left to find their value, as had been suggested by the author of the *Discourse*, 'as men list to take them after the estimation of the stuff'. But for those who had the good sense and nerve to hold on to such coins, their value as bullion, though well below the fiat value at which they had circulated before 1560, was a great deal more than the value to which they were called down and at which they had been current between 27 September 1560 and 3 January 1561. For, as with so many other measures of currency reform, the cost of the Elizabethan recoinage fell not on the government but on those unfortunate holders of debased coins who employed them in commodity transactions between the date of their being called down and the date of their ceasing to be current. More than that, the government not only restored the currency, but also made a net profit, estimated by Dr Challis at about £50,000, out of the recoinage. The government had been prepared to admit that this operation would be effected with some inconvenience, but sought to play this down as 'not much unlike to them that being sick receive a medicine, and in taking feel some bitterness, but yet thereby receive health and strength and save their lives'. It was at least right about the bitterness, for however essential currency reform and deflation might be, there can be no doubt that its burden fell heaviest on the poor and ignorant, the chief holders of the small and most heavily debased coins. Since they were also the principal victims of inflation, however, their hardship might be held to be a cruel, but necessary, element in the government's anti-inflation strategy. How successful was that strategy?

When a revised version of the *Discourse of the Common Weal* was produced in 1581, the author, who had ascribed the inflation of the middle decades of the century to the Great Debasement, had a great deal of explaining to do. How was it that 'the prices of all things fall not back to their old rate, whereas now long since our English coin . . . hath been again thoroughly restored to his former purity and perfection?' A glance at the figures in table 1 (p. 89) will confirm the truth of this depressing assertion. For while it is true that the rate of inflation after 1561 never approached that of the Great Debasement decade, Elizabethan statesmen were no more successful in bringing inflation under real control than their present-day successors who boast of their anti-inflationary achievements, when all that they have done is to bring down the rate of inflation from an intolerable to an unacceptable level. It used to be customary for price historians to draw attention to the second of the two causes of the continued inflation stressed in the *Discourse*: the abundance of Spanish-American bullion supplies, 'the great store and plenty of treasure which is walking in these parts of the world, far more in these our days than ever our forefathers have seen in times past'. But as Dr Kerridge observed in the early 1950s, the *Discourse* did not confine its attention to monetary factors.[11] More particularly, it drew attention to the natural reluctance of landlords – who had raised rents in response to what was seen as a debasement-inspired inflation – to lower them again once the currency had been restored. As we observed when examining the long-term movement of prices over the Tudor century, the phenomenon of rising rents fits satisfactorily enough into a thesis which emphasizes demographic expansion as the prime cause of Tudor inflation.

But while we may confidently assert that the most important causes of continued inflation after the Elizabethan recoinage were real rather than monetary, it would certainly be unwise to rule out the latter factor completely. The evidence for the contention that negative rather than positive trade balances – with a consequent drain, rather than accretion, of bullion – was the Elizabethan norm is certainly not so decisive as some of those who favour real, rather than monetary, explanations suggest. The balance of payments relating to war and diplomacy may have been unfavourable, but at least from the 1570s this was probably offset by the enormous amount of booty – a great deal of it in the form of specie – coming to England through the medium of privateering operations: £600,000 from Drake's circumnavigation voyage of 1577–80 alone, and extremely large sums in the two succeeding decades.[12] As in the earlier Tudor period, there may have been some increase in the effective supply of money from dehoarding and the increased use of money substitutes such as bills of exchange, though by how much is in each case very problematical. Of one other monetary factor, however, we can speak with rather more assurance. From 1566 onwards it was profitable for Englishmen to export gold to Spain, in return for silver, since, under the bi-metallic system of the day, a Spanish revaluation had overvalued gold as against silver. Now while the resultant influx of silver to England was paralleled by an outflow of gold, it would emphatically not be true to say that the two things cancel one another out in terms of the effective monetary supply. For in the nature of things gold coins were of a much higher denomination than silver, and therefore of little use in the vast majority of everyday transactions. On balance then, while the behaviour of prices after 1561 perhaps fits a real, better than it does a monetary, explanation, and bearing in mind the possibility that any increase in the effective supply of money may have been partially or completely offset by a decrease in the velocity at which it circulated or by the extension of the sphere of money economy to transactions where barter had obtained, the evidence is too uncertain for us to be able to pronounce confidently that one factor predominated to the virtual exclusion of the other.

(ii)

It was not only in terms of the need to check internal inflation and the desirability of paying off the foreign debt on the most favourable possible terms that deflationary currency reform was an important feature of government policy. It was also a vital element in the policy of conservative reconstruction which was characteristic of the new regime's attitude and policies towards the economy and society as a whole. Crucial to this question is the government's approach to the export trade. According to Professor F. J. Fisher,[13] English cloth exports, after expanding spectacularly in the early sixteenth century, became subject, during the period of the Great Debasement, to violent fluctuations. These were a consequence of the fact that the institutional rigidity of domestic prices prevented them from responding immediately to the inflationary stimulus of debasement, in contrast to the prompt response of the foreign exchange valuation of sterling, which plummeted. For so long as this gap existed between the internal and the external value of the pound, exporters were able to sell more cloth abroad by lowering the prices, without reducing the sterling equivalent of their proceeds per unit sale, whose purchasing power, moreover, remained the same. But as the gap closed and domestic prices rose, they had to raise their prices, with a resultant equally sharp fall in the physical volume of exports, requiring a further dose of debasement to set exports moving upwards again. There were in fact recurrent crises of excess capacity, as cloth production, which had expanded to meet the debasement-engendered export boom, equally suddenly contracted. The pre-debasement expansion of exports had certainly not been without its critics, who had argued that it was grotesquely distorting

Tudor society via the stimulus which it afforded to a free-for-all in foreign trade and the expansion of textile production and depopulating enclosure. As if this were not enough, these violent short-term fluctuations were to subject the economy to a strain which was likely to threaten the very survival of the regime.

This is a rather bald and over-simplified account of Fisher's brilliantly argued thesis. However not all economic historians have been convinced by it. In particular, Professors Lawrence Stone and J. D. Gould have urged that the very dramatic expansion of broadcloth exports in the early sixteenth century, as envisaged by Fisher, was spectacular only in respect of the trade of London in broadcloth in particular, as distinct from the trade of the whole realm in woollen products in general, which increased between the end of the fifteenth century and the beginning of the fifth decade of the sixteenth by something of the order of thirteen per cent, as distinct from the 105 per cent postulated by Fisher. Moreover it is hard to reconcile the figures produced by Gould with Fisher's account of debasement as a (however temporary) stimulus to exports and the engine of dizzy short-term fluctuations.[14]

In so far as Gould's or Stone's findings are accepted, rather than Fisher's – and it needs to be emphasized that their figures for provincial exports are more patchy and provisional than are Fisher's for London – then the role of monetary disorder in economic fluctuations and of monetary restoration in economic reconstruction was perhaps less central and certainly less dramatic. But that it had a vital role is hardly in doubt. In the first place, the resultant rise of sterling on the foreign exchanges would make exports dearer and reduce foreign demand for them. By the same token, of course, it would also cheapen imports, and it is in this context that we should view the government's discriminatory policies against imports, which provided the excuse for Margaret of Parma's embargo on the importation of English cloth. For it is not too much to see all these English measures as parts of an all-embracing policy whose principal features are memorably expressed in a State Paper of 1564, probably the work of William Cecil.[15] Severely restrictionist in its tone, this memorandum concluded that economic expansion was being bought at too high a price in terms of social and political instability. Most, if not quite all of the restrictive policies which it advanced met with an enthusiastic response from the commercial élite of the day, the large-scale exporting interest of London, who had deplored the commercial free-for-all seen as the regrettable consequence of a statute of 1497 which, so far as English exporters were concerned, had opened trade with the Low Countries to anyone who could afford to pay the relatively low entry fine of ten marks to the Merchant Adventurers Company. So a deflationary policy resulting in a lower level of exports suited the interests of this élite very well and harmonized with their restricting of entry into the trade by raising their entry fines in defiance of the statute of 1497, but with the connivance of the government. Even if the government was not immediately prepared (though it yielded later at least for a time) to go along with their wishes to be allowed to relinquish what they regarded as their unviable staple at Emden and to return to Antwerp, at least the reasons which the memorandum of 1564 gave for refusal to accede to this request were music to their ears: that the longer-distance trade to Emden would favour the substantial merchants at the expense of 'the unable and unsufficient merchants not meet to be favoured'.

This strongly expressed dichotomy was to be a feature of the debate on English commercial policy for at least another century, opposing the commercial élite – the professional, substantial, 'well-experimented' merchants bred to trade – and the 'straggling', 'pedlar-like' tradesmen, retailers and even craftsmen, trading indiscriminately, 'hugger-mugger' and on dangerously extended credit. Foreign trade, in the view of both the government and the metropolitan élite, was a 'mistery', a profession, to which men served a rigorous apprenticeship, or, if not, at least must pay the sort of entry fines which restricted access to the sons of the relatively well-to-do; or must be the sons of fathers who were already free of their companies. For, as Gresham had argued with characteristic hyperbole in a letter to the duke of Northumberland in 1553: 'how is it possible that either a minstrel-player or a shoemaker, or any craftsman . . . have . . . understanding of the feat of the Merchant Adventurers?'

In the reign of Elizabeth I Gresham's élitist notions were to find an increasingly receptive response from the government. The Merchant Adventurers received a new charter in 1564, confirming their *de facto* control of the trade to northwestern Europe. The Russia or Muscovy Company, founded in the previous reign, had its position strengthened following an incident in 1564, when, after the Russian capture of Narva from the Swedes, non-members flocked to the town on the excuse that it was not comprehended within the Marian charter of the Russia Company. The result was what was claimed to be scandalous over-trading and a disastrous fall in the price of English cloth, and this led to the official inclusion of Narva within the privileges of the Company. In the 1570s the Baltic and Spanish trades were to be brought within the company framework by the foundation of the Eastland and Spanish companies; and in the 1580s the trades to the eastern Mediterranean and north Africa were controlled by the foundation of the Levant and Barbary companies. Finally, in 1601, came company control of the trade to the Orient with the foundation of the East India Company. Many of these new companies were, like the Merchant Adventurers, 'regulated' companies, in which merchants traded on their own individual capital but subject to the regulations and under the control of the companies, all of which, by devices such as the 'stint', placed restrictions on the volume of goods handled by members as well as excluding all non-members. Others however, such as the Russia and East India companies, were joint-stock companies, taking subscriptions from the investing public, but with their directorates kept tightly in the hands of a restricted élite. This form of organization, which had also characterized the Levant Company in its early days before it changed over to the regulated pattern some time between 1588 and 1595, was deemed to be especially appropriate for long-distance trades in which the interval between investment of, and return on, capital was longer, and the need to spread risks correspondingly greater.

(iii)

The Elizabethan economic settlement was therefore in many respects the product of an intimate alliance between the commercial élite of London and the government. In almost every respect the keynote of this alliance was conservative restrictionism. The most notable exception to this rule is the relaxation of the usury laws in 1571. Here the government was responding not only to pressure from its City supporters, but also to its own financial needs now that the era of royal borrowing at Antwerp was coming to an end. It was not because the usury laws had posed an insuperable obstacle to royal borrowing at interest that the government threw its weight on the side of repeal. After all, the crown had dispensed with the operation of these laws in the past, and could, if necessary, do so in the future. Far more important was its awareness that to relax the usury laws was a condition of developing a flourishing money market in England and would help to keep interest rates down by reducing the element of risk. Technically, interest-taking remained an offence after 1571. However, if interest at less than ten per cent per annum was taken, the lender was subject to no other penalty than the return of interest on the suit of the borrower, a provision which was a virtual dead letter from the first.

Thus on this one, admittedly important, issue, the alliance between the government and big business found a liberalizing rather than a restrictionist expression. Nothing better illustrates the vital importance of this alliance than the government's willingness to part company with the church on this question. For it mattered not whether the arguments from economic liberalism advanced in the Commons debate which preceded the passing of the repealing statute held that the moral law condemned not all, but only excessive, interest; or whether they took the more radical view that the moral law had nothing to do with economic life, and 'we are no Saints . . . of no perfection to follow the Letter of the Gospel'. Both arguments were totally unacceptable to churchmen, who continued to denounce *all* interest in the most vehement and uncompromising terms.

Significant though it is, this instance of economic liberalism is also exceptional, for in general neither the government nor its business allies favoured freedom of economic enterprise. If, argued the author of the memorandum of 1564, the restriction of overseas trade to a mercantile élite, like the refusal to concede the return of the Merchant Adventurers to Antwerp, were to result in a diminution of cloth production, would this really be such a great loss? It would not, he argued, affect the production of coloured cloths, and, in so far as it made for a diminution of the production of undyed cloth, this was entirely compatible with the government's determination, as evidenced by the so-called Weavers Acts of 1555 and 1558, to diminish the number of untrained clothiers operating in rural areas, and to put the dynamic rural sectors of the industry at a competitive disadvantage with respect to the towns. For, as another Elizabethan memorandum was to put it:

> Cities and great towns are only or for the most part to be maintained by manual arts, occupations, misteries and sciences, And . . . apprentices should be there brought up . . . And not in such other towns [i.e. villages] and places where men ought to live by . . . labouring of grounds.

Industry was also better controlled in the towns, whose gilds offered some assurance that national regulations relating to the quality and size of products, and especially of cloth, would be better observed than in the case of uncontrolled rural production.

The motives which inspired the Elizabethan government in what looks like a determination to put back the economic clock were not simply, or even mainly, economic. Considerations of public order were probably uppermost in the decision to check the growth of cloth production, with its stimulus to rural depopulation and discontent, while the memorandum of 1564 expressed the belief that 'the people that depend upon making of cloth are of worse condition to be quietly governed than the husbandmen.' Considerations of external security and military strength loomed no less large. The glories of Crécy, Poitiers and Agincourt had not been won by shepherds – who, as one mid-Tudor treatise argued, made very poor archers – but by men who followed the plough, whose livelihood was threatened by the developments which it was the object of Elizabethan policy to arrest. Even less promising than shepherds as military material were handicraft workers and cloth producers, for, as Francis Bacon was later to observe, 'sedentary and within-door arts and delicate manufactures (that require rather the finger than the arm) have in their nature a contrariety to a military disposition.' Similarly, another product of the unrestrained expansion of cloth production and the stimulus which this afforded to pasture farming was the dangerous dependence on grain imports in times of dearth, not to mention the hardly less dangerous dependence on a single export commodity, or at least one which predominated over all others. Both factors made the realm especially vulnerable to economic strangleholds exerted by hostile foreign powers. These were further reasons in favour of the tighter control of cloth production and of encouraging that industrial diversification and import-substitution which the work of Dr Joan Thirsk has recently emphasized.[16]

Just as commercial was complemented by industrial restrictionism, so did both complement the government's agrarian policies. In the matter of the hardships of depopulation and enclosure there is some indication that the worst was now over – at least until the hardships of the 1590s. The wool boom was certainly past, though it is too easy to forget that depopulating enclosure was about grazing animals for meat and dairy produce as well as for wool, and that the grazier was assuming an increasing prominence as the Tudor century wore on. The most notable feature of the new anti-depopulation statute of 1563 was its conservatism; its scrapping of the innovatory machinery of enforcement in the form of the permanent commissioners appointed in the two previous reigns, and its ordaining that the statutes passed during the reigns of Elizabeth's father and grandfather should be revived. All arable land which had been converted to pasture between the seventh and the twentieth years of Henry VIII's reign should be restored to tillage, and further conversions were prohibited. But if there was nothing radically new about Elizabeth's agrarian policy *per se*, what was new was the way in which it intermeshed with, and was buttressed by, controls in virtually every other sector of economic life. The Elizabethan economic settlement was emphatically an integrated whole.

The most impressive monument of this settlement is undoubtedly the celebrated Statute of Artificers of 1563. Professor Bindoff's pioneering work on the origins and passage of the bill[17] clearly demonstrates that the final product was a great deal less crude and conservative than the original measure, which had been characterized by the notion that 'the problems of a relatively simple and predominantly rural society could be met by correspondingly simple and agrarian-minded regulation'. It is not necessary to deny this – still less to accept Thorold Rogers's celebrated and actively misleading description of the statute as 'the most powerful instrument ever devised for degrading and impoverishing the English labourer' – to endorse Professor Fisher's verdict that the statute is indeed 'a classic example of the restrictive legislation that great depressions tend to produce'. For, despite all the amendments and modifications which have quite properly been stressed by Bindoff, the basic conservatism of the statute mirrors and complements that restrictionism which dominated almost every aspect of Elizabethan economic policy.

It has already been remarked how the Elizabethan government sought to limit both the expansion of the woollen textile industry and the means of entry into foreign trade, and it was shown how, in the latter case, one loophole was stopped up by allowing the Merchant Adventurers to raise their entry fees in defiance of the statute of 1497. The Statute of Artificers went a significant step further by tackling the problem of entry by apprenticeship. It limited the right to take apprentices in anything but husbandry and allied crafts to householders of at least the age of twenty-four in corporate or market towns. It insisted on a minimum property qualification for the fathers of those apprenticed to certain specified trades, including the export trade and the manufacture of cloth, and it made that qualification higher (£3 as opposed to 40s) in the case of market towns, where there was a greater danger that industrial would impinge on agricultural employment. A similar purpose was served by the provision that no one who currently practised both agriculture and a handicraft or trade should take an apprentice to the two last occupations. Here then was a real effort to limit entry to certain occupations to the relatively well-to-do. As a memorandum of the next decade admitted, the object 'seemeth to be . . . that gentlemen or others of living might have some convenient means to bestow or place their younger sons in the commonwealth to live in reasonable countenance and calling'.

The clauses of the statute making arrangements for annual hirings and prohibiting the termination of such contracts either by employers or employees without the consent of at least one magistrate were designed both to prevent seasonal unemployment and to foster industrial discipline and public order. For order was indivisible, and rather than discharge their unruly, or otherwise unsatisfactory, employees, it was the duty of employers to correct them so that they might 'be reclaimed and brought to honest conversation that continue stubborn, and grow from evil to evil from naught to worse'. The same dual significance attaches to those striking limitations on the mobility of labour which have attracted a great deal of attention from historians. The statute initiated a procedure whereby wages were rated annually by the JPs who were themselves normally employers; it also provided that no workman might leave his city, town, parish or hundred without a testimonial from the local constable and two householders registered by the local parson, and that no-one elsewhere might employ such a person without the appropriate testimonial. Now it is perfectly true that the latter provision might easily be – and no doubt often was – used as a means of keeping local wage levels down by maintaining a local labour surplus, but at least as important as this are the reasons of public order underlying the clause. As the memorandum of the 1570s puts it: 'if servants could not be received without lawful testimonials, then so many would not rob their masters, get women with child, or do some other lewd Act in hope to run away and be received in another country [i.e. district] whereas they or their lewd Acts are not known.'

The Statute of Artificers was, in fact, a great deal more than simply a piece of economic legislation. It was no less – and perhaps even more – significant as an instrument of social control, police and public order, a means by which the government, lacking a civil service and a police force, sought to regulate employment and guard against unemployment; 'to help to advance husbandry, to banish idleness' (there was provision for compulsory direction of labour); 'to reform the unadvised rashness and licentious manners of youth; to avoid many untimely and discommendable marriages' (by insisting on a long apprenticeship of seven years); and 'to bring the aged Artificer to a staid state of living'. The statute was the government's first line of defence against poverty, unemployment and the dangers to public order associated with them. It was hoped that thereby 'the commonwealth shall not be in such sort burdened, as now it is, with lusty beggars, Rogues and vagabonds, whereby those that are poor and impotent may be the better relieved and sustained'.

In so far as the realm continued to be so burdened, the statute may be said to have failed in its purpose, and the second and final line of defence, the Elizabethan poor law, came into operation. A statute passed in the same year as the Statute of Artificers ordered the binding in recognizances of £10 and ultimately, if necessary, the imprisonment of those refusing to respond to the exhortations, first of the local parson and then of the bishop, to contribute to the cost of relieving the poor. England thereby took a further significant step along the road to the mandatory institution of a compulsory poor rate. It is true that some local authorities had for some time operated compulsory rates: London since 1547, Norwich since 1549, and Ipswich since 1557. The difficulty here was that the institution of a well-founded and efficiently administered system of relief by such enlightened municipalities was bound to draw a swarm of the indigent from other places. Nothing prompted the institution of a national system of relief more than this unevenness of the quality of local provision. What was needed in fact was the nationalization of the practices of the best local authorities, though it should be added that to enjoin such practices on all authorities by legislation was no guarantee that they would be administered with the same efficiency everywhere – not at least without that sort of pressure from the centre which, given Tudor administrative deficiencies, was inevitably sporadic rather than constant, a product of periodic panics about public order rather than the normal state of affairs.

While due allowance needs to be made for all these manifold deficiencies, it is nevertheless true that the legislation of the next decade wrote into the statute book the essential features of the system of poor relief and the repression of vagrancy which were to endure until the Poor Law Amendment Act of 1834 and required only relatively minor modification in the further statutes of 1597 and 1601, the products of the bad harvests and widespread fear of disorder of the last Elizabethan decade. These essential features, apparent in the statutes of 1572 and 1576, were the mandatory compulsory rate, the provision of stocks of material on which able-bodied paupers might be set to work, and the severe physical chastisement of vagrants. There was, of course, nothing new about the last of these things, except in its connection with doling out relief not only to the impotent but also to those able-bodied persons whose poverty was the result not of their own idleness but of economic circumstances. Horrific though the brutal treatment meted out to 'the froward, strong, and sturdy vagabond' might seem to the modern mind, there is a real sense in which it was a necessary, if crude and rudimentary, corollary of the state's recognition of the fact that not all the able-bodied poor fell into this category. No doubt in practice the separation of sheep from goats which this was designed to facilitate was very imperfectly achieved, vagrants often encouraged, and those genuinely seeking work whipped and sent to their places of settlement. But for all that – and our Tudor ancestors were far less squeamish about physical hardship and punishment than we – the Elizabethan poor law is a not unimpressive achievement. Above all, it needs to be viewed in the context of the integrated and systematic policies designed to maintain economic stability and hence to keep down the numbers of those who needed its ministrations. How far the government's attempts to keep the economy in the straitjacket which it had devised for it were attended with success is a matter for a later chapter, along with the challenges to the other aspects of the Elizabethan settlement whose fashioning has been the subject of this.

Chapter Four

THE CHALLENGE TO THE ELIZABETHAN SETTLEMENT: (I) THE EXTERNAL THREAT, c. 1564–1600

RELATIONS WITH SCOTLAND AND FRANCE, c. 1564–70

During the reign of Elizabeth I the recurrent nightmare which tormented the queen and her advisers was the danger that the rulers of Spain and France would join in a Roman Catholic crusade against Protestant England. However, as was shown in the last chapter, in the early years of the reign the danger from France, and more particularly from French influence in Scotland, loomed larger. Not only had the fall of Calais tightened the French grip on the southern channel ports. The second arm of a potential French pincer had been Scotland, though this danger had been removed, though perhaps only temporarily, by the treaty of Edinburgh of 1560. The death of the young Scottish queen's husband, Francis II of France, while not completely removing the danger of Franco-Scottish accord in support of Mary Stuart's right to succeed to the English throne (or perhaps even to supplant Elizabeth herself), certainly lessened the tension still further, not least on account of the apparent friendliness of the French regent, Catherine de Medici, towards England.

Given Elizabeth's natural distaste for the idea of the widowed Scottish queen marrying either another Valois or a

Habsburg, there was much to be said for Mary taking an English nobleman as her second husband. Even if she scorned to share her bed with the English queen's horsekeeper, as she contemptuously described the royal favourite Robert Dudley, soon to become earl of Leicester, and whom Elizabeth had suggested for the role, there were other possible candidates. Provided her choice fell on an Englishman acceptable to his queen, such a marriage might serve to strengthen the status quo established by the treaty of Edinburgh, and perhaps contribute to reducing Scotland to the role of a client-state of England, as distinct from the French client-state which it had been under Mary of Guise.

When Mary did remarry in July 1565, her choice, although an Englishman, was hardly designed to meet with Elizabeth's approval. For her second husband, the ill-fated Lord Darnley, was himself in the line of succession not only to the Scottish but also to the English throne, since his mother was the daughter of Henry VIII's sister Margaret formerly queen consort of Scotland, by her second marriage. (See the genealogical table on p. 439.) The fact that the main Scottish connections of Darnley's parents, the Lennoxes, were strongly Catholic in their inclinations posed a serious threat to the status quo established by the treaty of Edinburgh and to the hegemony of the anglophile Protestant noblemen led by Mary's half-brother the earl of Moray, who had dominated the Scottish scene since 1560. Moreover, if Elizabeth remained childless and Mary's position as heir presumptive to the English throne remained unchallenged, the Darnley match would also resurrect the terrifying prospect of a militantly Catholic succession in England, an eventuality which the proposed marriage of the Scottish queen to a reliable Englishman of Elizabeth's choosing had been specifically designed to avoid. These dangers were the more apparent in that Mary had already broken with her Protestant advisers even before her marriage with Darnley, and in August 1565, led by Moray, they took up arms against her in the so-called Chaseabout Raid, after whose failure they took refuge in England.

It may be that both the Chaseabout raiders and the English government exaggerated the threat to the settlement of 1560. At any rate, Mary had firmly declared her intention not to tamper with the Protestant religious settlement in Scotland, and, although married according to the rites of the old church, Darnley had ostentatiously not accompanied his royal bride to the subsequent nuptial mass. Moreover, it was not long before the total incompatibility of the newly-weds became glaringly apparent. Darnley's conspiracy with a group of bloodthirsty noblemen led by Lords Morton and Ruthven brought about the murder of Mary's Italian secretary Rizzio in March 1566, and the return of the Protestant magnates who had been in exile since the failure of the Chaseabout Raid. Admittedly this ill-assorted alliance was short-lived, and Mary and her husband were temporarily reconciled for a period of a few months. In June 1566 their son (the future James VI and I) was born, but on 9 February following Darnley was murdered. Mary's subsequent marriage to his murderer, the earl of Bothwell, the revolt of her outraged subjects, her defeat at Carberry Hill on 15 June 1567 and her subsequent imprisonment ended this sordid and bloody chapter of events.

The danger to the settlement of 1560 had been averted and Scotland was again under the control of Protestant and anglophile noblemen led by Moray, who was now regent to the new sovereign, Mary's infant son. But from Elizabeth's point of view, if not from that of her much-relieved ministers, there was one serious snag to this otherwise wholly desirable outcome. This was that it had been brought about by the revolt of Mary's Scottish subjects, a thing which the English queen was most reluctant to accept and which inhibited her from exploiting the revolt in a thoroughly Machiavellian manner in wholehearted cooperation with Moray and his colleagues. Indeed at one point she ordered that support should be given to the Hamiltonian

Marian faction against Moray. To Elizabeth the sanctity of monarchy and the inviolability of the person of an anointed ruler counted for more than cheap advantages to be gained by consorting with Mary's conquerors. Yet there was no doubt in the minds of her advisers that Mary's defeat and the restoration of anglophile government in Edinburgh removed one element in the threat of a linkage between Guisean Catholic forces in France and a Marian triumph in Scotland, which might once again raise the spectre of Scotland as a Catholic salient for a crusade against England.

The situation took a dramatic turn once again when Mary escaped from her island prison at Lochleven, joined forces with her supporters and was defeated again at Langside in May 1568, after which she fled to England, there to be an embarrassment and a potential danger to Elizabeth for almost two decades. For the next two years, with a pro-English regime in the saddle in Edinburgh, the problem of Mary Stuart turned, from Elizabeth's viewpoint, on the difficulty of securing her restoration to the Scottish throne, while at the same time avoiding a further recurrence of the threat to the settlement established by the treaty of Edinburgh which had brought about the crisis in Anglo-Scottish relations in the mid-1560s. Indeed from 1568 Mary Stuart was at least as much an internal English problem as an issue of England's foreign relations. Elizabeth's first impulse on hearing of Mary's arrival in England was to receive her at court with all the honour due to her royal status, and she seems to have been deterred from doing so only by the need not to alienate the anglophile rulers of Scotland, however much she disapproved of their rebellion.

Scottish cooperation was all the more necessary on account of the dangers presented by discontents in the north of England which were to burst forth in the next year in the revolt of the Catholic northern earls. In addition, the situation in 1568, and notably the seizure of La Rochelle by the French Huguenots, afforded an opportunity of dealing a blow at the other arm of the French pincer whose northern

Scottish arm had been effectively neutralized, for the time being at least. The last time Elizabeth had intervened in France had been in 1562, when, egged on by the Dudley brothers, she had jumped in with both feet and extricated herself only with difficulty, and without dignity or any notable advantage – least of all the hoped-for restitution of Calais – by means of the treaty of Troyes two years later. This time she was more cautious. There was no direct English intervention, and the aid given to the Huguenots was not lavish. The guiding spirit this time appears to have been Cecil rather than the Dudleys, though the former's pursuit of a policy of aid to foreign Protestants naturally involved him fairly closely with the latter.

The end of hostilities with the Huguenots in 1570 gave scope to the French crown to assert itself once again in international affairs. From the French point of view the time was ripe. The murder of the anglophile Scottish regent Moray in January had enormously swelled the hopes of Mary's Scottish supporters, the Hamiltons and Huntlys. This change of circumstances could hardly have come at a better time for France or a worse for England, with Elizabeth needing the cooperation of a friendly Scottish government to secure the extradition of those of the defeated northern rebels who had fled to Scotland. (On the northern revolt, see below, pp. 144–5.) It was not so much that Moray's murder had replaced a Protestant anglophile by a Catholic pro-Marian or pro-French government as that it had replaced it by anarchy. In these circumstances the dispatch of an English expeditionary force under the earl of Sussex to chastise those Scots who had been harbouring the fugitives from England should not have occasioned surprise, but, given the temporary lapsing of internal strife in France, neither should Charles IX's threat to send French troops to Scotland if the English force were not withdrawn. As a consequence Sussex was ordered to return to England.

The result was not so much a defeat or setback for England as a mutual Anglo-French agreement about non-intervention in Scotland, with Elizabeth undertaking to reopen negotiations with Mary and to work to secure her reinstatement in Scotland. Whether or not it was possible to restore the Scottish queen under strict conditions safeguarding English interests became the subject of fierce debates among Elizabeth's councillors, with Cecil violently against, and Leicester, somewhat suprisingly, in favour of restoration. The arguments of the latter group turned on the need to come to an agreement with France in face of the threat posed to both countries by the recent aggrandizement of Spanish power in the Netherlands. The proposed conditions were humiliating for the Scottish queen: to confirm the treaty of Edinburgh; to surrender all claims to the English throne during the lifetime of either Elizabeth or any of the heirs of her body; not to enter into alliances without the consent of the English queen; and to send her son – who had, of course, been proclaimed king of Scotland – to live in England as a virtual hostage. But the plan did not founder on Mary's objection to these harsh terms – she might well have accepted them and disregarded at least some of them once back in Edinburgh. The reason for the failure was the justified fear of the associates of the new regent Lennox, the nominee of the anti-Hamilton and anti-Marian party, of which the earl of Morton was the most powerful figure, that, however stringent the conditions of Mary's restoration, she would not be content until she had toppled them from power. So Mary remained in England, the centrepiece of plots and subversion, but at least out of harm's way insofar as the pro-English rulers of Scotland were concerned.

CRISIS AND DÉTENTE IN INTERNATIONAL AFFAIRS, *c.* 1567–77

The alarming build-up of Spanish power in the Netherlands which had helped to bring France and England closer together had begun with the arrival of the duke of Alva as Spanish governor of the Netherlands in 1567. The subsequent Spanish 'terror' was to precipitate a stream of refugees across the North Sea, many of them clothworkers whose skills in the manufacture of the light woollen fabrics which Englishmen came to call the new draperies was to help to transform the waning economies of declining textile towns, especially in East Anglia and Kent, and ultimately, in the next century, to facilitate an important reorientation of the English export economy away from north European and towards Mediterranean markets. (See below, pp. 355, 357–8.)

But more immediate was a mounting of English Protestant feeling against Spain. The closing months of 1568 saw the beginnings of that Anglo-Spanish hostility which was to culminate in war, though only after an intervening period of détente in the later 1570s and early 1580s. The causes were many. To those already mentioned must be added the Spanish attack on John Hawkins's slaving ships at San Juan de Ulloa in September, the English seizure of the Spanish treasure fleet carrying much-needed funds for Alva; and the Spanish retaliation against English merchants and shipping. All these things contributed to raising the international temperature and to England's drawing closer to France, where Catherine de Medici appeared both to be cultivating the support of the Huguenot magnates and sympathetic to the dissident forces who were giving Alva such trouble in the Low Countries. These are the years of a proposed Anglo-French entente to be cemented if possible by Elizabeth's marriage to one of Charles IX's younger brothers, at first the duke of Anjou (later Henry III) and later the duke of Alençon (later duke of Anjou). From an English point of view such an entente would have the dual advantage of concerting French and English strength against the overweening power of Spain in the Netherlands, and of removing the danger that the Scottish queen would again become a prime factor in the international scene and a threat to English security. Indeed in 1572 Elizabeth obtained some of her main objectives in the treaty of Blois with

France without having to enter into matrimony at all. In the previous year the Scottish regent Lennox, like his predecessor Moray, had been murdered by Mary's adherents, who had obtained control of Edinburgh. It is quite true that Elizabeth failed in her objective of getting the French to recognize the new pro-English regent of Scotland, the earl of Mar, but she had real grounds for satisfaction in the fact that the treaty made no mention of Mary, which, as Professor Wernham points out, was tantamount to the abandonment of her cause by France. In some measure French alienation from Mary may be connected with the disclosures about the Ridolfi Plot against Elizabeth, that the Scottish queen and her English supporters were looking for salvation to Alva and Spain rather than to Mary's traditional French connections.

At this stage of affairs the French regime seemed to many to present a notable contrast to the Spanish, as being prepared to accord at least a measure of toleration to its Protestant subjects. Indeed some English Protestant zealots, noting the growing influence of Admiral Coligny and other Huguenot magnates at the French court, entertained hopes of an Anglo-French crusade against Catholic Spain in conjunction with the Dutch, whose cause had taken a new turn of defiance early in 1572 with the seizure of Brill by Dutch privateers who had been expelled – whether or not with this end in view is an open question – from the English ports in which they had taken refuge.

These illusions were dispelled by the horrific massacre of French Huguenots on St Bartholomew's Day, 24 August 1572, an event which became etched deeply into the consciousness of Protestant Englishmen, contributing powerfully to the growth of militant Protestantism both at the council table and in the country. The resulting recrudescence of religious war in France naturally impelled English Protestant zealots, such as Secretary Walsingham, to urge the need to adopt a militantly Protestant foreign policy, involving active and determined intervention both in

France and the Netherlands. But the queen resisted, and alarmist rumours that the Huguenots were about to be crushed out of existence proved to be unfounded when Charles IX again concluded peace with them in June 1573. That was just too late to free the French king's hands so as to enable him to take effective action against Elizabeth's dispatch of an expeditionary force to Scotland in defiance of the terms which had been agreed with the French in the treaty of Blois. The English force was sent to the aid of the new Scottish regent, the earl of Morton, who had succeeded to that office in the month following Mar's death in October 1572. In the period between the capture of Edinburgh Castle from the pro-Marian party in May 1573 and Morton's fall from power in 1578, Scotland was perhaps more firmly than ever before in the hands of an anti-Marian, anti-French and strongly Protestant and pro-English regime. That back door was once more firmly shut.

The death of Charles IX and the accession of his brother, the strongly Catholic duke of Anjou, as Henry III in 1574 gave some cause for alarm that France might again pursue a determined anti-Huguenot and anti-English policy, and religious war did in fact break out again in 1576. But the danger of an international Catholic crusade against England in the 1570s existed chiefly in the minds of the militant Protestant group in court and country, for these years had seen a significant détente in Anglo-Spanish relations. The replacement of Alva by Don Luis de Requesens as Spanish governor of the Netherlands in November 1573 had ushered in a more conciliatory Spanish policy in the Netherlands which harmonized well with Elizabeth's own policy. The new regime at Brussels also went a long way towards meeting English demands which had been unacceptable to its predecessor in 1572: in matters such as the expulsion of English Catholic subversives from the Low Countries and the guarantee of toleration for English Protestant merchants in Spanish territory. In sharp contrast was the insistence of the Dutch leader, William the Silent, on terms of religious toleration for the Netherlands which Requesens did not have the power to grant. The Dutch also blockaded the Scheldt, thus threatening the English commercial lifeline with Antwerp which had been reopened following the improvement in Anglo-Spanish relations, and William proved ready to encourage French intervention in the Netherlands now that French civil strife seemed about to be settled again, at least for the time being. All these things served both to exacerbate Anglo-Dutch relations and to bring England and Spain closer together.

When considering Elizabethan foreign policy, and more especially policy towards the Netherlands, it is all too easy to fall into the errors of historical Whiggism. As Professor Wernham has pointed out,[1] we will never understand the motives of that policy if we see it as being designed to crush Spain completely and rid the Netherlands of Spanish rule, reducing the king of Spain – in Raleigh's famous phrase – to a king of figs and oranges. That might serve to describe fairly accurately the objectives of men like Leicester and Walsingham, who were the intermittent advocates of a militantly Protestant foreign policy; not so the queen, whose policy is better seen in terms of preserving a balance between the two superpowers, France and Spain, each of whose strength, at least when France was not preoccupied by internal civil war, enormously outweighed that of England. The last thing that Elizabeth wanted was the replacement of Spanish by French hegemony in the Netherlands. There was a distinct likelihood that this would be a product of the Dutch achieving nominal independence, with the resultant power vacuum exploited by France at the expense of Spain. What the queen strove for was not to extinguish Spanish sovereignty in the Netherlands – after all she remained as uneasy about supporting Dutch as she had about Scottish rebels – but rather to restore the position of the Netherlands before the coming of Alva: a decentralized Netherlands under loose Spanish sovereignty, but reversing that formidable build-up of Spanish military power which had seemed to add yet another Catholic dagger pointing at England's heart to that which already existed in the French channel ports.

THE DETERIORATING SITUATION AND THE COMING OF WAR, 1577–90

By the spring of 1577 Elizabeth's wider foreign policy aims seemed to be on the verge of achievement, notwithstanding the predicted setback arising out of the death of the statesmanlike and conciliatory Requesens in the previous year and the appointment of the great Catholic hero, the victor over the Turks at Lepanto, Don John of Austria, as governor of the Netherlands. In the meantime, however, the Spanish troops in the Low Countries had mutinied for want of pay, and Antwerp had been sacked in the ensuing 'Spanish Fury' of November 1576. One product of these horrifying events had been the creation of an unwonted unity between the provinces of the northern and southern Netherlands, concluded in the alliance known as the Pacification of Ghent, also in November 1576. Elizabeth, to the great joy of the militant proponents of a Protestant foreign policy, now acceded to the request of the States General for financial assistance; this took the form of a loan of £20,000 down, with the promise of a further £20,000 if Don John refused to recognize the Pacification. However, a combination of Spanish disarray, Netherlands unity, and diplomatic pressure and hardly veiled threats from the English government saved Elizabeth's money. Don John accepted the new status quo in the so-called Perpetual Edict of February 1577, although this proved in the event to be anything but perpetual.

All Elizabeth's foreign policy problems seemed to be solved. Scotland was in the friendly hands of Regent Morton and his anglophile allies; France was distracted by civil war and was having to postpone her ambitions in the Netherlands, where, in turn, Spanish power had been attenuated and the ancient privileges and liberties of the provinces restored although, as Elizabeth desired, under Spanish sovereignty. The only cloud on the horizon was the possibility that the Perpetual Edict might prove to be not the prelude to lasting peace but a clearing of the decks by Don John in preparation for a spectacular coup involving, so it was rumoured, the invasion of England, the marriage of Don John to Mary Stuart and the unseating of Elizabeth from the English throne. That Mary, at the time of the Ridolfi Plot, had already shown some inclination to look for assistance to Spain rather than to her traditional connections with France, added credence to this gloomier view of affairs, though the Spanish king appears to have entertained serious misgivings about the practicability of Don John's ambitions in this quarter.

Although these dangers never materialized, others arose when Don John seized Namur and recalled the Spanish troops whose departure had recently raised so many English and Netherlandish hopes. It seemed more than likely that he would join forces with the duke of Guise and a French Catholic army, the more so since the Catholic League was strongly entrenched in northern France. The whole settlement which centred on the Perpetual Edict seemed to be in jeopardy. Moreover, the new-found unity of the Netherlands which had found expression in the Pacification of Ghent was disintegrating, not least because the southernmost provinces were increasingly reluctant to put their forces under the command of the Calvinist William of Orange. In October 1577 the States General committed an act of total disobedience, which was deplored hardly less by the English queen than by the Spanish king, against whom it was directed. In inviting the Emperor's brother, the Austrian archduke Matthias, to take the place of Don John as their governor-general they were by implication repudiating not only Don John but Philip himself. The Spanish king's response was immediate and decisive, and it marks the opening of that final stage of development which was to culminate in war between Spain and England. In October 1578 Philip dispatched an army led by the man who was soon to acquire a deserved reputation as the greatest soldier of his day, the prince of Parma, son of the former regent Margaret of Parma. With the rebels routed by Parma's and Don John's forces at Gembloux on 31 January 1578, there was little left of the promising and hopeful situation which had prevailed less than a year earlier.

For England there was an additional unwelcome development. This was that the worsted rebels – not just the largely Roman Catholic Walloons of the south, to whom the Calvinist followers of William the Silent were no less of a menace than Parma's Spaniards on the rampage, but ultimately the Dutch also – were looking for a saviour in the person of the duke of Anjou, the devoutly Catholic but none the less anti-Spanish brother of the French king. Anjou's intervention was the more likely because France had been free from internal strife since the previous October, and the more acceptable on account of the tardy and inadequate support which had been forthcoming from Elizabeth. While Elizabeth herself was deeply concerned by the possibility of Spanish being replaced by French hegemony in the Netherlands, she was reluctant to run the risks attendant upon the strongly interventionist policies favoured by the Protestant zealots on her council, who wished to outbid Anjou in provision of men and money for the rebel cause. Elizabeth's own solution was characteristic, and a great deal cheaper into the bargain. It was to neutralize Anjou by revival of the old marriage project; or better still, to employ it to make him the instrument of her own policies. In the best of all possible worlds this would admittedly be an inferior solution to resurrecting the settlement under the Perpetual Edict, but there was no longer any chance of that happening, and so far as Elizabeth was concerned, compared with both of these alternatives the hotly canvassed militant solution of active English military intervention in a holy Protestant war came a very bad third. Confident, it would seem, of her ability to keep Anjou in tow, the queen was far less disturbed than some of her councillors by the agreement which he concluded with the States General in August 1578 to provide them with military assistance in return for some rather vague promises about his preferred position in the event of their repudiating Spanish sovereignty. Indeed it afforded her a good excuse to withdraw her own much less substantial offer of military assistance, with its awkward corollaries of expenditure which she could ill afford and a drastic deterioration of Anglo-Spanish relations.

To Elizabeth, then, the Anjou match afforded an opportunity of bending Valois schemes for substituting French for Spanish hegemony in the Low Countries to the ends of English policy. In addition, Elizabeth and her husband might play the part of protectors of the French Huguenots, which, it was hoped, would go down well with Protestant opinion at home, as well as helping to ensure that the Catholic League did not predominate in France, with the resultant danger of a Franco-Spanish alliance against both French and English heretics. For the French king the situation would have the advantage of providing some sort of guarantee of the loyalty of his Huguenot subjects. Moreover, the resultant check to Guisean ambitions would make it unlikely that the Scottish Marians would receive any support from France. The latter consideration loomed larger after March 1578, when Morton fell temporarily from power in Scotland. Although he was restored in the next month and was not finally ousted until the end of 1580, his position in the intervening period was a great deal less than the complete predominance which he had previously enjoyed, and a number of his opponents had to be admitted to the Scottish council.

The Anjou match foundered on the hostility which it evoked at home, not only from out-and-out Puritans such as John Stubbs, who lost his hand as punishment for a pamphlet criticizing the project, but also from most of Elizabeth's councillors, with the notable exception of Cecil (now Lord Burghley) and Sussex. The dangers of marriage to a Roman Catholic prince and the possibility of England becoming a mere appendage of France evoked fears similar to those which had haunted many Englishmen at the time of Mary Tudor's Spanish marriage. Such fears were too strong to be ignored, and Elizabeth relinquished not only the match but also her hopes of keeping Anjou's ambitions in the Netherlands under control.[2] By 1580 she seemed resigned to Anjou's acceptance of the offer of sovereignty from the rebel provinces and even ready to countenance full-scale French intervention against Spain in the Netherlands.

This very radical change in Elizabeth's attitude is explicable in terms of the transformation of the international scene consequent upon a series of events which came in quick and alarming succession. First, Spanish strength was significantly reinforced by the acquisition of Portugal – or, more correctly, by the accession of Philip II to the Portuguese throne – in 1580. The consequent unification of the entire Iberian peninsula, the addition of control of the spices of the Orient to that of the precious metals of the New World, and the substantial new resources of Portuguese shipping (which were to form an important part of the Spanish Armada in 1588) constituted an alarming boost to the resources of Spain, which now indeed appeared to bestride the world like a colossus. Second, there was the formal end put to Morton's anglophile regime in Scotland, when he fell from power – this time for good – at the end of 1580 and was executed in the following year. The young James VI now appeared to be the willing tool of Esmé Stuart, duke of Lennox, the first of a number of male favourites who were to play such an important part in the life of that king, both in Scotland and later in England. For a time there seemed again to be a danger that the back door to England would be laid open to a Catholic crusade, undertaken either by Guisean French or Spanish elements, or – most horrifying possibility of all – a combination of the two. This danger at least subsided in August 1582 when

James was taken over by militant Protestant noblemen in the so-called Ruthven Raid, and Lennox fled to France.

But in every other respect the situation looked disastrous. In the Netherlands Spanish fortunes were improving spectacularly, thanks first to the military prowess and political acumen of Parma, now himself governor-general following the death of Don John in October 1578, and second to the collapse of the Pacification of Ghent, itself the product of the temporary unity which had been created by the Spanish Fury of 1576. The Netherlands were hopelessly divided. On the one side were the French-speaking Walloon provinces of Hainault and Artois, the so-called union of Arras, which now made their peace with Spain, and on the other, the Flemish- or Dutch-speaking provinces of the union of Utrecht. In 1582 Parma began the long campaign to conquer the latter, and Anjou, their newly acquired protector, was powerless to stop him. By February 1585, when Brussels capitulated and Antwerp was under siege, Parma had restored Spanish fortunes to where they had been before the Pacification of Ghent, when Holland and Zeeland had stood virtually alone against the might of Spain. Thus he had not only won over the provinces of the Arras union, but had also undermined the Utrecht union. In the previous July the forces of resistance, and indeed the whole of Protestant Europe, had been shaken to the core by the assassination of William of Orange, the very soul and symbol of Dutch resistance. The death of Anjou a month earlier had removed another defender of the Dutch cause, though a vastly inferior one in terms of both character and ability. Could Elizabeth now avoid openly challenging Spain in the Netherlands? And could this be done without full-scale war?

In August 1585 Elizabeth concluded the treaty of Nonsuch with the Dutch, taking them under her protection and undertaking to send an expeditionary force of 5,000 foot and 1,000 horse, which was shortly dispatched under the command of Leicester. But the English commander almost immediately put his foot in it, both by his intrigues in Dutch internal affairs and by accepting the office of governor-general, the title traditionally given by the king of Spain to his representative in the Netherlands. This clearly implied that Elizabeth had replaced Philip as sovereign – the last impression she wanted to give, as being only too likely to precipitate that Spanish invasion of England which she was anxious above all to prevent. In addition to this Leicester was in disfavour for disregarding the cash limits which a still parsimonious queen had placed upon his expedition. In the two years which succeeded the treaty of Nonsuch, Leicester spent £313,000 as against an originally estimated £252,000. But he did at least achieve something positive by way of strengthening the Dutch defensive lines as a result of his operations deep into the Netherlands, the most celebrated incident of which was the encounter at Zutphen in August 1586 in which the poet, Renaissance luminary and staunch advocate of a Protestant foreign policy, Sir Philip Sidney, was mortally wounded.

Recalled to England in November 1586, Leicester was sent back again in the following summer to try to counter the offensive which Parma was now mounting against Sluys: an ominous prelude, it was feared, to an attack on Flushing. But though Sluys fell, Flushing remained in Dutch hands and the now imminent Spanish Armada was deprived of a deep-water base in the Netherlands. As Professor Wernham points out, even after the disaster to the Armada at Gravelines, there might have been a very different story if it had had such a refuge in which to refit. Similarly the worst horrors of the return journey of the Armada via the Scottish and Irish coast might have been avoided if James VI had reacted in a more hostile way to Elizabeth's execution of his mother, Mary queen of Scots, in 1587, and had been prepared to go beyond ritual protests and the making of outraged noises. But to James the English succession was far more important than the need to avenge his mother's death, in which circumstances there was no Scottish refuge for the stricken Spanish fleet. It was indeed fortunate for England that Elizabeth had not yielded to earlier temptations to return Mary to her Scottish crown. If she had done so, it might have been a very different story in 1588.

But the background to the Spanish enterprise of England and the defeat of the Armada is a great deal wider than this. Undoubtedly a consideration which exacerbated Anglo-Spanish relations was the expeditions of English mariners such as Drake and his fellows on the other side of the Atlantic and along the Pacific coast of south and central America, and of course it was the devastation wrought by Drake when he singed the Spanish king's beard in Cadiz harbour in 1587 which delayed the departure of the Armada for a crucial period. But at least as far as the former type of encounter is concerned, it is important to realize that peace in Europe and the idea of 'no peace beyond the line'* were, within limits, not mutually incompatible, and it is undoubtedly in the European theatre that the chief causes of the conflict are to be found. Something has already been said about England's more vigorous and committed participation in the Netherlands theatre following the treaty of Nonsuch, and it is probably these developments more than any other which finally convinced Philip of the need to put paid to the English queen and her heretic subjects once and for all.

Yet hardly less important was the situation in France. With Anjou dead and Henry III childless, the prospect of a Huguenot, Henry of Navarre, succeeding to the French crown was too much for the Guises and their Catholic League supporters to stomach, and to prevent it they now prepared to reopen civil strife in France. Worse, in December 1584 they concluded the treaty of Joinville with the Spanish king, accepting him as the protector of their interests and subsidizer of their operations. In the following

* The 'line' was a parallel of latitude (the Tropic of Cancer) not longitude as is sometimes thought. See G. Mattingly, 'No peace beyond what line?', TRHS 5th ser. xiii (1963), 145–62.

year, by the treaty of Nemours, Henry III capitulated completely to their demands to exclude Henry of Navarre from the succession. Elizabeth's long game of trying to neutralize France, operating at first via the Anjou match and later by encouraging Henry III to join forces with his heir presumptive, Henry of Navarre, against the Guises, was up at last. Philip II now had every reason to hope that France – and certainly northern France, which was so vital to his strategy – would largely be under the control of his allies, and that the board would be cleared for a triumphant Spanish invasion of the northern Netherlands or England or both. The danger that the French channel ports would fall into the hands of Spain's French allies was no less grave than that Flushing might fall to Parma.

In the event both dangers were averted, but the threat of a Franco-Spanish Catholic alliance against England was never greater than in 1587–8, and it lasted throughout the Armada crisis. It did not abate until the assassination of the hero of the Catholic League, the duke of Guise, in December 1588. This had been carried out by order of the French king, and was followed by his alliance with Henry of Navarre the following April. Elizabeth and England could breathe again, but it had been a very near thing. The assassination of Henry III himself in July 1589 and the accession of Navarre to the throne as Henry IV did not, however, bring an immediate improvement for England, for it had the effect of further strengthening the alliance between the Catholic League and Spain. Given the facts that Henry's chief strength lay south of the Loire, that the Catholic League was most powerful in the north, and that Parma's armies were for the moment at least partially disengaged from the struggle against the Dutch, the danger of the French channel ports being put at Spain's disposal seemed almost as great as ever. In these circumstances it was again necessary in 1589–90 for England to intervene in France to secure those ends of policy and national security which the southern-orientated Henry IV could not entirely be relied upon to implement if left to his own devices. Hence the dispatch of another English expeditionary force to Normandy and Brittany and of financial assistance to the new French king.

During the course of events whose main features have been recounted in the past few pages the English Privy Council had at first been the scene of serious differences of opinion between, on the one hand, men such as Leicester and Walsingham, the advocates of a militant Protestant foreign policy, involving active and larger-scale military intervention on behalf of both French and Dutch Protestants, and on the other the more cautious Lord Burghley and his allies. But the events of 1584–5, the total collapse of the European balance of power, were to bring even the latter round to the view that a showdown was inevitable, and English policy thereafter needs to be seen in the light first of the imminence of war and then of war itself, and the strategic needs of national defence against invasion.

MILITARY PREPAREDNESS AND LOCALIST OBSTACLES

At the accession of Elizabeth I, in matters of trained military manpower, military technology, weaponry and general military 'knowhow', England lagged a very long way behind the two superpowers France and Spain, both of which maintained large standing armies. One shudders to think what would have happened if large numbers of Alva's or Parma's troops had been successfully landed in England, though it is true that by the mid-1580s there had been substantial improvement in the organization, training and quality of at least a part of the militia, the nearest thing this country possessed to the national armies of France and Spain. In addition, some significant steps had been taken to close the alarming gap between English and continental armaments, which had widened spectacularly as a result of changes in military technology and strategic thinking in the mid-sixteenth century. The pace of such developments was to quicken still further over the remainder of Elizabeth's reign.

With regard to armaments, the only area in which England was not lagging far behind France and Spain in 1558 was in ordnance, that is, artillery. Elizabeth's father had laid down a good store, which advances in military technology had not rendered obsolescent, and the new government did its utmost to encourage the ordnance industry. Small arms, however, were quite another matter, and while the government endeavoured to foster native production – with some notable success by the 1580s – the deficiency in the early years of the reign was too great and manifest for it to be possible to avoid heavy imports of firearms. Here the contribution made by Sir Thomas Gresham in the first decade and a half of the reign is no less, and perhaps even more, important than his better-known achievement in liquidating the royal debt to the great international financiers at Antwerp. For Gresham was extraordinarily successful in evading the prohibitions laid by foreign rulers, and notably by the king of Spain, on the export of strategic materials, and under his directions large quantities of arms, armour, gunpowder and saltpetre were imported from the Low Countries and Germany. Later in the reign the right of domestic saltpetremen to search dovecots and other private buildings for this unsavoury commodity was to attain the dimension of a major national grievance.

Armaments, and more especially the latest types of continental firearms, were very expensive, and certainly could not be provided solely out of the hard-pressed ordinary revenue of the crown. An act which had been passed in the last year of the reign of Elizabeth's predecessor, 'for having of horse armour and weapon', provided for graduated contributions towards supplies of arms, though not for training in their use. Indeed, as a recent authority has argued, those who drew up the statute appear to have envisaged the use of traditional and well-understood weapons, however out of date, rather than any attempt to bring England abreast of the continental revolution in military technology.[3] The act made provision for two sorts of contribution. Substantial local individuals were required to provide arms on their own account (the so-called 'private arms'), while the remainder would contribute in cash towards the provision of local armouries, the so-called 'town arms'. Dr Hassell Smith has recently emphasized the gross inequities arising out of these modes of provision and the disgruntlement and unrest to which the system gave rise, and which, especially during the 1590s, resulted in widespread refusal to pay military rates in many parts of the country. For, in the first place, substantial landowners were assessed for private arms only in their places of residence. Hence in many parts of the country, and more especially in open-field England, where estates tended to be larger and absentee landowners more prevalent, the most substantial landowners were often not assessed at all towards the provision of private arms. Similarly, areas where a great deal of land was owned by the church also suffered, since the clergy were assessed separately for this purpose. Confronted by a situation in which there was, for the above reasons, a deficiency in the provision of private arms, local muster-commissioners or other local authorities responsible for contributions often reacted by jacking up contributions to 'town arms', which fell largely on less substantial persons for whom the real burden of contribution was heavier. Moreover, the fact that contributions to private arms were based on ratings towards the parliamentary subsidy, a tax notoriously regressive in its incidence, seriously exacerbated the problem. So did the extension of liability to other local charges of a military or quasi-military nature: after 1573 for militia training; and, after the outbreak of war with Spain in 1583, for coastal defences, the maintenance and repair of beacons designed to give warning of the approach of the enemy, and the payment of muster-masters.

But the provision of arms was only one part of the problem. In addition, those who sought to bring England to a state of proper military preparedness had to face the formidable task of training people to use them, and to overcome the no less formidable prejudices against their use. Nor were such prejudices confined to unsophisticated rustics alarmed at the erratic firearms which appeared to be as potentially lethal to their operators as to their intended targets. The general sentiment in favour of archery – reflected for example in the arguments against depopulating enclosure that it was, *inter alia*, robbing England of the ploughmen from whom the archers who had won the great English victories of the Hundred Years' War had been drawn – died very hard indeed, and are analogous perhaps to the predisposition of military authorities in favour of cavalry at the outset of the First World War. The decay of archery continued to be deplored well into the next century – John Stow's celebrated lament in his Survey of London is only one of many examples – though it is important to distinguish between its military practicability and its social utility as a manly alternative to a variety of unlawful games and other dubious pursuits. Nevertheless, Elizabethan England did not lack self-styled experts such as Sir John Smythe, who wrote a textbook extolling the virtues of bows and arrows and other comically obsolescent forms of warfare against all the innovations of continental weaponry and tactics. To the hard-pressed local contributor to military rates such arguments had the additional attraction of cheapness. Bills and bows and arrows were undeniably cheaper than pikes, harquebuses and calivers.

Although, with a few obvious exceptions such as clergymen, JPs, privy councillors and lords of parliament and their servants, all males between the ages of sixteen and sixty were liable for service in the militia, in actual fact only a small proportion received training. This can be illustrated by the example of the county of Suffolk in 1573, where there were reckoned to be about 19,000 males of military age of whom a mere 9,000 were adjudged as – in the words of a government memorandum of the previous year – 'able to bear arms or to use weapons on horseback or foot'. From about this time in England in general it became normal to enrol only such 'able' men, though in actual practice those enrolled were not always the most suitable, especially since not all recruiting officers were above accepting bribes to excuse individuals from service. Out of these 9,000 'able' men in Suffolk, 2,600 of the fittest, both in physical and economic and social terms – the proportion, of course, varied from county to county[4] – were chosen for special training for ten days in every year as members of the county trained bands. The emergence of this élite corps – though Alva or Parma would have found this use of the term laughable – was a recognition of the need for expertise acquired via specialized training in both manoeuvres and weaponry, as distinct from mere numbers, in conditions of modern warfare. It was insisted that membership of the trained bands should be open neither to persons of doubtful loyalty, such as Catholic recusants, nor to the lowest orders. As far as the latter provision was concerned, the government's desire to recruit the trained bands from relatively well-to-do householders and their sons was not always observed, and there were not wanting complaints against the infiltration of lower social elements, with consequent dangers to public order and state security.

Since it was thought desirable that the trained bands should be kept at home, English expeditionary forces abroad tended to consist largely of less reliable elements in both military and social terms, sometimes, as in the case of some of the soldiers sent to France in the 1560s, including rogues, vagrants and released gaolbirds. Indeed county particularism, which is so important a factor in the history of the period, strongly favoured restricting the operations of trained bands to the counties from which they were drawn. But the government was to insist that such conditions could not be applied in situations of national emergency, which, towards the end of the century, admitted of an increasingly broad interpretation. Moreover, there was normally a leavening of trained men among the troops sent abroad, and after the outbreak of war with Spain in 1585 one finds whole companies of the trained bands serving overseas. In this the history of the trained bands bears comparison with that of the Territorial Army before and after the outbreak of the First World War. There is, however, no modern parallel to the local protests against such things, and not least against the anti-invasion plans for concentrating the trained bands of several counties at strategic points in face of the probability or likelihood of enemy landings. As late as the English Civil War the strategic freedom of commanders on both sides was to be gravely hampered by similar localist objections.

The needs of military defence and military provision had brought an enormous accretion of power and influence to the most important agency of government policy in the localities, the lieutenancy; especially following the outbreak of war with Spain, when lord lieutenants were increasingly appointed on a long-term rather than an *ad hoc* basis, and most counties were assigned one, even though some lieutenants served several counties. The lieutenant and his deputies, the latter drawn from the élite gentry of the counties and themselves a significant minority of the JPs, were conceived as an effective centralizing agency to combat the foot-dragging of local magistrates in saving the realm against invasion. It was their duty to see that suitable muster-masters were appointed to instruct the trained bands, and if necessary to reduce the size of the companies of the trained bands, which ought to make for more efficient military training, even if it would also detract from the prestige and standing of the local gentlemen who served as captains, and therefore add a further reason for the unpopularity of the lieutenancy in the counties. The cost of the stipend of the muster-master and of the reforms he demanded became a major county grievance against the lieutenancy both in this and in the next two reigns. Matters were worsened in those cases where the right to appoint to the post, an important piece of lieutenancy patronage, was abused and those appointed lacked the necessary military experience and knowledge, as well as local connections.

There can be no doubt that war and the danger of war was a significant factor making for the diminution of the effective power of the local magistracy, the Commission of the Peace, in the counties. Many JPs no doubt felt that they were being reduced to the status of mere administrative assistants of the lieutenancy, except perhaps in the matter of granting the necessary military rates in Quarter Sessions, which was, in a very real sense, a sort of county parliament as well as an organ of administration and justice. If the trained bands were to be properly armed and trained, there could be little doubt that the military rates levied needed to be far in excess of those authorized by the Marian statute of 1558. If Quarter Sessions refused to be persuaded or bullied into this, some lieutenants were certainly not above exacting them on their own authority. Nor could considerations of national security be confined to preparations to resist foreign invaders. The war effort might itself be paralysed by internal disorder, and, in taking action in this field, the lieutenancy trespassed further on the functions of the JPs, even though, as mentioned earlier, most deputy lieutenants were themselves JPs. A good example is the appointment of provost marshals by lord lieutenants in the 1590s. At first the provost marshals were to oversee the discipline of soldiers, but this was later extended to disbanded troops and in actual practice to the bands of wandering vagrants from whom they were not always easily distinguishable. Here was another area in which the government, via the agency of the lieutenancy, was treading very hard on the toes of outraged county magistrates.

NAVAL STRENGTH AND COLONIAL ENTERPRISE

Fortunately the English militia was never put to the test, for the Spanish enterprise of England was defeated on England's own peculiar element, the sea. *Flavit Jehovah et dissipati sunt* ran the legend on a medal struck to commemorate the victory of 1588, significantly in Holland not England originally, for the English, while in no doubt that a Protestant God was on their side, would not have countenanced any version of events which failed to give full credit to the skill and valour of English seamen. The navy which fought the engagements of the summer of 1588 consisted of a mixture of royal, and impressed private, ships, among the latter the well-armed vessels of the Levant Company, built to withstand the attacks of Barbary corsairs in the Mediterranean. As to the royal ships, thanks especially to the reforms of John Hawkins as treasurer of the navy, his attack on corruption, streamlining of administration, construction of new and more manoeuvrable vessels and ingenious adaptation of older ones so as, *inter alia*, to increase their length relative to their width, they represented by the mid-1580s a formidable fighting force.

The English navy was built to fight at a distance. The Spaniards on the other hand, while certainly not wedded to the Mediterranean type of warfare based on the galley which had triumphed at Lepanto, still based their strategy on close-contact engagement, using their guns not to sink but to immobilize enemy vessels as a preliminary to boarding them. This is reflected in the construction of their ships; in their enormous superiority of trained soldiers carried in them; but not, it would seem, in their armament, since the view of one of the most eminent of English naval historians, Michael Lewis, that except in the matter of long-range guns, the armament of the Armada was more powerful than that of the English fleet, has since been decisively challenged. It may therefore have been not simply the Spanish shortage of powder which permitted English ships to shorten their range with impunity at Gravelines, at the start of that decisive course of events which sent the invincible Armada on its disastrous roundabout homeward journey via the North Sea and the Atlantic, strewing the coast of Ireland with Spanish wrecks.[5]

One of the more spectacular products of the naval reforms associated with the name of Hawkins was the transformation of a fleet designed to serve a preponderantly defensive function – its role in 1588 – into one capable of operating on the high seas. Elizabeth I has come in for more than her fair share of blame from naval and imperial historians, echoing contemporary naval experts such as Hawkins and Raleigh, for her failure to use this potential decisively to smash Spain and bring the war to a victorious conclusion. This might be done in a number of ways, the first of which was to mount attacks on Spain itself, as Drake had done in 1587 and Essex was to do – once again at Cadiz – in 1596. But, given England's lack of an efficient army, this strategy could at best inflict no more than temporary losses, however devastating these might be at the time. More attractive and promising perhaps was the idea of abandoning the periodic, inconclusive and occasionally disastrous English incursions on to the continent, which meant contesting on the Spanish rather than the English element, and replacing them by what in later centuries would be described as a 'blue-water' strategy, which, it was claimed, would quickly bring Spain to her knees. A permanent naval blockade spread out roughly between the Spanish coast and the Azores would afford the means of intercepting Spanish treasure fleets from the New World and, by cutting off Philip's lifeline, make it impossible for him to continue the struggle. Even if England had sufficient ships to effect the latter strategy, the appalling risks attendant upon leaving the British Isles vulnerable to attack was reason enough not to adopt it. As it was, most of the attacks on Spanish treasure ships were piecemeal, a form of naval warfare carried on by that characteristic Elizabethan form of private enterprise, privateering expeditions, financed on a joint-stock basis, with the queen herself sometimes acting as an investor. Such operations, however profitable, did no more than divert a tiny proportion of treasure from Spain, and, indeed, an increasingly lower proportion in the course of the 1590s as the Spanish treasure fleets became better armed and protected. Nevertheless, as the historian of Elizabethan privateering has urged, the Spanish need to concentrate more resources on the protection of the treasure fleet had the effect of leaving other Spanish ships relatively unprotected. He estimates that upwards of a thousand Spanish ships were captured in the course of the war, with a resultant growth of Spanish dependence on foreign shipping.[6]

Failing an east Atlantic blockade, similar ends might be achieved by operations in the western Atlantic from bases in the New World itself. Herein lay the germs of many schemes of transatlantic colonization. Of these the idea which most nearly approximated to the aims of the eastern Atlantic blockade was the frequently canvassed plan to cut Spanish America in two by occupying the isthmus of Panama, where bullion from South America was normally transhipped by the Spaniards. The operation, which was to be carried out with the aid of an allegedly friendly indigenous people, the Cimaroons, had come miraculously near to success – though in the event it was a total failure – as early as 1576 when conducted by a small force under John Oxenham. It continued to exert a powerful hold on the imagination of English naval strategists, and was literally to be the death of both Drake and Hawkins in their disastrous final expedition of 1595. The Cimaroons also figured in a fantastic project of the early 1580s to colonize the land bordering the straits of Magellan, whither they were to be transported from Central America. Their hatred of the Spaniards, along with their experience in servitude, 'in all toil far from delicacy', was regarded as sufficient guarantee both of their cooperation and of their ability to withstand the unaccustomed rigours of the cold climate of the southern extremes of the continent. The other settlers would include 'condemned Englishmen and women in whom there may be found hope of amendment', and a condemned pirate was to be reprieved on condition of undertaking the work. It is hardly surprising that this astonishing project 'whereby we shall make subject to England all the golden mines of Peru, and all the Coast and tract of . . . America upon the sea of Sur [sic] yet not fortified' was not put into effect.

The enterprise, however, offered a blend of settlement and colonization – the rich natural resources of extreme South America were warmly and over-optimistically stressed – and military strategy which was to become characteristic of a great many transatlantic schemes. No less characteristic was the idea of disposing of what the great propagandist of colonies, the younger Hakluyt, was to describe as 'the offal of our people' – an expressive if inelegant description for what was widely regarded as the surplus population of what appeared to some contemporaries to be an uncomfortably overpopulated England.

It is, of course, arguable that the greater the military success of such settlements the more they were likely to succeed in the long term as colonies; self-financed, that is, by serving as bases for privateering expeditions on the Spanish Main. But in actual fact the two aims, far from being complementary, were conflicting, and the bulk of the profits from such expeditions was bound to be swallowed up by investors at home. Far-sighted propounders of colonization, such as Sir Walter Raleigh, Sir Humphrey Gilbert and the two Hakluyts, were as voices crying in the wilderness in the emphasis which they laid on the long-term economic and social, as well as the military, arguments for colonies. They saw them not only as markets for English manufactures, and especially woollen textiles (a somewhat vain hope given the time it would take for such a market to develop and the absurdly over-optimistic notions entertained about demand from Indians who lacked both the purchasing power and the propensity to consume); but also as receptacles for English surplus population; as alternative sources of naval stores; and as an attractive opportunity for the younger sons of substantial gentleman, frustrated at home by impartible inheritance, to acquire their own large estates across the Atlantic, complete with facilities for hunting and other gentlemanly pursuits.

Such considerations were strongly stressed in Gilbert's project for colonizing Norumbega, the vast area north of the Hudson river on the eastern seaboard of the modern United States and Canada, and following Gilbert's death in the Atlantic in 1583, they were advanced again by Sir George Peckham and his associates. But they had a far stronger pull in attracting upper-class investment in colonization schemes much nearer home in Ireland, where considerations of national security bulked even larger. The revolt of the earl of Desmond which had broken out in 1579 and was not fully quelled until 1583 had left much of the province of Munster desolated, and large-scale plantations by English settlers were deemed to be a means of guarding it against future native uprisings. These settlers were to be what Professor D. B. Quinn has described as 'a whole cross-section of English society' – gentry, their servants, farmers, craftsmen and labourers. Large blocks of land, significantly called seignories, were to be entrusted to magnates known as undertakers, who, it was hoped, would bring with them settlers from their own parts of England. Raleigh for instance, was head of a group of undertakers from the West Country. But the actual course of the Irish settlements did not run at all smoothly. The original allocation of land had been hopelessly over-optimistic and made on faulty surveys, and those of the frustrated settlers who did not return home in disgust often had to contend with counterclaims from previous owners who had been attainted but subsequently pardoned. Moreover, contrary to the specific terms of plantation and to its objectives in terms of national security, many of the new landowners let their lands to Irishmen –

sometimes, no doubt, to the former owners – and themselves became absentees, a pattern to be repeated in the Ulster plantation of the next reign, and destined to bedevil Anglo-Irish relations down to and after the age of Parnell and Gladstone. But for all this the plantation undoubtedly helped to bolt England's back door or postern gate to a foreign invader, England's Scottish back door having already been closed by reducing Scotland to something akin to a client-state, ruled by an anglophile regime.

Both Ireland's strategic importance and its proximity to, and ease of contact with, England meant that Irish colonization was more popular and more vigorously pursued than transatlantic schemes such as Raleigh's successive Virginia settlements in the 1580s on the island of Roanoke off the coast of what is now North Carolina. In his essay *Of Plantations* Francis Bacon was to observe that 'the principal thing that hath been the destruction of most plantations [i.e. colonies] hath been the base and hasty drawing of profit in the first years. It is true, speedy profit is not to be neglected, as far as may stand with the good of the plantation, but no further'. But prospectors and investors in Elizabethan transatlantic colonization were obsessed by speedy profit. 'The discovery of a good mine . . . or a passage to the South-sea, or some way to it, and nothing else can bring this Country in request to be inhabited by our nation'. Thus wrote Ralph Lane, the governor of Roanoke, to Raleigh in 1586. The alternative prospect to the discovery of mines, privateering loot, was not stressed by Lane as an obstacle to successful colonization, since this was the main object of his quasi-military plantation, though, with its lack of deep-water harbourage, Roanoke was not suited for this either. But Raleigh's second Roanoke colony in 1587, where the settlers were not the employees of an England-based privateering syndicate but genuine settlers with a real stake in the land, was no more successful and vanished without trace, the probable victim of Indian hostility. For even given the right motives and attitudes, colonies could not stand as self-supporting enterprises, and insufficient help was forthcoming from the mother country to tide them over the long and difficult period of establishment and consolidation. Only the prospect of spectacular short-term gains attracted substantial support; above all the precious metal either from a 'good mine' or from loot from the Spaniards. These were the considerations which dominated Elizabethan transoceanic enterprises such as the schemes of Gilbert and his successors for Norumbega and Raleigh's plans for both Virginia and Guiana – Virginia as a base for privateering and Guiana containing the fabulous gold deposits of the mythical El Dorado. The effective beginnings of English transoceanic colonization are to be found not in the Elizabethan but the early Stuart period.

Chapter Five

THE CHALLENGE TO THE ELIZABETHAN SETTLEMENT: (II) THE INTERNAL CHALLENGE, *c.* 1565–1595

In chapter 3 it was shown how the comprehensiveness which Elizabeth had intended to characterize her religious settlement had been frustrated by her moving very much further in a Protestant direction than some thought desirable, even if not nearly so far as many of her more zealous Protestant subjects wished. In maintaining this settlement Elizabeth and her successors were challenged by Roman Catholics who viewed the newly reformed church with grave misgivings and by Puritans who wished the church to take on a more decisively Protestant character and who regarded the Catholics both as idolaters and as a potential fifth column available to be used by foreign Catholic invaders.

THE CATHOLIC CHALLENGE

That the reluctance of almost the whole of the Marian episcopate to go along with the Elizabethan settlement was not on the whole matched by a parallel reluctance on the part of the lower clergy must have been a matter for considerable relief to the government. Nevertheless, there were very real dangers in a situation in which the lower ranks of the early Elizabethan clergy contained so many parsons who were at worst crypto-Catholics and at best vicars of Bray, men who were not devoted and convinced Protestants and who might acquiesce with varying degrees of enthusiasm if the religious tide again turned, as it had turned so frequently over the previous two decades. Like so much else, the survival of the religious settlement depended on the survival of the queen herself. Elizabeth's strategy with reference to her Catholic subjects was based on the notion that, barring accidents, time was on her side. As such, it presents a marked contrast to the views of Puritan zealots who naturally had no patience for her notion of winning the Catholics over gradually by blurring as much as possible the distinctions between the practices of the old church and the new.

Elizabeth almost certainly had no expectation of immediate success in winning Catholic support for the new church. But as time went on, the chances of success would become progressively greater. The parish churches of England had after all been the hallowed places of worship of countless generations of English Catholics. Even if the new liturgy was unfamiliar – more unfamiliar than the queen herself had wished in her frustrated search for comprehensiveness – was it not better to attend services than not to go to church at all? And was it not likely that the habit of conforming would itself breed compliance and conformity, however unenthusiastic? Meanwhile the surviving Romish priests would gradually die off, and there was no obvious source from which they could be replenished. Thus a generation of Englishmen might arise which knew nothing of the old forms of worship, and the unenthusiastic conformism of many English Catholics – many attended church but left before the administration of the communion, for example – might be succeeded by a state of affairs in which their spiritual inclinations were brought into line with their outward practices. At the very least, conformity would be secured. Such hopes were reinforced by the isolation of the vast bulk of the English Catholics from the influence of the continental Counter-Reformation which was currently revivifying and stiffening the temper of international Catholicism.

Catholicism was indeed the traditional faith in more matters than those of doctrinal belief and liturgical observance. For instance, while Catholics were to be found in all parts of England, the old religion seems to have been more prominent and deeply rooted the further one moves from the central currents which were rapidly transforming English life: away from cities and in remote regions such as those which came to be described as 'the dark corners of the land': Wales, the far southwest and above all the north of England. This linking of conservative religious with conservative social and economic practices is, of course, by no means universal, and there were Elizabethan Catholics, such as Sir Thomas Tresham of Rushton in Northamptonshire, who were amongst the more notable agricultural entrepreneurs of their day. Nevertheless, the existence of such notable exceptions does not dispel the strong impression that English Catholicism was in danger of becoming the natural ideology of an old order which was on the way out, however gradual that process of decline might be. These factors, which have been given prominence in the brilliant work of a Catholic historian, Professor John Bossy,[1] tended to become even more pronounced after the papal bull of 1570 excommunicating the queen, when anti-Catholic measures became more stringent and the clandestine religious observances of great Catholic landowners put a higher premium on the loyalty of tenants and their consequent distaste for denouncing their superiors. For many Catholic landowners, to adopt more efficient methods of estate-management such as enclosure and rack-renting, however desirable in terms of their economic wellbeing, was unthinkable if only because it would subject such loyalties to an impossible strain. The sense of the mutual dependence of Catholic landlords and tenants, while not universal, undoubtedly reinforced any pre-existing tendency there might be for religious, social and economic conservatism to march hand in hand.

The revolt of the Catholic northern earls in 1569 is often represented as the most striking and eloquent expression of the connection between political, social and religious conservatism. But the truth is far more complex than is suggested by this simple statement. For while it is one thing to see the old-fashioned, paternalistic and lenient estate-management of Catholic landowners as helping to safeguard them against the possibility that their dependants would inform on them, it is quite another to see these things as conditioning a loyal tenantry to follow a Percy or Dacre into revolt against his monarch. As the work of Dr James has clearly demonstrated, few of the dependants of the earl of Northumberland were prepared to go so far as this in 1569, and while the support for the Dacres and the earl of Westmorland and his kinsmen in the northwest was more impressive, the rebel army of 3,000 men which was defeated by the queen's cousin, Lord Hunsdon, at Naworth in February 1570 contained far more Scotsmen than it did local dependants. According to an estate official of the earl of Northumberland, the secure terms on which many of his master's tenantry came to hold their lands militated against the sense of obligation which they would have felt if their tenure had been more precarious, but their lord had refused to take full advantage of this fact.[2]

The background to the northern revolt had been Catholic hopes following Mary Stuart's arrival in England and the prospect that she might be married to the greatest English nobleman, Thomas Howard, duke of Norfolk. While to some of Elizabeth's councillors, and especially Cecil, who came near to being toppled from power in 1569, the idea was anathema, it was not only to the wilder Catholic noblemen of the north that it appealed. The Norfolk match attracted them, of course, as being likely to have as its products the prompt recognition of Mary as Elizabeth's heir, an ultimate Catholic succession, and, more immediately, the downfall of Cecil and perhaps even the restoration of the old religion, or at least more lenient treatment of Catholics. But it also had attractions for others, among them the Protestant champion Robert Dudley, earl of Leicester, and the earl of Pembroke, both of whom saw the Norfolk match as a possible means of rendering Mary harmless by a safe marriage to a Protestant Englishman, for however conservative his style and inclinations, Norfolk was no papist. Their own support for the match would in turn help to secure their position in the event of Elizabeth's death and a Marian succession. The mutually contradictory hopes of both groups – and of Norfolk, who hovered ambivalently between them – were dashed when the queen peremptorily ordered Norfolk to abandon all thought of such a marriage and when he, after fleeing to the safety of his palace at Kenninghall in south Norfolk, returned meekly to face royal displeasure and imprisonment. His subsequent execution in 1572 came about in consequence not just of his aspirations to obtain the hand of the Scottish queen, but of disclosures connected with the Ridolfi Plot of 1571, which implicated him in a plan to bring about, by treasonous support for a foreign invasion, what he had failed to achieve by policy.

The northern revolt was a blind and despairing protest by Catholic noblemen who had felt themselves to be near to success only to see their triumph snatched from under their noses. Norfolk had tried unsuccessfully to dissuade his dubious and hot-headed northern allies from a revolt which, in the event, could hardly have been worse timed – unless it is argued that the bad timing lay with the papal bull *Regnans in Excelsis*, which excommunicated the queen but did not appear in England until after the revolt had been crushed in 1570. For all that, the bull marks the real English beginnings of the militant strategy of the Counter-Reformation papacy, which was ultimately to frustrate Elizabeth's hopes of absorbing her Catholic subjects within the established church. The bull was more than a declaration that they must have no truck with this heretical body. It both excommunicated the 'pretended queen and the servant of crime' and absolved her subjects of obedience to her. It was an act in the great tradition of papal *plenitudo potestatis*, the tradition of Gregory VII, Innocent III and Boniface VIII. And even if for Elizabeth there was to be no Canossa, for her Roman Catholic subjects the easy way of acquiescence in the authority of the established church was finally barred by the supreme authority of the pope.

But, it may be asked, in the context of 1570 could the bull be anything more than a very grand gesture? How was the unyielding spirit of tridentine Catholicism to get through to England to arrest the danger of a slide away from Catholicism as the product of conformity and habit? Here the Jesuit and other Catholic missions which came to England from the later 1570s onwards were the crucial lifeline. These English Catholic missionaries, trained in foreign seminaries to expect martyrdom not only as their more than probable fate but also as the glorious consummation of their careers, brought by their example an inspiration and a stiffer backbone of resistance to their co-religionists to whom they ministered. Yet, faithful servants of the Counter-Reformation papacy though they were, the success of their operations was if anything hindered rather than helped by papal intransigence. However resounding a clarion call to Catholic action the papal bull might be, this precipitate action of Pope Pius V, which was significantly deplored by the unimpeachably Catholic king of Spain, made things unnecessarily difficult for the missionaries as the papal shock-troops on the English front. Most of them were probably sincere in their profession that, in Edmund Campion's moving words from the scaffold: 'We are dead men in this world; we only travailed for souls; we touched neither state nor policy.' But the terms of the bull seemed clearly to contradict this and to strengthen in the minds of English Protestants the identification which they were all too prepared to make between popery and potential treason – a connection strengthened in their view by the involvement of Catholic hotheads like Throckmorton and Babington in the plots associated with Mary Stuart in the 1580s. Matters had, if anything, been made worse by the so-called *Explanatio* issued by Pius's successor, Gregory XIII, in 1580, which took pains to explain that the bull of 1570 did not oblige English Catholics to rise immediately against Elizabeth, but rather to continue to obey her until the time was ripe. Against such a background both the popular and government disbelief in the sincerity of the missionaries' repudiation of political action is hardly surprising.

The achievement of the Catholic missionaries was very great. Their determination to stem the process of minimal conformity with the established church on the part of English Catholics, and the example of the lives and the heroism of the deaths of so many of them, were factors whose importance it is difficult to exaggerate in the survival of Catholicism as a force in English life. Nevertheless, when judged against the exacting criteria of their own standards and aims, their success was only partial. For they did not succeed in winning back to the old faith even the bulk of those (or their descendants) who had been Catholics at the beginning of the reign. Indeed, it has recently been argued with force that by tending to favour the strongly Protestant south and east at the expense of the more backward but potentially more fruitful highland zone, the main thrust of the missionaries' effort was in a real sense misdirected. In 1580 the north of England had two-fifths of the detected (and probably a much higher proportion of the undetected) recusants, but only one-fifth of the priests. This misdirection was a product of a number of circumstances: of the normal convenient routes from continental seminaries into England; sometimes even of the far greater likelihood of achieving the glorious crown of martyrdom in the more hostile environment of London and the militantly Protestant south and east; but sometimes also of the number of opportunities provided by these regions for a relatively comfortable existence as chaplains in the halls and manor houses of recusant nobility and gentry. For, it could be argued both plausibly and sincerely, such places offered the most secure bases from which to proselytize and to minister to the spiritual needs of Catholic congregations. It is not altogether surprising that spiritual duties in the manor house often took precedence over congregational ministration. This no doubt was partly due to the fact that the former duties were more attractive to missionaries who were mostly well-born and well-educated men who found ministering to their own kind or to social superiors more congenial and rewarding than work among the peasant faithful whose brand of Catholicism was often a compound of gross superstitions and neo-magical beliefs. But another important factor was the embarrassment and danger of extensive proselytizing and congregational activity to the missionaries' hosts, who may frequently have urged the priests to keep their heads down. All these factors help to explain the 'concentration on the least promising areas and a neglect of the majority of Catholics'; at worst a 'strategy of disaster', as Dr Haigh has described it; at best a very serious limitation on the successful accomplishment of the aims of the mission.[3]

The government met the Catholic challenge by resorting to increasingly repressive measures both against the missionaries and popish priests and against Catholic laymen. By an act of 1581 it was, *inter alia*, declared treasonous to attempt to withdraw support not only from the queen but also from the established church, and the same act raised the fines for recusancy (non-attendance at church) to £20 a month. An act of 1585 made it treasonous simply to be a Jesuit or seminary priest, while another of 1593 increased the already heavy disabilities imposed on Catholic laymen, who were ordered not to go further than five miles from their places of residence. In what were, it needs to be remembered, times of war, when Catholics were viewed as potential fifth columnists, they lived in constant fear of raids from government officials, while in addition to the fines for recusancy, every imaginable form of harassment was employed to wean them from the old faith. For instance, their marriages, when not conducted in the parish church, were not legally recognized, and their children regarded as bastards. Inevitably many of the weaker brethren – and even some of the Catholic clergy – yielded, and by the last decade of the reign there were signs that the tide of return to active Catholicism had been stemmed. It would probably be true to describe the net result of the later Elizabethan drive against Catholic recusancy as being to reduce the number of Catholic families, but it is also true that, because of the activities of the missionaries, the temper of those remaining in the old faith had hardened and the number of 'church-papists' who enjoyed minimal conformity had been reduced. Although there were fewer Catholics, there was no longer danger that the faith would be crushed out of existence. That is the real achievement of the missionaries.

As Professor Bossy has emphasized, in concentrating on the missionaries' impact on the English Catholic community there is a danger of neglecting a reciprocal flow of influence. Hidden in the houses of Catholic gentlemen (at considerable risk to their hosts), disguised as their servants or dependants, it would not be surprising if many of the missionaries themselves absorbed something of the character of the community they came to transform. Without becoming any less intransigently Catholic or losing anything of the spirit of Counter-Reformation idealism and resolution with which they had set out to save and rejuvenate the English Catholic community, they may, in the process of doing so, have become more English, less international, in their outlook, and more capable of appreciating the general ambivalence which characterized the attitudes of so many of their hosts. These patriotic Catholic gentlemen who accepted their ministrations gladly, but rejected the political claims of the bull of 1570, no doubt felt themselves to be acting no differently from the countless Catholics in the English past who had opposed the political demands of popes to dispose of empires and dethrone kings.

Needless to say, not all of the missionaries underwent this process of anglicization. One of the factors which set important limits on the influence they exerted was their often bitter disputes with existing Catholic priests, who had been there before the missionaries arrived, and who regarded themselves as the bulwark of traditional English Catholicism against these unwelcome intruders. Such difficulties had existed ever since the arrival of the first missionaries, but since it was in the closing years of the reign that they came to a head, they are best left to discussion in the chapter which follows.

THE PURITAN CHALLENGE

(i)

It is now necessary to turn to the challenge to the Elizabethan settlement posed not by those who believed it had gone too far in a Protestant direction, but by those for whom it had not gone far enough, and whom contemporaries described as Puritans, or sometimes Precisians. This is the way the term has been used in the pages which follow, and it must immediately be apparent that it covers a very great deal, ranging from moderate but determined reformers to wild-eyed extremists such as John Penry, Henry Barrow and John Greenwood, who ended their days on the scaffold. It included noblemen and courtiers, such as the Dudley brothers, earls of Warwick and Leicester, the earl of Bedford, the queen's relations, the earl of Huntingdon and Sir Francis Knollys, and Secretary of State Sir Francis Walsingham; influential country gentlemen such as Sir Nathaniel Bacon, son of Elizabeth's lord keeper, in Norfolk, and Sir Richard Knightley in Northamptonshire; even perhaps strongly reformist bishops such as Edmund Grindal, bishop of London and later archbishop both of York and Canterbury, Thomas Bentham, bishop of Coventry and

Lichfield, and Matthew Hutton, bishop of Durham and later archbishop of York; anti-episcopal Presbyterians such as Thomas Cartwright, Walter Travers and John Field; and separatists such as Barrow and Greenwood, who, despairing of achieving what they regarded as truly Protestant ends through the established church, broke away to form their own illegal 'gathered churches', consisting only of those whom they regarded as God's elect, and advocating reform 'without tarrying for the magistrate'. It is, of course, arguable that what divided such widely ranging categories from each other was a great deal more significant than what they held in common. But from time to time contemporaries used the word 'Puritan' to describe all of them, and this is the practice which will be followed here.

In general it is true to say that, at least in the reign of Elizabeth, it was not matters of theology which divided Puritans from their opponents in the established church, as they were to come to divide them under the Stuarts. Even Archbishop Whitgift, Elizabeth's third Primate and the most resolute and successful harrier of the Puritans, remained a good Calvinist predestinarian to his dying day, opposed to Calvinist notions about church government but not to Calvinist theology. What in fact characterized Puritan attitudes from the beginning was an uncompromising opposition to ecclesiastical abuses, which less precise churchmen were inclined to condone as regrettable but unavoidable. Such an abuse was the licensing of churchmen to hold benefices in plurality, which left many parishes without resident parsons. In fairness, the church had not been wholly inactive in seeking to set limits to this abuse. In 1571 Convocation promulgated canons which limited the number of such benefices held by one man to two, as well as insisting that they should be 'compatible' – that is, within twenty-six miles (later increased to thirty) of one another. But some pluralism there must be, insisted its defenders, if learned men were to be attracted into the ministry, if the universities were to be properly served and the chaplains of queen, bishops and noblemen adequately rewarded. The most impressive answer to this was to come in an essay on the subject by the great Francis Bacon, who argued that the chaplains of noblemen – he did not mention royal chaplains – ought to be maintained by their patrons and not at the expense of parishioners being denied resident parsons. But Bacon was also realistic enough to admit that 'to desire that every parish should be furnished with a sufficient preacher' – the *sine qua non* of all Puritan programmes – 'and to desire that pluralities be forthwith taken away is to desire things contrary; considering *de facto* there are not sufficient preachers for every parish . . . [and] there is not sufficient living and maintenance in many parishes to maintain a preacher'.

Such arguments might have had more force if it were not for the fact that there were large numbers of more than adequate and learned preachers who had been deprived of their benefices for refusing to observe a variety of rites and practices which offended their precise Protestant consciences. In July 1566 the Puritan ministers Laurence Humphrey and Thomas Sampson appended to a long letter to the Swiss divine, Henry Bullinger, a list of 'some blemishes which still attach to the church of England'. Prominent among these were the increasing use of church organs and 'the exquisite singing in parts', probably on the grounds that both rendered the service unintelligible. Not that the liturgy itself was above reproach, for though containing 'nothing impure, there is, however, a kind of popish superstition', for instance in the failure emphatically to repudiate the real presence, and in the use of unleavened cake instead of bread in the eucharist. There was a great deal to complain of in the sacrament of baptism, including the use of the sign of the cross and the emphasis on the responsibilities of godparents rather than of the natural parents of the child. The widespread practice of baptism by midwives in private houses when the infant was in danger of not surviving was deplored, probably because it implied that baptism was essential to salvation. Rings were given in betrothal and marriage, a deplorably popish survival, and women were not allowed to be churched unless veiled, a practice which turned an act of thanksgiving for safe delivery in childbirth into a sort of ritual purification, or so it might be interpreted. The Protestant ideal of godly congregational discipline was neglected, and discipline was enforced instead by ecclesiastical courts presided over by laymen, which, moreover, licensed abuses such as pluralism and non-residence as well as fining persons for contravening popish prohibitions, such as those against eating meat on forbidden days. Clerical marriage was officially disapproved, and the children of such marriages widely regarded as illegitimate. Humphrey and Sampson may be exaggerating somewhat here, for although the queen's own disapproval of clerical marriage was well known, it did not stop many of her bishops taking wives. The Puritans objected to clerical celibacy not only because it was a popish practice but because it set parsons apart from their congregations, considerations which also applied to the insistence that parsons wear vestments when conducting services and distinctive dress when outside church.

This last issue was to provoke the first serious dispute within the ranks of the new church. The official view of vestments was that since they were *adiaphora*, that is things indifferent, it was perfectly proper to enjoin their use as a matter of order and decency. In actual fact, of course, vestments were an important aspect of Elizabeth's determination to blur the distinction between the practices of the old church and those of the new, so as to minimize the amount of observable change to those who favoured the former. But it was surely questionable, argued Thomas Sampson, one of the main opponents of the use of vestments, whose views were later to cost him his office as dean of Christ Church, Oxford, 'whether the nature of things indifferent admits of coercion' – in other words if they were matters indifferent, why enforce their use? Moreover, to

Sampson, his ally Laurence Humphrey, the President of Magdalen College, and to countless other Puritan conscientious objectors to vestments, they were anything but indifferent. For the fact that they marked off the ministry as a distinct species of men from the laity in turn reinforced their association in the popular mind with the service of the papal Antichrist.

To some of their continental Protestant advisers such as Henry Bullinger and Rodolph Gualter at Zürich, the objections of vestiarian purists like Sampson and Humphrey verged upon pedantry, not least in their insistence that, indifferent or not, vestments did not tend to edification and therefore could not be countenanced. They were quick to point out that the danger of making mountains of principle out of such molehills was that their objectors would be deprived of their livings and the way left clear for crypto-papists and Lutherans. Nevertheless, there was certainly point in Humphrey's and Sampson's insistence that simple people were inclined to believe that without vestments 'we can neither be ministers, nor that the sacraments can be rightly administered'. Educated Protestants might ridicule 'that comical dress', but in these circumstances vestments were anything but comical, and 'neither can nor ought to be reckoned among things indifferent'. They were the distinctive garb of the Catholic priests, of the sorcerers whose failure to wear them would be as inimical as the incorrect repetition of the ritual incantation to the act of magic whereby bread and wine was transubstantiated into Christ's body and blood. When hard-line Protestants referred to Catholic priests as sorcerers and magicians, they wished to be taken quite literally.

Some of the bishops, such as Parkhurst at Norwich, Pilkington at Durham and Bentham at Coventry and Lichfield seem to have been prepared to countenance some degree of conscientious divergence from the standards of vestiarian conformity laid down by Archbishop Matthew Parker's *Advertisements*. Parkhurst, the former Zürich exile, in his very large diocese of Norwich, seems to have been more or less a law unto himself in such matters. At London, Edmund Grindal, soon to be the archetypal godly Protestant bishop in the Foxeian mode, temporized but ultimately gave in, and on 26 March 1566 was present with Parker at Lambeth Palace, where the correct vestments and clerical outdoor dress were paraded before 110 London clergymen, thirty-seven of whom were suspended for refusing to undertake to comply with them.

(ii)

Despite the liberal attitude of bishops such as Parkhurst and Bentham, it was the disciplinary actions taken, sometimes reluctantly, by bishops, especially in vestiarian matters, which brought about the first really strong and widespread criticism of their role. While such criticism was certainly not confined to those who opposed episcopacy as an institution, it may well have had the effect of swelling their ranks at a difficult time. The first and virtually the only time in the early history of Puritanism – before the Root and Branch Petition of 1640 – when a significant part, as distinct from a small minority, of the movement took a decided lurch to the left and adopted a strongly anti-episcopalian programme was to come in the 1570s and 1580s. The two Admonitions to Parliament of 1572 were public manifestos of a new Presbyterian and anti-episcopal Puritanism. The second Admonition, in particular, made a determined attack on the office of bishops which was 'drawn out of the pope's shop' and whose government was condemned as 'Antichristian and devilish and contrary to the scriptures'.

The new radical emphasis is usually dated from Thomas Cartwright's lectures on the Acts of the Apostles in Cambridge in 1570, which brought about his dismissal from the Lady Margaret chair of Divinity in that university. Cartwright had argued that the primitive apostolic church had been organized along Presbyterian lines with an equality of the ministry, and that in consequence this form of church government was indeed divinely ordered (*iure divino*). As Professor Collinson has pointed out, Cartwright was not the first Englishman to put forward such views, and, quite apart from the matter of its *iure divino* sanctions, the idea of a non-episcopal Protestant church was familiar enough to many Englishmen, not only as a result of their experiences as Marian exiles, but also of their observation of the ordering of Protestant refugee churches in England. But while the advocates of a Presbyterian form of church government, with their genius for propaganda and self-advertisement, might appear to occupy the centre of the stage in the 1570s and 1580s, it would be a grave mistake to assume that they completely took over the Puritan mainstream. For instance radical anti-vestiarians, such as Humphrey and Sampson, although critical of episcopal persecution, were never absorbed into the Presbyterian movement. Indeed, after that movement had been effectively crushed by Archbishop Whitgift in the course of the last two decades of the reign, the mainstream continued to flow much as before.

That Presbyterianism never took very deep root in England is not altogether surprising. For one thing, in stressing, in the words of the first Admonition, the need to remove 'advowsons, patronages, impropriations . . . and to bring in that old and true election . . . by the congregation', it threatened some of the most cherished rights and emoluments of the well-to-do. It is true that this form of patronage, the right to present to benefices in their gift, was in fact one of the means whereby influential Puritan sympathizers succeeded in spreading the word in various parts of the country: in Essex and Norfolk, for example, where the Rich family and Nathaniel Bacon respectively had extensive livings in their gift. But theirs was a moderate, mainstream Puritanism, not in any sense anti-episcopalian or Presbyterian in character. Nor was it only the interests of well-to-do gentlemen and aristocrats which were threatened by Presbyterianism. The godly prince and the godly bishop were the centrepiece of mainstream Foxeian Puritanism.

Not so under Cartwrightian Presbyterianism, which not only had no place for bishops but also cut princes, however godly, down to size. As civil magistrates, monarchs might be supreme in secular affairs, but in ecclesiastical matters it behoved them, in Cartwright's own words, 'to subject themselves unto the church, to submit their sceptres, to throw down their crowns . . . to lick the dust of the feet of the church'. No statement of papal *plenitudo potestatis* – not even Boniface VIII's notorious bull *Unam Sanctam* of 1302 – had put ecclesiastical power on a higher pedestal than this. James VI of Presbyterian Scotland was to experience the full force of the doctrine when he was told by the fiery Presbyterian Andrew Melville at Falkland in 1596 that there were in fact not one but two kingdoms in Scotland: there was the lesser kingdom over which he ruled, and, more important, Christ's kingdom, 'the Kirk, whose subject James the Sixth is, and of whose kingdom, not a king, nor a lord, nor a head, but a member'.

Although Cartwright and his Presbyterian colleagues were prepared to allow of Elizabeth exercising some authority within the church, even this concession, made in flat contradiction of their more extreme utterances, would give her far less power than she already exercised. To John Whitgift's argument that an episcopal form of church government, though humanly rather than divinely ordained, was necessary in England, because a monarchical regime called for an hierarchical form of church government, Cartwright replied that this 'is as much as to say as if a man should fashion his house according to his hangings'. On the contrary, 'the commonwealth must be made to agree with the church and the government thereof with her government'. This gave Whitgift a golden opportunity to point the contradiction between this view and Cartwright's own notion of church and state as two strictly autonomous kingdoms, with a democratically organized church in no way incompatible with a monarchically organized state. Surely, he insisted, the logic of Cartwright's argument was to have 'all monarchies overthrown and reduced either to a popular or an aristocratic estate, for these two types of government he [Cartwright] only alloweth of in the church'. But there was also a sense in which Whitgift's case for episcopacy, resting as it did on human rather than divine ordinance, was at a real disadvantage in the face of the Cartwrightian insistence that Presbyterianism was *iure divino* not *iure humano*. It may have been such considerations which account for the assertion by some defenders of episcopacy, though not by Whitgift himself, that episcopacy itself was divinely ordained, a view which horrified good mainstream episcopalian Puritans such as Sir Francis Knollys. In a letter to Lord Burghley on 4 August 1598 Knollys was at great pains to emphasize that an episcopal claim to hold office by divine ordinance logically short-circuited the royal supremacy. However, far from elevating the status of bishops by resting their authority on a higher sanction than mere human ordinance, the insistence of a minority of bishops on their *iure divino* authority was, probably, more responsible than any other factor for the eventual discrediting and collapse of episcopacy under the early Stuarts.

But all this was as yet far into the future. Under Elizabeth as has already been emphasized, the Puritan mainstream – even in the Presbyterian heyday of the 1570s and 1580s – was not anti-episcopalian. On the contrary, most Puritans probably accepted the thesis of the great John Foxe, that the work of godly reformation was to be brought about by godly bishops working hand in hand with the godly prince. That each of these Protestant champions was to fall sadly short of moderate Puritan expectations must not be allowed to obscure the fact that among the first generation of Elizabethan bishops were many zealous reformers cast in the Foxeian mould, some of them former Marian exiles like John Parkhurst at Norwich, James Pilkington at Durham, John Jewel at Salisbury and Edmund Grindal at London. It is true that Elizabeth's first primate, Archbishop Matthew Parker, was a far more conservative churchman, as his enthusiasm for vestments and dislike of radical reform clearly reveals. The succession of Grindal to Parker's see at the end of 1575 (he had in the meantime been archbishop of York) was in fact to provide the greatest test for the notion of the godly bishop as a prime agency of godly reformation. Grindal's effective primacy was to be a pitifully short episode, and in the early summer of 1577 he was suspended from the office, and he remained under a cloud until his death in 1583. But in his short period of effective power he had given abundant evidence of godly Protestant intentions: in his proposal to reform his Court of Faculties, which to many Puritans resembled a Romish court; in his encouragement of the printing and dissemination of the Geneva Bible, which had been suppressed by his predecessor, and of other Genevan devotional texts; in his stand against pluralism and non-residence and encouragement of preaching; and perhaps above all in his support for the exercises known as 'prophesyings'. His refusal to suppress these at the queen's behest was to occasion his downfall.[4]

In essence, the prophesyings were orderly meetings of clergymen for the purpose of mutual edification; in a sense large-scale clerical seminars, to which laymen were sometimes admitted but not allowed to participate. The twin objects of the meetings were the interchange of views and the improvement of the standard of learning and preaching among the ministry. And beyond doubt there was room for radical improvement in this respect. The surveys of the state of the clergy in different counties, which became a notable form of Puritan propaganda, offer numerous examples. In case this be thought a biased form of evidence, a similar picture is obtainable from archdeacons' visitations. In the 1560s while fifty-four out of the 247 beneficed clergymen in Gloucestershire were certified as capable of preaching, there were only twenty such in neighbouring Wiltshire, twelve in Devon, six in Cornwall and – lest this be thought a peculiarity of the backward southwest – only five in the whole of the diocese of Rochester. The ignorance of many of the parochial clergy was such as to be hardly credible. To cite but one example out of many, in 1583 one Nottinghamshire vicar was reported as being unable to distinguish between Jesus and Judas![5]

To the Puritan mind there were few clerical deficiencies more shocking than ignorance and consequent inability to preach the word. Churchgoing and the taking of sacraments were worse than useless without edification, of which preaching was the pre-eminent means. There is some justice in the criticism of Francis Bacon and others that the Puritan obsession with preaching involved the neglect of things of at least equal importance, even though 'the house of God be denominated . . . a house of prayer, and not a house of preaching'; also that the Puritans were far too ready to countenance inadequate preachers. Be this as it may, it is certainly not a charge which can be brought against Grindal. Chiding the queen gently but firmly in a letter of 20 December 1576 about her command that he suppress the prophesyings, the newly appointed Primate marvelled 'how this strange opinion should once enter into your mind, that it should be good for the church to have few preachers'. But in Elizabeth's view 'three or four [preachers] might suffice for a county, and . . . the reading of homilies to the people was enough'. The homilies, prefabricated published sermons to be read from the pulpit, were uncontentious and designed to foster obedience rather than the seditious notions which, some believed, stemmed from Puritan sermons. Grindal and like-minded churchmen might plead that it was not because of preaching that men strayed from the path of obedience, but because of their own ignorant misinterpretation of scripture, which was the less likely to occur in proportion as competent preachers were available. But the queen was not convinced.

Sir John Neale's defence of Elizabeth's near-hysterical attitude to the prophesyings and his characterization of Grindal and his colleagues as men unwittingly playing the part of '"fellow-travellers" in a revolutionary movement', rests largely on his analogy between the prophesyings and, on the one hand, the public exercises in self-criticism and mutual correction practised in Geneva, and, on the other hand, the party cells within revolutionary movements in our own time.[6] The second analogy is somewhat far-fetched. As to the first, the queen's general dislike of preaching to the masses may have predisposed her to confuse the reported excesses of the prophesyings at Southam in Warwickshire, where a more radical and less tightly controlled type of exercise was carried on, with the orderly exercises which were encouraged and defended by Grindal. Indeed the latter had no less reason than his queen to deplore the goings-on at Southam, which were suppressed in 1576. Grindal knew well that such things could easily upset the whole applecart of godly and moderate reform. In vain he stressed the fact that the exercises of which he approved were not of that sort; that they commanded widespread episcopal support, and were kept firmly under episcopal control. But to Elizabeth they were all of a piece: among other things, a means whereby 'the vulgar sort, meet to be otherwise occupied with honest labour . . . are brought to idleness and seduced and in a manner schismatically divided amongst themselves into a variety of dangerous opinions'.

It is difficult to over-emphasize the significance of Grindal's fall from power, which came with his suspension from office in 1577. The notion of a godly partnership between prince and bishop was put in serious question, at the very time when the Presbyterians were most vociferous in their emphasis on the idea of an autonomous church of which princes were ordinary members and in which bishops had no place at all. An interesting postscript to the issue of the prophesyings is, however, to be found in the monthly preaching exercises which were instituted at fourteen places in the northern diocese of Chester in 1584, in the first year of the archiepiscopate of Grindal's successor Whitgift, with the approval of the bishop and the strong support of local Puritan clergymen. The object was the same as that professed by Grindal: to improve the learning of clergymen and the standard of their preaching as part of the uphill battle against popery in these backward parts. Evidently what was frowned upon in more civilized southern and Midland parts was deemed appropriate in the backward and popish north-west.[7]

All over England, however, there were parishes where, thanks to weekly or even more frequent lectures, which were either endowed or paid for by subscription, the opportunity to hear the word of God ably expounded did not depend entirely on the preaching ability of the incumbent. Such lectures were sometimes attached to one parish and sometimes shared between several. In some cases the lecturers and the incumbents were one and the same person, but more often – especially when the incumbent was a 'dumb dog' incapable of delivering a decent sermon – the lecturer was an unbeneficed clergyman, who, as likely as not, had been prevented from taking a living by conscientious scruples such as objections to vestments or ceremonial. Often enough the lecturer and the incumbent were at daggers drawn, the former getting his often much more substantial remuneration from public subscription or from the income derived from capital which had been specially invested for this purpose. To some members of the hierarchy there was a very real danger that, as Bishop Wren of Norwich was to put it in the 1630s, the lecturer would in these circumstances be 'forced to suit his business to the fancy of his auditors'. The chaplains of Puritanically inclined noblemen were often in a sense also a species of lecturers, in cases where public access was permitted to the private chapels where they preached.

This was but one of a number of ways in which Puritan influence could be spread within the church. A document which came into the hands of Richard Bancroft, chaplain to the strongly anti-Puritan Sir Christopher Hatton, Whitgift's great ally on the Privy Council, offered a number of suggestions as to how radical Protestant, and even neo-

Presbyterian, practices might be exercised within the framework of established Anglican procedures. A powerful potential instrument for modifying established practices in a Presbyterian direction was the so-called 'classis' – conference of godly, like-minded ministers working within a limited, but quite extensive, area – which might, as in the case of the best-known classis at Dedham in Essex, overlap diocesan boundaries. For example, one of the main Puritan objections to established practices related to the fact that clergymen were ordained indiscriminately by bishops instead of waiting until called to serve a particular congregation. However, if a congregation where there was a vacancy could communicate its need to the classis of local godly ministers, the latter might make a selection of a suitable candidate who, if acceptable to the congregation in question, might then be recommended for episcopal ordination, in cases where there was a sympathetic bishop. In the placing of such parsons, the institution of lay patronage might be put to good use in the numerous cases when the holder of the advowson was a Puritan sympathizer such as Sir Nathaniel Bacon in Norfolk, Sir Richard Knightley in Northamptonshire and Sir Andrew Corbet in Shropshire, with whom the members of the local classis, if there were one, might 'deal earnestly . . . to present fit men'. Once ordained and installed, the minister might modify the service by, for instance, omitting objectionable parts of the Prayer Book, in so far as this could be done 'without danger of being put from the ministry'.[8] Indeed on occasions it might be possible via the election of suitable churchwardens to turn them into something not dissimilar from Presbyterian lay elders, exercising that congregational discipline which was so dear to Puritan hearts. Professor Collinson suggests that such cases may have been relatively rare, however, since their successful operation postulates a state of complete harmony and mutual confidence between incumbent and churchwardens which was probably very much the exception rather than the rule.

(iii)

It has been emphasized that Grindal's suspension in 1577 had administered a sharp shock to those who had held out great hopes for an episcopally-led reformation. No less of a shock was the character of what may be described as the second generation of Elizabethan bishops. The 1570s and early 1580s saw the death of a number of bishops who had been ex-Marian exiles: Parkhurst of Norwich died in 1575, Pilkington of Durham in 1576, Bentham of Coventry and Lichfield in 1579, Horne of Winchester in 1580 and the suspended Primate Grindal in 1583. Most of the new bishops were of a quite different temper and churchmanship. An exception is John Woolton, whose appointment to the see of Exeter in 1587 can probably be ascribed to the territorial influence of the strongly Protestant earl of Bedford. Some of the other new bishops, like Whitgift, who became bishop of Worcester in 1571, and was to succeed Grindal at Canterbury in 1584, and Edmund Freke, who moved from Rochester to succeed Parkhurst at Norwich, had themselves been through a radical phase, but were now, like Freke's two immediate successors at Rochester, Piers and Young, stern anti-Puritan disciplinarians. Of this genus, next to Whitgift himself, there is no better example than John Aylmer, who became bishop of London in 1576.

In dioceses such as Norwich and Coventry, where sympathetic bishops had kept Puritan parsons on a pretty loose rein in matters such as vestiarian conformity, the transition was sudden and violent, especially at Norwich, where Freke's anti-Puritan drive brought him into alliance with local Catholic and crypto-Catholic gentry. But the shock was greatest in such dioceses only because of the laxity – or rather the puritan-sympathies – of the previous bishops. In many other dioceses also there was a marked tightening of the drive for conformity, which was further intensified when Whitgift became Primate in 1584.

As will be shown later, the 1580s were also a decade when the attempt to use parliament as a means of pushing the established church in an emphatically Presbyterian direction reached its height. But Whitgift's assault, backed at court and the council table by the queen and the royal favourite Sir Christopher Hatton, was by no means confined to the Presbyterians and the even more radical congregational separatists, three of whom, Barrow, Greenwood and Penry were executed in the 1590s. It was also directed at the more moderate Puritan mainstream, consisting of the sort of people who had taken such heart at Grindal's promotion and had been so cast down by his suspension.

The central weapon of Whitgift's campaign was his insistence on subscription by all clergymen to three articles, the most contentious of which involved agreement that the Prayer Book contained nothing contrary to the word of God, and the acceptance of all of the Thirty-Nine Articles of 1563 and not simply those relating to theological doctrine. It was probably due to pressure from Burghley and Walsingham that some of the more obnoxious – from a reformist point of view – elements were subsequently removed from the articles to which subscription was required. While such concessions cut no ice with radicals such as John Field and the other members of the Presbyterian London conference of ministers, they were welcome both to more moderate Puritan clergymen and to their supporters among the laity. Even so, the mode of investigating suspects via the Court of High Commission rendered the Whitgiftian regime the object of opprobrium, not only to Puritan extremists, but also to many common lawyers whose dislike of civil law procedures helped to forge what was to become a momentous alliance between them and moderate Puritan reformers. Among the most violently disliked of these procedures was the *ex officio* oath, which forced suspects to give truthful answers to the questions put to them, subject to the penalties of perjury. Since the object of the oath was to elicit admissions of guilt from suspects who were made to incriminate themselves, often without prior knowledge of the nature of the charges brought against them, such objections, both lay and professional, are hardly surprising.[9]

In chapter 2, when dealing with the phenomenon of patronage, stress was laid on the role of magnates such as Bedford, Leicester, Warwick and Huntingdon in securing positions for, and offering protection to, churchmen of a Puritan persuasion. In the first of these respects, of course, such influence was never again to be so strongly felt as it had been in the matter of the first appointments to the Elizabethan episcopate. Around the end of the 1580s some of the most powerful patrons of the Puritans were to die, and their removal from the scene helped to make Whitgift's persecuting task so much the easier. The earl of Bedford died in 1585; Leicester in 1588; his brother Warwick and Secretary of State Sir Francis Walsingham in 1590; the Puritan-sympathizing chancellor of the Exchequer and founder of Emmanuel College, Cambridge, Sir Walter Mildmay, in 1589; and the earl of Huntingdon in 1595. It would be difficult to overstate the importance of such powerful lay patrons and of other secular agencies in this period, which one ecclesiastical historian, Dr Claire Cross, has characterized as a time which saw 'the triumph of the laity in the English church'. And of these agencies none was more important than parliament.

(iv)

It was only to be expected given the considerable, even if not total, success of the more radically Protestant MPs in the matter of the religious settlement of 1559, that those whose Protestant expectations had not been fully met by that settlement should redouble their efforts in parliament to push the infant church further along the Protestant road. If Elizabeth's next parliament in 1563 was relatively quiet in such matters, this can no doubt be explained by the fact that Puritan hopes for a variety of godly reforms on matters such as vestments and the Prayer Book were concentrated on the church's own legislative organ, Convocation. It was only after the very narrow failure of the determined Puritan effort, backed by sympathetic bishops such as Parkhurst and Sandys, to get a reform programme through the first Convocation of the newly reformed church in 1563 that attention turned once more to parliament as the agency of godly reformation. According to Sir John Neale, it was only the preoccupation of the parliament of 1566 with the crucial and extremely delicate issue of the succession which prevented religious issues from bulking much larger in that parliament than in fact they did. As it was, the queen quashed a bill for giving statutory confirmation to the Thirty-Nine Articles of 1563 (which was allowed in the next parliament in 1571). That this was not a notably Puritan measure is clear enough from the fact that Archbishop Parker and a number of his episcopal colleagues favoured it. But the reasons for the queen's distaste for it are not difficult to divine, and are certainly not unrelated to the Puritan challenge. Elizabeth was in fact determined to emphasize that ecclesiastical and spiritual matters formed an indisputable part of her prerogative. Parliament had undeniably played a central part in the original Elizabethan settlement, but this was to be treated as an exceptional circumstance and not as a precedent allowing parliament to take the ecclesiastical initiative or even to discuss religious matters at all. But these were the very matters which many MPs felt were the most important of all, and beside which, as one of them was to put it in the House of Commons in 1571, other things were 'but terrene, yea trifles, in comparison'.

The Elizabethan House of Commons contained a large number of MPs who were by no means Puritan activists, but who looked on the Puritans as a sort of super-Protestant, anti-papist ginger group, whose cause was especially popular when the Protestant regime seemed to be in particular danger, whether from within or without, or both. Certainly the stiffening of anti-recusant legislation, which was always a prominent part of the Puritan programme, commanded a great deal of support from outside the ranks of the godly zealots in times of crisis. Especially important in this respect were the events of the parliament of 1571, coming so shortly after the revolt of the northern earls and the papal bull excommunicating Elizabeth; the parliament of 1572, coming after the revelations about the Ridolfi Plot, though (happily for the Catholics) before the Massacre of St Bartholomew's Day in August; the parliament of 1584–5, following the panic arising out of the murder of William the Silent and discovery of the Throckmorton Plot against Elizabeth's life; and that of 1586, which learnt of the Babington Plot that was ultimately to bring the Scottish queen to the scaffold in the following year.

But while the aspirations of godly Puritans for further instruments of reformation to complete the Protestant settlement, which in their view had only been begun, not completed, in 1559, gained a good deal of support from outside the ranks of Puritan zealots, especially in such times of apparent crisis, this was only in so far as such plans were relatively moderate in temper. For example, wide support might be forthcoming for demands for tougher recusancy laws; for measures against pluralism, non-residence and simony (as in 1566 and 1589); for attacks on the archiepiscopal Court of Faculties (as in 1571); for the enforcement of annual attendance at communion (as in 1571, 1572 and 1576); for the correction of unfit clergymen (as in 1584–5); for the reform of ecclesiastical law (as in 1571); and against the Court of High Commission and the *ex officio* oath (as in 1584–5, 1589 and 1593). But when, in 1572, the failure of more moderate proposals for reform produced the more extreme courses outlined in the two celebrated Admonitions to Parliament which threatened the very existence of episcopacy, the ranks of those who had supported moderate Puritan reforms thinned out notably.

Nothing better demonstrates the hostility of the reforming Protestant mainstream to theocratic Presbyterianism than the events of the parliament of 1584–5. Here once again moderate reforming measures obtained wide support, but the Presbyterian Dr Turner's proposals for his so-called 'bill and book' – a Presbyterian form of church government and a Genevan form of worship – were received unenthusiastically. Far more subtle and less objectionable to moderate men had been the proposal in the previous parliament in 1581 for what Professor Collinson describes as 'a kind of blueprint for a reformed and episcopal Church of England', which, *inter alia*, while going a long way towards the Presbyterian notion of ordination in cases where livings were vacant, nevertheless saw the system as operating within an essentially episcopalian framework.

The high point of parliamentary Presbyterian campaigning came in the parliament of 1586–7. The Presbyterian plan found expression in Anthony Cope's 'bill and book' for the adoption of a Genevan form of worship and the abrogation of all ordinances relating to ceremonies of the established church. Unlike its predecessor in the previous parliament, the bill was emphatically not a damp squib. It differed from it both in form and content, and notably in its greater stress on the role of neighbouring Puritan 'classes' in the election of ministers. The Presbyterian strategy, managed within parliament by men such as Cope, Job Throckmorton and the irrepressible Peter Wentworth, and outside by Walter Travers and the Presbyterian organizing genius John Field, meeting at the same time in conference in London, was twofold. If the bill and the book were not acceptable to parliament, their main provisions might still be put into effect by godly ministers in the country. In the event the programme failed in parliament, and the attempt to implement its provisions more or less clandestinely in the country met with successful resistance and fierce persecution from Archbishop Whitgift and his episcopal colleagues.

THE SCOPE OF PARLIAMENTARY PRIVILEGE

Religion provides the most striking example of the attempts of Elizabethan MPs to influence policy, and the apparently parliamentary nature of the royal ecclesiastical supremacy afforded some scope for such action, which, however, was firmly disallowed by the crown. Other issues over which MPs' knuckles were rapped more than once for trespassing outside their proper bounds were the connected matters of the queen's marriage and the succession. Both issues were raised in the House of Commons in 1563, when the problem of the succession dominated the scene, the queen having come near to death from smallpox in the previous year, while in 1566 the Commons tried to write a royal promise to marry into the bill for the subsidies which they were granting. The queen urged on the House both the dangers of naming an heir presumptive, which might produce an unwelcome reversionary interest in the realm, and the fact that this was anyway none of its business and it had no right to discuss it. One MP, Paul Wentworth, daringly inquired whether this were not contrary to the Commons' privilege of freedom of speech, and the queen ultimately allowed a debate to take place. In doing so, she was simply making an *ex gratia* concession which in no way implied her acceptance of Wentworth's constitutional point. Indeed Paul Wentworth's brother Peter was to get into hot water for again trying to raise the matter of the succession in the parliament of 1593.

In the royal view the parliamentary privilege of freedom of speech amounted to a great deal less than the assertions of the likes of the Wentworths suggested. As her lord keeper was to emphasize in his reply to the Speaker's petition for the privileges of the House in 1593, MPs must distinguish between liberty and licence. The former was 'not, as some suppose, to speak [in parliament] of all causes . . . and to frame a form of religion or a state of government as to their idle brains shall seem meetest'. In other matters falling clearly within the royal prerogative, such as the ordering of royal government, foreign policy and – at least down to 1597 – economic policy, the queen's attempts to keep parliament off her territory were largely successful, if not completely so. In fact, in maintaining that those matters which difficult

MPs such as Strickland, the Wentworths and Cope most wanted to discuss were outside the bounds of free speech, Elizabeth managed to frustrate most attempts to encroach on the prerogative.

PARLIAMENT AND ROYAL FINANCE

One of the ways offering some scope for parliament to increase its power was via control of the purse-strings. To appreciate this it is necessary to understand some central features of contemporary fiscal history and prevailing ideas about the ordering of royal finance. Here a preliminary word of warning will not be out of place, for the actual visible side of royal finances, formally represented in official statements of royal revenue and expenditure, is somewhat analogous to the visible tip of an iceberg, since the vast bulk of royal revenue and payments was indirect and invisible. The crown might be relatively short of funds, but it was also relatively rich in perquisites of one sort or another which individuals could easily convert into cash – things such as the purchase of royal wardships at bargain prices, granting beneficial leases of land below the economic rent, or allowing some royal officials to supplement their inadequate cash stipends, whose fixed value was continually eroded by inflation, by charging fees for their services to the public.

On occasions such indirect forms of revenue might become causes of contention in parliament; the purveyance of provisions for the royal Household at fixed undervalues is a case in point, especially during the early years of the next reign. However, in so far as we are concerned with the problem of parliament's using finance as a means of exacting leverage to enable it to be called more often, to meet for longer periods, and perhaps also to obtain redress of grievances, it is legitimate to concentrate our attention on the visible side of the royal account. In this context it is imperative to appreciate the significance of the dichotomy between ordinary and extraordinary revenue and expenditure, which finds its most familiar expression in the idea that the monarch must live of his (or her) own; that is, that the regular annually recurring charges of state, the maintenance of the royal Household and organs of central government (in so far as these were not paid for by indirect means), should be met out of ordinary, annually recurring revenue. Only one branch of this ordinary revenue, the customs and subsidies of tonnage and poundage, was voted by parliament, and since this was normally done (before 1625) at the beginning of each reign to cover the duration of the whole reign, it afforded no opportunites thereafter to those desiring to use finance as a means of increasing parliamentary power. As to the other branches of the ordinary revenue, such as the income from royal estates, the profits of justice, and income from sale of wards, these were all prerogative revenues, in no sense within the control of parliament.

While ordinary expenditure ought properly to be met only out of ordinary revenue, neither of Elizabeth's first two lord treasurers, the marquis of Winchester, whom she inherited from Mary Tudor, and his successor William Cecil (later Lord Burghley), who held office from the year of Winchester's death in 1572 until his own in 1598, worked on the assumption that extraordinary expenditure must be met only out of extraordinary revenue, the most important item of which was the occasional parliamentary taxes on real and movable property, the subsidies, fifteenths and tenths. On the contrary, the cumulative surpluses of ordinary revenue over expenditure were seen as constituting an emergency fund to defray future extraordinary charges such as those arising out of war or other occasions of national emergency; not necessarily capable of meeting the whole of such charges but at least able to contribute significantly towards them. The remaining extraordinary need, if any, would then be met by parliamentary grants or, if necessary, by sales of capital, and notably of royal lands. The latter expedient, it might be thought, ought to have been avoided as far as possible, because of its necessary corollary of a decline of future income. Yet given the fact that, in the view of the queen and some of her ministers, parliaments had a tendency to be difficult and fractious bodies, one can readily appreciate both the government's determination to build up an emergency fund out of cumulative ordinary surpluses and even its occasional willingness to liquidate capital resources rather than call parliament; as Elizabeth did, for example, when she employed the proceeds of sales of royal lands towards the expenses of the Scottish campaign of 1560, even though war expenditure was the classic example of extraordinary need, for which a monarch might expect parliamentary assistance.

Elizabeth succeeded in maintaining a surplus on her ordinary account throughout her reign,* and by the 1570s this surplus had risen from a very modest sum in the opening years of the reign to more than £70,000, remaining around this level down to 1589. Down to the mid-1570s the ordinary surplus was achieved by ruthless economies in ordinary expenditure rather than by increases in ordinary revenue. There were, however, some increases in ordinary revenue over the reign as a whole, of which royal landed revenues are one example; a somewhat surprising one, in view of the queen's need to sell off substantial quantities of land in order to finance war deficits, especially in the last years of the reign. Nevertheless, over the reign as a whole accretions were greater than sales. Notable examples of these accretions were the lands of attainted noblemen, such as the northern earls and the duke of Norfolk, and the compact blocks of episcopal land which Elizabeth obtained in exchange for scattered spiritual revenues in her possession, such as rectories and tithes, which consumed much of their yield in the costs of their collection. Thus, although there is little evidence of any determined campaign to screw up the rents of the royal lands, the landed revenues of the

* It should be noted, however, that in the naval ordinary, for example, it became the practice to treat ordinary changes over and above a fixed sum as extraordinary.

crown were, it has been calculated, £22,319 higher in 1603 than they had been in 1558.[10]

Of the other branches of the ordinary revenue, the customs were by far the most important. The net customs receipts in the first year of the reign were about £80,000, spectacularly above the yield of £29,315 for the fourth year of Elizabeth's predecessor's reign. This was largely due to the introduction of a new book of rates at the end of Mary's reign. But the improvement was not maintained, and customs receipts dropped in subsequent years. They were brought up with difficulty to above the £70,000 mark by 1578, and did not attain the yield of the first year of the reign until 1584. During the last decade of the reign, net exchequer receipts from customs never fell below £81,000 in 1599, varying between this level and a top figure of £120,000 in 1595. Burghley leant strongly towards the idea of maintaining certainty in customs yield via the practice of farming piecemeal branches of the customs to operators who paid a fixed rent, assumed the charges of collection, and pocketed the remainder. However, some of the customs were never put to farm during Elizabeth's reign. The export duties for London, for example, which accounted for more than half of the total customs revenue, were always directly administered by the crown. Moreover, from 1588 onwards Burghley showed an inclination to favour a return to direct administration by not renewing the leases of at least some of the farms as these fell in.[11]

Careful management of the ordinary account was not designed only to restrict the government's demands for funds from parliament to the extraordinary occasions when a parliamentary grant might reasonably be expected; it could also serve to reduce the amounts demanded of parliament even in such cases. It was therefore not so much a matter of the queen's desiring to avoid calling parliaments. There were, after all, three parliaments in each of the first two decades of the reign, four in the 1580s, and only three in the last decade, when her need for extraordinary revenue was obviously at its peak on account of the Spanish war and the revolt in Ireland. It is rather that the political product of her financial providence in the years of peace was that she was the less vulnerable – certainly before 1590 – to the sort of leverage which might have resulted from her financial dependence on parliament. In these circumstances parliament's role as the institution whereby the political nation was associated, financially and otherwise, with royal policies could be carried on with the minimum of danger that it would attempt to exercise any sort of control over that policy. If it is argued that Elizabeth's cumulative ordinary surpluses were a mere drop in the ocean of extraordinary requirement after 1588, it needs also to be emphasized that parliament did not display a notable willingness to vote adequate sums even in times of the greatest national danger. While something could be done by expedients such as shifting the responsibility for the militia from national taxes to local rates, and by requisitioning private ships in a national emergency, the former expedient in particular was, as was shown in the last chapter, attended by much local grumbling and foot-dragging. As to the latter, while the defenders of restricted trade by chartered companies were quick to argue that the great ships which the companies used – as distinct from the smaller ships of interlopers – provided a sort of supplementary naval reserve, this was no guarantee that their use by the crown was ungrudgingly conceded when this idea was put to the test. There were, in fact, very clear limits on what could be done, and Elizabeth's ministers were all too aware that for their demands to exceed these would be counter-productive. Unlike her father, Elizabeth had no monastic spoils out of which to finance a state of national military preparedness. Again, unlike Henry VIII, she would not resort to currency manipulations as a means to this end, since this would threaten the success of the policy of economic and social stabilization to whose progress we now briefly turn our attention.

THE CHALLENGE TO THE ECONOMIC SETTLEMENT

In chapter 3 it was shown that the restrictionism which characterized the economic and social aspects of the Elizabethan settlement and which finds its most spectacular expression in the great Statute of Artificers of 1563 was the product of economic depression; and that associated policies continued to be developed throughout the reign, as evidenced by, for example, the proliferation of restrictive chartered companies with area privileges in foreign trade, and the statutes establishing a national system of poor relief and vagrancy control in the 1570s and their consolidation in 1597 and 1601. But the system did not go unchallenged, nor was the government itself completely immovable in face of such challenges.

It is a commonplace that the reach of Tudor governments was not matched by their grasp. Despite regulations and statutes to the contrary, the rural textile industry continued to grow, unapprenticed workers to be taken on, commons to be enclosed, land to be converted from arable to pasture, and 'interlopers' to trade in defiance of the area monopolies conferred by charter on bodies such as the Merchant Adventurers and the Muscovy companies. Indeed it was not only interlopers, men free of no company, who were complained of, for the companies themselves were frequently at one another's throats. The Merchant Adventurers trod on the Levant Company's toes in the closing years of the reign by their practice of importing from their privileges in the Low Countries currants and other commodities brought from Turkey and the Levant by the Dutch. They also aroused the hostility of the Eastland Company by similar practices in respect of Baltic naval stores. But the Merchant Adventurers in turn felt that they had ample grounds for complaint against merchants who were free both of their own company and of the Spanish Company, which had been founded in 1577. These merchants, they claimed, were able to undercut 'mere Merchant

Adventurers' in the sales of their cloth in Germany, because of the triangular nature of their trade, of which the most profitable aspects were not the cloth exported to Germany – the meat and drink of ordinary Merchant Adventurers – but the German goods they shipped to Spain and the Spanish wine, oils and other commodities which they brought back to England with the proceeds.

In two areas in particular – the spheres of agrarian and commercial policy – the government seems, for a time at least, to have been prepared to modify the rigid framework of regulations and restrictions which it had established. Here the controlling agents were respectively parliament and the Privy Council. The repeal of the anti-enclosure and anti-depopulation legislation in 1593 seems to have been based on the mistaken assumption that the social dangers against which these statutes had been intended to guard were now past. The recrudescence of enclosure and depopulation which followed suggests both that parliament and the government had been over-optimistic, and that parliamentary economic legislation was not quite the dead letter that some historians have too readily assumed it to have been. At any rate the few years which followed not only saw a succession of bad harvests and the danger of starvation for people on the margin of subsistence but, according to the preamble of one of the two statutes which were hastily passed against enclosure and conversion of arable land to pasture, 'many more depopulations, by turning Tillage into Pasture, than at any time for the like number of years heretofore'. This new legislation marked the regime's return to the traditional restrictionist agrarian policies from its new-found, but temporary, economic liberalism of 1593.

An even more temporary experiment in economic liberalism – lasting less than a year – was concerned with foreign trade. The winter of 1586–7 saw serious and widespread distress in the textile industry. The clothiers complained that no reasonable prices could be obtained for their cloth in

London, and the Merchant Adventurers bewailed deficiency of demand and other difficulties abroad. There was dislocation both in the Low Countries, following the prince of Parma's military offensive, his capture of Antwerp and the blockade of the Scheldt by the Dutch; and in Germany, following the Spanish offensive in Gelderland, which cut off access via the Rhine, and the Hanseatic intrigues against the Merchant Adventurers at their German staple at Emden. The Privy Council responded to complaints from clothiers, and woolgrowers in particular, by ordering the Merchant Adventurers to make their usual purchases of cloth from the clothiers at the customary prices. This was very hard in times of acute depression, but the council backed it up by ordaining that the trade should be thrown open to all if the cloth were not taken off the clothiers' hands, first by the Merchant Adventurers and then by the Staplers, by a certain time in every week. Indeed in the following year the trade was thrown completely open for a time.[12]

In the hands of the Merchant Adventurer John Wheeler, the incident became a classic part of the argument against a free-for-all in overseas commerce, though it is obvious enough that the prevailing conditions of acute economic dislocation were hardly favourable circumstances for this short-lived experiment in free trade. What makes the incident significant in the longer term, however, is that it may mark the historical beginnings of a fundamental change in the nature of the reaction of government to the phenomenon of economic depression. Whereas it had responded to the mid-century depression by clapping a straitjacket on the economy, in that of 1586–8 it took tentative steps towards the economic liberalization which was to be its remedy, admittedly under pressure from parliament, for the great depression of the 1620s. All the same, one must not discount the extent to which the moves of 1586–7 were a threat designed to produce a response from the Merchant Adventurers, rather than a considered economic remedy in its own right. However, at the beginning of the next reign the commercial restrictions which were so crucial a part of the Elizabethan economic settlement were to meet with a challenge in a very different economic context: not of economic depression but of expansion, following the end of the war with Spain and the widening of English commercial horizons.

Chapter Six

THE DISINTEGRATION OF THE ELIZABETHAN SETTLEMENT, *c.* 1595–1612

(I) THE CLOSING YEARS OF ELIZABETH

It used to be customary to see the defeat of the Armada in 1588 as heralding the opening of the glorious climax of the reign, the so-called 'spacious days' which were also to witness the greatest achievements of Elizabethan culture, extending into the first decade and a half of the Stuart era; Shakespeare, for instance, did not die until 1615. This book does not aim to deal with the astonishing artistic achievements of the age of Shakespeare and Jonson; of William Byrd and John Dowland; of Inigo Jones, Nicholas Hilliard and Isaac Oliver; achievements which are incomparably greater than those of any equivalent period in English history. What needs to be emphasized, however, is that the idea of the developments of the closing years of Elizabeth's reign as providing an appropriate background of national confidence, strength and unity to these stupendous cultural achievements no longer finds much favour with historians, most of whom now see this as a time of economic crisis, dislocation and hardship, financial bankruptcy, political disintegration, declining political morality and burgeoning corruption: an age in which things turned horribly sour.

ECONOMIC DISLOCATION AND FINANCIAL CRISIS

Nowhere is this note of crisis and desperation more apparent than in the economic conditions of the mid- and later

1590s, which provide the background to crucial policy measures which have already been described elsewhere: notably the codification and stiffening of the poor law in 1597–8 and 1601, and the hasty reintroduction in 1597–8 of anti-enclosure and anti-depopulation legislation which had been unwisely abandoned in 1593. (See above, pp. 176, 177). The fear of widespread starvation and, above all, the threat which this presented to public order – in Kent alone there were as many as eleven food riots between 1585 and 1603[1] – were too great to be ignored. In the country as a whole, starvation pure and simple may have been the cause of very few, if any, deaths, as distinct from disease for which malnutrition resulting from the scarcity and high price of foodstuffs had provided the breeding ground. However, the distinction between formal starvation and the lethal ingestion of rotten meat, grass or other things which only the stark desperation of famine conditions could induce even the hungry to consume is somewhat unreal. Professor Appleby's researches suggest that starvation in this broader sense was a crucially important factor in the spectacularly increased mortality in Cumberland and Westmorland in 1597; and indeed that the north in general suffered worse than the south and Midlands. But there can be no doubt that the mid- and later nineties – down at least to 1598, when the succession of disastrously bad harvests ended – were a terrible time for those on the margin of subsistence everywhere.[2]

Of course, it was the poorest who bore the heaviest brunt of the depression. Nevertheless, the combination of economic depression and heavier taxation to meet the wartime needs of the government also pressed heavily on taxpayers whose burden, moreover, was not confined simply to meeting the heavier taxes voted by parliament. In addition there was a number of locally rated levies: for ship money, which from 1596 was raised from maritime counties and not just from port towns; for 'coat and conduct money' for the troops impressed for service in France, the Low Countries and Ireland; and for the charges of equipping the county militias, paying the stipends of the professional soldiers employed as muster-masters to train the militiamen, and compensating the latter for wages lost during training.

Although the figure of between £90,000 and £100,000 for the annual surpluses of ordinary revenue over expenditure during the 1590s may be somewhat inflated by rather dubious contemporary accounting practices,[3] there can be no doubt whatever that the overall deficits which characterized these closing years of the reign were a product of extraordinary rather than ordinary imbalance. Their root cause lay in the charges of war, and above all of the revolt in Ireland. Over the last thirteen years of the reign a total of £1,063,338 in cumulative savings on past ordinary accounts was applied towards an extraordinary charge of £3,636,226. Some of the deficiency was made up by parliamentary grants and other items of extraordinary revenue, and the remainder came from the proceeds of the sale of royal lands. Another product of the government's financial difficulties was its increased recourse to making payments in kind instead of in cash: in privileges, perquisites and concessions. It was the questionable practices arising out of the consequent growth of jobbery at government level which caused the greatest of modern historians of Elizabethan England, Sir John Neale, to argue that there was a sharp decline in public morality at the time, heralding the even greater enormities of the next reign. That many contemporaries took a similar view is clear from the outburst against patents in Elizabeth's last two parliaments.[4]

Dr Joan Thirsk has demonstrated how, during the 1580s and 1590s, genuinely innovative projects making for industrial diversification and often facilitating what modern economists would describe as 'import-substitution' came to take a very poor second place to projects which were not designed to serve these laudable ends.[5] Many of the latter were, in fact, little more than ingenious economic rackets for the benefit of the courtiers, who acted either as principal lessees at a beneficial rent from the crown, subletting at a profit to the businessmen who operated the privileges, or as intermediaries who took a rake-off by using their influence at court to obtain privileges for others. Although constructive projects, some of which also owed something to courtly influence and even courtly capital, did not disappear entirely from the scene, in general the 'constructive phase' in the history of projects gave way to the 'scandalous phase'. It was against the perpetration of such outrages that Elizabeth's subjects sought redress in parliament in 1597. Following the failure of parliament's representations in 1597, the enraged MPs in the next parliament in 1601 were seriously contemplating the introduction of an anti-monopoly bill, which would, of course, have directly infringed the royal prerogative. It was the queen herself who saved the situation by abolishing the most obnoxious patents by proclamation and conceding that the remainder were liable to testing at common law. In her celebrated 'Golden Speech' she succeeded in turning what had been the occasion of one of the nastiest anti-government demonstrations in any Tudor parliament into a major triumph, regaining the love and admiration of her parliamentarians.

By no means all the patents complained of related to monopolies. Among them were the courtly poet Sir Edward Dyer's patent 'to pardon, dispense and release all forfeitures and abuses committed by Tanners contrary to the statute [of 1563]'; 'A Patent to one Kirke et aliis, To take the Benefit of Sowing Flax and Hemp'; another to an unnamed person 'to have the benefit of forfeiture by gig-mills'; and another to one Arthur Bassaney to export 6,000 calf-skins. All these patents relate to the enforcement of existing statutory regulations concerning respectively the prohibited use of gig-mills for raising the nap of woollen cloth, the tanning of hides, the requirement that owners of more than sixty acres of land grow hemp, and the prohibited export of calf-skins. In the absence of developed bureaucratic machinery, the ambitious Tudor code of economic regulation made use of private interests as a mechanism for the discharge of what would today be regarded as public duties, as well as serving as a form of courtly out-relief. The anomalous nature of these concessions lay in the fact that the pursuit of the private profit of the patentee and the enforcement of government economic regulations, far from being complementary, were in fact contradictory aims. For at least as often as not, and certainly in all the examples cited here, the patentees made their profits by licensing people to disregard statutes rather than by enforcing them. A situation in which licences to disregard the law are issued by private individuals for their own profit is, to say the least of it, hardly conducive to fostering respect for the observance of the law. But it was to remain a central feature of government, and far from receiving their quietus in 1601, patents and other courtly concessions were a hydra which was to grow new and more scandalous heads in the next reign.

FACTIONAL STRIFE AND THE ESSEX REVOLT

The last decade of the reign was a climacteric in other spheres than those of war finance and the consequently increased need for the government to have recourse to more indirect modes of payment and reward. The shortage of such perquisites and concessions relative to the demand of magnates and their followings for them was to have crucially important consequences for the stability of the body politic. Elizabeth in fact found it more and more difficult to maintain a balance between the leaders of court factional groups, the very skill which one Jacobean courtly observer, Secretary of State Sir Robert Naunton, saw as distinguishing her from her successors. The later 1590s were a time of transition between the high Elizabethan and the Jacobean situations; the former characterized by the successful, if somewhat precarious, maintenance of balance between factional groups, and the latter by the hegemony of one group, until it in its turn was overthrown by a rival group – a pattern that was to characterize English court politics until the assassination of the duke of Buckingham, favourite of both the early Stuart kings, in 1628.

In the last years of his life the ageing Burghley had come to concentrate a great deal of power in his own hands. The *regnum Cecilianum*, of which the earl of Essex and his followers complained so bitterly in the late 1590s, was in fact the creation of Burghley, who was also desperately anxious that he would be succeeded at the helm of the ship of state by his meticulously trained and supremely able younger son Robert. There are indeed two significantly different and mutually contradictory interpretations of factional struggles at court in the later 1590s. The first and most familiar view is that the virtual hegemony of a single faction, the so-called *regnum Cecilianum*, was the reluctant creation not just of Burghley but also of the queen herself, forced by the overweening ambition and jealousy of Essex, who would brook no rivals, and in fact sought an equally, if not more, complete hegemony for himself. The contrary interpretation is that, far from being the product of an outraged royal reaction to Essex's precipitancy, the *regnum Cecilianum* was instead the cause of it: in other words that Essex was driven to despair and ultimately to self-destruction by the Cecilian stranglehold on office and preferment. Both views are oversimplifications, but since both were versions of reality firmly believed by the opposing factions, they influenced profoundly the course of events. Certainly Essex's demands and his alarming popularity both inside and outside the court made Elizabeth feel it necessary to put more real power into Cecilian hands than she might have judged desirable in more normal circumstances. Equally certainly, to Essex the Cecils appeared to have their hands on all the crucial levers controlling the distribution of office, power and perquisites, and it became increasingly clear to him that their grip could be loosened only by force.

It needs to be stressed that the queen was careful not to confer all of Burghley's offices on his son following the former's death in 1598. Robert Cecil, who had been secretary of state for the past two years, now took over his father's post as chancellor of the duchy of Lancaster. However, Burghley's greatest office, that of lord treasurer, went not to his son but to Lord Buckhurst, the later earl of Dorset. Robert had to wait till Dorset's death in 1608 before becoming lord treasurer, and until May 1599 before getting the much coveted post of master of the Court of Wards, which also had been held by his father. This was a place of great potential profit, offering enormous possibilities of gratifying one's clients by securing them wardships at bargain prices. As such it was also coveted by Essex, whose worsting at the hands of his rival stoked up the bitterness and jealousy which were to plunge him into treason in 1601. Elizabeth herself seemed to recognize that there had been an undesirable concentration of power in Cecilian hands when, after the Essex revolt in 1601, she removed the chancellorship of the duchy of Lancaster from Cecil's hands and gave it to Sir John Fortescue. But by that time Essex was in the grave.

Essex had been increasingly obsessed by what he took to be the reasons for his inability to reward his clients with the sorts of offices and perquisites which a first-rate patron needed to have at his disposal if his following was not to melt away at the edges. It was a consequence of the polarization of factions in these years that there was no place for a man who was unwilling to plump firmly for one side or the other, or who, like Essex's friend and wise counsellor, Fulke Greville, desired to reconcile the warring groups. Indeed, so far as office and profit were concerned, Essex might argue with force that there was no place for anyone who was not an out-and-out Cecilian. In 1596 he had tried to obtain the office of lord chamberlain for Sir Robert Sidney, the brother of the great Sir Philip, alongside whom Essex had fought at Zutphen. But the office went to Lord Cobham, Cecil's father-in-law. Following Cobham's death in the next year, Essex tried to get one of his offices for

Sidney. This was the lord wardenship of the Cinque Ports, which carried with it considerable powers of patronage. But Sidney was again unlucky and the post went to Cobham's son. The fact that Sidney was among those ranged against Essex in the great testing time of the Essex revolt in February 1601 should not, however, be taken as an indication that he had deserted his friend on account of his conspicuous failure to find him preferment, but rather that his duty to the queen overrode the ties, however strong, of friendship. The charge of deserting his patron for careerist reasons may well be more applicable to Francis Bacon, for whom Essex had failed to obtain the office of attorney-general, which went instead to the Cecilian Sir Edward Coke in 1594; or even in the following year that of solicitor-general, which was vacant as a result of Coke's promotion. It certainly did not require the stark issue of treason to make Bacon look elsewhere for a patron, and there are signs of his moving into the Cecilian camp well before the final show-down in 1601.

Essex's popular reputation had reached its apogee in 1596 with the brilliantly successful Cadiz expedition. His attempt to strike another deadly blow at the heart of Spanish naval strength and to frustrate the possibility of another Armada, the so-called Islands Voyage of the next year, was unsuccessful, but his reputation and popularity hardly suffered, except where it most mattered, with the queen herself. Yet even at his most brilliantly successful in the martial exploits which dazzled his contemporaries, he was at his most vulnerable through leaving the field of domestic power politics open to his enemies. Thus before leaving for Ireland at the beginning of 1599 in command of the expeditionary force to put down the earl of Tyrone's rebellion, he observed bitterly that, armed with a breastplate but not a cuirass, he was protected from attacks in the front, but not from the rear.

There is no need to accept the arguments put foward by some contemporaries – not all of them Essexians – that

Essex's appointment to his Irish command was a Cecilian plot to encompass his ruin, brought about by starving him of necessary supplies. In actual fact, no such Machiavellian ruses were necessary. Frustrated by an ever retreating but never defeated enemy; unable to gain the decisive victory he sought in this graveyard of English reputations, including that of his own father; tormented by psychotic visions of plots against him at court, he made an unauthorized truce with Tyrone and stormed back to court in September 1599 to justify himself to the queen. From then on his affairs went from bad to worse. Excluded from the court, the great man who had chafed at his inability to help his friends to preferment was now condemned to obscurity himself. He was, no doubt, now prepared to admit that he had erred badly in his precipitate return from Ireland. But, he might reflect, he had served his mistress well, even spectacularly well, in the past. Did he really merit her refusal to acknowledge any of his letters pleading for reinstatement or at least for some recognition of his just deserts? Were not his services at the very least as great as those who were now prospering by his disgrace?

> Of all the swarm I only did not thrive.
> Yet brought I wax and honey to the hive.

Elizabeth's refusal in September 1600 to renew Essex's patents for the farm of the duties on sweet wines and for issuing wine licences set the economic seal on his political decline. This action, which destroyed his credit and inhibited further borrowing to meet his financial difficulties, Elizabeth undertook, on her own admission, because 'an unruly horse must be abated of his provender that he may be the easier managed'. But its effect was the reverse of what was intended, and far from reducing him to obedience, it drove him to despairing revolt. For it underlined the stark choice lying before him: retirement from active life and savage retrenchment of his style of life, or seizure of power by force. Frustrated of what they felt to be their just deserts, Essex and his associates resolved, in the words which a contemporary attributed to one of them, to 'seize the queen and be our own carvers'.

In the forefront of the revolt were the four earls, Essex, Southampton, Bedford and Rutland, the first in his early thirties but the others all in their twenties. All four had been former wards of Burghley and displayed in their wild and extravagant life-style the antithesis of Burghley's concern for restraint and decorum. Did Southampton's great dependant, William Shakespeare, have Burghley in mind in his merciless portrayal of Polonius in *Hamlet*, or Cecil, Raleigh and Cobham in mind when recounting the fate of Bushy, Bagot and Green, caterpillars of the commonwealth, in *Richard II*? At any rate, disregarding the sort of counsel which Polonius gave to Laertes, all the earls were up to their ears in debt. Admittedly their landed resources were such that the exercise of restraint and economic retrenchment might have restored their fortunes. But not even this choice of action, which to these wild and angry young men was out of the question anyway, was open to the lesser and older Essexian peers, Lords Sandys and Cromwell, whose debts were far more serious relative to their real and potential resources. Cromwell, who had sold off lands to the tune of £10,000 over the past decade, was a comparatively late recruit to the ranks of the Essexians, having first failed to find favour with the Cecils. But as an impoverished soldier he was perhaps better placed than any other of the noble rebels to appreciate the burning resentment which consumed lesser men: long-standing campaigners like Sir Christopher Blount, Sir Ferdinando Gorges, Sir William Constable and Sir John Davies. Such men were moved by the contrast between what they regarded as the government's base ingratitude for their services and the open-handed magnanimity of Essex, whose prodigal bestowal of knighthoods, which so infuriated the queen, has been seen as a calculated attempt to build up a personal following of swordsmen who would make his cause their own.[6]

The Essex-Cecil conflict operated in the provinces as well as at court. The rivalry between the Essexian Sir Robert Sidney and the Cecilian Lords Cobham, father and son, over court office had a distinct Kentish dimension to it too. Similar factional rivalries were to be observed in Norfolk, where for a time the Essexian Heydons were part of the lieutenancy 'in-group', even though Essex failed to secure the office of lord lieutenant for Lord Cromwell in 1596. North Wales too was rent by factional strife between Essexian and Cecilian gentry. South Wales, however, was an area of Essexian hegemony, where there were extensive Devereux estates and the Commission of the Peace and other local offices were dominated by Essexians. Thanks to Sir Gelli Meyricke, Essex's Welsh steward, this was to be the recruiting ground *par excellence* for the swordsmen who it was later hoped would flood up to Essex House in London to take part in the *coup d'état* of 1601; a move which proved in the end to be a very damp squib.[7]

How far was the Essex Revolt more than a revolt of frustrated malcontents, of 'outs' determined to get themselves an innings? Essex certainly seems to have seen himself as Leicester's successor, the leader of the group favouring a militantly Protestant policy at home and abroad. But if the Essexians are to be seen as a militantly Protestant party, how does one explain the inclusion within their ranks, even if on the fringes, of popish recusants such as Sir Christopher Blount, Sir Charles Danvers, Robert Catesby and Francis Tresham, the two last of whom were later to be involved in the Gunpowder Plot of 1605? As to foreign policy and the conduct of the war, Essex certainly favoured a more vigorous and daring strategy in the Netherlands, in France and in carrying the war to the enemy on the high seas. His aggressive line certainly contrasts with the more cautious Cecilian policy of reducing continental commitments where possible, and reserving the navy for less ambitious and more strictly defensive use. But even this difference of policy does not mark a completely clear-cut division between the opposing factions, for Essex's deadly enemy Raleigh also stood for an aggressive and expansionist naval policy, and yet was at the same time allied to Cecil, even though he too was soon to fall victim to him. All in all, then, for all its ideological overtones, one must conclude that the Essex revolt was first and foremost a struggle for power and influence, in which issues were of minor significance. As such, it heralds the power struggles at court in the next reign, as does the ultimate product of the Essexian discontents, the hegemony of a single faction. Although Elizabeth had another two years to live, the end of the Essex revolt heralds the final triumph of the Cecilians and the beginning of a distinct era in court politics. In this sense at least the Elizabethan age hardly outlived the century.

RELIGIOUS DISSENT IN THE CLOSING YEARS OF THE REIGN

For all his being billed by moderate Puritans and even by the separatist John Penry as an aristocratic patron and the prime hope of the godly cause, Essex was in reality very far from being the successor of those influential Puritan-sympathizing peers such as the second earl of Bedford (d. 1585), Leicester (d. 1588) and Huntingdon (d. 1595). If indeed his Puritanism had been serious and consistent, it would be more reasonable to regard him as the first of a new line of Puritan noblemen such as Viscount Saye and Sele, the earl of Warwick and the second Lord Brooke, who were rigorously excluded from power and influence at court. Yet if 1588, the Protestant *annus mirabilis*, also marks, paradoxically, the beginnings of the decline of Puritan influence at court with the death of Leicester, this decline affects only the role of Puritanism at court and in parliament after the high point of Puritan parliamentary activity in 1586–7, rather than its spirit in the country as a whole. The 1590s, it is true, were to see the continued success of the Whitgiftian assault on both the remnants of the Cartwrightian Presbyterians and the more extreme separatists, who were denounced by episcopalians and Presbyterians alike. Three such separatists, Henry Barrow, John Greenwood and John Penry, men who sought reformation without tarrying for any, through the means of gathered congregations of the elect come together of their own volition, met their end on the scaffold in 1593. But the assault of Whitgift and the hierarchy was not directed only at extremists, and they sought to tar even moderate Puritan reformers with a Presbyterian or even a separatist brush. Yet because such moderates were not at this stage anti-episcopalian, it is arguable that Elizabeth and her successor were to lose a marvellous opportunity – as Elizabeth had already done in the time of Grindal, and as James I was to do at the Hampton Court Conference in 1604 – of harnessing these forces by associating the church with the cause of moderate, as distinct from radical, reform.

Another feature of the religious history of the closing years of the reign was the fierce internecine disputes within the ranks of the English Catholics between the Jesuit missionaries, to whom the Catholic revival had owed so much, and the secular priests, many of whom resented Jesuit intrusion and mistrusted Jesuit ambitions.[8] The first issue in dispute was whether the English Catholics were to be subject to a Catholic 'bishop' or to a so-called 'arch-priest', a new device favoured by the Jesuits. The organization of the clandestine English Catholic church under a bishop was favoured by the seculars not only on account of their traditionalism and the appeal to them of an office which had existed in pre-Reformation days. It also argued for a degree of autonomy and self-regulation for English Catholicism, rather than organization under an 'arch-priest', which, as the seculars rightly concluded from the lesser dignity as well as the unfamiliarity of the office, suggested closer subordination to foreign and Jesuit direction. The Jesuits won, and the appointment of the Jesuit George Blackwell as arch-priest in 1598 precipitated not only two unsuccessful appeals from the seculars to Rome in

1598 and 1600, but also negotiations between a small group of the appellants and Sir Robert Cecil.

To understand the significance of this last move it is necessary to make reference to the other issue which divided the Jesuits from most of the seculars. This was nothing less than the succession to the English throne itself. Recognizing that the succession of James VI of Scotland was a more or less foregone conclusion, the seculars seem to have calculated that, in the interests of obtaining a better deal for English Catholics, it would be prudent to offer their enthusiastic support to James, whose own mother had, after all, herself been a Catholic. The Jesuits, on the other hand, rejecting the idea that one heretic should succeed another, favoured the Spanish Infanta, whose claim rested on her descent from John of Gaunt, the son of Edward III. Indeed, the Jesuit Robert Parsons had been at pains to put out the rumour that, partly because of Essex's allegedly close relations with James VI, Cecil himself favoured the Infanta. This, however, may have been a shrewd way of putting a spoke in the wheel of the concordat which Cecil may have been planning with the seculars, whose disillusionment, following the accession of James, was soon to be expressed in a particularly futile plot against him.

(II) THE CECILIAN ASCENDANCY, 1601–12

FACTION AND POWER AT COURT

While the execution of Essex had removed the main obstacle to Cecilian hegemony, Cecil was disposed to be conciliatory, at least to the Essexian peers, who probably owed to him their lenient treatment and release from prison at the beginning of the new reign. He probably sensed the need to go carefully, given the likelihood that the queen had not long to live, and that the accession of a king who had reportedly been favourably disposed towards Essex carried with it a threat to his own position. Indeed on the queen's death Raleigh's close associate, the earl of Northumberland, planned to exploit the constitutional technicalities of the situation by insisting on the resignation of all existing office-holders and the interim exercise of power by the peerage as the Great Council of the realm. But the peers refused to play, and James confirmed existing office-holders with only a very few exceptions. The survival of the Cecilian ascendancy may well have owed much to the conciliatory policy pursued by Cecil in the interim between the Essex Revolt and the death of the queen.

One of the noblemen whom Cecil had been at pains to conciliate was Lord Henry Howard, the son of the poet earl of Surrey who had been executed by Henry VIII in 1547, and brother of the duke of Norfolk who had suffered the like fate in 1572. Both had much to gain from the connection. The Howards were in eclipse, but their fortunes were to burgeon spectacularly in the new reign until their own ascendancy followed Cecil's after the latter's death in 1612. Howard was *persona grata* with James, who unlike Elizabeth relished the unctuous brand of flattery which was a particularly distasteful part of his courtly stock-in-trade. He became a valued ally of Cecil, not least in his consummate use of the poison pen to blacken Northumberland, Raleigh and Cobham in the eyes of the Scottish king. At first sight more surprising than Cecil's alliance with Howard is the favour which he showed to the Essexian peers while turning against not only Fulke Greville, who had dispensed moderate but unheeded advice to the Essexians, but also Cobham and Raleigh, his former allies against Essex. As to Greville, Cecil certainly had not shared the old queen's appreciation of his fruitless attempts to influence Essex in the direction of moderation, which he recognized had as their object the restoration of the earl to royal favour. But for so long as the old queen lived, Greville continued to enjoy her favour, and it was not until the new reign that Cecil was able to exact a delayed retribution. Greville was supplanted as naval treasurer by the Howard client Sir Robert Mansell, an appointment which spelt doom to the naval reforms so dear to Greville's heart. In addition he had to buy back the offices in the Council of the Marches which James had conferred upon one of the numerous Scottish fortune-hunters who had followed him to England. It took an astonishingly long time for it to dawn on him that he had Cecil to thank for his misfortunes.[9]

But why did Cecil turn against his former allies in the struggle which had culminated in the Essex Revolt? This is at best only partially explicable in terms of his Machiavellian consciousness of the convenience of conciliating the Essexian grandees by making Raleigh and Cobham plausible scapegoats for the disaster to their fortunes in 1601. A more significant clue is presented by Cecil's foreign policy and the significance of his alliance with Howard in this respect. Pro-Spanish and crypto-Catholic, Howard strongly favoured Cecil's plan for peace with Spain, which was concluded in the treaty of London in 1604. Raleigh, on the other hand, was a passionate advocate of hotting up the war. Raleigh may have been a useful ally in the conditions of the Essex-Cecil struggle for hegemony, but in the reign of *Rex Pacificus* he was a positive embarrassment. Raleigh saw the peace of 1604 as a base desertion of England's Dutch allies; James mistrusted the Dutch as rebels against monarchical authority. It was not difficult to poison the new king's mind against him, and with the aid of Lord Henry Howard that process was well under way before 1603. Shortly after James's accession Raleigh was dismissed from the post of captain of the guard (supplanted by yet another Scotsman) and from the lord wardenship of the Stannaries. In addition he lost his lucrative wine licensing patent and was made to leave the London residence of the bishop of Durham in the Strand, which he had occupied for twenty years. His economic condition was now as desperate as that of some of the lesser Essexians in 1601, and his feelings towards Cecil probably similar to theirs. He was shortly to be in deeper trouble through his associate Lord Cobham, whose brother

George Brooke, though not himself a Catholic, had become implicated in the Bye Plot instigated by the secular priest Watson. (For details see below, pp. 217–18). Both Brooke and Watson were to be executed for their part in the plot, but more important to Cecil was the fact that the examination of Brooke had revealed that Cobham had been involved in another plot, the so-called Main Plot, to replace James on the throne by Arbella Stuart. Further evidence was held to implicate Raleigh, absurd though the idea of Raleigh's plotting along with the ambassador of the Habsburg archduke might appear to the unprejudiced observer. Both Cobham and Raleigh were condemned to death, though the sentence was suspended, to be put into effect in Raleigh's case thirteen years later.

The sentences completed the work which had been done during the last two years of the old queen's reign by the clandestine correspondence between Cecil, Howard and James. Cecil was to become earl of Salisbury in 1605, and on the death of Dorset (the former Buckhurst) in 1608, he succeeded to his father's old office of lord treasurer. He now held in his hands that combination of offices which Elizabeth had wisely seen fit to deny him. As for the Howards, Lord Henry became earl of Northampton, lord privy seal and lord warden of the Cinque Ports, the last office being forfeited by the condemned Cobham. His nephew, Lord Thomas Howard, became earl of Suffolk and succeeded to another of Cobham's offices, that of lord chamberlain. Another Howard, the earl of Nottingham, the former Lord Howard of Effingham, the lord admiral and victor over the Armada, now got his hands on the wine licensing patent which Raleigh had once enjoyed.

But the Cecil-Howard alliance was to be fairly shortlived. When Cecil – or Salisbury as we must now call him – whose part in the unmasking of the Bye, Main and Gunpowder plots had been a spectacular demonstration of his apparent indispensability, began to run into more difficult times, his Howard allies, and notably Northampton, were to turn against him without the least compunction. To Salisbury's policies we will turn in a moment, but in the meantime we must note the appearance on the scene of a new factor which perhaps more than anything else was to mark the difference between the Elizabethan and Jacobean political scenes. This is the key role which was played by beautiful young men to whom the king's affections were drawn and whom he delighted to honour. To obtain and keep the favour of these persons was to become the essential condition of the exercise of power and influence, and not even the most accomplished statesmen were exempt from this condition. As a teenage king of Scotland James had experienced between 1579 and 1582 the first of such passions: for Esmé Stuart, whom he created duke of Lennox and from whose clutches he had to be forcibly extricated, like Edward II from Gaveston, in the celebrated Ruthven Raid in 1582. While court gossips and scandalmongers had been quick to single out a number of likely aspirants for the role of favourite in the opening years of James's English reign, it was not until 1607 that their expectations were realized in the person of the young Scotsman Robert Carr, who had come to England with the king in 1603, but had taken himself off to France in the meantime. It soon became clear that the highway to royal favour and influence lay through the cultivation of the royal favourite.

Here was a state of affairs as unlike the Elizabethan as could be. For never did a Leicester or a Burghley exercise the monopoly of influence over the sovereign that became the prerogative of Carr – who was made Viscount Rochester in 1611 – and later of Villiers, who supplanted and surpassed him. When an Elizabethan favourite like Essex had aspired to enjoy such a monopoly, he had been driven into the wilderness and his ultimate destruction. But now Carr's favour was the key to power, and the competition for it of Salisbury and the Howards, hardly less than of aspirant courtiers, was one of a number of signs that the alliance between Cecil and the Howards was under severe strain.

Another was the heat generated by Northampton's attempt in 1607 to supplant the syndicate of customs farmers which was backed by Salisbury, by exposing their malpractices and putting forward his own alternative candidate for the farm, a development reminiscent of some of the bitterest incidents in the Essex-Cecil struggle of a decade earlier.

THE FAILURE OF FISCAL REFORM

One clear sign that some of the basic Elizabethan certainties no longer obtained in the new reign was the nature of Jacobean financial deficits. As in the closing years of Elizabeth I, the royal finances were in overall deficit. But whereas the causes of later Elizabethan financial imbalance were the extraordinary charges of war and the Irish revolt, and the ordinary account remained in surplus, the first decade and a half of James's reign was characterized by (from 1604) peace and a cumulative deficit on the *ordinary* account. The king, in other words, was failing to live of his own. In consequence the royal debt, which had stood at £350,000 at the beginning of the reign, had risen to £735,000 at the beginning of 1606, and by Michaelmas the current ordinary deficit was to swell it by a further £81,831 and an extraordinary charge by £17,792. Neither inflation nor the fact that James, unlike Elizabeth, had a family are sufficient to extenuate, for example, the increased average annual expenditure of the royal Wardrobe from £9,535 in the last four years of Elizabeth to an annual average of £36,377 over the first five years of the new reign, or a rise of about £8,000 in royal Household expenditure, as an annual average, using the same years as a basis for comparison. James's prodigality in cash rewards, pensions and perquisites in kind was no less spectacular than his inflation of titles of honour, which was dealt with in an earlier chapter (see above, pp. 49–50), and no less damaging to the royal fortunes and prestige, not least since many of the beneficiaries were immigrant Scotsmen. As Bishop Godfrey

Goodman was later ruefully to admit, 'his time being a time of peace, we fell to luxury and riot'.

Although it is appropriate to characterize the decade following the Essex Revolt as the era of Cecilian ascendancy, Salisbury, as Robert Cecil had now become since 1605, did not become lord treasurer until the death of Thomas Sackville, earl of Dorset, in 1608. His predecessor, 'fill-sack' as he was popularly known in a not altogether inappropriate play on his family name, must therefore bear his own share of the blame for the deteriorating financial situation. By the same token he must also take some of the credit – if credit is due – for such measures as were taken to rectify the situation. These fall broadly into two categories: measures designed to keep the debt from rising; and measures to reduce it.

Given the extreme difficulty of restraining the king's open-handedness, revenue improvement offered a more promising field than expenditure reduction.[10] At the end of 1604 a crucially important decision was taken in the sphere of customs administration. Following Burghley's death in 1598 there had been a reversal of the policy of resumption by the crown of piecemeal farms of the customs which had marked the previous decade. The government of James I was to accentuate this process by opting for customs farming on a hitherto unprecedented scale. All those duties not currently in farm were brought together in one consolidated farm of the customs and let to a syndicate whose principals were the Levant Company merchants William Garway and Nicholas Salter and the customs house official Francis Jones, for a rent of £112,400. Before the lease had technically expired, the rent was screwed up to £120,000 by Dorset in 1606, and to £136,226 by Salisbury in 1611. It has been argued, however, that more could have been done if Salisbury had not been inhibited by his own personal indebtedness to the farmers,[11] and that what little was done was due to his hand being forced by Northampton's espousal of the cause of Sir John Swinnerton, who, wishing to obtain this concession and others for himself, had published damaging revelations about the current syndicate's malpractices.[12]

The custom and subsidy of tonnage and poundage, whose administration is referred to above, were – at least until 1625 – granted to the monarch by parliament for life; not so the so-called impositions which were levied not by parliamentary grant, but by royal prerogative. A number of new impositions had been introduced by Dorset since 1598. It was no doubt the decision of the Court of Exchequer in Bate's famous case in 1606 about the payment of impositions on currants which encouraged Salisbury, during his first year as lord treasurer in 1608–9, to expand the scope of impositions so as to bring in an estimated additional revenue of £70,000. The official constitutional case for impositions as a prerogative levy was that they flowed from the royal right and duty of protecting trade, and that any fiscal spin-off was entirely incidental. But it is difficult to see Salisbury's new impositions, especially those on exports (other than exports of raw materials needed in English manufactures), as satisfying these exacting criteria, and these considerations fuelled the parliamentary opposition to impositions, which will be dealt with later. While in no doubt that impositions served a preponderantly fiscal purpose, Salisbury was not, however, averse to making occasional adjustments with protectionist and general economic considerations in mind: by putting higher duties on luxury imports and imports competing directly with native English manufactures; by excepting vital raw material and strategic imports (e.g. naval stores) from duty; and by lowering the especially contentious impositions on imported sugar and currants. Indeed the neo-protectionist adjustments which he made to the tariff in 1610, when he was anxious to placate parliament, actually resulted in a loss of £20,000 to the royal revenue.

Income from the royal estates was the second of the two great twin pillars of the ordinary revenue. Over the first nine years of the reign James I sold off royal land of annual value of

£27,311 for a capital sum of £645,952. The greatest volume of sales took place under the administration of Lord Treasurer Salisbury as part of the process of reducing the royal debt. This alienation of capital resources involved, of course, the reduction of the income derived therefrom, though, as far as possible, care was taken to sell small, detached properties, which consumed a significant proportion of their revenues in the charges of collection and administration. Although the land market would be depressed by being flooded with large quantities of land, by making use of syndicates of city businessmen acting as contractors for crown lands, who bought in large quantities and then re-sold over a period, Salisbury may have secured a better return than he would have done by selling direct. Needless to say, the contractors themselves did very well out of it.[13] Sales were a regrettable necessity in view of the horrifying rise in the royal debt. They also inhibited the prospect of success for Salisbury's landed policy of instituting extensive and expert surveys of royal lands with the object of screwing up rents and other landed revenues to more economic levels; as did the crown's continued need to reward its dependants by beneficial leases of royal land.

In the matter of debt-reduction Dorset and Salisbury were a great deal less successful than might appear at first sight. For to have reduced the debt from about £735,000 at the beginning of 1606 to about £280,000 by 1610 is not a very impressive achievement, given the fact that more than £1,185,000 was made available for this purpose from the subsidies voted by parliament in 1606 (about £453,000), the sale of lands and wood (more than £445,000) and from a variety of other measures.[14] The reason why the debt was not liquidated completely was the continued operation of the causes which had made it rise, the cumulative ordinary deficits. Such a state of affairs was hardly likely to predispose parliament to respond favourably to the imaginative programme of fiscal reform, the so-called Great Contract, presented to it by Salisbury in 1610, when he pleaded that 'seeing the ship of state drive so near the port', they should not suffer it to perish. For if things had been managed properly, it should already have been home and dry.

Salisbury was asking for two things: in his own words, for Supply and Support. Supply, an extraordinary parliamentary grant of £600,000, was at least straightforward. It was also contentious, in that, like the parliamentary grant of 1606, it involved the use of an extraordinary parliamentary grant to finance the consequences of the king's inability to live of his own. Support, on the other hand, was completely novel: an annual parliamentary revenue, in return for which the crown would sacrifice politically unpopular and socially anachronistic feudal dues such as wardship and purveyance.

From the time when Sir Robert Cecil (as he then was) had succeeded his father as master of the Court of Wards in May 1599, he had reversed the prevailing policy of using wardship as an expenditure-reducing device and a means of rewards in kind – wardships at bargain prices and the like – and opted instead for tangible cash returns. These he aimed to maximize via a variety of administrative improvements, while not neglecting the opportunity of taking juicy pickings for himself. Since this policy ran counter to the general tendency running, since the 1590s, in the direction of indirect modes of finance, it is reasonable to suggest that Salisbury may have been contemplating his Great Contract scheme nearly a decade before he advanced it. For if the feudal revenues were to be bargained away for cash, it was obviously in the crown's interest to have a firm figure for their yield. By 1607 the revenues of the Court of Wards had risen to more than £17,000, about £3,000 above their average Elizabethan level. But Salisbury urged parliament to think beyond what wardship was currently yielding, to what it could be made to yield if no Contract was agreed – it was in fact to yield £84,000 by 1640.

But this very point emphasized one fundamental disadvantage of the proposed Contract to the crown: the substitution of a fixed agreed sum whose real value would decrease with continued (even if falling) inflation, for a revenue which was capable of substantial expansion, even if at considerable political and social cost. Nor was this the only reason why the king came to have second thoughts about the value of Salisbury's Contract. In addition, there was the not unjustified suspicion that the sort of parliamentary grants made in 1606 and 1610 might become things of the past. 'The King,' observed Sir Julius Caesar, Salisbury's chancellor of the Exchequer but an opponent of the Contract, 'may undoubtedly resolve to receive no more subsidies or fifteenths from his subjects in time of peace. For that is a parcel of the ground whereupon they [viz. MPs] are purposed to win their countries' [viz. constituencies'] consent to that contract.' One must also attach some importance to James's reluctance to lose what he regarded as a precious flower of his prerogative, though Francis Bacon was surely exaggerating when he argued that the sacrifice of a prerogative for a parliamentary revenue would afford 'a ready way to a democracy'. But, political considerations aside, there was plenty of room for down-to-earth doubts about whether the Contract was really value for money. Caesar estimated the total annual yield of wardship and purveyance (the royal right to levy goods and carriage service below the market price or compositions paid in lieu of this) at £115,000. Given that £200,000 was as high as parliament would go, this left a net gain to the crown of £85,000 per annum, and considerably less than this, if it, and not parliament, was to bear the cost of compensating redundant officials. Small wonder that James first hesitated, and then demanded £200,000 *de claro*, that is, in addition to the value of the revenues he was proposing to surrender. This, of course, made the proposition totally unacceptable to parliament.[15]

It seems highly probable that when MPs did consult their constituents about the Contract during the parliamentary recess in 1610 – and as Dr Hirst has demonstrated, early Stuart MPs were far more responsive to the wishes of their constituents than was once supposed[16] – they received a pretty frosty response. The precise objections can only be guessed at, but some of them probably reinforced the doubts of the MPs themselves. As to the projected abolition of wardship, it might be argued that the total tax burden would be distributed more evenly and less capriciously, not falling simply on those unfortunate enough to hold their land by feudal tenure of the crown and to succeed to their inheritance while still minors. But such considerations were not likely to appeal to those who were anyway not subject to the burdens of fiscal feudalism, but now saw themselves as likely to become liable to pay for what replaced it. Uncertainty as to who exactly would bear the brunt of this charge – would it be a tax on landowners in general to replace a tax falling capriciously on certain sorts of landowners, or would it extend less or more widely than this? – was an important factor inducing parliamentarians to opt for the devil they knew, to whose exactions a large number of them were anyway not liable.

Mutatis mutandis, similar considerations are applicable to doubts about the abolition of purveyance.[17] Here again the crucial difference as to interest in or opposition to abolition rested on the matter of differential tax burdens; not, this time, as in the case of wardship, between different sorts of landowners, but between different counties. It is roughly true that the nearer a county was to London and the court, the greater burden of purveyance it had to bear. In these circumstances the advantages of doing away with purveyance, as they might appear to a gentleman from Kent, Essex or Buckinghamshire, might evaporate when seen from the standpoint of a man of Lancashire, Yorkshire or Devon.

Moreover, if some of the crown's advisers opposed the contract as 'a ready passage to a democracy', to some MPs the reverse seemed the more likely outcome: that it might make the crown financially independent of parliament.[18] But it seems unlikely that even James's final and rejected demand of £200,000 *de claro* would provide an adequate financial basis for royal independence. It would in fact be more likely to precipitate further royal extravagance, a consideration which provides the final, and perhaps the most powerful, reason for the parliamentary opposition to the Contract. 'To what purpose is it for us', argued Thomas Wentworth, MP for Oxford and son of the formidable parliamentarian Peter Wentworth, who had given such trouble to Elizabeth I, 'to draw a silver stream out of the country, if it shall run out thence by private cocks?' Or, as another MP, John Hoskyns, put it, how could one be sure that 'the whole benefit [of the Contract] might come to the King's purse'? One could not, of course, be sure, and, in identifying himself with the fortunes of the Great Contract, Salisbury, normally a supremely realistic politician, seems to have lost his grip on political reality. In the words of his master's cruel, but not entirely unjust, rebuke, Salisbury had been 'a little blinded with the self-love of your own counsel in holding together of this Parliament, whereof all men despaired . . . but yourself alone'. Thereafter he was an isolated and discredited figure. Although he clung to office for the remaining two years left to him, the days of his ascendancy, unchallenged since the death of Essex, were over. To all intents and purposes the *regnum Cecilianum* ended in 1610.

PARLIAMENT AND REFORM

The failure of the Great Contract was a crushing defeat for Salisbury rather than a victory for parliament over the crown, as it is too often represented by historians. As the highly critical memorandum on the Contract compiled by Salisbury's own chancellor of the Exchequer, Sir Julius Caesar, indicates, the Contract had influential opponents at court as well as in parliament. Like so much else of what used to be regarded as the winning of the initiative by the Commons,[19] the episode provides an example of what was to be one of the central features of early Stuart political history, the transference of court disputes on to the parliamentary scene. The work of a number of historians, and notably of Professor Conrad Russell, has recently emphasized the danger of considering the history of Jacobean parliaments in terms of the search for the origins of the Civil War,[20] a corollary of which has been to postulate the anachronism of a coordinated parliamentary opposition to royal policies long before such a movement came into being. This is an offshoot of that Whig interpretation which takes as the central theme of English institutional history the broadening of freedoms and the development of representative institutions at the expense of personal monarchy. But the historian who concentrates his attention on the events of James I's first parliament, which met intermittently between 1604 and 1610, and puts the history of Cromwellian (not to speak of Victorian) England out of mind, is more likely to be conscious of what many parliamentarians regarded as a threat posed by the crown to the Elizabethan constitutional equipoise than of a parliamentary assault on the royal prerogative. As the so-called *Apology and Satisfaction* drawn up by a parliamentary committee in 1604, but never approved by the House of Commons for presentation to the king, put it: 'the prerogatives of princes may easily and do daily grow: the privileges of the subject are for the most part at an everlasting stand.'

One point taken up in the *Apology* typifies the fears of some MPs that the crown was seeking to make all sorts of constitutional inroads into their cherished freedoms. This related to the celebrated dispute over the election of MPs for Buckinghamshire in 1604. It has recently been argued convincingly that this dispute, arising out of the failure of the privy councillor Sir John Fortescue to top the poll, and the government's attempt to exclude the victor, Sir Francis Goodwin, on a technicality, was less a dispute between court and country than between different factions at court, and that the king himself had no particular liking for Fortescue, whom anyway he had relieved of two important offices in favour of a Scot.[21] Nevertheless, there can be little doubt that the royal insistence that Chancery not the House of Commons was the proper judge of the validity of elections to the latter body raised genuine alarm that here was the thin end of a wedge through which the composition of the House might come to be determined by the crown; that, in the colourful expression of one MP, it 'opens a gap to thrust us all into the Petty Bag. A Chancellor may call what persons he will by this course.'

Similar fears, which had been pooh-poohed by Chief Baron Fleming in giving judgment for the crown in Bate's case in 1606, afflicted MPs in the matter of royal impositions. In their brilliant speeches in the great debate on impositions in the House of Commons in June 1610, the two lawyer MPs, William Hakewill and James Whitelock, deployed powerful constitutional arguments against the royal right to impose. The customs tariffs were controlled by common law, and, since the common law abhorred uncertainty, were for fixed amounts, changeable only by parliamentary consent. No one disputed the king's prerogative right to close the ports in the national interest. But to argue that the greater right of closure justified the lesser right of imposing in lieu of restraint was 'to sell government, trust and common justice, and most unworthy [of] the divine office of a King'. 'So we see,' argued Whitelock, 'that the power of imposing and power of making law are *convertibilia et coincidentia* and whatsoever can do the one can do the other.' An unrestricted power to impose, he argued, would spell the death of parliaments.

Some also feared that the legislative authority of parliament was under threat from another source: from proclamations. According to a House of Commons petition of grievances of 7 July 1610, which also condemned impositions and abuses in the Court of High Commission and the Council of the Marches and Wales, 'there is a general fear . . . that proclamations will . . . increase to the strength and nature of laws'. No one had, of course, challenged the supremacy of statute, but what was feared was not so much that proclamations might contradict existing statutes, as that they might, for example, be used 'shortly after a session of Parliament for matter directly rejected in the same session'. Not even the pronouncement of the two lord chief justices that proclamations were neither common law, statute law nor custom could completely dispel such fears.

One issue on which parliament could plausibly represent itself as successfully challenging royal innovation relates to the king's heartfelt desire to bring about the union of his realms of England and Scotland, which was not to be achieved for another century. To the modern observer it is far too easy to contrast the fearful resistance to change which prevailed in parliament with James's far-sighted and imaginative plans, whose success might have brought, in his own words, 'Peace, Plenty, Love, free Intercourse and common Societie of his two great Nations'. There is an element of truth in this, but it is no more than a half-truth. For there can be little doubt that here, as in so much else, the king's main interest lay in his own self-glorification. Even when all due allowance is made for the conventions of a very different age from our own, there is an unattractive arrogance about James's assumption that the case for union followed naturally and unchallengeably from his occupancy of both thrones, which had removed 'that partition wall which by God's providence in my blood is rent asunder'. But many MPs saw things differently, and it is not difficult to appreciate their misgivings. What would become of the cherished liberties of Englishmen? Would they survive the absorption of England into Great Britain, a name which James included in his royal style in October 1604 after parliament had rejected it? Such questions reflected very real fears and were not simply obstructive rhetoric.

Moreover, while James was ultimately to opt, *faute de mieux*, for something less than complete or 'perfect' union, this was, if anything, even less attractive to critics of the proposals, since such a scheme would appear to confer the maximum benefits on the inhabitants of the poorer country in return for the minimum of liabilities in terms of taxation and other obligations. In some ways the crux of the matter lay in the proposals which were made by *ad hoc* commissioners of both kingdoms about naturalization. They suggested that all Scots born after James's accession to the English throne in 1603 (the so-called *post-nati*) were also English subjects as a matter of common law, and that a statute should be passed to confer English nationality on those born earlier (*ante-nati*). Reciprocal benefits were to apply to Englishmen, but this was hardly the point. The rich pastures of England, complained Nicholas Fuller, in an apt and telling metaphor used in a speech in the House of Commons on 14 February 1607, would be invaded by lean and hungry Scottish cattle, while their English equivalents would find few attractions in the reciprocal Scottish facilities extended to them. Negotiations had already dragged on for almost three years, and James displayed impatience with such objections to what he now affected to see as a reasonable compromise which should prove to be a significant step on the way to that perfect union which he had previously espoused, but which he was now prepared to admit might have been premature; like putting a couple, whose marriage was proposed, to bed without 'mutual Sight and Acquaintance of . . . one with another'. But to many Englishmen the increased sight of, and acquaintance with, the Scots, which had resulted from the incursions of the despised blue-caps, as they were called, following James's accession, had if anything increased rather than mitigated the contempt and hostility with which they regarded their northern neighbours. James may have derived satisfaction from the decision of an English court that a Scottish *post-natus* born in 1605 was also an English subject, but, on balance, victory went to parliament on the issue of Anglo-Scottish union, just as it had gone to the crown in the matter of the impositions which it continued to levy despite parliamentary protests.[22]

In each of these cases, however, it was royal rather than parliamentary innovation that was at issue. By contrast, one case where it can plausibly be argued that parliament was aggressively challenging royal policies and the Elizabethan settlement itself lay in the sphere of economic policy. This was the attack which was made on the privileges of some of the chartered companies in foreign trade in the House of Commons in 1604. This was to some extent a logical extension of the successful anti-monopoly campaign in Elizabeth I's last parliament in 1601, though monopolies were to spring up again under James I. The fact that parliament was now attacking trading companies as well as domestic patentees was a potent factor cementing the different elements of the London concessionary interest; at least until the later 1620s, when parliamentary attitudes were to change significantly, along with the degree of support which such concessionaires could expect from the government. This is not to deny that there were many matters on which the interest of different varieties of concessionaires were conflicting rather than complementary. For instance, there were numerous complaints from the chartered companies against both the customs farmers for their exactions and domestic monopolists for their import restrictions. The companies also complained against each other. The Levant Company, which imported currants, objected, for instance, to the Merchant Adventurers' importation of currants from the Low Countries, brought there by the Dutch in competition with the Levant Company. Nevertheless, faced with the fierce attacks mounted in the parliaments of 1601 and 1604, it behoved concessionaires to sink their own differences in face of a far greater menace from without.

At first sight it might seem as if the attacks on the companies – and the Merchant Adventurers and Muscovy companies were singled out for particular blame, while some of the other companies got off scot-free – were unavailing. The Merchant Adventurers survived a particularly savage attack without having to make concessions such as widening their membership, while attempts to prevent the re-formation of the Levant Company, which had gone into liquidation at the end of the previous reign, were unsuccessful. However, the fact that the Levant Company's new charter of 1605 was relatively liberal as to qualifications for membership and size of entry-fines may owe something to its sponsors' awareness of the need to placate the parliamentary free traders, representing, in great measure, outport, as distinct from metropolitan, interests. It can be argued with force that this was only a minor gain for the so-called free-traders, when set against a succession of defeats in their attacks on other companies. But they had something more spectacular to show for their efforts in the sphere of Anglo-Spanish trade, which was to expand spectacularly following the peace of 1604 (see below, pp. 356–7). Here the combined mercantile, fishing and landowning grain-exporting interests of the southwest prevailed over the London interests who were attempting to resuscitate the Elizabethan Spanish Company, which had gone into liquidation in consequence of the war.[23] In 1606 an act was passed for free trade with France and the Iberian peninsula. In the case of trade with France, the free trade victory was not to endure for more than three years, for a London-dominated French Company received a charter from the crown in 1609. In Spain, however, it was to be permanent. But this apart, the inroads made into that part of the Elizabethan economic settlement which was characterized by a close alliance between government and chartered companies were very slight. Indeed this alliance was to survive not only a change of dynasty in 1603, but a change of regime at Westminster in 1642.

RELIGION AND REFORMATION

A good case can be made for the view that the disintegration of the Elizabethan religious settlement had begun before the

1590s; that it was the joint product of the admittedly unsuccessful Presbyterian challenge to the episcopalian organization of the church, and of the energetic response of Archbishop Whitgift and his bishops to that challenge. One somewhat extremist response to the notion of Presbyterianism by divine right was the idea of episcopacy by divine right, a notion which later was to be favoured by Charles I, but was detested by his father, who rightly saw it as a challenge to his own ecclesiastical supremacy. But at the moment, this was a small cloud on the Puritan horizon, unlike the persecution by Whitgift and his episcopal colleagues of almost every variety of non-conformity. Yet mainstream Puritanism remained episcopalian, even though not all Puritan opinions at the accession of James I were so moderate as those expressed in the so-called Millenary Petition which was presented to the king in 1603, and whose authors were at pains to emphasize that they were neither anti-episcopalian, 'affecting a popular parity in the Church, nor schismatics aiming at the dissolution of the state ecclesiastical'; nor as those held by the Puritans at the conference called by the king at Hampton Court at the beginning of 1604. These put forward a moderate programme of reform in the mainstream Puritan tradition. They looked for the reform of pluralism and clerical ignorance, the improvement of clerical remuneration, the abolition of 'popish' ceremonies and garments such as the surplice, and the reform of the liturgy, all within the context of the Book of Common Prayer and an episcopalian ecclesiastical polity. Was there not some hope that the new king from Calvinist Scotland, with his known interest in Calvinist theology, might have some sympathy with such a programme of moderate reform?

Whoever bears the responsibility for the failure of the Hampton Court conference, it is difficult to escape the conclusion that a marvellous opportunity was lost. Professor Mark Curtis has argued with some force that James was far more sympathetic to the moderate Puritan demands than generations of historians, misled by the biased contemporary account by William Barlow, dean of Chester, have given him credit for.[24] In Curtis's view it was not so much that the conference itself failed as that the episcopate failed to implement its recommendations on matters such as pluralism and non-residence, the encouragement of preaching, the modification of the Catechism and the abuses of excommunication. However, in correcting a long-standing bias Professor Curtis may perhaps have swung a little too far in the opposite direction, discounting for example the king's own account, in a private letter to a friend, of how he had trounced the Puritan divines at Hampton Court. And whatever else failed at Hampton Court, generations of English men and women have had occasion to be thankful for one product of agreement there: that imperishable contribution to English worship and literature, the Authorized Version of the Bible.

The villains of Professor Curtis's piece are the bishops, not all of whom, however, were totally unsympathetic to the moderate Puritan point of view. Some indeed looked forward with enthusiasm to the revival of that process of Protestant reformation in which their early Elizabethan predecessors had played so important a part. Such a man was Matthew Hutton, archbishop of York at the beginning of the reign. But both Whitgift and Richard Bancroft, who succeeded Whitgift at Canterbury in 1604, were emphatically not cast in this mould.[25] Bancroft was responsible for the formulation of new canons in 1604 which established a coherent body of regulations for the government and discipline of the church, and for continuing and intensifying that drive for conformity which had been the most notable feature of the rule of his predecessor. Those parsons who refused to conform were, in the last resort, deprived. In addition the thirty-sixth of his new canons required subscription at the time of ordination or institution to a stiffened version of the Three Articles which had been issued by Whitgift in 1583, and which asserted, among other things, that there was nothing contrary to the word of God in the Book of Common Prayer and all of the Thirty-Nine Articles. Although Bancroft's modern biographer, Dr Babbage, insists that only about ninety cross-grained and intransigent parsons were deprived, and that some were later reinstated on promising to conform in future, this did not prevent the deprivation of the ministers becoming one of the most contentious issues in parliament; accompanied by attacks against the new canons, which produced bills which got no further than the lower house in 1604 and 1610.

Additional point was given to the problem of the deprived clergymen by the agitation against pluralism and non-residence. Francis Bacon's famous argument that 'to desire that every parish should be furnished with a sufficient preacher and to desire that pluralities be forthwith taken away is to desire things contrary' lost much of its force when so many of the deprived parsons were 'sufficient' men in both the Baconian and the Puritan sense; learned and educated men as distinct from 'dumb dogs'. Thus, as Dr Babbage shows, nine of the fourteen clergymen deprived in the diocese of London, seven out of the nine in that of Lincoln, and five out of the eight in that of Norwich, had university degrees, and some of them higher degrees. In these circumstances it is hardly surprising that complaints against pluralism, non-residence and deprivation of ministers often went hand-in-hand, as they did in a petition of the House of Commons in April 1610. Three years earlier a bill against pluralism and non-residence had successfully passed through the House of Commons, but failed to negotiate the upper house, where, of course, the bishops had seats.

The House of Commons was not the only forum for criticism of Bancroft's policies. The prominence of lawyer MPs such as Hakewill and Whitelock in the opposition to royal prerogative exactions has already been noted. One opportunity for Puritan and legal opposition to come together was afforded by the conflict between secular and ecclesiastical courts, the latter, of course, being manned not by common but by civil lawyers, with their very different legal training and traditions.[26] The main point of contention was the issue by common law courts, such as King's Bench and Common Pleas, of writs of Prohibition. These writs called cases out of ecclesiastical courts on the ground that the nature of the cases in question demanded a hearing in a common law, as distinct from an ecclesiastical, court. One of the most cogent objections of Bancroft to this practice, which he explained in a schedule of 1605, dubbed by his great antagonist, the common lawyer Sir Edward Coke, the *Articuli Cleri*, was that the common law courts were in effect acting as judges in their own cause in such matters of disputed jurisdiction. Bancroft recommended that the king should arbitrate in such matters, and even that on occasions James should dispense justice himself, both of which suggestions horrified Coke. It was not until Coke's dismissal from the post of chief justice of the King's Bench in 1616, though over a quite different matter, that the flow of Prohibitions, which were never again to be so numerous as they had been during the previous decade, fell sharply off.

Dr B. P. Levack has estimated that more than three-quarters of the Prohibitions issued related to impropriations. Impropriations were former ecclesiastical revenues, such as tithes, which, for one reason or other, had come into the hands of laymen; as distinct from appropriations, where they were in the hands of clerics, though not of those exercising cure of souls in the parishes to which they appertained. Bancroft's predecessor, Archbishop Whitgift, had estimated that the church lost about £100,000 a year through impropriations. Now while Bancroft's Puritan critics advocated an increase in the stipends of resident clergymen through the surrender by the hierarchy of their appropriated tithes, Bancroft himself sought to achieve a similar aim by urging the need to restore lay impropriations to their original spiritual uses. He averred that he would have been only too happy to see the abolition of pluralism and non-residence, provided that the stipend attached to each benefice could be increased to an appropriate level. He rightly bewailed the manifest unfairness of the unsuccessful anti-pluralism bill of 1610, which sought to forbid parsons to receive tithes from more than one benefice, while imposing no such restrictions on lay impropriators. Bancroft also sought to jack up the real value of those tithes which were still in clerical hands and which had palpably failed to maintain their real value in face of inflation, especially in cases where tithe payments in hand had been commuted for a *modus decimandi*, or money composition. Civil lawyers and ecclesiastical courts not surprisingly tended to favour clerical attempts to revert to receiving tithes in kind. Since the common law courts did not necessarily take the same view, such cases in the spiritual courts naturally occasioned the frequent use of writs of Prohibition calling cases from the spiritual courts. It was matters such as these which helped to give a particularly sharp edge to the disputes between Bancroft and Coke.

Archbishop Bancroft is remembered by history as much for his work as a great ecclesiastical and administrative reformer as for his continuation and intensification of Whitgift's assault on the nonconformists. Indeed, as an administrative reformer his efforts were attended with greater success than those of his great counterpart in the secular field, Salisbury. In a speech made in 1610 in the House of Lords during what was to be the last year of his life, Bancroft adumbrated some of the main reforms for which he was striving, and in some of which he had already achieved more than a modest degree of success. They included the improvement of the yield of tithes, and in certain cases the substitution of tithes in kind for cash payments; the transfer of as many impropriations as possible from the lay owners, for which he suggested that parliament might consider making a grant; episcopal augmentations of clerical stipends when no other supplementation was available; the restoration of glebe (viz. parsonage) land and the prohibition of its alienation in the future; measures against simoniacal contracts between lay patrons and clerical incumbents; and, finally, a sort of rational, enlightened pluralism which anticipated the practice of our own time whereby adjacent parishes were combined under the cure of a single parson.

If Bancroft's success was only partial, this should not be surprising. His policies, like Laud's after him, ran counter to many powerful interests which were themselves the beneficiaries of the abuses and anomalies which he wished to remedy. Among them were bishops, deans and chapters and colleges at the two universities, and not least, lay impropriators, all of them loaded with the revenues which were needed if Bancroft's reforms were to come to full fruition. Since he was sixty-six when he died in 1610, a good age by contemporary standards, it would obviously be wrong to regard his uncompleted achievement as that of an able reformer cut short in his prime. It was rather that of one who battled against impossibly heavy odds: against idealistic Puritans and self-interested elements, who at times made odd but very effective partners. But the long primacy of Bancroft's successor, George Abbot, bishop of London, a surprise choice as Primate, was to see a significant change of archiepiscopal direction. As an old-fashioned, strongly Calvinist churchman, with more than a sneaking sympathy for Puritan moderates, Abbot slackened the drive to conformity. As one who valued the good will of his gentry and aristocratic associates and neighbours more than the need to improve the economic position of the church, he also slackened the drive to recover impropriated revenues for the church. As an unenergetic, easygoing man, he let fall the reins of thoroughgoing administrative reorganization and reform, which were not to be taken up again until he was succeeded by William Laud in 1633.

The opening years of the reign of James I saw two desperate Catholic plots against the king, the Bye Plot of 1603 and the Gunpowder Plot of 1605. Both were the product of frustration and disappointment at the failure of the accession of the son of the Catholic Mary Stuart to bring any alleviation of their position, supplemented in the case of the Gunpowder plotters by a sense of isolation as a result of having been betrayed by the Spaniards, who had made peace in 1604, apparently without attempting to secure better conditions for their English co-religionists. Each plot was the work of a small and desperate minority. At the heart of the Bye Plot was the disappointed secular priest, William Watson, who had backed James's succession against the Jesuit-backed Infanta, and had been discredited by its failure to yield any of the promised fruit for the Catholics. The Gunpowder plotters, Robert Catesby, Sir Everard Digby, Francis Tresham, Guy Fawkes and their associates were wild extremists, and, as Lord Salisbury was at pains to point out, no less desperate in their economic fortunes than in their religious outlook. Some of these 'Gentlemen spent in their Fortunes . . . and fit for all Alterations' had also participated in that other futile revolt of desperate men, the Essex Revolt of 1601. The Gunpowder Plot was, in Professor Bossy's words, 'the last fling of the Elizabethan tradition of a politically engaged Catholicism'.[27] The plotters were the direct successors of the northern earls, and of Throckmorton and Babington. To most Catholics they were a menace whose activities brought undeserved retribution on the king's peaceable and law-abiding Catholic subjects.

The smell of gunpowder lingered in the air for a long time after 1605, and there was a reinforcement of that anti-Catholic xenophobia born of deeply seated fears which the plot had seemed to corroborate.[28] One product of this situation was more severe enforcement of the recusancy laws. Another was the introduction in 1606 of an oath of allegiance to be administered to all Catholics below the nobility. By making Catholics renounce the doctrine that they could depose or even murder rulers who had been excommunicated and deposed by the pope, the oath was conceived as a device to distinguish what the government regarded as loyal Catholic sheep from potentially seditious

Catholic goats. As the king himself was to emphasize in his treatise *An Apology for the Oath of Allegiance* (1608), the oath touched only civil matters and did not extend to spiritual considerations. This did not mean that those who took the oath – who included, surprisingly, the Jesuit Arch-priest, George Blackwell, and Thomas Preston, the leader of the Benedictine mission newly come to England – were accorded lenient treatment in respect of the recusancy laws; simply that those who refused to take it were guilty of sedition. It was not until the closing years of the reign that the application of the recusancy laws was to be relaxed, as part of James's bid to obtain Spanish support for the restoration of the Palatinate to his son-in-law.

Chapter Seven

FACTIONS, FAVOURITES AND PARLIAMENTS, 1612–29

(I) THE HOWARD ASCENDANCY, 1612–18

THE ACHIEVEMENT OF POWER 1612–14

In the period following Salisbury's death in 1612 there were three main, though admittedly rather fluid, factions at court and at the council table: first, and least important, a group of francophile Scottish noblemen chief among whom were the duke of Lennox, Lord Hay and Lord Fenton, who favoured close relations with France and a French marriage for the prince of Wales; secondly, a pro-Spanish, largely crypto-Catholic group dominated by the Howard family and led by the earl of Northampton, who favoured a Spanish match for the prince; and thirdly a strongly anti-Howard group, some of whom favoured a militantly Protestant foreign policy. The most important figures in this group were Archbishop Abbot, Lord Chancellor Egerton (later ennobled as Lord Ellesmere), the earl of Pembroke, Lord Zouch and the chancellor of the Exchequer, Sir Julius Caesar. Unlike the Howards, most of the group seem to have favoured the calling of a parliament which would almost certainly look upon their policies with favour and execrate those of their rivals. On its fringe stood Sir Thomas Overbury, a crucially important figure on account of his influence over the favourite Rochester. Associated with Overbury was Sir Henry Neville, who had been an Essexian in 1601 and was a former ambassador to France. Neville had played an important role in opposition to some of the government's designs in the last parliament, and it was hoped that he would use his influence to sweeten the next.

In the filling of the offices made vacant by Salisbury's death, the king showed his concern to preserve factional balance. Rather than appoint Neville, the anti-Howard faction's candidate, whom he anyway distrusted, as secretary of state, James announced that for the time being he would be his own secretary. Sir George Carew, who became master of the Court of Wards, was not associated with any faction, and when he died at the end of 1612 the king appointed Salisbury's old client, Sir Walter Cope, now a lone figure of no political factional associations and virtually the only apologist for his former patron after his death. There was to be no question of the mastership becoming an object of factional struggle, as it had been in the time of the Cecil-Essex rivalry. Salisbury was to have no immediate successor in the most important of all his offices, that of lord treasurer, as the Treasury was put into commission. Prominent among the treasury commissioners were Northampton, Suffolk and Wotton from the Howard faction and Caesar and Zouch from the anti-Howard group. But of these Northampton was to be much the most important, and his undeniably unattractive personal qualities have until recently blinded historians to his energy and ability as an administrative reformer.[1] Nevertheless, taken as a whole, the work of the Treasury Commission can hardly be described as impressive. A report which it produced in 1613 showed that, despite extensive land sales, royal and courtly extravagance had caused the debt to rise to the alarming level of around £500,000 from the £280,000 to which it had been reduced by 1610.

Northampton might dominate the Treasury Commission, but a serious obstacle in the way of securing the ascendancy of his faction was the association of the favourite with Sir Thomas Overbury. One possible way out of the difficulty was to exploit the amorous relationship between Rochester and the countess of Essex, the former Lady Frances Howard, daughter of the earl of Suffolk. Overbury had formerly been of assistance to his friend in this affair. However, it was one thing to compose amatory verse and elegant *billets doux* with the agreeable object of prostituting the daughter of one's political opponent; quite another to contemplate the proposed annulment of the countess's marriage and her remarriage to Rochester. Overbury not unnaturally took alarm, for he quite correctly deduced that such a marriage would spell the extinction of his influence over Rochester, as the favourite moved into the Howard family connnection.

That to some members of that connection the matter extended beyond the extinction of Overbury's influence to the extinction of Overbury himself suggests that he knew far too much about the countess's relations both with the favourite and with her husband, the son of the Elizabethan rebel, including perhaps, as was later rumoured, her administering drugs to Essex to render him impotent. While there is no reason to suspect that Rochester had any hand in the course of events which resulted in Overbury's committal to the Tower on 21 April 1613 for refusing to accept a diplomatic appointment abroad, there can be no doubt that it was convenient to the favourite to have him safely out of the way. And Rochester's convenience was his mistress's opportunity. Whatever the degree of culpability attaching to Rochester, Suffolk and Northampton for the situation which led to Overbury's murder in the Tower, the guilt of the countess is not in doubt.

With Overbury out of the way, the plan to annul the Essex marriage went forward, though not altogether smoothly. A prime difficulty was the resolute opposition of the Primate on the commission appointed to examine the matter. How far Abbot was moved by moral scruples in risking the displeasure of both king and favourite and how far by his awareness of the political disadvantage which would follow from Rochester's subsequent marriage into the rival connection at court is a moot point. Conceivably both moral scruples and political advantage for once pointed in the same direction. At all events an enlarged commission ultimately granted the annulment on the grounds of the impossibility of consummating the Essexes' marriage. The countess quickly regularized her relations with the favourite (now raised to be earl of Somerset to make him of equal rank with his bride) in a spectacular and, to some, profoundly shocking wedding, at which she wore her hair long as emblem of a virginity which it was common court knowledge that she had long ago lost.

Overbury's removal had lost Sir Henry Neville one powerful advocate in his candidacy for the office of secretary of state; his other advocate who also died in 1612, at the age of eighteen, was Henry, prince of Wales. The king had long tired of the chores of office, and the appointment went in 1614 to the English ambassador at the Hague, Sir Ralph Winwood, a staunchly Protestant and anti-Howard partisan. However, factional balance was preserved by assigning some of the secretary's duties to the Howard client, Sir Thomas Lake. Winwood was immediately plunged into a situation for which he was ill-equipped, but for which Neville had had almost unique qualifications: grappling with one of the most contentious and futile of Stuart parliaments, which royal financial difficulties had made it necessary to call, though in the event it was to contribute nothing to their solution.

THE ADDLED PARLIAMENT AND ITS AFTERMATH, 1614–15

For a parliament which turned out to be so devoid of positive achievement, the aptly named Addled Parliament seems to have been preceded by some surprisingly well thought out schemes designed to secure its success.[2] One of these was Bacon's plan to win over potential troublemakers by offers of preferment, a procedure which was to be employed in a number of cases in later years.[3] Another was Neville's scheme of 'undertaking' to win over such persons and others with the aid of a programme of judicious concessions. One product of the temporary rapprochement in the months before parliament assembled on 5 April 1614 between the earls of Suffolk and Pembroke may well have been that Suffolk became privy to the anti-Howard faction's schemes to adopt Neville's 'undertaking' proposals as a means of managing parliament. Such schemes were anyway frustrated by Neville's failure to obtain office, but in the hands of the Howards and their following, and especially of the earl of Northampton, rumours were skilfully spread which distorted them into alleged attempts to tamper with elections to secure a compliant parliament. The ensuing agitation against 'undertakers' was a prime factor hindering the House of Commons from getting down to the king's business. This suited the Howards' book perfectly, since it resulted in the growing impatience of the king with parliament and his eventual dissolution of it on 7 June, only nine weeks after it had first assembled.

But it was not simply the Commons' dilatoriness which infuriated the king. In addition, there were more positively hostile acts: the expulsion from the House of the privy councillor, Sir Thomas Parry, chancellor of the Duchy of Lancaster, a victim of the rumours about 'undertakers'; further attacks on royal impositions; the relentless pursuit of Bishop Neile, who had argued against a conference between the two Houses on the grounds that it would force the peers to listen to 'undutiful and seditious speeches unfit for us to hear'; and, finally, the attacks on court corruption and favourites, whom Christopher Neville, the son of Lord Bergavenny and no relation of Sir Henry Neville, described provocatively as 'spaniels to the king and wolves to the people'. Another MP, John Hoskyns, attacked the Scots, among whom, of course, the favourite *par excellence* was numbered, in a speech in which he made ominous and inflammatory reference to the Sicilian

Vespers, and which landed him in gaol after the parliament had been dissolved.

The facts that Hoskyns was a client of the earl of Northampton, and that one of the most vociferous opponents of impositions, Sir Edwin Sandys, had been found a seat through the agency of the naval treasurer, Sir Thomas Mansell, himself the client of another Howard, Lord Admiral Nottingham, are suggestive. It may well be that the Howards, having reluctantly decided that parliament would have to be called on account of the appalling state of the royal finances, resolved to make the best of a bad job by conspiring to ruin it so spectacularly that it was unlikely to be called again for a very long time. This end might be achieved by securing the election of persons who would be inclined to make trouble and affording them every encouragement to pursue contentious lines of action which would probably shorten parliament's life. Whatever the truth of the matter, there is no disputing the fact that the dissolution of the Addled Parliament was a triumph for the Howard earls of Northampton and Suffolk.

The dissolution marks the apogee of Howard fortunes at court. The Treasury Commission was shortly dissolved, and Northampton undoubtedly could have had the office of lord treasurer for the asking, but he died within a week of the dissolution of parliament, and the regime was deprived of his unquestionable administrative ability. Instead his nephew Suffolk, a very different character, became lord treasurer. One of Suffolk's sons-in-law, Lord Knollys, became treasurer of the royal Household and master of the Court of Wards, and another, the favourite, Somerset, was lord chamberlain. Admittedly the strongly Protestant and anti-Howard Winwood remained secretary of state, but from the beginning he had been viewed as a '*secretarius ordinarius*', and it was Somerset – and through him the Howards – who had the effective ear of the king.

Suffolk's administration of the royal finances was in every way disastrous, and not simply on account of his own laxity and inefficiency. In addition there was the peculation of his wife and her creature, Suffolk's auditor of the Exchequer Sir John Bingley, and probably that of the treasurer himself, which contributed *inter alia* to the cost of building his prodigiously expensive palace at Audley End, as Salisbury's practice had helped build Hatfield. But Salisbury at least had striven for some notable financial reforms. Under Suffolk the annual ordinary deficit reached the horrifying figure of £160,000. Although there were some increases of revenue, in expenditure profligacy reigned, and there was no obstacle to the disastrous rake's progress of king, favourite and court. With Somerset as lord chamberlain and Lord Hay, no Howard partisan but a byword for extravagance even in a Jacobean context, as master of the Wardrobe, courtly propensities to consume conspicuously were at their most lavish and given full scope by the regime at the Treasury. In this unpromising context there was hardly any scope for the well-meant reforming aspirations of such an honest and experienced Elizabethan administrator as Sir Fulke Greville, who, after a decade in the wilderness under Salisbury's regime, replaced Sir Julius Caesar (promoted to master of the Rolls) as Suffolk's chancellor of the Exchequer. That this former friend of Sir Philip Sidney and proponent of a Protestant foreign policy should consent to serve under a pro-Catholic, pro-Spanish Howard lord treasurer speaks volumes for the way in which the appetite for preferment could dull even the strongest ideological objections in early Stuart England. Nor was there scope enough for the exercise of the talents of Northampton's business expert and administrative reformer, Sir Lionel Cranfield, who before long was to move into the anti-Howard camp, where they were better appreciated. The post-Addled-Parliament, Howard-dominated regime took its tone from a very different sort of person: the disreputable Bingley at the Exchequer, and the hardly less disreputable Sir Arthur Ingram and Sir William Cockayne in the City.

Bingley's extortions, bribe-taking and diversion of royal

revenue into private uses were to become the occasion of public scandal which shocked even hardbitten Jacobean statesmen. Ingram and Cockayne were respectively the authors of two destructive economic projects with which the Howard regime became involved. Ingram himself seems to have done well out of his schemes for the royal production of alum at Whitby between 1613 and 1615, and thereafter for the farming out of the enterprise to himself and two partners. But investigation in 1618 was to reveal that over the whole period of its involvement the crown had received only about £5,000 on an investment of £67,700.[4] The main losers from Cockayne's project were far more widely dispersed and less exalted interests: cloth exporters and manufacturers and all those many occupational groups whose prosperity was bound up in one way or another with that of England's premier manufacture. Under the guise of a project to export fully finished, instead of unfinished cloth, the main aim of the projectors seems rather to have been to take over the Merchant Adventurers' lucrative monopoly of the export of unfinished cloth to the Netherlands and northwestern Germany.[5] The project was propounded in 1614, and in the following year a new company was formed by the projectors and given a royal charter under the significant title of the King's Merchant Adventurers; significant because it was licensed to export *unfinished* cloth, though with a progressively increased quota of finished cloth in each of the three subsequent years. The new company failed to meet its obligations or even to export anything approaching the volume of unfinished cloth that its predecessor had done. The result was a disastrous slump and a serious shock to the alliance between crown and Merchant Adventurers which had been a central feature of royal economic policy since the opening year of the previous reign.

THE END OF THE HOWARD ASCENDANCY, 1615–18

The business of bringing down the Howards was long drawn out, and began at least three years before Suffolk was dismissed as lord treasurer in July 1618. The first important phase was a two-pronged attack on Somerset's position as royal favourite: first by insinuating into the king's favour another handsome young man, who, it was hoped, would be amenable to control by the Howards' opponents; and secondly – the work especially of Secretary Winwood – by instituting an investigation into the mysterious circumstances surrounding the death of Sir Thomas Overbury in the Tower in 1613. An account written by Archbishop Abbot more than a decade after the event tells the story of the ruthless and determined way in which he and his colleagues achieved the first of these objectives: by obtaining the originally reluctant support of James's queen for their bid to oust Somerset, whom she loathed, from the king's affections, in favour of their candidate, George Villiers.[6] Villiers was successfully launched, knighted and admitted a Gentleman of the royal Bedchamber in 1615, made a viscount in the following year, earl of Buckingham in 1617, a marquis in 1618, and finally a duke, the first in England since Norfolk's execution in 1572, in 1623. The queen had warned Abbot that he and his associates would live to regret their plot, and she spoke prophetically. For while Somerset had proved amenable to almost every crack of the Howard whip – at least once Overbury had been put out of the way – Villiers was to be less obliging to his sponsors. No marionette content to be manipulated by the anti-Howard magnates, he was shortly to strike out on his own, and his rise signifies not so much the ascendancy of a court faction as a unique and unparalleled personal hegemony.

As to the second objective of the anti-Somerset drive, the increasing shift in the king's affections away from Somerset and towards Villiers made it easier for him to bear the revelations about the favourite's role – or more correctly his wife's – in the murder of Overbury and their subsequent trial, conviction and banishment from court in 1615. In the face of such revelations it is hard to see how James could continue to extend his favour to Somerset, but, without

Villiers to console him, Somerset's fall might well have recoiled on those who planned it. As it was, it was only the first step in the plan to bring down the Howards, whose position at court might be more vulnerable than it had been, but was still a position of strength from which a formidable counter-attack might be launched. In so far as such a counter-attack may be said to have materialized, it was a mirror-image of the tactics of the Howards' opponents. It was not, however, until February 1618, when the Howard prospects were beginning to look desperate, that a Howard young hopeful was launched on the scene in hope of weaning the king's affection from Buckingham. This was William Monson, a nephew of the Sir Thomas Monson, master of the Armoury in the Tower, who himself had been implicated in the Overbury murder and had been lucky to escape scot-free. It was reported that Lady Suffolk took enormous pains with young Monson, 'tricking and pranking him up, besides washing his face every day with posset-curd'. But it was all to no effect, for James was too hopelessly infatuated with Buckingham, and Monson was ordered to forbear the royal presence.

The other element in the Howards' counter-strategy began earlier and lasted longer, but once again was a direct attempt to go one better than their opponents. Given the rapid deterioration of the royal finances after 1614, Howard incompetence had been an obvious target for the opposing faction, in whose campaign for economical reform Sir Lionel Cranfield, who had once been Northampton's financial adviser and efficiency expert but had moved into the rival camp after Northampton's death, was a crucially important figure. Amongst other things, Cranfield advanced proposals for thoroughgoing tariff reform and the enforcement of the so-called Statutes of Employment whereby alien importers would be compelled to employ some or all of their proceeds in the purchase of English wares. In addition, his sustained, informed and ultimately unanswerable arguments against the Cockayne projectors were an important factor in putting an end to this Howard-backed racket and restoring Cranfield's old company, the Merchant Adventurers, to its former privileges in January 1617. In his proposals for economical reform Cranfield took care not to alienate the king and his new favourite by blaming royal extravagance for the problem, choosing rather to stress the inefficiency and corruption in the royal service presided over by the Howards. It was this rising clamour for economical and administrative reform that the Howards endeavoured to counter with their own schemes to cut, as they hoped, the ground from under their opponents' feet, using their own efficiency expert, Sir Arthur Ingram, against their opponents' Cranfield. But the appointment of Ingram as cofferer of the royal Household, early in 1615, was foiled by the resultant outburst of gentlemanly outrage on the part of Household officials at the prospect of serving under 'such a scandalous fellow'. There was something approaching a strike in the Household and Ingram had to go. What the protesters feared most were the economical reforms which he would have effected. In future, Suffolk had to content himself with using Ingram in an advisory capacity, though few of his sensible proposals for reform made later in 1615 were put into effect.[7]

It would, however, be wrong to give the impression that the anti-Howard strategy met with complete success all the way along the line. One stratagem which failed dismally was the scheme, favoured by Pembroke and pushed particularly hard by the strongly anti-Spanish secretary of state Sir Ralph Winwood, to obtain the release of Sir Walter Raleigh from the Tower to mount an expedition to search for precious metals in the Orinoco region. When it was reported in 1618 both that the expedition had failed to discover the hoped-for mine and that it had engaged in armed conflict with the Spaniards, the king, not without reason, saw the whole scheme as a cheap and dangerous device to discredit the pro-Spanish Howards and perhaps to embroil him in conflict with Spain. Following Spanish pressure

Raleigh was executed, under the suspended sentence of 1603, after his return, and if Winwood had not died in October 1617 he would almost certainly have been dismissed for his part in the business. Following his death, he was replaced by a new secretary of strongly Protestant and anti-Howard leanings, Sir Robert Naunton, who was – significant sign of the times – a client of Villiers. Despite the disappointed anti-Spanish expectations, the failure of Raleigh's expedition cannot be counted as a disastrous setback to the anti-Howard forces, since by the time of Raleigh's return to England, power was visibly slipping from the Howards' hands.

It was not simply incompetence and inefficiency which brought the Howards down. The exposure of scandals only less horrific than those which had brought down Somerset in 1615, and notably one form or other of peculation of public money and receipt of bribes, in which Bingley and Lady Suffolk were central figures, and of which the treasurer himself could hardly have been unaware, brought about Suffolk's dismissal in July 1618, and a fine of £30,000 following a trial in Star Chamber in November 1619. Bingley was fined £2,000 and imprisoned. The Treasury was put in commission, and Suffolk's dismissal was followed by the removal of other Howard office-holders including Lord Admiral Nottingham and the master of the Wards, Lord Wallingford (the former Knollys), on the pretext of scandals spread by his wife. The Howard ascendancy was over.

(II) THE HEGEMONY OF BUCKINGHAM: REFORMS AND PARLIAMENTS, 1618–29

REFORM AND THE TREASURY COMMISSION, 1618–20

As was shown earlier, departmental reform was in the air long before the replacement of Lord Treasurer Suffolk by the new Treasury Commission in July 1618. Apart from Sir

Fulke Greville, who despite being Suffolk's chancellor of the Exchequer had never been an out-and-out Howard man, the Commission was packed with members of the anti-Howard faction, including Abbot, Caesar, Naunton and Sir Edward Coke. Coke's judicial independence and intransigence in face of royal pressure had resulted in his dismissal as lord chief justice of the King's Bench in 1616, but he was now working his way back to favour with the aid of Buckingham, and almost certainly had designs on the office of lord treasurer. Francis Bacon, Coke's enemy since the 1590s and now lord chancellor (Ellesmere having died in the previous year), was also on the Commission. But the most active of all the reformers, Sir Lionel Cranfield, was not a member until early in 1619. Cranfield was strongly backed at this point both by Bacon, who had his own plans as lord chancellor for thoroughgoing legal reform, and by Buckingham, who had enthusiastically embraced the cause of reform as a suitable stick with which to beat the Howards.[8] Cranfield was a member of the Privy Council sub-commissions for the Household and the Ordnance Office. In addition he replaced Wallingford as master of the Wards and the profligate Hay as master of the Wardrobe, appointments which set courtly tongues to wag, as they had over Ingram's aborted appointment as cofferer three years earlier.

It must have given particular satisfaction to Sir Fulke Greville, who had lost his place as naval treasurer to the corrupt Howard client, Sir Robert Mansell, in 1603, to find himself a member, along with his erstwhile colleagues on naval matters, John Coke and Sir Thomas Smythe, of the sub-commission for the navy which exposed Mansell's and other malpractices. Mansell was removed in 1618 and was replaced by Sir William Russell, a commercial magnate who bought the office. But the uprooting of Howard influence in the navy went much higher than the treasurer, when the aged Lord Admiral Nottingham himself was replaced by Buckingham; he paid £3,000 for the office to Nottingham, who in addition received a pension of £1,000 per annum from the crown. The naval commissioners' reform plan was not confined to expenditure cuts and weeding out fraud and peculation. In addition there was a programme to build ten much-needed ships and two new dockyards at a cost of £30,000. The naval ordinary charge thereafter ran at a greatly reduced cost of £20,000 per annum.

Mrs Prestwich has calculated that the reforms of the Treasury Commission and associated bodies made an additional £121,700 per annum available to the government. About seventy per cent of this came from reduced expenditure and the remainder from increased revenue, probably from new and rather contentious customs dues. Substantial savings in annual expenditure included about £18,000 in the royal Household; about £20,000 in the Ordnance Office, a notable area of Howard influence ever since the days when it had been presided over by Sir Roger Dallison, who had been dismissed back in 1616; and more than £20,000 in the Wardrobe, where Cranfield was in his element insisting on purchases in the cheapest market and on the nail, and pocketing, by agreement with the king, all savings below an expenditure of £20,000, an arrangement which was later to be brought up against him. But despite these impressive reforms, the royal debt had risen from about £700,000 to about £800,000 by Michaelmas 1619 and was to rise further by a similar sum over the following year. Although the ordinary account was in surplus by more than £40,000, the ordinary revenue of future years had already been anticipated to the extent of £117,000 in 1619. The truth is that *ordinary* savings were more than offset by the alarming growth of *extraordinary* charges, which, as during the later years of Elizabeth I, were to dominate the fiscal scene over the next decade. The savings achieved had been impressive but insufficient, and, moreover, increasingly difficult to augment, for, beyond a certain point, they ran up against the opposition of both king and favourite.

There may be another reason why the achievements of the reformers may not have been so great as appears at first sight. One of the main grievances of parliament in 1621, as in 1597 and 1601, was to be patents of monopoly, and there had undoubtedly been a growth in the number of such patents granted during the previous three years. This raises the question of how far expenditure reduction was achieved via the substitution of perquisites for cash payments in such matters as gifts and stipends. Intimately concerned with sanctioning and approving these new patents were Lord Chancellor Bacon, now Viscount St Albans, and Henry Montagu, Viscount Mandeville, who had succeeded Coke as lord chief justice in 1616 and was made lord treasurer when the Treasury Commission was wound up in November 1620. He paid £20,000 for the office, which he enjoyed for only a few months.[9] To Coke, the appointment of the man who had replaced him at the King's Bench to the office which he now coveted as the next stage in his return to power must have been a great frustration, and his thwarted ambitions were to loom large in the parliament which was shortly to be called.

ECONOMIC AND INTERNATIONAL CRISES AND THE PARLIAMENT OF 1621

The parliament of 1621, the first for seven years, met against a sombre background of economic depression and international conflict.[10] In 1619 the king's son-in-law, the Elector Palatine, had exacerbated what was to be the Thirty Years' War as a result of his rash assumption of the Bohemian crown, to which he had been elected in defiance of tradition and the claims of the Habsburg emperor. In the autumn of 1620 he had been driven from his new kingdom after a humiliating defeat at the so-called battle of the White Mountain. His own hereditary dominion of the Palatine had also been invaded, and he was in danger of being totally dispossessed. The latter threat and the paramount need for the realm to display strength and unity of purpose and for adequate supplies to be voted were undoubtedly the main reasons why parliament was called. And, since, as one MP put it, 'Grievances and supply like twins . . . go hand in hand', hardly less important was the economic dislocation experienced as a result of a general European economic depression; more particularly since many blamed government restraints on economic activity for exacerbating difficulties, and indeed in some cases for being their principal cause. At all events, the cloths exported from London by Englishmen had fallen from 102,332 pieces in 1618 to 85,741 in 1620, and were to fall still further by 1622, the worst year of the depression. Over-abundant harvests in 1619–20 had relieved hardship somewhat by lowering the price of grain but had cut back agricultural purchasing power, while the atrocious harvest of 1621 was to result in rocketing grain prices and severe hardship among artisans without producing much benefit for any but very large-scale farmers. There was widespread textile unemployment, which in the main took the form of drastic reductions in the amount of work put out to domestic artisans by clothiers.[11]

However gloomy the economic and diplomatic outlook, the auguries for harmonious relations between king and parliament were quite good. James was in the happy and unusual position of being able to parade the achievements of a genuinely reforming, if by no means completely united, administration since 1618. Moreover, the two subsidies which were voted very early in the new parliament, however inadequate they might be in terms of the realities of international diplomacy and warfare, were a hopeful sign and it was expected that the king would respond by redressing manifold grievances, which included patents of monopoly, the malpractices of informers and the lax enforcement of the recusancy laws.[12] But, as one MP observed: 'All grievances . . . are trifles, compared with the decay of trade.' Contemporary diagnoses of the causes of the depression were many, and some of them, as the work of Professors Gould and Supple has demonstrated, got a great deal closer to the heart of the matter than used to be admitted by economic historians. The English woollen industry was indeed increasingly confronted by the growth of international textile competition, but this was a long-term factor, existing before and continuing after what was, after all, a short-term depression. One short-term factor of which informed contemporaries were very well aware was the orgy of currency manipulation undertaken by the numerous mints in Germany and Central Europe. Currency enhancement meant that English exporters had to raise their prices if they were to obtain the same sterling equivalent (in terms of precious metals) as previously. But to raise their prices meant a steep diminution in the demand for their products, more especially since – as had been the case with the English debasement of the 1540s – prices of local cloth did not respond immediately to the inflationary stimulus of a depreciated currency.

In the circumstances it was natural that MPs should be highly critical of new burdens on trade such as the pretermitted customs on cloth and the levies imposed by the Merchant Adventurers to meet their expenses and the fine to the crown after Cockayne's Project. It was no less natural that, moved by the sufferings of hungry and desperate textile workers, they should scream for the widening of the channels of export. Thus the parliament of 1621 saw the most violent attack on the restrictive practices of the great chartered companies – and notably the Merchant Adventurers, Levant, Russia and East India companies – since the great free trade debate of 1604. Moreover, there was a significant tendency to lump the companies together with domestic concessionaires such as monopolists and customs farmers, characterizing all of them as metropolitan agencies draining away the lifeblood of the provinces and outports. Concurrently with this, the king's intervention on 3 May to prevent parliamentary scrutiny of the Merchant Adventurers' records was an eloquent reminder of the total dependence of concessionaires on the Crown.[13]

The king might rescue the Merchant Adventurers, but both he and his favourite were inclined to let domestic monopolists and other patentees go to the wall.[14] Patents of monopoly were intensely unpopular; not only the monopolies of economic production, but also the administrative patents, which were bitterly resented by local magistrates whose functions were thereby usurped by this alternative means of centralist control. It was originally in connection with its attack on the most notorious of all monopolists, Sir Giles Mompesson, that parliament took the momentous step of reviving the medieval process of impeachment, that is, the judicial process in which the lower house acts as accuser and the peers as judges. Important though this revival of parliamentary judicature is, however, it is no less important to appreciate its limitations. As Professor Russell has reminded us, its main political significance was as a further medium for the extension of court factional strife on to the parliamentary scene, rather than as an attempt to assert the responsibility of ministers of the crown to parliament.[15] For when the Commons turned their attention from monopolists such as Mompesson and his associate Sir Francis Mitchell to Bacon and Mandeville, who had given advice in their ministerial capacity about patents, their success was severely limited. The king made it clear that, while he would not disallow proceedings against his ministers – any more than against patentees – for misdemeanours or crimes, if their ministerial advice was called in question this would strike at the very roots of ministerial responsibility to the sovereign. So the Commons obediently desisted from their intention of impeaching Bacon as a referee for some of the patents and impeached him on different grounds, for gifts, allegedly in the nature of bribes, which he had received while acting in a judicial capacity as lord chancellor. To Coke and Cranfield the nature of the charge was relatively unimportant, for they sought not to establish the responsibility of ministers to parliament, but to destroy Bacon, who was fined £40,000 and imprisoned during the king's pleasure. The sentence was later mitigated but his career was ruined.

Given the superabundance of Protestant zealotry at Westminster in 1621, the danger that parliament might overstep the mark and trespass on the royal prerogative was perhaps even greater in the field of foreign affairs than it was in that of impeaching ministers.[16] Parliament's initial vote of two subsidies was, of course, hopelessly inadequate to meet the real cost of military preparedness and the mounting of an expeditionary force to relieve the Palatinate. The Commons were not found wanting when it came to grandiose declarations of readiness to assist the king if he chose to go to war over the Palatinate, or to extreme manifestations of Protestant zealotry such as were produced by the indignation against the unfortunate Catholic barrister Edward Floyd, who had made slighting remarks about the Elector and his wife and against whom MPs vied unedifyingly with one another to devise appropriately savage forms of punishment. When it came to providing hard cash, they were a good deal less forward.

It is especially in the events which occurred after the summer recess that historians have depicted parliament as overstepping the mark. The reality was not quite so dramatic as the classic Whig interpretation of this course of events suggests, though it may amount to rather more than is allowed by Professor Conrad Russell, who at all points plays down the argument that the Commons were challenging the royal prerogative. He is certainly correct in emphasizing that the House initially took it upon itself to discuss foreign policy in response to a royal invitation, or even command, to do so, in a speech by Lord Keeper Williams on 21 November. But the fact that the king and parliament were at one in their preparedness to go to war if necessary over the Palatinate must not be taken to imply that parliamentary zealots for a Protestant foreign policy accepted the royal distinction between the interests of the emperor and those of the king of Spain. They were justifiably sceptical about the likelihood of the latter being prevailed upon to bring effective pressure to bear on the former to keep the Palatinate inviolate.

On 29 November parliamentary critics of what indeed looked like an absurdly over-optimistic pro-Spanish policy were to receive encouragement from an unexpected quarter when Buckingham's client, Sir George Goring, proposed that the Commons should petition the crown to declare war on Spain in the event of there being no Spanish response to James's request to cease support for the emperor over the Palatinate. Goring's proposal has been seen as indicating that Buckingham, contrary to the king's wishes, was already playing the virulently anti-Spanish game which was to win him such popular favour in the next parliament. Alternatively it has been suggested that Goring's patron was moved by considerations nearer to those of Northampton in 1614, seeking to provoke the House to action which would both precipitate its dissolution and redound to his own credit in Spain. But Buckingham's latest biographer offers the most satisfactory explanation of the incident, arguing that Goring's motion was designed not to force, but to strengthen, the king's hand by demonstrating to Spain the strength of parliamentary feelings about the Palatinate and the king's crucial role in restraining with great difficulty the bellicose anti-Spanish sentiments of his subjects.[17]

The parliament was ultimately dissolved because MPs went far beyond the terms of Goring's motion. Not only did they voice criticism of royal diplomatic strategy, appealing to nostalgia for Elizabethan days by trumpeting the merits of a diversionary war at sea against Spain coupled with an invasion of the Spanish Netherlands in cooperation with the Dutch, rather than the unpopular and far more expensive expedient of a continental campaign in the Palatinate. In addition such arguments led easily and naturally to criticism in the House, and in a petition to the king, both of the proposed Spanish marriage for the prince and of the leniency being shown in enforcing the recusancy laws in deference to Spain. No wonder the king in an irate letter of 11 December accused the Commons of leaving him no part of his prerogative unviolated save the striking of coin! No doubt in reply to James's quite constitutionally correct assertion that such matters were 'unfit things to be handled in Parliament except your King should require it of you', the Commons might protest that this was exactly what the king had required of them, but their response had gone far beyond the limits of what he deemed appropriate. Moreover their Remonstrance of 18 December went further than this, in its assertion of their freedom to discuss any matter, prerogative or otherwise, even without royal invitation. It may well be that James's further insistence not simply on the nature and limits, but also on the origins, of the parliamentary privilege of freedom of speech as proceeding from his grace not from right, was supererogatory and bound to have the effect of inflaming MPs on a very delicate subject. But there can be no doubt that James firmly believed that, as he put it in his proclamation dissolving parliament on 6 January 1622, the Commons had wasted valuable time in seeking 'the enlarging of the limits of their liberties and divers other curious and unprofitable things'.

LORD TREASURER MIDDLESEX AND HIS ENEMIES, 1621–4

In October 1621, during the parliamentary recess, Mandeville was succeeded as lord treasurer by Cranfield, who had been made a baron the previous July and was to become earl of Middlesex in the following year. When he became treasurer, the royal debt stood in the region of £900,000, with something like £124,000 of future revenue anticipated, in which circumstances the small ordinary surplus was but a tiny drop in the ocean. Successful cooperation with parliament issuing in a substantial grant of subsidies seemed essential, and the royal dissolution of parliament on 6

January 1622 without its vote of subsidies being finalized in a statute must have come as a sad disappointment to the new treasurer. Yet if the cooperation of any future parliament was to be obtained, the impression of continued reform and vigilance against extravagance had to be sustained. In the circumstances it is not surprising that Middlesex, as we must now call Cranfield, was more active in the sphere of expenditure control than in that of revenue improvement, though his term as lord treasurer did see some modest increase in ordinary revenue – from £503,804 to £539,903 per annum – the most important of which came from improvements in the customs revenue, including a net increase of £4,000 in the rents from the now combined great and silk farms from 1621; quite an achievement in a time of deep depression.[18]

The core of Middlesex's policy as lord treasurer consisted in a continued attack on departmental expenditure, but, as Mrs Prestwich has suggested, it was far more difficult for an isolated and vulnerable lord treasurer to put such unpopular policies into effect than it had been in the days of the collective leadership of the Treasury Commission. At any rate, the royal Household and Chamber were spending £11,000 more in 1624 than they had been in 1619. Effective expenditure control was ruled out in the navy now that Buckingham was lord admiral; and in the Wardrobe now that his brother-in-law, the earl of Denbigh, had replaced Cranfield as master. The lord treasurer's plans to institute a rigorous scrutiny of new applications for pensions by making them all pass through him, and even to achieve a temporary suspension of the payment of existing pensions, which were reckoned to cost £74,000 per annum, enjoyed at best only temporary success, coming up against the king's notorious inability to resist suitors. The pensions bill had in fact risen to about £90,000 by 1624.

Events abroad were producing a massive rise in extraordinary expenditure for such matters as extraordinary embassies like those of Lord Digby to Vienna and Madrid, and most of all the madcap expedition of Prince Charles and Buckingham to Spain in 1623 in pursuit of the hand of the Infanta. They spent over £46,000, in addition to £16,000 on jewels and gifts, and the fleet assembled to bring back the Spanish bride cost more than £52,000. It would have been some consolation to the distracted treasurer if Charles and Buckingham had returned with the Infanta, the prospect of a dowry of around £600,000 and the promise of the restitution of the Palatinate without the expense of war. But there was to be no Spanish bride, no dowry, and, above all, no peace. Instead the two knights errant returned smarting against alleged Spanish breaches of promise and real or imagined indignities to which they claimed to have been subjected in Madrid and clamouring for war against Spain.

For Middlesex this must have been the last straw, and, relying on the king's known love of peace, which, in the event, stood the treasurer in very poor stead, he earned the enmity of the prince as well as of his former patron the duke (as Buckingham had now become) for his opposition to their bellicose and expensive policies. Nor was this the only reason why he fell foul of prince and favourite, who had also complained of his tardiness in supplying them with funds when in Spain. Moreover, Buckingham's departure for Spain had been the signal for some intrigues against him both on the part of Southampton, who had been behind the unsuccessful attack made on him by the former attorney general, Yelverton, in the last parliament, and of Pembroke, who detested the upstart favourite and resented his embracing of what looked like the pro-Spanish Howard policies which he had originally been raised to combat. They might have met the approval of Thomas Howard, earl of Arundel, but this embodiment of aristocratic *gravitas*, who regarded himself as the rightful duke of Norfolk, the premier dukedom in England, was alienated by Buckingham's dukedom and also by the new duke's return to England vituperating against all things Spanish, a development which put Arundel alongside Middlesex and Lord

Keeper Williams in the Council.[19] On the other hand, the duke's new-found belligerency may have won over Pembroke, though even he abstained in the vote at the council table in February 1624, when Buckingham tried unsuccessfully to obtain a repudiation of the marriage negotiations with Spain. As to the treasurer, he had even attempted to interest the king in a young male relative of his wife (herself a kinswoman of Buckingham), in the same sort of equally vain hope as the Howards had once entertained of weaning his affections from Buckingham.

It is difficult to judge quite how much credence should be attached to rumours, assiduously fostered by the Spanish ambassador, that Buckingham had fallen out of James's favour, or, if true, whether it mattered very much. For since his return from Spain, it was plain for all to see that the duke was in high favour with the prince, in which circumstances what a later age would describe as a reversionary interest was developing. This fact would certainly give ambitious noblemen such as Pembroke and Southampton second thoughts about opposition to the duke, more particularly when the latter had suddenly assumed an acceptable anti-Spanish stance. As to Middlesex, he was surely doomed, not only for his intrigues against Buckingham and opposition to his policies, but also for his apparent presumption in forgetting that, though now a peer of the realm, he was still the client of the favourite. For what sort of a client was this man, who as lord treasurer showed such a marked disposition to favour the needs of his courtly ally, the duke of Lennox (whose death at the beginning of 1624 was a great blow to the treasurer) and to ignore those of his patron? The jumped-up tradesman had indeed forgotten himself and must be taught a lesson. When the time came, there were numerous other enmities aroused by Middlesex which would come to the fore in the fierce onslaught which was to be launched against him by prince and duke: enmities of courtiers outraged by the attempts of a low-born treasurer to limit the royal bounty at their expense; of landowners horrified by increases in wardship fines; of officials fearful of redundancy or the exposure of corrupt practices; and, not least, of creatures from Middlesex's own natural element, the City, whether customs farmers smarting at being faced by a treasurer who knew all the tricks of their trade, and moreover acted on his knowledge, or suppliers of goods for the court, whose prices were beaten down by an ungentlemanly insistence on competitive tender and buying in the cheapest market. Such were among the animosities which were to come to a head in the parliament called in 1624, one of whose products was the fall of the reforming lord treasurer.

THE PARLIAMENT OF 1624 AND THE END OF JAMES I'S REIGN, 1624–5

The period between the return of the prince and the duke from Spain and the death of James I on 27 March 1625 is often characterized as a time when the king totally lost his grip on affairs, and all, including the favourite, were turning their eyes from the setting to the rising sun. The events of James's last parliament in 1624 saw the king under irresistible pressure to break off the negotiations with Spain which he hoped would result in the restoration of the Palatinate; to sacrifice his reforming lord treasurer, Middlesex, who knew better than anyone else that England was incapable of bearing the cost of war; and to accept the anyway inadequate grant of subsidies on humiliating terms which imposed parliamentary control over their appropriation. The source of their pressure in each case was the alliance between the prince and duke and some of the elements who had been most critical of the latter, and of royal policies, in the previous parliament. It was even rumoured that Charles and Buckingham planned to shut the king up in Theobalds, his Hertfordshire house, while the prince took over the realm, and following James's death allegations were not lacking that the duke had speeded him on his way by the application of noxious plasters and potions.

To repudiate the most absurd of these allegations does not necessarily involve a denial that there were some serious differences of policy and opinion between James and his son and favourite. Nor is the notion of a reversal of political alliances following the return from Spain in serious question. In the apt description of a contemporary, the duke, having failed to persuade the council in February 1624 to repudiate the treaty with Spain, 'fled from the Council of State and disclaimed it for a Parliament by way of an Appeal'. This appeal was made in alliance with strongly anti-Spanish noblemen such as Southampton, Pembroke and Saye and Sele, and a number of their clients and associates in the lower house, such as Sir Robert Phelips, Sir Edwin Sandys, Sir Dudley Digges and Sir Edward Coke. The prince and the duke played not only on their anti-Spanish and strongly Protestant inclinations but on the personal ambitions and hopes of preferment which the new turn of events allowed them to indulge without any sacrifice of principle.

One element in the traditional view of these events which is open to criticism is its representation of Buckingham's reversal from a pro-Spanish policy to an alliance with some of its bitterest opponents as an aberration. For, in terms of the duke's career to date, it was surely the Spanish journey of 1623 and not his subsequent anti-Spanish alliance with Puritan and other parliamentarians that was the aberration. He had, after all, risen to power through the anti-Howard, anti-Spanish faction on the Council, led by Pembroke and Archbishop Abbot, and, while he had long freed himself from its leading-strings, it would be quite wrong to assume that this necessarily involved dissociating himself from its ideology. His patronage of the eminent Puritan divine Dr John Preston, and his care to secure numerous preferments for him, including that of chaplain to the prince himself in 1621, was a further earnest of his inclination and had strengthened the ties between him and militant Protestants such as Lords Saye and Sele, Warwick, Brooke (Fulke Greville) and Sir Richard Knightley.[20] Moreover, it is not impossible that, far from returning to his Protestant senses in 1624, Buckingham had never really left them: that once it had become clear that there was virtually no possibility of Spanish cooperation over the Palatinate the duke had chosen deliberately to wreck negotiations at Madrid by his boorish behaviour and flagrant disregard of Spanish court protocol and religious susceptibilities.

No less misleading is the usual verdict that Charles and Buckingham joined forces with a virulently anti-Spanish and pro-war parliament to push into war a prematurely senile king, who had begun his reign by making peace with Spain. As Professor Russell has observed, it is far too easy to confuse opposition to the Spanish marriage, which was very widespread in parliament, with a desire for war, which was not. For one thing MPs were all too conscious of the unpopularity of taxation with their constituents. Indeed parliament's ultimate vote of three subsidies and three fifteenths was ludicrously inadequate, and the product of an exercise in self-deception bolstered by the arguments of Buckingham's followers, Sir Edward Coke and Sir John Eliot, about the likely profits of a sea war – 'England never prospered so well as when Wars with Spain'.

Too much has also been made of the arrangements for parliamentary control of the appropriation of this grant. Like the revival of impeachment in 1621, the arrangements in the 1624 subsidy act that treasurers responsible to parliament should be enjoined to issue money only on receipt of warrants from the newly created Council of War, which in turn would be held responsible for the purposes for which such warrants were issued, were a product of struggles at court rather than of struggles between court and country. As Professor Russell has observed, Charles and Buckingham wanted a royal declaration of war to precede a parliamentary grant of subsidies, fearing that otherwise no war would follow and the grant would be diverted to other uses. James, on the other hand, feared that the grant might be inadequate and that he 'would be left committed to a war for which he could not pay'. In these circumstances the appropriation clause in the subsidy act was in the nature of a procedural compromise for breaking the deadlock, and if anything it favoured the king, who 'got his money in return for a scrap of paper'. The point is underlined by James's subsequent refusal to engage in all-out war, confining himself to the financing of a mercenary expedition to the Palatinate, which was nevertheless forbidden to relieve the key city of Breda *en route*. Moreover, once parliament was dissolved, the king resumed full control of events.

But before the dissolution there was one very important piece of business to undertake. By far the best illustration of the reversionary interest's ability to get its own way was the successful impeachment of Middlesex, and the king's feeble, halfhearted and unavailing attempts to save his lord treasurer. Contemporaries need not have marvelled at what they called 'the Prince's Undertaking' to bring down the royal minister as an attack on the royal prerogative, since, as in Bacon's case three years earlier, the charges which stuck against Middlesex were not those relating to ministerial advice about impositions and other matters, but those relating to bribes from the customs farmers and extortions in the Wards, the Wardrobe and the Ordnance. After some uncertainty about the charges Middlesex was not held responsible to parliament for ministerial advice or actions as distinct from crimes and misdemeanours. This may have been comforting to both king and prince, but was no consolation to the fallen minister, who was sentenced to pay a fine of £50,000 (subsequently greatly reduced), to be debarred from holding office for ever, and to be imprisoned during the king's pleasure (like Bacon he was soon released). His fall illustrates a main characteristic of the Jacobean system: that political success was dependent either on retaining the favour, or, at the very least not contradicting the interests of the current favourite; or on supplanting him. Middlesex had offended against the one, without succeeding in his attempts to achieve the other. It is highly significant that among Buckingham's clients in the lower House who gave crucially important evidence against the treasurer were the latter's own subordinates, Sir Miles Fleetwood in the court of Wards and Sir Robert Pye in the Exchequer; while Sir Benjamin Rudyerd, another subordinate as surveyor of the Wards, was a client of the duke's new ally, Pembroke.[21]

The case against Middlesex had first come to the attention of parliament via a report from Sir Edwin Sandys's parliamentary Committee of Trade, which stressed, *inter alia*, the grievance of impositions, some of which had been recently introduced by the lord treasurer, in its account of the causes of the economic depression. By the time that parliament met in the early spring of 1624 the worst of the great depression had in fact passed, though no one could be sure of that at the time and the Commons listened to some heartrending accounts of distress in the textile industry. In the circumstances complaints against the restrictive practices of the chartered companies were bound to be heard again, and the government yielded to parliamentary pressure and forced the Merchant Adventurers Company to widen its membership, accept a measure of free trade to its Dutch and German privileges in some sorts of cloth, and lower the impositions which it levied on its members. The Levant and Eastland companies came off relatively lightly in this parliament, though there was some hostility towards the East India Company for its export of specie, and there was even a motion that its ships should be arrested. But the real force of this feeling arose as much from the power struggle extending over three companies in which Sir Thomas Smythe and his city and courtly associates were mounting an effective counter-attack against the opposing faction led by Sandys and the earl of Southampton, who had ousted them from control of the Virginia Company in 1619 and the Somers Islands (Bermuda) Company in 1621. The Smythe faction was to regain control of the latter company at its elections in December 1624, while the Virginia Company, thanks to the same faction's attacks, had been made the subject of a commission of inquiry in 1623, and was to be dissolved in 1625. But Smythe was also governor of the East India Company, and the ferocity of the parliamentary attack on its directorate in 1624 ought to be seen as the Sandys faction extending the struggle both to parliament and to another company.

But, for all the continued criticisms of companies, the tendency to lump them together with domestic concessionaires, which had been such a feature of the parliament of 1621, was absent from that of 1624.[22] Highly significant in this respect was the most important legislative enactment of the parliament, the Statute of Monopolies. While prohibiting domestic monopolies, except when concerned with genuine innovation, the statute made an exception in favour of corporate bodies, thereby opening a significant loophole for the chartered companies, whose members were freed from the nightmare which had obsessed them ever since the anti-monopoly agitation of 1601. Among the least advertised events of the parliament of 1624 was this split among business concessionaires and the possibility of a new *modus vivendi* between the chartered companies and all but the most implacable of their parliamentary critics.

TWO WARS, TWO PARLIAMENTS AND THE ATTACK ON BUCKINGHAM, 1625–7

It is frequently argued that in their stormy relations with parliament in the opening years of the new reign, Charles I and Buckingham were reaping the whirlwind of their reckless impetuosity in 1624. There is some truth in this, but it is by no means the whole truth, for if it had not been for James I's failure to create a state of military preparedness despite the events of his last parliament, Charles's and Buckingham's good relations with parliament might have carried over into the next reign. Moreover, to the failure to prosecute the war energetically were added justified suspicions that the substitution of a French for a Spanish marriage for Charles (to Henrietta Maria, the sister of Louis XIII) would nevertheless involve unwelcome concessions to English Catholic recusants. Finally, some importance should probably be attached to the disappointed expectations of some of Charles's and Buckingham's parliamentary allies of 1624, who, as one contemporary put it, were to find themselves not 'so countenanced by the Duke as they expected'. This combination of factors produced an atmosphere of suspicion and criticism early in the second session of Charles's first parliament, which, on account of the ravages of the plague in London, was adjourned to Oxford in the summer of 1625. The fact that no subsidies were granted in the Oxford session and only two during the first session was largely responsible for the disastrous failure of the English expedition to Cadiz which followed the dissolution of parliament in August.

The bill to grant the king tonnage and poundage for one year only, instead of for life as hitherto, is probably the best-known instance cited in favour of the classic Whig view that parliament was using the power of the purse to ensure the king's continued dependence upon it. Here again Professor Russell has demonstrated that this is an over-simplified view of a very complex situation. He shows that it was the original intention to draft a bill which would put an end once and for all to the contention which had surrounded royal impositions by incorporating them within a tonnage and poundage bill. But, with MPs desperately anxious to get away from plague-ridden Westminster, there was insufficient time to prepare such a complex measure, while a suitable stop-gap bill was prevented by the insistence of some West Country MPs on the need to shock Lord Admiral Buckingham into drastic action against the North African pirates who were currently cruising off the Cornish coast. The grant of tonnage and poundage for one year only was the chosen instrument for this end, appropriately enough, since the avowed purpose of the customs duties was protection of the seas. But the House of Lords refused to accept such a bill, and as a result the king collected not only the impositions but tonnage and poundage without a parliamentary grant.

In the Oxford session of parliament, Charles's French marriage proved to be as contentious an issue as the Spanish match had been in 1621 and 1624, though alliance with a major continental power was essential if there was to be any hope of winning back the Palatinate. But, fearing the conditions which went with the marriage treaty, the Commons petitioned for a royal declaration that the recusancy laws against Roman Catholics would be strictly enforced. Significantly, Charles chose to give satisfaction to parliament at the risk of alienating the French and forfeiting the second instalment of Henrietta Maria's dowry of £240,000, though he got not a penny by way of a parliamentary grant in return.[23] Further fears both of the religious consequences of the French marriage and of the favourite who had pressed for it were reinforced when Buckingham, as lord admiral, acquiesced in the loan of English ships to the French without any guarantee that they would not be used against the Huguenots in La Rochelle.

Anti-Catholic feeling was also fed by the growth of what many, understandably if incorrectly, saw as a sort of popish fifth column within the Anglican church, the so-called Arminian movement. Like so many issues this split the court as well as the bench of bishops, but was not yet the court-versus-country issue that it was to become in the 1630s. At this point it was the opponents of the Arminians – including, but certainly not exclusively consisting of, Puritan parsons and laymen – who saw themselves as the conservative defenders of tradition and orthodoxy and the Arminians as liturgical and doctrinal innovators in their emphasis on ritual, their determination to raise the status of clerics, their insistence on the *iure divino* authority of bishops, and their questioning of the orthodox doctrine of predestination. A central figure of controversy over these years was Richard Montague, a parson who had in 1624 published an allegedly anti-papist pamphlet with the curious title *A gag for the gospel! No! a new gag for an old goose*. But to many Protestants Montague's pamphlet was more notable for what it condoned than for what it condemned in Catholic practice and beliefs. The Commons in 1624 had referred Montague's case to Archbishop Abbot, who recommended him to revise or remove the offending passages. Instead Montague appealed directly to James I in a further tract with a title, *Apello Caesarem*, which was likely to please that monarch who licensed its publication. There was a renewal of parliamentary attacks on Montague in 1625 and he was saved only by Charles I taking him as his chaplain and ordering the Commons to desist from attacking his servant.[24]

If this incident made the king's ecclesiastical position abundantly clear, what of the duke's? Buckingham's former allies among the Puritans, and notably Lords Saye and Sele and Warwick, determined to bring his churchmanship to the test, and their chosen instrument was a conference at Buckingham's London residence, York House, in February 1626, shortly after Charles's second parliament had assembled. At the conference Arminian views in general, and Montague's in particular, were debated, and Buckingham's refusal to repudiate the Arminian position, which was ably expounded at the conference, meant an irreparable break with his parliamentary Puritan allies of the early 1620s. The favourite had too clear an appreciation of the king's growing preference for the new brand of churchmanship to be prepared to range himself alongside its opponents.

The parliament of 1626 was to vote Montague's impeachment, but was to be dissolved before this could be put into effect. Dissolution also saved a far more exalted figure, the duke himself, from the same fate. The York House conference had marked the final breaking point with his former Puritan allies, but even more significant was the turning away of his old clients and allies, Sir Dudley Digges and Sir John Eliot. In his capacity as vice-admiral of Devon – an office which he owed to the duke – Eliot had no doubt observed the chaos attending the departure of the expeditionary force for Cadiz in 1625 and the pitiful condition in which its remnants had returned; certainly no repetition of the successful Elizabethan expeditions of Drake and Essex to the same port, as a means of restoring the duke's heavily tarnished reputation. In addition Buckingham could no longer rely on the support of Pembroke, and of Pembroke's able and eloquent clients in the lower house, Sir Benjamin Rudyerd and William Coryton. This notable widening of opposition to the duke rendered futile the government's attempts to spike the guns of his opponents by picking as sheriffs six of the most awkward MPs in the previous parliament, including Sir Robert Phelips and Sir Edward Coke, and denying writs of summons to the earl of Arundel, who was in the Tower for countenancing the marriage of his heir into the royal family, and the earl of Bristol, who was under house arrest because he knew too much of what had gone on in Spain in 1623.

There can be no doubt that one of the major causes of parliamentary disquiet in 1626 – not least to the way of thinking of Pembroke and his clients – was that although the war with Spain had so far gone disastrously and the Palatinate seemed to be irrevocably lost, England appeared to be drifting relentlessly in the direction of a second war: with France. Among the causes of the alarmingly rapid deterioration of Anglo-French relations were English seizures of French ships alleged to be carrying contraband of war to the enemy and French retaliation against English merchants in France. Added to these were Charles's taking the part of the French Huguenots in their quarrel with Louis XIII, and his disregard of the provisions of the marriage treaty in regard to both the relaxation of the recusancy laws and the composition of the queen's household. The dispute about the household culminated in August in the expulsion of all but a mere handful of Henrietta Maria's French attendants. Not all of these things were Buckingham's fault, least of all the matter of the recusancy laws, but as lord admiral he bore the responsibility for the arrest of French ships and, more particularly, the re-arrest of one of them, the *St Peter* of Le Havre, which was to become something of a *cause célèbre*. Moreover, he had played a central part in the humiliation of the queen over her household, and was even reported to have reminded her that queens of England had lost their heads before now. The duke in fact was the obvious scapegoat, whose removal might placate the French and thus enable England to concentrate on fighting the Spaniards.

Yet to state the desirability of this end was a great deal easier than to devise means of bringing it about. It had been all too easy to find witnesses against Bacon in 1621 and Middlesex in 1624, in the latter case subordinates of the treasurer but clients of the duke and secure in his protection. But who could be found to give evidence against the greatest subject in the land, secure in the favour and protection of his king? Certainly not the members of the Council of War, whom the king quite properly forbade to answer any inquiries as to whether the lord admiral had disregarded the Council's advice on any important matters. On other issues such as the re-arrest of the *St Peter*, the duke was able to plead having acted by the king's command, and his plea was borne out by Charles himself.

These obstacles were ingeniously circumvented when, on 11 March, Dr Samuel Turner, a court physician and client of Pembroke, who had found him a seat, told the Commons that evidence of this sort was unnecessary to mount an indictment against the duke as distinct from convicting him. For was it not a matter of common fame that as lord admiral he had lost control of the Channel and been responsible for the disaster at Cadiz; that the royal revenue had been impoverished by gifts to him and his kindred; that he had engrossed and sold offices to the ill government of the kingdom; and that recusancy had been encouraged by the example of his mother and his father-in-law, the earl of Rutland? Further charges were later to be added in the articles of impeachment drawn up against the duke; including, on Eliot's insistence, the re-arrest of the *St Peter*; the loan of English ships to France for use against the Huguenots; the extortion of £10,000 from the East India Company as a penalty for its capture of Ormuz from the Portuguese in 1624; and, most spectacular of all, the administration of a potion and plaster to the late king on his deathbed, described as 'an act of transcendent presumption and of dangerous consequence'. The king's furious demand that the Commons should investigate Turner's outrageous conduct was brilliantly turned into an investigation of his charges as an excuse for preparing a detailed case against the duke.[25]

On 27 March the Commons decided on a vote of three subsidies and three fifteenths – another absurdly inadequate grant – but not to embody these in a bill until their grievances had been redressed, and here they meant not just the passing of bills to remedy the primarily local and regional grievances which most MPs always regarded as the most important parliamentary business of all, but this time also a settlement of what was aptly described as 'the grievance of grievances', the duke himself. Two days later Charles peremptorily told the Commons to desist from further attacks on the duke and to make an unconditional grant of subsidies without further delay. The refusal to comply raises the question of why the king allowed parliament to drag on until 15 June before dissolving it. Charles may indeed have been confident until the very last moment that the peers would acquit Buckingham.[26] Professor Russell has recently suggested that there may have been a distinct possibility of constructive compromise whereby the charges would be dropped in return for some ministerial changes including the resignation of Buckingham from the office of lord admiral (Warwick was an obvious candidate to replace him), but not from his court and household offices. In addition, the king would get his subsidies as well as what Sir Benjamin Rudyerd described as 'an orderly warrantable revenue proportionable to his ordinary charge' – whether in the form of including impositions in a tonnage and poundage bill or of some other increase in ordinary 'support' there is no way of telling. Also in the air was the nostalgic and attractive notion of sea war by private enterprise via the foundation of a West India Company, through whose judicious mixture of naval aggression and private profit 'his Majesty shall have no more to do at sea but to defend the coasts'.

If indeed such a compromise had seriously been entertained, it would ultimately have been wrecked by the publication of Bristol's charges against the duke that he had plotted with the Spanish ambassador to take the prince to Spain and other revelations about the events in Spain in 1623. The Lords refused to condemn Bristol without a hearing, and in the nature of things the case for Bristol was the case against Buckingham. Compromise was impossible and the parliament had to be dissolved to save the duke. Bereft of grants of both tonnage and poundage and subsidies, Charles had to continue to collect the former without parliamentary sanction, and, in place of the latter, to raise a forced loan, significantly known as the Loan of Five Subsidies, which yielded about £264,000 over 1626–8, and which in its turn was to become a prime grievance in the next parliament.

In the circumstances of the inadequacy of parliamentary grants to meet the expense of conducting two wars, there were bound to be very heavy government borrowings, sales of royal land and anticipations of future revenues. By 1628, £325,000 of the ordinary revenues of the next two years had been hypothecated by quartering what was in effect war debt upon them and this legacy of the war years was to be a burden which was not shaken off during the subsequent decade.[27] It is impossible to say how far both the enormous sums borrowed during the war years – over a million pounds in all between 1624 and 1628 – and other demands on economic resources for the war effort had the effect of retarding recovery from the economic depression of the earlier 1620s. In the first year of the reign war certainly did less damage than plague. From May to November 1625, 35,417 people died from plague in London, and there was panic in the metropolis as deaths rose to a peak of about 4,000 a week in August. The economic effects of the paralysis of metropolitan activity were particularly disastrous because of London's importance as the bottleneck through which so large a proportion of England's foreign trade passed. There was a severe, though temporary, check to the recovery in broadcloth exports from London, which, however, were up again to 91,000 in 1626 as against 38,000 in 1622 at the height of the depression and 59,000 in 1624. While it had been the broadcloths, kerseys and other 'old draperies' which had been hardest hit during the early 1620s, the war against Spain had a disastrous effect on the new draperies, whose most important markets were in Spain and the Mediterranean lands. The seizure of French ships in 1626 on pain of carrying contraband of war was not only a step closer to war with France, but also precipitated French retaliation, with disastrous effects on the exports of the London French Company and on the wine trade. When war broke out, the ravages of Dunkirk privateers, operating under letters of marque, inflicted serious damage on the east coast fishing trade and the coastwise trade in coal from Newcastle to London and east coast ports. As to textiles, the new draperies again were more vulnerable than the old, which were mostly shipped by chartered companies sailing in protected convoys.

Just as the Spanish war had its humiliating débâcle in the failure of the Cadiz expedition in 1625, so did the French war see a similar disaster in Buckingham's attack on the Isle of

Rhé from July to October 1627 in an ill-conceived attempt to afford assistance to the hard-pressed Huguenots at La Rochelle. 'Since England was England,' lamented Denzil Holles, 'it received not so dishonourable a blow.' In Buckingham's successive attempts to win back the esteem of his countrymen in 1624, 1625 and 1627, each failure seemed worse than the last. He did indeed fight gallantly at Rhé, but no amount of gallantry could make up for inadequate supplies and scant reinforcements, which were in turn, as Professor Russell reminds us, to no small extent a product of 'the failure of local administrators to place sufficiently harsh pressure on their countrymen'. Nevertheless, it is the weight and unfamiliarity of the pressure on both which needs to be appreciated if the issues which engaged the attention of Charles's third parliament, which assembled on 17 March 1628, are to be fully understood.

THE END OF BUCKINGHAM AND THE END OF PARLIAMENTS (?), 1628–9

By the time that Charles's third parliament met, the country had become war-weary, and any enthusiasm for war which had once existed had long since evaporated, to be replaced by profound uneasiness about the burdens of war and the necessary inroads which it had made into English liberties and, more particularly, into local and county self-government. It was not, of course, that the 1620s saw the beginning of centralized pressure on local government. The work of the JPs both in and out of quarter sessions had long been subject to a general oversight exercised on the government's behalf by justices of assize on circuit, and the government had long endeavoured to circumvent JPs and usurp their functions by the use of a wide variety of administrative patents, which produced such a storm in the parliament of 1621 and were not to survive that of 1624.[28] But there can be no doubt that war produced an enormously increased volume of pressure from the centre, a development in which, as in the days of the late Elizabethan war against Spain, lord lieutenants and their deputies were of crucial significance.

Here again, in the matter of military preparedness and training, the conflict between the lieutenancy and the vast bulk of those local JPs who were not themselves deputy lieutenants had made itself felt long before the war, and was to continue long after. The conflict had constitutional overtones in that the repeal of the admittedly hopelessly inadequate Marian statute on musters and military provision in 1604 had meant that the military functions of the lieutenancy were clearly based on the prerogative and not, as hitherto, on statute. Moreover, besides the provision of arms, counties had also had to pay the stipends of the professional soldiers known as muster-masters who undertook the training of the raw rustics, which local gentlemen felt they could do themselves with at least equal efficiency and at much lower cost. Finally, the local rates imposed for these purposes were often levied by lords lieutenant with scant regard for quarter-sessional authority. This, when coupled with the repeal of the Marian statute in 1604 and the extra-parliamentary levies of Charles I in wartime, made for a highly significant linkage between the royal flouting of the authority of parliament on the national, and of quarter sessions on the local level.[29]

In wartime the duties heaped upon the lieutenancy enormously multiplied, and although there is evidence that some lieutenants did their best to represent to the government the hardships inflicted on their counties, it was more or less inevitable that they should bear the bulk of the unpopularity for forced loans, coat and conduct money for local levies, billeting, ship money in the maritime counties, and a large number of other incidents. Thus it was that the actions of the lieutenancy were among the main grievances against which MPs were to voice complaint in 1628. The need to cope with so many disorderly men under arms had led to the issue of commissions of martial law, which raised the question of how far soldiers were subject to the law of the land. Moreover the billeting of soldiers on unwilling householders was not only a grievance itself but had raised fears that martial law might be extended to civilians in what were virtually 'occupied' districts. The need to levy local troops had led to demands for coat and conduct money, and the need to pay them to the levying of forced loans in 1625 and 1626–8. Further, the need to make an example of those who declined to contribute had led to arbitrary imprisonment, of which the most celebrated example is the imprisonment of five recalcitrant knights in 1627 for refusing to contribute to the so-called loan of Five Subsidies; and, above all, to the judicial decision that the keeper of the Fleet prison had been right to refuse, in answer to a writ of Habeas Corpus, to give the cause of their imprisonment other than that it was through the king's special command.

Anyone who has lived through any war knows that for its duration certain basic freedoms have to be forgone. But the doubts which afflicted many MPs in 1628 arose out of genuine fears that a permanent despotism might be ushered in under the guise of wartime necessity. And it is a most arresting paradox that it was such suspicions and the forthright way in which they were expressed which turned these fears into a self-fulfilling prophecy, in the shape of the so-called eleven years tyranny of the 1630s, when non-parliamentary levies became what began to look like a permanent feature of English life without the emergency conditions of war to justify them.

Charles needed another parliament in order to equip another expedition to La Rochelle, where the Huguenot cause was now in desperate straits, while most MPs needed one in order to take action for the redress of the grievances of their constituencies which have been outlined above. There seems to have been general agreement not to renew the attack on Buckingham,[30] since this would precipitate a speedy dissolution with grievances unredressed. Accordingly, it was not until the king's first and unsatisfactory answer to the parliamentary Petition of Right on 2 June, that the issue of the duke came again to the fore, as the result of Sir John Eliot's initiative. The Petition of Right can be understood only in terms of the fears of Englishmen that the curtailment of their liberties might be more than temporary. It reflects not so much the need for the rule of law as uncertainty as to the nature of the law, fed by the judicial decision in the five knights' case. As Eliot succinctly put it on 6 May: 'All the question is what the law is.' What was needed was that the particular interpretation of the law desired by parliament in the matters of forced loans and arbitrary taxes, arbitrary imprisonment, billeting and martial law, should be regarded as the correct interpretation. At first the Commons attempted to embody these matters in a bill, so as to give to the desired interpretation the supreme authority of statute. When the king refused to agree to this mode of procedure on the grounds that this would be changing the law, Sir Edward Coke hit on the brilliant idea of a Petition of Right, which would both define the law on the contentious issues and insist that this was the traditional interpretation. It was highly appropriate that this ingenious way out of the difficulty should come from the great lawyer. Its adoption is a prime illustration of the Cokean view of the law and the constitution as immemorial and unchanging, which was to be part of the essential stock-in-trade of those parliamentarians who, like the anti-Arminian Puritans, saw themselves as the conservative defenders of tradition against courtly innovation. Like their ancestors, argued John Pym, they were 'demanding their ancient and due liberties, not suing for any new'.[31]

The king's first reply to the Petition of Right on 2 June, 'that right be done according to the laws and customs of the realm', gave no satisfaction, since it was the precise interpretation of the law, not its mere existence, that was at stake. The Commons had decided to vote five subsidies, a substantial even if still inadequate grant, but they would require more than this answer if they were to complete the subsidy bill. With the king's second answer on 7 June, using the required formula, '*Soit droit fait comme il est désiré*', parliament was satisfied, and the subsidy bill went through, though Charles's insistence that he was conceding no more than he had intended to in his first answer ought perhaps to have given grounds for caution.[32] The four days between the king's two replies saw parliamentary frustrations boil over into violent attacks on two matters on which MPs had hitherto – no doubt with great difficulty – restrained themselves: Buckingham and the Arminians. Nor did the more satisfactory second answer altogether quell the storm, and the king must have been particularly irritated to receive two Remonstrances from the Commons: the first, voted on 11 June, demanding rigorous enforcement of the recusancy laws, complained about the favouring of Arminian over orthodox Calvinist clergymen, and condemned the multiplicity of offices and 'the excessive power of the Duke of Buckingham and the abuse of that power'; the second, on 25 June, was directed against the continued royal collection of tonnage and poundage, not granted in a parliamentary way. Religion and tonnage and poundage were to dominate the second session of the parliament in 1629. Buckingham did not become an issue only because he was assassinated in the interim.

The parliament was successively prorogued a number of times before it reassembled on 20 January 1629. In the meantime a great deal of moment had happened. Until October 1628, when La Rochelle fell to Louis XIII after enduring horrible privations, a second naval expedition there had been at the top of royal priorities, to restore the king's honour by redeeming his promise to the Huguenots. After securing his base by making his peace with Arundel and – more surprisingly – with Bristol, Buckingham took off to Portsmouth to supervise naval preparations, and it was there that he was murdered on 23 August by a discontented naval lieutenant, John Felton. The murder of

Buckingham – greeted with popular exultation which made a permanent impression on Charles – and the fall of La Rochelle greatly improved the prospect of peace, at least with France and perhaps also with Spain. There was also a spectacular improvement in Charles's relations with his queen, which had hitherto been inhibited by his relationship with the duke. The beginning of the long love affair between Charles and his consort certainly gave hope for an improvement in Anglo-French relations. So perhaps did the appointment of the queen's favourite, the francophile earl of Holland, as constable of Windsor Castle and his election to succeed Buckingham as chancellor of the university of Cambridge. As for hispanophiles, the return of Arundel to the council and the promotion of his associate Sir Richard Weston to succeed the pliant and easygoing earl of Marlborough as lord treasurer, and of Sir Francis Cottington as chancellor of the Exchequer all seemed to improve the chances of an end to the Spanish war too. Another product of Buckingham's death was that it enabled one of the bitterest parliamentary critics of the muddle and mess of his policies, Sir Thomas Wentworth, to accept a peerage and office as president of the Council of the North. Wentworth's inclinations too were strongly in favour of peace.

For all the extensive 'legislative programme' of government-sponsored bills planned for this session,[33] it was in fact dominated by two great issues, tonnage and poundage and religion, and while some MPs, such as Eliot and John Selden, tended to give a higher priority to the former, others, such as John Pym, Francis Rous and Sir Nathaniel Rich, were especially hot for the latter.[34] On both issues the king was not unconciliatory. While correctly repudiating the allegation that his continued collection of tonnage and poundage was in violation of the Petition of Right, he was at pains to emphasize that he collected the duties not of right but of necessity, and that he was simply anticipating parliament's declared intention of making a retrospective grant. As to Arminianism, while the promotion of Montague to the episcopal see of Chichester in 1628, in succession to the orthodox Calvinist Carleton, can hardly be seen as a conciliatory move, the king had at least taken measures to ensure the withdrawal of Montague's contentious *Apello Caesarem* from publication. However, nothing could damp down the atmosphere of near-hysteria which prevailed in the lower house over Arminianism, and it was now more than a small, even if vocal, minority who were obsessed by it. Furthermore, while it is important to distinguish between the two great issues of this session, it is no less important to appreciate that, in the minds of MPs, they were clearly connected. Indeed at one point Pym and his colleagues attempted to make the passing of a tonnage and poundage bill conditional upon a royal undertaking to abandon Arminianism, just as the subsidy bill had been made conditional upon a satisfactory royal answer to the Petition of Right in the previous session. Moreover, as Professor Russell observes: 'Just as the 1628 House had been driven towards giving legal force to Parliamentary interpretation of the law, the 1629 House was driven towards wishing to give legal authority to Parliamentary interpretation of religion'. Indeed, there were not wanting those who saw Arminian influence behind the fact that Charles had insisted on the Petition of Right being printed with his first and not his second answer attached.

When the debate on religion petered out on 17 February over differences about finding an acceptable statement of Calvinist orthodoxy, the Commons reverted to the matter of tonnage and poundage, from which they had originally been deflected by Francis Rous and others. Leaving aside the interesting and contentious question of whether to concentrate, as Eliot desired, on the matter of parliamentary privilege – one of the merchants whose goods had been confiscated for failure to pay tonnage and poundage was the MP, John Rolle – or, as Pym desired, on the general issue of unparliamentary taxation, the general strategy favoured by both groups was to try to pin the blame firmly on the customs farmers, since the customs had been alienated to them by the king (but were they his to alienate in the first place?). But the king would not allow this to happen. Those farmers who had taken part in confiscating the goods of recalcitrant merchants were also salaried collectors of customs and, moreover, had been acting on his express command.

The royal defence of, and parliamentary onslaught on, the customs farmers in 1629 produced a further split in the London concessionary interest. Just as the Statute of Monopolies of 1624 had marked a clear distinction between the interests of trade corporations and those of individual domestic monopolists, so had the events of 1629 pointed to a clear incompatibility between the interests of the companies and those of the customs farmers. By 1629 a pattern had emerged which was to endure through the next decade and into the Long Parliament. The long-standing Elizabethan alliance between crown and chartered companies had been weakened by a combination of growing parliamentary sensitivity to company interests and diminishing royal regard for them.[35] At the same time the barely latent hostility between the companies and domestic concessionaires (monopolists and customs farmers) had been accentuated. The most eloquent expression of this new alignment of forces came in the virtual strike by members of the companies, and notably the Merchant Adventurers and Levant companies, against the payment of tonnage and poundage to the customs farmers. This they did in direct response to the Protestation which the Commons had passed on 2 March in that most theatrical of parliamentary scenes, with the Speaker held down in his chair as Black Rod came to dissolve the House. The Commons protested that anyone who counselled the exaction of unparliamentary tonnage and poundage was 'an innovator in the Government and a capital enemy to the Kingdom and Commonwealth', and also that anyone who paid such duties was 'a betrayer of the liberties of England, and an enemy to the same'.

The first clause of the Protestation attacked, as capital enemies, another sort of innovator: papists and Arminians, now significantly yoked together. Thus those who in the previous session had devised the Petition of Right as a reassertion of immemorial liberties, not the creation of new, now castigated those whose innovations in religion and government threatened both the Reformation settlement and the ancient constitution. The king not unnaturally saw things differently. Eliot (shortly to be committed to the Tower, from which he was never to emerge), Pym and their colleagues might be convinced of the existence of a coordinated plot against both the church of England and the constitution. Charles was no less convinced, as he averred in his declaration of 10 March 1629 explaining the reasons why he had dissolved parliament, of the existence of a quite different plot: a plot 'to abate the powers of our Crown, and to bring our government into obloquy, that in the end all things may be overwhelmed with anarchy and confusion'.[36]

Charles's declaration makes a tolerably good text for the Whig interpretation of history. But he was as mistaken about the true intentions of his opponents as they were about his. With the exception of his addiction to Arminianism – arguably his greatest misjudgment – the things they complained of were largely the product of emergency wartime needs and their own reluctance to make adequate provision for them, rather than of any deep-seated plan to establish absolutist government on the continental model. Likewise, far from planning to usurp the functions of government, the parliamentary leaders were seeking to safeguard what they regarded as ancient liberties whose existence was incompatible with a state of war. That state of war was to end with the conclusion of peace in the following year. But one corollary of peace was that the king would have less need to summon parliaments, even if many of the incidents which had made for stormy relations with his parliaments would be removed by the end of the war. How far was Charles able to use the period of peace and non-parliamentary rule that lay ahead to re-establish himself in the affection of his people, thus creating a basis for harmonious relations with future parliaments? Or how far was England now set on the course which the French monarchy had followed since the last dissolution of the States-General in 1614? Was the ending of the parliament of 1629 to be an end to parliaments in general?

Chapter Eight

THE PERSONAL RULE OF CHARLES I, 1629–40

FACTIONS AND POLICIES

With Buckingham dead, parliament dissolved and peace with both France and Spain concluded in 1629 and 1630, it was hoped that there would ensue a period when peace and concord would replace war and contention, even if at the price of abandoning hope of restoring the Palatinate to Charles's unfortunate brother-in-law. The fact that upholding what many thought of as the cause of international Protestantism – and through it the interests of the Elector – was left to Sweden and later to Catholic France, while England lifted not a finger, might be an occasion of shame to some Englishmen. But there were others who were all too aware that England's record in international affairs in the 1620s, when parliaments were meeting and making admittedly inadequate grants to the King, was emphatically nothing to be proud of. Some, like Sir Richard Fanshawe in his great ode of the early 1630s, rejoiced unashamedly in the good fortune of Englishmen, since, in contrast to the war-torn continent:

> White Peace (the beautifullest of things)
> Seems here her everlasting rest
> To fix, and spreads her downy wings
> Over the nest.[1]

But whatever the advantages of peace, unity and concord were not among them, either at court or in the country. We will later be concerned to trace the survival of country opposition despite the fact that it lacked a parliamentary focus. This section, however, is particularly concerned to stress how the continuance of factional struggle betokened a deeply divided court. Until the death in 1635 of the highly efficient, if also highly corrupt, Lord Treasurer Sir Richard Weston, who had been raised to the peerage in 1628 and become earl of Portland in 1633, probably the simplest way of characterizing court divisions is via the distinction between the treasurer's faction and those of his opponents. The former group was headed by Portland, Cottington, his chancellor of the Exchequer,[2] and Secretary of State Sir Francis Windebank, who had owed his appointment to that office in 1632 to Laud's influence, a fact which increased Laud's hostility towards the treasurer when Windebank drifted into the latter's camp. Also associated with Portland's group were the grandee Thomas Howard, earl of Arundel, and John Williams, bishop of Lincoln, the former lord keeper and Laud's bitter enemy.

Strongly opposed to the lord treasurer, who was backed by Charles, were Laud and his followers and a group of courtiers around the queen. Laud was appalled by what he deemed to be a total lack of financial probity in the lord treasurer, while the queen disliked Portland both for his insistence on economies in her household expenditure and for what she regarded as his pro-Spanish foreign policy. On both matters she found natural allies, not among the courtly Catholics and crypto-Catholics of the traditional picture, but as has recently been demonstrated,[3] among a group of Protestant, and even moderate Puritan, noblemen who favoured a renewal of war against Spain and even the calling of a parliament. Such were the Rich brothers, earls of Holland and Warwick, and the earls of Pembroke, Northumberland and Leicester and Viscount Dorchester, opponents no less of Laud's than of Portland's policies. Isolated during the hegemony of Buckingham, the queen is seen as responding enthusiastically to the attentions of these courtiers, of whom Holland was at one and the same time both the most charming and attentive and the most empty of statesmanlike qualities. To Henrietta it mattered less that such persons were Protestants than that she found them personally sympathetic. Indeed it was arguable that unimpeachably Protestant supporters could do more for her English co-religionists, and especially for court Catholics, than could avowed Catholics or those whose religious affiliations were dubious. Her courtly Protestant followers were in fact valuable allies against both the religious intransigence of Laud and the financial economies and pro-Spanish inclinations of Portland.

Thus while Laud and the courtiers around the queen might share a dislike of Portland and his policies, this was about all that they had in common. The queen resented the archbishop's persecution of her co-religionists no less than she did the lord treasurer's designs to reduce her household expenditure. Indeed, perhaps because the latter was somewhat less determined than the former, Henrietta and Portland seemed for a time in 1633 to be on the point of joining forces against the jumped-up cleric, much to Holland's and his associates' alarm, not because they favoured Laud but because they disliked Portland and all that he stood for. While the threatened rapprochement between the queen and the treasurer was an aberration and came to nought, it does serve to illustrate the fluid and indefinite character of court faction at the time. So does the fact that while there seems from the very first to have been no love lost between Laud and Portland, the former's distrust of Cottington was relatively slow to develop before the middle of the decade. Similarly, Wentworth, whom one tends instinctively to regard as Laud's close ally, cannot be said to be firmly in any camp, at least before about 1633 at the earliest. Drawn strongly towards Laud on some matters, he was, however, deeply obliged to the lord treasurer for having pressed his appointment to the Privy Council in 1629 and to Cottington for helping to persuade the king to make him lord deputy of Ireland in July 1631. Indeed, unlike Laud, he seems to have remained on friendly terms with Cottington throughout the

1630s. Finally from 1637 the queen's Protestant entourage seems to have fallen away. During that year Senterre, the French ambassador, who had offered constant encouragement to the queen's anti-Spanish Protestant associates, returned to France, and there arrived in England the French queen mother, Marie de Medici, and Henrietta's childhood companion, the duchesse de Chevreuse: both of them strongly pro-Spanish in their outlook. It is from about this time that we should date the queen's surrounding herself with her co-religionists and encouragement of Catholic proselytes at court, among them her former Protestant associates Wat Montagu and Henry Jermyn.

This account of the shifts in court factional groupings has taken us a long way forward, to within a year or two of the time when the queen's former associates Holland, Pembroke, Northumberland, Warwick and Secretary of State Sir Henry Vane are to be found among the parliamentarians who went to war against the king in 1642. It will now be necessary to retrace our steps and turn to those financial policies of Lord Treasurer Portland which both Henrietta's associates and Laud found so distasteful, though for very different reasons. Expenditure reduction was the most important of these policies, both in the matter of economies on court spending and in maintaining peace, the latter being the most important economy of all, and one which, as has already been emphasized, ran counter to the policies favoured by the queen's faction. The crown had, of course, accumulated a huge debt during the war years of the later 1620s, most of which had been quartered on the ordinary revenue of at least two years ahead. The charge had been reduced from £277,680 at the beginning of the decade to £204,674 by 1633, though it was to rise again to £315,816 by 1637, two years after Portland's death. The fact that a significant proportion of each year's ordinary revenue was anticipated to meet past debt, a situation which precipitated further cumulative anticipation, casts some doubts on Professor Dietz's thesis that the years of personal rule were a time of progressive financial improvement and that, if it had not been for this, Charles might never have embarked on his disastrous Scottish exploits.[4]

If increases of revenue have attracted more attention from historians than decreases in expenditure, this is not because they were a more important part of Portland's financial policies – they were not – but because of the opposition they provoked and the contribution which they made to the wider unpopularity of the regime. Among the minor increases achieved was a rise in the revenue from clerical tenths to about £14,000 in 1635, which may well have contributed to worsening relations between Laud and the treasurer. Recusancy fines rose from about £5,200 in 1630 to about £12,000 in 1635, though they had been as high as £26,000 in 1634. This particular increase indicates that Portland's alleged crypto-Catholicism does not seem to have affected his revenue policies. Licences to retail tobacco, introduced in 1633, yielded £9,320 in 1633–4, and £8,919 in the following year. The revenues of the Court of Wards rose from about £45,000 to about £50,000 between 1630 and 1635, and were to rise still further after 1635, when Cottington became master of the Court of Wards, reaching a peak of £83,100 in 1639, and yielding £76,200 in the following year.

In the more important field of the customs revenue, Portland achieved an annual increase of £16,000 on the rent of the three farms of wines and currants by amalgamating them into one consolidated farm. But his failure to increase the rent of the great farm above £150,000, that is £10,000 below the rent which had been negotiated by his old chief, Lord Treasurer Middlesex, in 1621, at the height of the economic depression, led to allegations from some of his enemies that, like Lord Treasurers Dorset and Salisbury at the beginning of the previous reign, Portland was in the pocket of the farmers. However, while he lost on the rent, he gained in terms of the substantial advances made by the farmers. These took the form of allowing the crown both to overdraw its rent to amounts varying between £12,669 in 1629–30 and £53,067 in 1633–4, and to anticipate the rents of future years to the tune of sums varying between £30,000 in 1630–1 and £73,569 in 1632–3. At a time when the range of credit facilities open to the government was contracting sharply, such services were of vital importance. In addition the revival of trade and the issue of a new Book of Rates in 1635 brought substantial increases in the revenue from impositions.[5]

Impositions were, of course, a prerogative revenue, although the fact that tonnage and poundage had also not been voted by parliament makes the distinction between the two somewhat tenuous. Another very important prerogative revenue in this period of prerogative rule *par excellence* was ship money. Over the whole period from 1634 to 1640 ship money yielded more than £730,000, not counting the very substantial contributions of London, which were made in terms of ships rather than of money in lieu of ships, except in the case of the 1639 writ collected in 1639–40. Despite the very large sums yielded by ship money, all of which were genuinely devoted to naval provision, the growing gap between the government's expectations and the actual receipts, culminating in the enormous shortfall of over £170,000 in 1639–40, was a cause of increasing consternation to the government.[6]

Fines in distraint of knighthood and fines for encroaching on royal forests are both examples of the government's determined exploitation of prerogative rights with little concern for anything but their fiscal yield. It was in fact only too happy that gentlemen who had possessed land worth £40 per annum and upwards should have failed to take up the now dubious honour of knighthood at the time of Charles's coronation, since if they had done so, this would have further swollen the inflation of honours which had deliberately been halted since Buckingham's death. It suited the government's book much better to fine such gentlemen for not taking up knighthood. This was a highly successful fiscal device which added £173,537 to royal revenues between 1630 and 1635, though it also, not surprisingly, occasioned a great deal of irritation amongst the gentry. The insistence on the ancient and often forgotten boundaries of the royal forests, established via pressure on local juries, and the re-establishment of forest courts imposing swingeing fines on those who were deemed to have encroached on them, was a similar device, in that the crown had no wish to clear out such encroachers, desiring only to profit by the fines they paid. Here certainly the hostility which its action aroused was disproportionate to the revenue gained, which amounted only to £37,400 over the period 1636–40. In the hands of Holland, who was appointed chief justice in Eyre of all forests south of the Trent, the revival of forest jurisdiction became a weapon to be used in factional warfare against dependants and associates of Portland, such as his secretary John Gibbons and his friends Sir Basil Brooke and George Mynne, all of whom were fined for forest offences which could not but reflect on the lord treasurer himself.[7]

The exact fiscal value of monopolies is uncertain, since this was not only a matter of the rents which they yielded to the crown, but also of the expenditure they saved through affording a rake-off for courtiers who acted as intermediaries in the market for such concessions, which, since the statute of 1624, now took a corporate form. The most notorious of Caroline domestic monopolies, the Westminster Soapmaking Company, is of additional interest in the context of court factional struggle because it provided an important cause of contention between Laud and Portland, and, after the latter's death, Cottington. The fact that the Westminster Company, established in 1632, was backed by the lord treasurer and a number of his Catholic and crypto-Catholic associates caused its product to be popularly known as 'popish soap'. Laud became a determined supporter of the claims of the ousted independent soapboilers, who had offered to form a company paying double the tax per ton paid by the Westminster Company to the crown. Portland's death solved nothing, for Cottington took up the cudgels on behalf of the monopolists, arguing that it would be dishonourable for the king to go back on his undertaking to the company, though not opposing an increase in their dues. Ultimately, after many frustrations, Laud did obtain his desire, and the Westminster Company was ousted in favour of his independent protégés, who, however, now formed an association as restrictive as its predecessor, except for its wider membership and the fact that the ban on the use of fish-oil was lifted.

Another issue over which Laud and Cottington clashed was the king's desire to enlarge Richmond Park for hunting, which involved interference with the property rights of a number of local people. Laud disliked the scheme for good social reasons as well as deploring the expense of building a long wall around the new circuit of the park at a cost of £10,900. As chancellor of the Exchequer and, like Laud, a member of the Treasury Commission which had taken over following Portland's death, Cottington also had argued against the scheme in private conversation with the king. However this was unknown to Laud, who was conscious only of Cottington's support for it in public and of the banter in which he indulged at the expense of its opponents.

But if Laud got his way only very belatedly over the soap monopoly and was worsted by Cottington over Richmond Park, there was another issue of far greater moment on which he emerged completely victorious. This was the matter of the choice of a successor to Portland, following the lord treasurer's death in 1635. As in the case of the succession to Salisbury in 1612 and, though perhaps not quite so clearly, to Suffolk in 1618, the Treasury Commission which took over on Portland's death was clearly a very temporary expedient. While there were certainly no grounds for presumption that chancellors of the Exchequer automatically succeeded to the vacant higher office, the highly experienced and able Cottington had some reason to consider himself as favourite for the succession. But Laud, moved partly, no doubt, by considerations of factional advantage, but also by his sincere conviction that the appointment of Cottington would spell the end to all hopes of thoroughgoing financial reform, persuaded the king to appoint William Juxon, who had succeeded him as bishop of London in 1633.

Juxon's appointment as lord treasurer in March 1636 may be said to mark something of a watershed and, if not the beginning of a Laudian ascendancy and the rule of 'Thorough', at least a very notable strengthening of the archbishop's position. Nevertheless, one must also beware of exaggerating its importance. Although he had acquired a reputation as an administrative reformer in his large and complex diocese, the new lord treasurer was very inexperienced in matters of royal finance, and had to rely to no small extent on the expertise of just those persons – and notably of Cottington, who continued to be chancellor – whose influence he had been appointed to combat. Moreover, there was a large number of influential persons scattered across the whole range of court factional groupings who would do their utmost to frustrate thoroughgoing economic reforms in so far as these menaced their own interests: among them the earl of Pembroke, head of the royal Household since 1630; the earl of Holland, who took over the royal Bedchamber in 1636; the earl of Denbigh, master of the Wardrobe since the previous reign; and the earl of Dorset, the queen's lord chamberlain, to mention but a few of them. In these circumstances it is perhaps surprising that the new lord treasurer achieved as much as he did, not least in the matter of reduction of the royal pensions bill.[8] While his policies in general were likely to bring him into disfavour with the queen, as had Portland's, in one of his changes he worked hand-in-glove with one of Henrietta's favourites, the courtly multi-concessionaire Lord Goring. This was the prising away of the great and petty customs farms from the grip of the syndicates which had been so strongly maintained by Portland. From the end of 1637 a new syndicate led by Goring – containing, it is true, some members of the old – managed both farms at a notably improved rent of £172,500 for the great, and £72,500 for the petty farm. But a corollary of the higher rent seems to have been a much lower level of credit provision from the farmers, who in the crisis of royal affairs in 1640 were replaced by a new group, dominated by the most powerful figure of the pre-1637 syndicates, Sir Paul Pindar.[9]

It has become something of a commonplace to play down the significance of much of royal social policy by pointing out that it was activated more by fiscal than by paternalistic considerations. Long ago George Unwin showed how the royal concern to foster – especially in London and especially during these years – new organizations of small masters striving to free themselves from the mercantile interests which dominated their parent gilds was a good deal less altruistic than might appear at first sight; in fact that it was too often bound up with the provision of one form or another of out-relief for courtiers who secured a substantial rake-off from such concessions. Certainly, given the somewhat incongruous mixture of paternalism and fiscalism in royal policy towards the gilds, the former consideration, though always present, too often took second place to the latter.[10] Fiscal considerations also loomed very large in the government's anti-depopulation policies, which were especially active in the decade. As in the case of distraint of knighthood and forest fines, it was often easier to take fines and tacitly condone depopulating enclosure than to right the social evils which the Caroline depopulation commissions had been ostensibly created to remedy. But, as in the case of the gilds, to say this is not necessarily to go completely along with Dr Joan Thirsk's verdict that 'the punishment of enclosures degenerated into a money-raising device and little else'; though this is certainly true of the many cases where, as Professor Beresford has shown, it was landowners who had participated in enclosure by agreement rather than depopulators who were mulcted.[11]

One argument against completely discounting the paternalistic, as distinct from the fiscal, element in social policy is to be found in the energy which the government devoted to the supervision of policy at the local level in matters where there was nothing financial at stake. The immediate origins of the so-called Orders and Directions which were issued by the Privy Council in January 1631 was the disastrous harvest of the previous year, and the need for drastic measures was to be reinforced by another bad harvest in 1631. The resulting hardship and near-famine conditions accentuated the need for efficiently administered poor relief and vagrancy control, control of food supplies and of grain consumption by brewers and alehouses, supervision of the arrangements for apprenticing the children of the indigent and a variety of other matters. The Orders and Directions were an attempt to galvanize local government into taking effective measures to deal with what seemed to the central government to be a highly dangerous situation both in terms of human distress and of the consequent threat to public order. The 'Orders' provided for regular divisional meetings of JPs to deal with these matters, while the 'Directions' dealt with the specific measures which were called for by the crisis. A commission of privy councillors was set up, and divided into small groups, each of which was attached to a particular assize circuit and given a general oversight over these matters within this geographical compass; along, of course, with the assize judges, who had indeed been charged with exercising this particular oversight ever since the previous century. The main medium of central control was to operate via the quarterly certificates of their actions sent by local JPs for the scrutiny of the new conciliar commissioners. These measures are eloquent testimony to the seriousness with which the government regarded the crisis and its determination to devise an appropriate mechanism for dealing with it.[12] Undoubtedly the immediate impact of the Orders was spectacular. But while Professor T. G. Barnes insists that the improvement was sustained in Somerset throughout the following decade, county studies of Sussex, Kent and Cheshire suggest an initial spectacular improvement followed by a falling off of both magisterial energy and rigorous conciliar supervision, a picture which is borne out by Dr Quintrell's recent survey of the general problem.[13]

A significant contrast with this state of affairs is provided by the rigours of Wentworth's personal rule as lord deputy of Ireland. On the face of it Wentworth's achievement was spectacular, or, to use his own favourite adjective, 'thorough'. He freed the English Exchequer from the need to make regular contributions towards Irish solvency; he made significant and determined moves in the direction of a Laudian type church, and indeed, in the matter of the resumption of former ecclesiastical lands and impropriated revenues, his efforts were attended with a great deal more success than those of his friend the archbishop back at home. In a word he succeeded in establishing a personal supremacy such as was enjoyed neither by his predecessors nor by his successors. Yet the last fact serves to emphasize the limits of his achievement: its most important effect was probably the fright it gave to Englishmen who watched with horrified fascination the implementation of policies which it did not require much imagination to see as a trial-run for what might later be done at home. And, as Professor Kearney has been at pains to emphasize, the most lasting effect of the rule of the earl of Strafford (as Wentworth became in 1640) in Ireland was the creation of an improbable alliance between its opponents, the dispossessed Ulster Catholic Irish and the Catholic Old English. This was to come to terrible fruition in the great Irish massacres of 1641.[14]

RELIGION: LAUD AND HIS OPPONENTS

Following his promotion to the episcopal see of London in 1628, William Laud had to wait another five years before Abbot, the old-style Calvinist primate, died, and he succeeded him at Canterbury, to be replaced at London by his faithful follower William Juxon. In the previous year, 1632, Laud's former patron, Richard Neile, had become archbishop of York. The dominant Arminian party was now successfully placing its adherents in the most strategic sees in the church. For example, John Buckeridge had moved from Rochester to Ely in 1628; Matthew Wren became bishop of Hereford in 1634, of Norwich in 1635 and (following Buckeridge's death) of Ely in 1638; being succeeded at Norwich by the man who was probably the most notorious ritualist of all, Richard Montague, the author of *A New Gag*, who had previously succeeded the Calvinist Carleton at Chichester in 1628. William Pierce had become bishop of Peterborough in 1630, and of Bath and Wells (Laud's old see) in 1632.

It is difficult to over-emphasize the importance of the Arminian ascendancy, in terms of the reputation both of the monarchy and of the institution of episcopacy. In the short run the emphasis on liturgical and ceremonial innovation and on what Laud described as the beauty of holiness encouraged the popular identification of Arminians with disguised papists whose goal was to create Protestant disunity and to soften up ecclesiastical resistance against the ultimate Roman assault. The same popular interpretation found confirmation in the anti-Calvinist, anti-predestination, doctrinal emphasis of the Arminians, as well as in Laud's determination to raise the esteem in which clerics were held – an aim which, as some were not slow to observe, accorded ill with the mean social origins of many of the most prominent Laudian clergymen, as did their insistence on divine right episcopacy. Laud was particularly insistent that bishops and deans and chapters should employ only short-term leases when letting out ecclesiastical land to laymen. For in addition to the very obvious economic advantages of this practice, there was also, as Laud's contemporary biographer and follower Peter Heylin emphasized, the further motive that short leases would make lay tenants – some of whom were themselves quite important people – more frequently beholden to the ecclesiastical landlords on whom they were dependent for a renewal of their tenure. Also singularly lacking in tact and discretion were those Laudian churchmen who went out of their way to deplore the church's losses in material wealth, and therefore of influence, since the Reformation, a view which further underlined the popular identification of them with papists. But in England, unlike Germany and Scotland, the issue of restoring church property revolved more around impropriated tithes than confiscated lands. By attempting either to buy back these revenues or, given an insufficiency of funds to do this, to get lay impropriators to devote a greater portion of their tithe revenues to spiritual uses, and to screw up the yield of such tithes as remained in ecclesiastical hands, Laud was pursuing a policy not unlike that of his predecessor, Bancroft, though this was hardly likely to commend his action to his critics.[15]

One way of making the church's influence more strongly felt in the land, and a way which certainly commended itself to Laud, was to increase the power of the spiritual courts. The conflict between ecclesiastical and temporal jurisdiction, which had been especially manifested in the first half of the previous reign by the dispute over writs of Prohibition calling cases out of the spiritual into the temporal courts, had quietened following the dismissal of Sir Edward Coke as lord chief justice in 1615. Not only were such writs less easily obtained thereafter, but during the reign of Charles I judges were under very considerable pressure to exercise the utmost restraint in this matter. To many common lawyers the virtual removal of such checks to ecclesiastical jurisdiction appeared as a direct threat to their professional livelihood and had heightened their antagonism to the civil lawyers to whom practice in the spiritual courts provided the most important of their professional opportunities. Moreover, given the fact that the ecclesiastical courts were the main instruments for enforcing spiritual and moral discipline not only on laymen for numerous offences which today are no longer crimes, but also on Puritan dissidents, there was obviously abundant scope for community of interest between Puritans and common lawyers.

Despite its apparent defeat in the 1640s, Laudian innovation has left a permanent mark on the Anglican church. For all the fury which such issues aroused at the time, the altar is now railed off at the east end of churches, the congregation bows at the name of Jesus and organs are used in services. Such issues, unlike those which have their origins in the Anglo-Catholic revival of the nineteenth century, no longer divide high from low church Anglicans. Yet in its own day Arminianism polarized churchmen between the Laudians and the moderate Calvinists. For Calvinism was not only the doctrine of Puritan dissidents, most of whom were in any case loyal episcopalian churchmen. It had also been up to that time the orthodoxy of the church of England as professed by Archbishops Whitgift and Abbot and Bishops Davenant, Carleton and Morton. But it was now treated as heterodox and even heretical. Moderate Church of England Calvinists were castigated as Puritan extremists, and the conservative Foxeian episcopalians William Prynne and John Bastwick were mutilated on the same scaffold in 1637 as the radical anti-episcopalian and future Independent Henry Burton. Puritan sabbatarian beliefs were outraged by the reissue in 1633 of James I's Declaration of Sports of 1618. Puritan stipendiary lecturers in churches came under more rigorous episcopal scrutiny and many of them had their licences withdrawn. They had become an object of suspicion to Laud not only because of their Puritan views, but also because they were able to preach without holding livings and therefore having to say the liturgy, and because the finance for their stipends often came from secular bodies who, paying the piper, would, it was argued, be all too likely to call the tune.[16] In addition, following a case in the Court of Exchequer instigated by Laud in 1633, the Puritan Feoffees for Impropriations were suppressed. Founded five years earlier, the Feoffees had been enormously more successful than Laud in recovering impropriated tithes for spiritual uses. Where they offended was in applying such revenues to augment not the resources of the parishes to which they appertained but those of orthodox anti-Arminian parsons elsewhere, and especially in using them to endow Puritan lectureships.

The logic of Laudianism was the logic of polarization, and the squeezing of the moderate ecclesiastical centre by the extreme wings. Moderate mainstream Foxeian Puritan churchmen who up to now had reverenced godly bishops as the partners of the godly prince in the work of godly reformation, and as the descendants, if not of the apostles, at least of Marian Protestant martyr-bishops, now came increasingly to look upon episcopacy with distaste, as the institution became hopelessly tarred with the Laudian brush. There still remained some old-fashioned non-Arminian bishops, such as Morton, Ussher and Laud's enemy the worldly John Williams of Lincoln: men who favoured *iure humano* episcopacy and who insisted that Laud's *iure divino* episcopacy was an aberration and corruption of an honourable institution. But they were voices crying in the wilderness, and it is one of the major tragedies of Stuart history that Laud, the great exalter of the powers of episcopacy, was the most powerful single factor in bringing about its downfall.

Laud might popularly be viewed as a crypto-Catholic fifth-columnist, but his attitude towards recusancy makes it abundantly clear that this reputation has no foundation in fact. Frustrated in his desire to do much about Catholicism at court on account of the queen, and all too aware that this reinforced popular suspicions about his own pro-Catholic attitude, it was as if he compensated by turning with particular severity on Catholics in the country who did not enjoy this protective aura. Provincial recusants had every reason to make unfavourable comparisons between relaxed application of the recusancy laws in the later years of James I, when the Spanish marriage had been contemplated, and their reinforcement under his son; and between the rough treatment accorded to them and the leniency shown to courtly recusants.

THE SURVIVAL OF OPPOSITION

Following the dissolution of parliament in March 1629, some of those whom the king undoubtedly thought of as parliamentary troublemakers found themselves in prison, but most of them, including Selden, Valentine and Holles, made their peace with the king, were prepared to give security for good behaviour in future and were quickly released. Only Eliot remained in the Tower, from which he was never released. Indeed the regime itself was notably strengthened by taking in tow some of the parliamentarians who had been among its chief critics in the days of Buckingham's hegemony. As was shown in the last chapter, Sir Thomas Wentworth had been made president of the Council of the North in December 1628 and was to be made lord deputy of Ireland in 1631; Sir Dudley Digges became master of the Rolls in 1630, and Sir William Noy attorney general in 1631. Noy was to expiate his sins as one of the more awkward critics of government in the 1620s by playing a crucial role in laying the legal foundations for levies such as ship money, forest fines and fines in distraint of knighthood.

But it would be wrong to conclude that all opposition was either cowed into submission or placated by being taken aboard the bandwagon of Personal Government. Parliament might appear to be a thing of the past, but there were not lacking other foci of discontent through which opposition continued to smoulder: among them the institutions of local government, such as quarter sessions; the great chartered companies for foreign trade, disillusioned at the bitter fruits of their old connection with crown and court and aware of the new and more sympathetic response of the recently dissolved parliament to their problems; the great country houses of magnates such as the earls of Warwick and Bedford; and not least, as was first emphasized by the late Professor A. P. Newton, three companies formed to engage in transatlantic colonization. The earliest of these companies, as well as the most successful and least élitist in terms of its membership, was the Massachusetts Bay Company, founded in 1628. The names of the members of the other two, a few of whom were also subscribers in the Massachusetts Bay Company, read like a roll-call of the most influential lay Puritans in England – among them Lords Saye and Sele, Brooke and Warwick, Sir Thomas Barrington, John Pym and Oliver St John. In economic terms the Providence Island Company, founded in 1630 to colonize a Caribbean island as a base for action against the Spanish colonies, was a pretty disastrous flop, while the Saybrooke

Company, for which a patent was granted in 1630 for a colony in New England taking its title from the two godly peers of these names, was hardly a roaring success. But economic failure or not, one does not have to swallow whole the conspiracy theories of royalist pamphleteers in the 1640s to be conscious of the fact that, like the country houses of Puritan aristocrats, the Providence Island Company's rooms in Gray's Inn Road were a place where a great deal more almost certainly went on other than discussion about the dubious business prospects of colonial ventures.[17]

What exactly went on one can only guess at. But one such guess might be that discussion sometimes turned on Laudian religious innovations and sometimes on the discontent aroused by some of the methods which the government was employing to finance itself. Conscious of the fact that those who opposed such measures would be likely to take their stand on the defence of traditional and time-honoured ways of doing things, the government, no doubt heeding the advice of legal antiquarians such as Noy, strove to represent some of its most bitterly resented fiscal devices as having a firm basis in tradition and being in no sense innovatory. Needless to say, the fact that it appealed to the unquestioned practices of an often remote historical past in defence of its exactions did not make them any the more acceptable to those who had to pay. Many of the latter were all too conscious of the fact that the crown was pushing its demands beyond reasonable limits in, for example, the restoration of ancient and long-forgotten forest boundaries to the financial detriment of those who found themselves – often to their astonishment – dwelling within them.

Similarly, the fact that there were Elizabethan as well as Caroline precedents for the exaction of ship money did not prevent it from being the most contentious of all the fiscal levies of the Personal Government. Here indeed there was a sufficient number of novel elements about the levy to allow its opponents to take their stand on grounds of custom and tradition. Not the least significant of these was the government's insistence on the adoption of novel assessment systems designed both to increase the yield of the levy and to make its incidence more socially equitable; an aim which certainly did not endear it to the normally under-assessed county élites, who were thus afforded the opportunity of reconciling the defence of tradition with that of their own pockets. But, quite apart from the mode of assessment, there were objections to the tax *per se*, more especially once it appeared to have become an annual levy. Even before then, the city of London, although not pushing its objections to the first ship money writ of 1634 to the extent of refusing to supply the required ships, had by its protest provided a text for individual refusers. Prominent among these was the indomitable Richard Chambers, who had already been one of the heroes of the tonnage and poundage dispute of 1628–9.

But it was not until the aftermath of John Hampden's celebrated trial in the Court of Exchequer Chamber in 1637–8 for refusing to pay the sums assessed on him in accordance with the third ship money writ that opposition to the levy became sufficiently widespread to become the occasion of really serious alarm to the government. Hampden's case, which was conducted by two lawyer clients of the earl of Bedford, Oliver St John and Robert Holborne, the first of whom was to make his formidable reputation on the case, rested not on the innovation of sending the writ to inland as well as to maritime counties nor on the king's right to levy such a tax in a time of undoubted national peril. What was challenged was the appropriateness of raising such an extra-parliamentary tax except in circumstances in which the bypassing of parliament was justified by the extreme urgency of the occasion. But this was itself belied by the long period elapsing between the date of the writ and the date at which the ships or the wherewithal to purchase them had to be provided. The fact that Hampden lost the case by the narrowest possible margin, five of the twelve judges deciding in his favour, was a technical victory but a moral defeat for the king. The case itself fuelled growing resistance to the levy, which extended in some cases to local officials such as JPs and even to some deputy lieutenants. The sheriffs, who were held personally responsible for any shortfall in the sums collected in their counties, were at their wits' end, subject to relentless conciliar pressure on the one hand and the dilatoriness of their subordinates and the resistance of taxpayers on the other. A number of them, including the sheriffs of London and Middlesex, were rebuked in the strongest terms for their alleged lack of enthusiasm for the levy, while two successive sheriffs of Northamptonshire had to suffer the indignity of going about the business of supervising the collection in their counties in the hardly disguised custody of a sergeant-at-arms, who was instructed to see to it that they discharged their duties properly.

Ship money was only the most spectacular of the issues over which continued central pressure on local authorities produced a breakdown of royal authority at local level. The classic description of the resentment of the local magistracy at the burdens imposed by the conciliar Orders and Directions of 1631 is that given in Professor Barnes's account of Somerset under the Personal Rule. But it has already been remarked that developments in other counties offer a very different picture, and it would be dangerous to assume that the burden was uniform both over the whole of the decade and the whole of the country. As Dr Quintrell observes, it is significant that in that ragbag of charges against royal government in the 1630s, the Grand Remonstrance of 1641, which loses no opportunity of including anything of moment, the Orders and Directions do not even rate a passing mention.

More solid grounds for magisterial discontent probably derived from the king's continued pursuit of his aim of creating the 'perfect militia'.[18] Resentment about the raising of local rates based on the prerogative function of the lieutenancy rather than on quarter-sessional authority dated back to the time of the repeal of the Marian statute relating to militia provision in 1604. Much was made of the coincidence of the absence of both parliamentary (statutory) and quarter-sessional authority for the rates for militia training. This point was urged by the deputy lieutenants of Herefordshire upon the lord lieutenant, the earl of Bridgwater, in October 1633, and it is impossible to be certain how far such objections proceeded from a genuine sense of constitutional outrage and how far they simply served as a respectable excuse for not paying up. In the later 1620s such rates had been only one of a vast accumulation of financial burdens relating to military preparedness during the war years. Such burdens were naturally lessened following the coming of peace in 1630, but far from being the occasion of thankfulness, the absence of war simply served to pinpoint the continued burden and alleged unconstitutionality of the militia rate. In 1630 it was reported that the Dorset muster-master's stipend was two and a half years in arrears because the Dorset gentry were failing to pay their rates. In 1635 the grand jury of Shropshire declared the muster-master's office superfluous and the levying of a rate for his stipend a grievance. And from December 1637 the king was increasingly infuriated by the way in which the reluctant city fathers of London dragged their feet over paying the stipend of the muster-master whose appointment he had pressed upon them.

In concluding these remarks about central pressure on local magistrates, a word ought to be said about two institutions whose operations affected only limited areas, the six northern counties on the one hand and Wales and four border counties of England on the other. Of these two great Tudor creations, the hold of the Council of Wales seems if anything to have slackened in the 1630s, perhaps because it had powerful enemies at court as well as in the country. But, according to the later royalist Edward Hyde, Wentworth as president of the Council of the North, 'every day procured new authority and power to oppress' the northern counties, and to keep local magistrates up to the mark.[19]

COURT AND COUNTRY

For all the fact that the Caroline court of the 1630s was nothing like so homogeneous in outlook as used to be thought, there can be no doubt that Laudian pressures, unpopular financial policies, the development of a selfconscious and élitist court culture and an accentuated emphasis on exclusivism and lineage – 'the privileges of generous blood are more to be cared for than heretofore', it was announced in 1634 – did make for polarization between court and country. The inflation of honours had ended with the death of Buckingham, and the growing exclusivism of the court became a factor to be reckoned with even at the highest social levels. As Professor Stone observes of the peerage, 'political and religious opposition combined with enforcement of government regulations about residence in London and the drying up of the flow of favours sharply to reduce the number of court peers to between a third and a half of the whole body. Charles, Henrietta Maria, and Laud thus contrived to restrict the Court to a narrower circle than had been seen for over a century.'

This narrowing of the basis of the court finds a further reflection in the court connection in the City of London, though this development had been noteworthy during the previous decade, beginning with the exemption of the chartered companies from the provisions of the Statute of Monopolies in 1624 and culminating in their role during the tonnage and poundage dispute in 1628–9. The resulting split within the concessionary interest, with the chartered companies increasingly alienated from the court and domestic concessionaires such as monopolists, licensees and customs farmers, continued to characterize the 1630s. It was, if anything, intensified by new developments such as the king's support for his Scottish relative, the duke of Richmond and Lennox, in his dispute with the Merchant Adventurers over the price of his cloth export licences; the Levant Company's distaste for the ambassadors to Constantinople, appointed by the crown but paid by the company; and the royal countenancing both of court-backed privateers in the Red Sea and of a rival East India association organized by Sir William Courteen and some courtly associates. As in other areas, the basis of the court-orientated interest in the City had narrowed in a way which was to make it relatively easy for the Long Parliament in 1640–1 to pick off its chief remaining elements, the customs farmers and domestic monopolists, without in any way alienating the vast bulk of concessionaires in the chartered companies.

As if this was not enough, the City government of London, in which directors of the chartered companies figured quite prominently, became engaged in a number of bitter disputes with the crown. Here, as elsewhere, the latter displayed an astonishing propensity for alienating people who ought to have been its natural supporters. We have already seen how the government encountered opposition in the City over two issues in which it was also running into difficulties in other parts of England: militia training and ship money. But these are only two of a large number of contentious issues over which the crown and the London City fathers clashed. Among the others were two court cases brought by the crown against the City: in the Court of Exchequer in 1633 over its malpractices in the sale of royal lands which had been conveyed to the City's trustees in 1628 in satisfaction of royal debts; and in the Star Chamber in 1635 over the City's alleged mismanagement of the Londonderry plantation. In both cases the City lost and was fined and humiliated in the process. Further causes of dispute were the renewal in 1636 of formerly abandoned royal claims to fees for encroachment on London streets and wasteland; the stiffening of royal building controls and the activities of the royal building commission; the creation in 1636 of a royal Corporation of the Suburbs, more especially since it was given control over the so-called 'liberties', pockets of former monastic land within the boundaries of the City, but, for the most part, outside its jurisdiction; and disputes with Laud over tithes and the City's contribution towards the rebuilding of St Paul's cathedral. Finally, far from supporting the City fathers against the commoners, as Professor Stone has suggested, Charles infuriated them by putting his authority behind the attempts both to form breakaway incorporations of craftsmen, and – ignoring the so-called custom of London which allowed any member of any City gild to exercise any trade – to translate gildsmen to the gilds which bore the name of and claimed to control the crafts which they pursued.[20]

If the last of these causes of contention between crown and City appears to run counter to the notion of a royal tendency to favour hierarchy and exclusivism in every walk of life, the apparent contradiction is partly explicable by the incongruous mixture of fiscal advantage and genuine paternalism which, as indicated earlier, characterized the royal attitude in this matter. But if there is one area where the growing exclusivism of the court and its consequent alienation from the country is apparent, it is in the sphere of cultural history, and more particularly in the genuine innovativeness associated with the court in this, as in so many other matters.[21] The reign of Charles I marks the apogee of what was undoubtedly a distinctive court culture. Even if this was not the concern of the court in general, but of minority groups of cultivated courtiers within it, the fact that many of these activities, in contrast to those of the previous reign, centred on the king himself tended to identify the sovereign with an innovative and exotic culture, which in turn helped to confirm the already conservative suspicions of many of the chief critics of the regime.

Thus Charles's collection of great Renaissance and mannerist paintings and his patronage – on a scale not known at the English court since the reign of Henry VIII – of great baroque masters such as Mytens, Van Dyck and Rubens, made him the object of suspicion rather than admiration to most of his contemporaries. The moderate Puritan William Prynne dismissed the royal art collection as significant evidence of a popish design to exploit the king's artistic taste as a means of subverting true religion in England. Similarly, while what impresses the modern observer of the neo-Palladian architectural masterpieces of Inigo Jones (who had also enjoyed the patronage of James I who had commissioned both the Queen's House at Greenwich and the new Banqueting House in Whitehall) is their classical chasteness and astonishing anticipation of the quintessentially English Georgian style, contemporaries saw his work only as an exotic importation. Just as the religious iconography of Charles's pictures tended to confirm the suspicions of Puritans like Prynne, so did the use to which Jones's buildings were put – allegedly Italianate masques in the Banqueting House, Laudian ceremonies behind the new west front of St Paul's, and popish masses in Henrietta Maria's chapel in St James' – serve to reinforce the transalpine and Counter-Reformation connotations of Jones's neo-Palladian idiom.

In the world of music and drama the supreme age of Byrd, Dowland and Shakespeare had now passed. However in both secular and sacred music the court and the chapels royal remained the centres of innovation *par excellence*. At the court foreign, and especially Italian, musicians continued to find a warm welcome. Indeed one English composer, John Cooper, thought it advantageous to italianize his name to Giovanni Coperario. It was at court that the new Italian style of declamatory writing for solo voice flourished, while the chapels royal were as innovatory in the matter of music as they were in that of liturgy. Indeed, organs and polyphony were as objectionable to conservative and Puritan worshippers as were altars, crucifixes and wafer-bread. While it has recently been observed that the Puritans were less unequivocally hostile to all forms of drama than was once imagined,[22] the early Stuart period did see the development of an important distinction between public playhouses such as the Globe, the Fortune and the Red Bull and the fashionable coterie theatres such as those at Blackfriars and Salisbury Court. Moreover, the Caroline period saw the emergence of a new theatrical genre, the so-called 'Cavalier drama'.[23] Of relatively minor importance to the historian of drama, compared with the massive achievements of the age of Shakespeare, the phenomenon is nevertheless of great interest in this context, since it reflects, in its emphasis on platonic as distinct from corporeal love, the efforts of the king to clean up the court. But it also reflects the growing exclusivism of the court in the heavy stress which it lays on considerations of proper courtly behaviour and punctilio.

Such considerations apply *a fortiori* to the most characteristic and exclusive of all early Stuart art forms, the court masque. It is arguable that the greatest days of the masque had now passed following the irreconcilable quarrel between two collaborators of genius, Inigo Jones and his librettist Ben Jonson. For Jonson's masques had at least consistently held up to the court a model of what it ought to be, whereas his successors in the 1630s were less exacting in the demands they made of courtly audiences, on most of whom the neoplatonic subtleties of the entertainment were completely lost and who went simply to gawp at Inigo's spectacular scenic effects and to conform to courtly fashion. However, the masque is a phenomenon significant to the political as well as to the cultural historian. Celebrating the closed world of the court and culminating in the ritual glorification of the monarch, the masque presented as potent an image of monarchy and court and all that they stood for as Van Dyck's equestrian portraits of the king or Rubens's ceiling panels in the Banqueting House; as potent perhaps, but less permanent, for one of the things which made masques an object of criticism was their combination of extravagance and ephemerality. They were rarely put on more than a very few times, and sometimes only once.[24]

In this as in their élitist emphasis, masques symbolize perhaps better than any other art form the growing distance between court and country. Even if the two were never quite the completely distinct entities envisaged by some contemporaries and some modern historians, there can be no doubt that they were growing dangerously apart. In that high art-form which perhaps best epitomizes the contrary ethos of the country, the country-house poems of Ben

Jonson, Thomas Carew, Robert Herrick and others, the country tends to be identified with tradition and virtue and the court with innovation and vice: function as opposed to ornament; resident as opposed to absentee landownership; hospitality as opposed to neglect of local duties; paternalism as opposed to exploitation; temperance as opposed to excess; sexual simplicity and chasteness as opposed (rather unfairly in a Caroline context) to both homosexual and heterosexual licence; and with plain speaking as opposed to grovelling servility. Of course, the contrast was grossly overdone, but it plays a crucially important role in the fabrication of a popular image of courtier and countryman and the creation of what might perhaps be described as an ideology of the country.

What other elements went into this ideology? Given the fact that a principal reason for the shrinkage of support for royal policies is to be found in the consequences of what was arguably one of Charles I's worst mistakes, his espousal of Laudian Arminianism, it is appropriate to inquire how far Puritanism, the religious antithesis of Arminianism, came to acquire an extra-religious significance as an ideology of alienation, in a word, of the country against the court. Such questions need to be approached with the greatest caution, since, for all the sweeping claims which have been made for the ideological significance of Puritanism by the proponents of a variety of different explanations of the struggles of the mid-seventeenth century, there is certainly nothing to suggest that it drew its adherents from, or was the ideology of, any particular social, political or economic grouping. Puritans are to be found in virtually every social milieu: among noblemen, gentlemen, businessmen, master-craftsmen, yeoman-farmers and labourers. Of course, it has been pointed out by Max Weber and others that the Calvinist emphasis – not all Calvinists were of course Puritans – on the virtues of godly application to one's worldly calling and abstinence in the expenditure of the fruits of that diligence makes for a marvellous ready-made ideology of capitalism.[25] But, as the master of Peterhouse has reminded us, it might also serve as an ideology of economic retrenchment for impoverished gentlemen striving to make ends meet and grateful for a creed which stressed the ideological merit of that abstinence and parsimony which to so many contemporaries were incompatible with gentility.[26] Other historians, among them Dr Michael Walzer, have seen the Puritan psychology as a sort of blueprint for modern revolutionary psychology. Walzer points out how, in its relentless emphasis on the direct and unmediated connection between man and God, Puritanism acted as a powerful solvent of local and kinship associations.[27] Yet the history of the seventeenth century offers numerous examples of the strongly localist temper of godly Puritan magistrates such as Sir Nathaniel Bacon in Norfolk and Sir Richard Knightley and Lord Montagu of Boughton in Northamptonshire. These were men, the temper of whose localism was sustained and not destroyed by their Puritan faith; not least since among the many centralist pressures to which they were subjected were pressures for religious conformity. The identification of their Puritanism and their localism was the easier in that, as opponents both of high-church ritualism and of centralist government pressures, they could plausibly represent themselves as the opponents of innovation and the upholders of tradition.

In their avowed emphasis on the need to return to the practice of the primitive, apostolic church, the Puritans found a significant constitutional parallel in the emphasis of Sir Edward Coke, John Pym and other MPs, on the ancient and immemorial constitution. In this and other respects they again saw themselves as defenders of tradition against innovators who argued that what had been appropriate practices in the days when Christians were a persecuted minority were no more necessary or appropriate to the modern church than were the primitive constitutional arrangements prevailing in the primeval forest to the modern state. Moreover, since Arminian divines such as Roger Mainwaring and Robert Sibthorpe defended both divine right episcopacy and the divine right of monarchs to raise unparliamentary taxation, their Puritan and other opponents were the more easily able to equate resistance to the one with resistance to the other. Prynne, the vehement Puritan opponent of divine right episcopacy, was also the author of the most celebrated of all tracts against ship money. Of course, it is not argued that all opponents of ship money were Puritans, nor even that all Puritans were opponents of ship money. Similarly, when considering Puritanism's role as an ideology of exclusion, it is important to remember that while some men were attracted to the creed because of their exclusion from court and office, others were excluded because they were attracted to the creed.

While it is incontestable that the 1630s saw increased polarization between court and country, there is no need to assume that this alone would have been sufficient to bring England to civil war. The tensions which had accumulated in English politics by 1629 did not have issue in civil war, though they might conceivably have done if the wars against France and Spain with their associated pressure and burdens had continued beyond 1630. Just as war had been the parent of political tension in the later 1620s, so did the wars with the Scots between 1638 and 1640 make the calling of parliament necessary. Without war, it is arguable that Charles's personal rule might have continued indefinitely.

THE SCOTS AND THE BISHOPS' WARS

Before the Act of Union of 1707 English and Scottish history were separate entities. However, the 1630s and 1640s, like the early years of Elizabeth I's reign, are decades for which the main trends of English history are totally incomprehensible without close reference to events north of the Tweed.[28] To seek the causes of Scottish disaffection with Charles I it is necessary to go back to at least the beginning of the reign. The numerous cases of Scottish monarchs succeeding to the throne during their minorities had led to the practice whereby it was generally understood that a monarch might, between the ages of twenty-one and twenty-five, issue an Act of Revocation withdrawing grants of royal property which had been made during his minority. Ignoring the fact that, since he was twenty-four when he succeeded his father, he had never been both the king and a minor simultaneously, Charles nevertheless issued an Act of Revocation before becoming twenty-five in November 1625. Moreover his act was breathtaking and innovatory in its scope, annulling all grants not only of royal but also of ecclesiastical property (including tithes) which had been made since 1540. Here indeed was the sort of reform which, if it had been put into effect in England, would have rejoiced the hearts of Laudian churchmen. Small wonder that a contemporary Scottish annalist describes Charles's revocation as 'the ground stone of all the mischiefs that followed'.

Yet it probably need not have been so, if it had not been for the undue secrecy with which Charles cloaked the precise nature of his intentions, and his characteristic lack of concern to explain to his Scottish subjects that he did not intend to take away their lands without compensation. This, given the very limited financial means at his disposal, would severely restrict the scope of the proposed redistribution of property. It is not argued, however, that a statement of the limits of his practical ambition would have nullified opposition to the king's policies, more particularly since the opposition of the Lords of Erection, the magnates who had profited materially from the Scottish Reformation, related to the potential loss, not simply of some of their landed gains, but also of the feudal superiority which they had retained over persons to whom they granted away such land. But it is undeniable that secrecy and lack of explanation maximized the hostility engendered by the sense of chronic insecurity which afflicted Scottish landowners.

Opposition to the Act of Revocation, however inspired it may have been by self-seeking motives, easily acquired respectability by representing the act as a significant move in a Romeward direction. Similarly, just as the appointment of Bishop Juxon as lord treasurer in England in 1636 occasioned undue disquiet at the apparent reversal of the post-Reformation trend to the secularization of office, so the admittedly unsuccessful attempt to get the Scottish treasurership for the bishop of Ross, and, more important, the appointment of the veteran Archbishop Spottiswoode as chancellor in 1635, caused anxiety in Scotland, where, as in England, there were also complaints about the high-flown pretensions of low-born bishops. But it was especially the liturgical innovations which pointed to the Romeward tendencies allegedly favoured by Charles. The closing years of the previous reign had seen a number of royal ecclesiastical innovations of which the most notable were the so-called Five Articles of Perth, 'the sound of the feet of popery at the door', as one Scottish Presbyterian had described them. But the Articles had not been very strictly enforced in the last years of James's reign, nor indeed in the early years of his son's, when the Act of Revocation, rather than liturgical and ceremonial innovation, occupied the centre of the stage. The first real omen of what was to come was perhaps the ceremonial splendour at Charles's coronation in Edinburgh in 1633. Even then it was not until 1636 that a new set of canons appeared, promulgated by royal fiat and not by the General Assembly of the Scottish kirk, and in the following year the new Prayer Book was introduced. Even with the substantial modifications which had been inserted at the urging of Scottish bishops, its use in Edinburgh provoked riots, fanning a flame which was hardly less nationalistic than religious in temper and finding ultimate expression in the National Covenant of February 1638.[29]

The Covenant is in some ways more noteworthy as a gesture of resistance and solidarity than for its precise recommendations. It left room for concerted action between those who had no objection to moderate Jacobean episcopacy and those who looked on all episcopacy as falling within the scope of the Covenant's denunciation of recent innovations, along with the new canons and the Prayer Book. To Charles, however, the Covenant was anathema.

'So long as the Covenant is in force,' he told the marquis of Hamilton, whom he dispatched to Scotland in May 1638 to act as his commissioner, '. . . I have no more power in Scotland than as a Duke of Venice.' Hamilton's instructions reveal the least attractive and most damaging aspect of Charles's statecraft: what the nineteenth-century historian, Lord Macaulay, was to describe as 'an incurable propensity to dark and crooked ways'. For while Hamilton took with him a royal proclamation suspending the hated canons and Prayer Book, and was empowered to promise that the king would sanction the calling both of a parliament and a General Assembly of the kirk, provided the Covenant was withdrawn, his secret instructions were 'to flatter them with what hopes you please . . . until I be ready to suppress them'.

In addition to the above concessions and the abolition of the Scottish High Commission and the Five Articles of Perth, Charles endeavoured to find a harmless substitute for the Covenant by authorizing the signing of the so-called Negative Confession of 1581. Although this 'King's Covenant', as it was derisorily called, preceded James VI's episcopalian innovations and was therefore capable of being interpreted in an anti-episcopalian sense, it met with bitter hostility from the Covenanters, though it was subscribed quite heavily in Aberdeenshire and the strongly episcopalian northeast. But when the long-awaited General Assembly met at Glasgow in November 1638 it was packed with Covenanters. Despite Hamilton's unavailing attempts to get the assembly dissolved when it was clearly proceeding to measures which would infuriate the king, it not only annulled the new canons, the Prayer Book and the Five Articles, all of which had been suspended but not annulled by Charles, but went on to depose the bishops and abolish the High Commission. With the die irrevocably cast, Charles prepared for the military solution which he had always planned but had hoped to delay by his temporizing policies. Recruiting also began by the Covenanters, with the aid of a number of experienced soldiers returning home after distinguished service in the continental wars, most notably the near-illiterate but supremely capable Alexander Leslie, who had served with the great Gustavus Adolphus and ranked as a field marshal in the Swedish service.

The ignominious failure of the king's intended threefold strategy, involving attacks from Ireland on the southwest, landings at Aberdeen by Hamilton and an overland offensive led by the king himself, caused Charles, who was all too aware of the Scottish preparedness to mount a counter-offensive into England, to accede to a cessation of hostilities at Berwick in June 1639. He agreed to come to Scotland for a meeting of parliament in the early autumn. Both sides were to disband their armies, but since the king had not consented to ratify the acts of what he described as the 'pretended assembly' at Glasgow, the Scots kept their forces under arms. They were wise to do so, for Charles had no intention of treating their request seriously, and was simply playing for the time he needed before trying again for a military solution, notwithstanding the débâcle of the so-called First Bishops' War. On 12 August 1639 another General Assembly of the kirk met at Edinburgh, this time with the earl of Traquair as the king's commissioner, and, nothing daunted, proceeded not only to confirm the acts of its predecessor at Glasgow, but also to declare that episcopacy was contrary not only to the constitution of the kirk but also to the word of God. When it became clear that the Scottish parliament, which opened on 31 August without the king, was also dominated by Covenanters, and would probably not only ratify the acts of the General Assembly but also introduce constitutional changes weakening the royal prerogative, Traquair prorogued it until June 1640. By that time Charles hoped to have gained sufficient resources to mount an invasion of Scotland.

If proroguing the Scottish parliament was one part of the royal plan, the other was to call an English parliament, whose financial support was necessary and whose cooperation Charles hoped to win by revealing how the Scottish rebels had appealed to Louis XIII of France. But he was sadly disappointed. When the assembly which was to become known to history as the Short Parliament met on 13 April 1640, it ignored the royal appeal for funds and concentrated its attention on English grievances. Thus it was that the revolt of the Covenanters facilitated the very thing which had so far been lacking in the simmering discontent of the years of personal rule, and without which it might never have come to the boil; a central focus for discontent in the form of parliament which had not met for eleven years. Although it was to be the Short Parliament's successor which saw these things brought to fruition, the royal dissolution of parliament on 5 May left Charles in a much worse position than if he had never summoned it, since its short life had nevertheless been sufficient to make abundantly clear to the Scots that they faced a deeply divided England.

On 20 May, the same day that the king, lacking the hoped-for parliamentary grant, moved with his forces to York, the Scottish army crossed the Tweed. An English force was overpowered at Newburn and on 30 August Newcastle was occupied. Following this further humiliation – the so-called Second Bishops' War – a treaty was signed at Ripon, whereby the Scots were to occupy the two northern counties and be paid £850 a day until permanent peace was concluded. In the meantime Charles summoned a great council of the peers of the realm to York to advise him both on the terms of peace and on what further action would be appropriate. Peace was not finally concluded until June 1641, when Charles undertook to ratify the legislation of the Scottish parliament which had reassembled a year previously, and not to garrison the border fortress towns of Berwick and Carlisle. There was to be consultation on ecclesiastical reform in both countries and the Scots would receive an indemnity of £300,000. After the payment of the first instalment of this, their army finally left England, but the fact that negotiations had lasted so long and that the financial implications of the settlement were beyond the unaided royal means continued to be an effective guarantee that the parliament which Charles, following the advice of his council, had summoned to meet at Westminster on 3 November 1640 would not be another Short Parliament.

Chapter Nine

CONFLICT AND REVOLUTION, 1640–9

THE WAY TO CIVIL WAR 1640–2

While about 400 of the 493 MPs who assembled at Westminster on 3 November 1640 came determined to make the world safe for Protestantism, parliament and local liberties, and to get rid of what they regarded as the excesses of royal personal government, at least fifty-five MPs were to go over to what was fast becoming a royalist party before the outbreak of Civil War in the late summer of 1642, while an additional thirty-five were to join Charles in the course of the war.[1] However, the first session of what was later to be called the Long Parliament, ending with adjournment on 9 September 1641, saw the achievement of a programme of reforms which commanded a wide measure of agreement, including that of some moderates who were later to defect from John Pym and those reformers who were seeking further limitations on the king's power. These achievements can be briefly summarized as effectively dismantling the apparatus, punishing the personnel, and discountenancing the measures, of royal absolutism.

As to the apparatus, the High Commission, the Council of the Marches and Wales and the Council of the North were all abolished, the 'undue proceedings' of the Privy Council and the Star Chamber in recent years were brought within the purview of a parliamentary committee, and arrangements were made on 14 December 1640 to prepare a bill for the regulation of the lieutenancy. As to personnel, the earl of Strafford was impeached, and when that procedure looked as if it might be unsuccessful, he was sent to his death via a bill of Attainder, which the king reluctantly signed, in May 1641. Articles of impeachment were prepared against Archbishop Laud, who, however, was to languish in the Tower until his execution at the beginning of 1645. Secretary Windebank and Lord Keeper Finch of Ship Money fame escaped a worse fate by fleeing the country. The leases of the customs farmers were sequestered and they were fined £150,000 for their delinquency in collecting tonnage and poundage which had never been voted by parliament. Most of the domestic monopolists – though not the London soapboilers – lost their privileges and were punished, while those monopolists and customs farmers who were also MPs were expelled from the House. The vital distinction, which had developed over the 1620s, between such domestic concessionaires and the chartered companies in foreign trade also characterized the attitude of the Long Parliament, and the companies continued to bask in the parliamentary favour which they had so unaccustomably enjoyed in the early years of the reign. As to the unpopular measures of the years of personal rule, ship money, forest fines, fines in distraint of knighthood, patents, monopolies and Laudian ecclesiastical innovations were all roundly condemned. In addition, two important bills were passed and received the royal assent in 1641 which both made recurrence of a long period of non-parliamentary rule impossible by severely curtailing the royal prerogative of summoning and dissolving parliament. These were the Triennial Act, which laid down that a parliament must be summoned to meet within three years of its predecessor's dissolution, and the 'act for a perpetual parliament', as it later came to be called, which forbade the dissolution of the present parliament without its own consent.

The fact that these and other reforms received the royal consent, however unwillingly given in practice, was later to be skilfully used by royalist propagandists emphasizing the new image of the king as model constitutional monarch. But while undoubtedly such concessions disposed some moderates favourably towards the king, their ultimate defection to the royalists probably owed more to what they came to consider to be the excesses of Pym and his associates than to the concessions made by the king. Now while there were incidents during the first session, such as the debate on the petition for the extirpation of episcopacy root and branch in February 1641 and the recourse to a bill of attainder to dispatch Strafford, which shocked some moderates and helped to produce the defection of a few of them, there can be little doubt that it was the numerous extreme measures advanced in the tenser atmosphere of the second session, beginning on 21 October 1641, which must bear the main responsibility.

Beyond all doubt the most important contributory factor to the heightening of tension early in the second session was the revolt which broke out in Ulster at this time. For not everyone was disposed to disbelieve the Irish rebels' contention that they were acting on the king's behalf and that he had countenanced their rebellion. This in turn raised the spectacle of a royal design to subvert Protestantism, and of the mass murder of Protestant settlers by Irish Catholics as the prelude to similar horrors at home. But even if the wild claims of the Irish rebels were completely discounted, there remained the problem of how they were to be quelled. Could the king be trusted with the army which would have to be raised for this purpose? Or should control of such forces be vested in parliament? This would, of course, be a clear violation of the royal prerogative, and one which, in the great controversy over the militia bill and ordinance in 1642, was to incline many men to the view that Pym and his associates had badly overstepped the mark, and that it was now time to part company with them. The skill of some formerly reforming MPs such as Edward Hyde and Lord Falkland in capitalizing on this growing unease was an important factor in producing this significant flow of sympathy back towards King Charles and away from King Pym.[2]

No better indication could be had of the way things were going quite early in the new session than the fact that the Grand Remonstrance, Pym's great device to justify a radical programme, passed the House of Commons by only eleven votes in November as well as occasioning a serious rift between the two houses. This tiny majority suggests that many more MPs than were ultimately to defect to what was from about this time in process of becoming a moderate royalist group in the House clearly had doubts about Pym's policies. Such doubts were to be increased by the decision to publish the Remonstrance, 'to remonstrate downwards to the people', as one former, but now rapidly retreating, radical, the Kentish MP, Sir Edward Dering, put it. The Remonstrance contained a number of positive and far-reaching proposals: among them those depriving bishops of their votes in the House of Lords and abridging their power over the clergy; the 'removing of oppressive and unnecessary ceremonies' in the church; and the removal of bad councillors and their replacement by such councillors 'as your Parliament may have cause to confide in'. In addition, it provided a highly slanted synthetic history of the reign, whose central feature was a grand papistical plot in which the Laudians, no less than avowed Catholics, had played a crucial role and which had culminated in the revolt which had recently broken out in Ireland.[3]

The royal declaration in reply to the Grand Remonstrance in December 1641 was the first of a remarkable series of moderate royalist pronouncements which were to culminate the following June in Charles's justly celebrated answer to parliament's Nineteen Propositions. The declaration was careful to hit out at extremists wherever they were to be found, both courtly papists and the wild-eyed sectaries whose excesses were confirming the fears of many moderate but conservative men and women that things had gone far enough and that their cherished, ordered world of deference and hierarchical subordination was in danger of dissolution. Now surely was the time to stop the rot by joining forces with those who were seeking to prevent further inroads on the royal prerogative, without in any way desiring to fly to the other extreme and revive the personal rule of the previous decade.

It is perhaps at first sight surprising that such apprehensions did not produce a larger flow of defectors than was in fact the case. But the truth was that Charles did not consistently live up to the image of a reformed constitutional monarch which his more moderate advisers were doing their utmost to create. For the king was by no means clay in the hands of moderates such as Hyde and Falkland, and was at least equally susceptible to the counsels of extremists such as the renegade ex-reformer Lord Digby and the queen herself. Hearkening to the counsel of Hyde and Falkland produced the statesmanlike and conciliatory reply to the Grand Remonstrance. Turning to Digby and the queen had as its disastrous products the appointment on 23 December 1641 of the swashbuckling Cavalier, Sir Thomas Lunsford, as lieutenant of the Tower and the even more disastrous invasion of parliament on 4 January 1642 to arrest five members of the Lower House (Pym, Hampden, Hesilrige, Holles, and Strode) and one peer, Lord Kimbolton, the later earl of Manchester. Each move was equally unsuccessful, and the king had in fact got very much the worst of both worlds. On the one hand, his resort to extremist action had failed miserably, and, on the other, the hollowness of his recent professions of constitutional moderation had been mercilessly exposed for all to see.

Needless to say, Pym and his colleagues exploited to the full the propaganda advantages thus presented to them, and Hyde and Falkland must have approached despair at the thankless task of resuming their labours from scratch. From now on they pursued a twofold strategy: to undo the damage done by the royal recourse to extremism in December and January by abandoning the charges against Kimbolton and the five members; and to make the maximum capital out of the further inroads on the prerogative which Pym claimed had been necessitated by royal extremism and were a violation of the letter of the constitution only in order to preserve its spirit. Such actions were the seizure of the royal magazine at Hull and the refusal to grant the king entry to that town when he stood before it on 23 April; and the parliamentary claim to control the militia and to nominate to the lieutenancy. In addition a great deal was made of the tumultuary assemblies in London, fomented, it was claimed – and not without reason – by Pym's City allies, and which had the effect of forcing the king to leave London for York in March.

Potentially the most important of all the defections from Pym's party was that of the municipal government of London. If it had not been for the municipal revolution which effectively began with the election of a radical majority in the City Court of Common Council in December 1641, continued with the creation of a Committee of Safety which usurped the lord mayor's right both to summon Common Council and to control the militia, and culminated in the deposition of the royalist Lord Mayor Sir Richard Gurney in July 1642 and his replacement by Pym's ally Isaac Penington, London might well have been royalist rather than parliamentarian in the coming war. However while one modern authority sees the municipality as a royalist bastion from the beginning, which had to be captured if the City was to be made safe for Pym and his associates, another argues that the governors of London had been alienated from the court by 1640, both in their capacity as commercial magnates and (often) concessionaires and as municipal governors.[4] In these circumstances their behaviour in 1641–2 would be explicable in the same terms as can be applied to the erstwhile reformers of 1640, who were increasingly alienated by what they took to be parliamentary extremism, as well as reacting favourably to royal concessions.

One means of establishing rapport between king and parliament which had been consistently advocated by moderates such as Hyde and Falkland, as well as by Pym, was to make ministerial appointments which would command general parliamentary approval. Such were the appointment of Oliver St John as solicitor general early in 1641 and the hotly canvassed proposal for Bishop Juxon to be replaced as lord treasurer by St John's patron the earl of Bedford, which was frustrated by Bedford's untimely death in May. But the ideas of Hyde and his moderate royalist colleagues on such 'bridge-appointments' differed crucially from those of Pym as the latter developed in the course of 1642, largely under the impact of royal extremist actions at the beginning of that year. While to Hyde the essence of such an arrangement lay in trusting the king to appoint ministers acceptable to parliament, his opponents took the view that either – as expressed in a House of Commons resolution of 31 January – the king should appoint ministers nominated by parliament, or – as in the Nineteen Propositions presented to the king in June – that parliament should at least have a negative voice, that is, the right to veto royal nominees.[5] Pym might argue that parliament had perforce to press its constitutional offensive still further if its achievements of 1640–1 were to be safeguarded. But his royalist opponents claimed – nowhere more brilliantly than in the masterly royal reply to the Nineteen Propositions – that he and his colleagues were indulging in unwarranted constitutional aggression, stepping right outside the bounds of parliamentary power as envisaged in the notion of 'mixed monarchy' which constitutional royalists had now found it convenient to revive: that they were in fact ravishing the ancient constitution and proposing to reduce the king's powers to the equivalent of those of a Venetian doge.

But what indeed was the ancient constitution? In the coming struggle its virtues were extolled by both Roundheads and Cavaliers. Certainly the royalists argued with some justification that it was being violated by parliament in such matters as the control of the militia and the lieutenancy and in some of its demands in the Nineteen Propositions: a negative voice in the appointment of royal councillors and military commanders; control over the education of the royal children; disqualification of Catholic peers from the House of Lords; the alteration of the condition of judges' tenure; and the right to interfere in foreign policy (one of the Propositions recommended an Anglo-Dutch alliance). But the vast majority of those who were soon to go to war, not, as they were at great pains to emphasize, against the king, but rather for king and parliament, refused to see themselves as constitutional aggressors. They aspired not to innovate, but to restore what they conceived to be their ancient liberties.

It ultimately came to war largely because of the profound mutual distrust which divided the two sides and caused each to take up a position which precluded compromise. Indeed in some respects it is surprising that war did not come earlier, given the fact, on the one hand, that the parliamentarians were trying to raise forces under the Militia Ordinance which their opponents rightly denounced as illegal, since, like all subsequent parliamentary legislation, it lacked the royal consent; and, on the other, that the king, despairing of the loyalty of a lieutenancy appointed by his enemies, resorted to reviving the Commissions of Array. These were a long-abandoned mode of raising levies, which, parliamentarians complained with some justice, had been rendered obsolescent by the Marian militia statute of 1558 and had certainly not been restored as a result of the repeal of that statute in 1604. Thus with two competing and mutually antagonistic authorities for the raising of troops, there were violent scenes in, for example, Leicester in late June, Devonshire in July and Gloucestershire and Somerset in August. Torn between the competing demands of king and parliament, men suffered agonies of indecision, and some entered into agreements to try to keep both armies out of their native counties.

Some time before the king raised his standard at Nottingham on 22 August war had become about as inevitable as anything ever is in history, if only because each side feared that the other would try to gain a crucial and perhaps decisive advantage by striking first. While the voice of reason and moderation tends to be hushed in wartime, there were nevertheless moderate men in plenty on both sides.

However, among the royalists, the extremists who had favoured the attempt on the five members and other examples of Cavalierism red in both tooth and claw were again in the ascendancy, as were Pym and his followers at Westminster. Nevertheless, for all the vociferous radicals among the king's opponents, republican principles were almost unknown, and the wild statements of exceptional people such as Henry Marten and Sir Henry Ludlow were both a great embarrassment to Pym and the parliamentary leadership and marvellous material for royal propaganda. In its initial phases the Great Rebellion was for the most part a rebellion of conservatives.

POLITICAL GROUPINGS AND THE COURSE OF THE WAR, 1642–3

After the outbreak of war John Pym and the other leaders of the parliamentarian cause had at least as much need of strong nerves and political judgment as they had had in the preceding months. The main objective of Pym's leadership was to fight the war in a sufficiently determined manner to enable parliament to obtain a settlement not far different from the terms which had been unsuccessfully pressed upon the king in the Nineteen Propositions of June 1642. Pym led a number of MPs described by Professor J. H. Hexter as a 'middle-group', which sought to strike a balance between extremist war-groupers such as Sir Arthur Hesilrige, Henry Marten and Alexander Rigby who favoured war *à l'outrance*, a crushing victory and a dictated peace, and the peace-groupers such as Sir Simonds D'Ewes, John Maynard and Denzil Holles.[6] While it would be an exaggeration to characterize these latter as favouring peace at almost any price, they certainly were inclined to propose or accept peace on far less stringent terms than were both the middle and war groups. They were appalled by the apparently radical consequences which, as the royalists were quick to emphasize, had been set off by the act of disobedience and revolt; by the excesses of the religious sectaries; by the threat to men of property posed by popular disturbances of which those in the Stour Valley in Essex and Suffolk were only the most frightening of a number of examples; and by the way in which Pym and his followers made use of – and perhaps even fostered – disturbances in London as instruments of policy without appreciating the danger that attacks on the persons and property of papists and Cavaliers might all too easily become attacks on property in general.[7]

Profoundly disturbed at the consequences of civil strife and desiring a return to normal at the first possible opportunity, the peace-groupers trembled at almost every constitutional or military innovation which was necessary if the war was to be conducted efficiently and parliament was not to be crushed. Among the new taxes introduced in the first half of 1643 which they opposed were the excise and the weekly assessment, the latter being particularly objectionable to them since it employed the same sort of innovating assessment which had provoked such a storm when used by the king for ship money in the 1630s. Not the least pernickety of their objections was that such fiscal innovations had been introduced, in D'Ewes's words, 'by a mere Ordinance of both houses', as distinct from a genuine act of parliament, which would, of course, have required the royal assent.

Unlike Marten, Hesilrige and their war-group associates, Pym and his middle-group colleagues shared with the peace-groupers a desire for a negotiated rather than a dictated peace. But, unlike the peace-groupers, they were all too aware that the price of a peace which was anything more than abject submission was military preparedness, and resolute prosecution of the war. The alternative was royalist victory, for the king was certainly not held back by any such inhibitions. Indeed for a time during the summer of 1643 a complete royalist victory seemed very likely. After the failure of the royalist attempt to take London following the indecisive first real battle of the war at Edgehill in Warwickshire on 23 October 1642, there had ensued a lull in hostilities, and early in 1643 there were unsuccessful peace negotiations at the royalist capital, Oxford.[8] The campaigns of the ensuing months brought parliament almost to its knees. In the far southwest, the largely Cornish royalist force raised by Sir Ralph Hopton, who had left his native Somerset following the failure of the earl of Hertford to raise that county for the king the previous summer, routed that of the parliamentarian earl of Stamford at Stratton on 16 May 1643. Sent to retrieve the disaster in the west, a more competent commander, Sir William Waller – William the Conqueror as he was optimistically known – was also crushed by Hopton at Roundway Down on 13 July, and on 26 July Prince Rupert took the vitally important port and stronghold of Bristol for the king. In addition the royalist advance posed a serious threat to the strategically crucial town of Gloucester. The parliamentarian hold on the southwest had crumbled spectacularly, with the exception of a very few places of which Plymouth was the most important. Moreover, in the north, the earl of Newcastle had crushed the parliamentarian force under the Fairfaxes at Adwalton Moor on 30 June. Although Hull survived both the threat from his army and the attempt of its parliamentary commanders, the Hothams father and son, to hand it over to the king, Newcastle pressed on through Lincolnshire to threaten the parliamentary heartland in East Anglia.

As it happens, these spectacular victories constitute the high point of royalist military success, although no one could know this at the time, when the parliamentarian cause seemed to be in desperate straits indeed. Moreover, that cause was threatened by internal dissension as well as by royalist military victories: by the continued sniping of the extremist war-groupers at the indecisive leadership and alleged military incompetence of the parliamentarian commander-in-chief, the earl of Essex, whom at one time they strove to replace by Sir William Waller; and by the danger of subversion from within through a royal attempt to promulgate a Commission of Array in London, which, however, Pym skilfully turned to advantage in May 1643 by using it to discredit the idea of renewed negotiations with the king for which the peace-groupers were again clamouring. In this, Pym and the war-groupers were at one, but he stood very firm against them in their attacks on Essex, the continuation of whose supreme command was vital to preserving the respectability of the cause and its continued appeal to the faltering moderates.

Not only was the challenge to the authority of Pym and Essex successfully warded off. In addition, the tide of royalist military success receded. On 8 September Essex relieved Gloucester, and 20 September, in the bloody first battle of Newbury, he forced the royalist army, which attempted to bar his return to London, to yield him passage. The balance of advantage in the war might still seem to lie with the royalists, but in his steadfast support of the at last victorious commander-in-chief, his careful piloting of crucial measures such as the ordinances for the weekly assessment and the excise through parliament, and in his final achievement of bringing Scotland into the war, Pym had created the conditions which would bring about a reversal of parliament's fortunes.

SCOTLAND'S ENTRY INTO THE WAR, 1643–4

To many Scottish Covenanters the main lesson of the history of the previous decade was that their Presbyterian kirk was not safe for so long as the church in Charles's southern kingdom was organized on an episcopalian basis. A victory for the king in the English Civil War would afford him the opportunity of turning his unimpeded attention to Scotland and enforcing the ecclesiastical settlement of which he had been foiled in the later 1630s. To prevent this it would be necessary for the Scots to intervene against the king in the war. But for a variety of reasons the Scottish alliance with the parliamentarians was not concluded until the autumn of 1643. In the first place it was not until the military situation became desperate for the English parliament that parliamentarians, most of whom were no more sympathetic to Presbyterian than they had been to Laudian theocracy, were prepared to accept what appeared to be the religious implications of such an alliance. Secondly, it was not until well into 1643 that the out-and-out interventionists in Scotland, led by the earl of Argyll, had gained the complete ascendancy which enabled them to put their policies into effect. Before that time they had had to contend with strong opposition from a variety of quarters.[9]

Since 1638 there had been a number of momentous changes in Scotland which went far beyond the avowed aims of the National Covenant and the overthrow of episcopacy. Indeed before 1642 the forces making for the limitation of royal power had achieved even more success in Scotland than in England. Not only had a Scottish triennial act preceded its English equivalent by a year, but in 1641 the king conceded to his Scottish subjects something near to what he was to refuse to yield in England in the Nineteen Propositions of June 1642. He agreed that his Scottish councillors should be chosen with the advice of parliament, and, when parliament was not meeting, of other privy councillors. Moreover, these and other inroads on the prerogative of the Scottish king appeared to critics to have been paralleled by the increasing aggrandizement of Argyll and his faction. Among the enemies of this group were Montrose and his faction who, beginning from a moderate Covenanting position, ultimately came to favour intervention in the English war on the side of the king, and the faction led by the marquis of Hamilton, who took up a non-interventionist stance, since, royalist though they were, they reckoned that it was necessary only to frustrate Argyll's aim of intervention on the side of parliament to ensure a royalist victory in England. Hamilton's negative non-interventionist policy made him a much more influential opponent of Argyll than was Montrose, since it engaged the active support of genuine Scottish neutralists who wished a plague on both contending English parties and desired only to keep Scotland out of the war.

If the above considerations explain why Scottish intervention in the war was delayed, there still remains the problem of why Argyll and the interventionists ultimately prevailed. In the first place, the disdain with which Charles greeted the Scottish commissioners who were sent to Oxford in March 1643 with an offer to mediate between him and his English parliament was arrogant and ill-judged and very badly received in Scotland. But the ultimate triumph of the interventionists is certainly not attributable to any single cause. In addition, since December 1642 the king's alleged relations with his Catholic subjects had been an important cause of Scottish suspicions, which extended far beyond Argyll's faction. Charles's refusal to condemn the allegedly extensive employment of papists in the earl of Newcastle's army in the north of England was to be one of the most effectively employed propaganda points against him in both England and Scotland. In Scotland the revelations about the so-called Antrim Plot for a ceasefire in Ireland, to be followed by an attack by the Catholic Irish on the Western Isles and Western Highlands, were probably the last straw, and taken as a clear indication that the king had no objection to using Catholic savages as a means of reducing his Scottish subjects to obedience. The horrors of the massacres of Protestant settlers in Ulster in 1641 might soon be repeated in Scotland, a possibility which afforded marvellous confirmation of Argyll's argument that if Scotland did not strike before the king had crushed the English parliament, the Scots in their turn would surely be struck down.

The disclosures about the Antrim Plot were undoubtedly of crucial importance in producing an overwhelming majority in favour of an alliance with the English parliament in the Scottish Convention of Estates which met on 25 June. But now there were delays on the English side. Just as Argyll's interventionist policies had powerful enemies in Scotland, so was Pym's plan for a Scottish alliance anathema to the peace-groupers at Westminster, who feared that to bring in a foreign power – Charles's own subjects to make matters worse – against the king could only have the effect of exacerbating relations with him to a quite unacceptable degree. Moreover, an alliance with the Presbyterian Scots multiplied the already formidable difficulties in the way of concluding peace with Charles, who was most unlikely to budge an inch on the matter of the episcopal organization of the English church. In addition, there was a strong disinclination on the part of many Englishmen to see a Scottish army once more on English soil. However the desperate military situation plus some skilful use by Pym of the disclosures about the Antrim Plot as revealing the full perfidy of the king ultimately won over parliament to sending a commission to Scotland to negotiate an alliance.

Does this mean that the Scots were able to dictate the terms of their alliance with the English parliament? How far did the Solemn League and Covenant concluded in September 1643 go towards committing England to the establishment of a Presbyterian system *à l'écossaise*? That no such unequivocal undertaking was contained in the Solemn League and Covenant is attributable partly to skilful negotiating on the part of the English commissioners in Edinburgh led by Sir Henry Vane the younger; partly to the fact that the Scots needed the alliance hardly less urgently than the English; and partly that they appear rather naively to have assumed that the English determination to abolish episcopacy necessarily betokened an equal determination to establish Scottish-type Presbyterianism. But many of the most influential of their new English allies, among them Erastians like Pym and St John and Independents like Vane, while recognizing the need for the new church settlement to conform, at least nominally, to the Presbyterian pattern, were determined to do their utmost to avert the worst rigours of thoroughgoing Presbyterianism.

Accordingly, to the disappointment of their Scottish equivalents, Vane and the English commissioners in Edinburgh could not go anything like all the way with them. In the original draft Solemn League and Covenant they accepted that the Scottish kirk was constructed 'according to the word of God'. However, while the future settlement of the English and Irish churches was also to be 'according to the word of God', it was in addition to conform with 'the example of the best reformed Churches'. What exactly did this caveat mean? Was it a significant loophole? Was it conceivable that the word of God might be different in respect of England from what it was in respect of Scotland? Moreover, even this modified Covenant negotiated by Vane and the English commissioners produced further objections at Westminster, and on 1 September the formerly agreed description of the Scottish kirk as 'according to the word of God' was removed from the final form of the Solemn League and Covenant agreed by the English parliament.[10] There were no longer any grounds to regard the Covenant as a pledge for identical forms of church government in both countries.

By the terms of the treaty concluded at about the same time, Scotland was to send an army to England, and the English parliament was to contribute £30,000 monthly towards its charges and pay any additional arrears after the end of the war. In case of rebellion in Scotland, England was to offer similar assistance, a clause which was conveniently forgotten during Montrose's royalist rebellion in 1645. Both parties pledged themselves not to make a separate peace with the king. On 10 January 1644 a Scottish army once again crossed the Tweed, in pursuit of war aims of which the most important was the establishment of Scottish-type Presbyterianism in England, on which the Solemn League and Covenant had offered no firm assurance. It was not to be long before the difficulty of achieving this end, together with the English parliament's failure to honour the financial terms of the alliance, turned Anglo-Scottish relations sour.

THE SUCCESSION TO PYM AND THE CRISIS IN THE PARLIAMENTARIAN HIGH COMMAND, 1644–5

December 1643 saw two important events both of which occasioned what turned out to be unfulfilled hope for the royalist cause. The first was the death on 8 December of John Pym, whose political skill and statesmanship had guided parliament through its darkest hour; and the second the issue of a royal proclamation on 22 December summoning a parliamentary assembly to meet at Oxford. The latter event marks a victory, however temporary, for Edward Hyde and the moderate royalists, whose strength at Oxford had been sorely weakened by the death of Secretary Falkland at the battle of Newbury in September and his replacement by the now extremist Digby. Calling the Oxford assembly was designed to attract MPs from Westminster to join those other MPs who had already gone over to the king. In this it was singularly unsuccessful. Nevertheless, the presence of some sort of representative assembly at Oxford was not without value for those who, like Hyde, wished at all costs to avoid giving the impression that there had been a reversion to the atmosphere and notions which had prevailed during the personal rule of the 1630s. But even this mild and deferential assembly, which first met on 22 January 1644, and thereafter only very sporadically until it was adjourned for the last time on 10 March 1645, was too much for hard-liners like Digby and Prince Rupert, and for the courtiers and officials who did not relish even its very mild scrutiny of their expenditure and procedures. If the experiment had produced a more positive response from the peace-groupers at Westminster, it is just possible that something might have come of it. As it was, it fizzled out, unloved and unwanted, a 'mongrel parliament', as the king was later to describe it.

The Westminster parliament, which rejected with contempt the overtures from Oxford, had not been thrown into total disarray as a result of Pym's death, and the view that this resulted in the immediate disintegration of Pym's middle-group following is no longer generally held.[11] Dr Valerie Pearl has argued that the middle-group found an able and worthy successor to Pym in Oliver St John and that it survived as an independent political force at least down to the middle of 1644 and as a distinctive political attitude of mind long after that. St John's role as Pym's political heir was manifested in his support for the earl of Essex against the continued attacks of the war-group; in his attempts to reconcile the needs of Essex's army with those of Waller and the regional associations; in his determination to negotiate from a position of strength which, like Pym, brought him into frequent cooperation with the war-group; and in his support for the Accommodation Order of September 1644 by which parliament reminded the intolerant Presbyterians in the Assembly of Divines of the need for the coming religious settlement to reconcile the diversity of religious views in the Assembly, and, in the event of the failure to do so, to make adequate provision for tender consciences. Similarly, in his support for the Ordinance of February 1644 establishing the Committee of Both Kingdoms – and for its subsequent renewal as the directing agency of the strategy and war effort of parliament and its new Scottish allies – St John was pursuing a policy of which Pym would certainly have approved. Even if the break-up of Pym's political system and the subsequent transformation of politics had to wait only a matter of months following Pym's death, the respite was of the utmost importance to the improvement of parliamentarian fortunes in 1644.

With the great victory of the earl of Manchester, Oliver Cromwell and the Scots over Rupert and Newcastle at Marston Moor at the beginning of July 1644, a great deal of the north of England fell into the hands of the king's enemies, although the fact that in England the main credit for the victory was given to Cromwell was strongly resented by the Scots and contributed to the growing Anglo-Scottish contention which was soon to become a central feature of the political scene. From this time too seems to date the beginning of Manchester's foot-dragging and temporizing which was to become a major issue in the quarrel about the conduct of the war with his subordinate Cromwell. Mutual recriminations among army commanders had, of course, not been unknown previously, either in the royalist or in the parliamentarian high commands. The most celebrated manifestation of the latter had been the antagonism between Essex and Waller, which Pym, and after him St John, had been at such pains to prevent from assuming disastrous proportions. But in the second half of 1644 such internecine disputes assumed a new and unprecedented intensity following two notable reverses to parliamentarian military fortunes which threatened to give to the earlier victory of Marston Moor something of the character of a false dawn. The first and more serious of these reverses was the disastrous culmination of Essex's West Country campaign when his army capitulated at Lostwithiel in Cornwall in September. But it was the second, the failure to follow up the parliamentarian advantage gained at the second battle of Newbury in late October, thereby allowing the royalists to relieve Donnington Castle on 9 November, which produced a real frenzy of mutual recriminations between Manchester and Cromwell, neither of whom was also averse from diverting attention from himself by attacking Essex for the disaster at Lostwithiel. Essex in turn publicly accused Manchester and, needless to say, Waller, of failing to come to his assistance during his western offensive, and consulted with some peace-groupers and Scottish statesmen about the feasibility of impeaching Cromwell, a project which he was persuaded to abandon.

It was out of these bitter internecine disputes, which threatened to fracture irreparably the fragile unity of the parliamentarian cause, that there was ultimately to emerge a new national army, the so-called New Model Army, under a new commander, Sir Thomas Fairfax. With one notable exception all army commanders who were also office-holders or had seats in parliament – and both Manchester and Essex as peers had no choice in the latter matter – had to resign their commands according to the terms of the second Self-Denying Ordinance which passed through parliament on 3 April 1645, an earlier ordinance having failed to get through the House of Lords the previous December.[12] The exception was Cromwell, who was allowed to retain his command in face of the dangers arising out of the royalist offensive in the Midlands in the early summer of 1645. This exception naturally came in for much criticism, especially from peace-groupers, but was crucial to the success of the New Model Army which, after the fright caused by the royalist capture and sack of Leicester on 31 May, won the most decisive parliamentarian victory of the war when it defeated the royalist army at Naseby on 14 June.

It used to be customary to regard the creation of the New Model Army as the main turning-point on the road to republicanism as well as to victory in the war. But it is important not to read back the highly politicized army of 1647–8 into the conditions of 1645.[13] Nor was it the first army in which religious Independents and sectaries succeeded in attaining high rank. Before the disputes in the Eastern Association Army during 1644, Manchester and Cromwell had cooperated enthusiastically in creating an interdenominational Puritan force.[14] On the other hand, while emphasizing the contrast between the New Model Army of 1645 and of 1647–8, its latest historian lays great stress on the bitter disputes of the months preceding its establishment as inaugurating a new and fiercer sort of parliamentary activity, the replacement of 'consensus' by 'adversary' politics, which was thereafter to increase in intensity and culminate in the bitter strife of 1647–8 both inside and outside parliament.[15] Nevertheless, this contrast may also be too stark. The bitterness of the parliamentary exchanges of 1644 and 1645 over issues such as the conduct of the war and the Self-Denying and New Model ordinances is not in doubt. But it is open to question whether these were different in kind, as distinct from degree, from, for example, the disputes over the Grand Remonstrance in 1641, the Militia Ordinance in 1642, the agitation for negotiations with the king in 1643, or the establishment and power of the Committee of Both Kingdoms in 1644. This is not to deny that one of the products of the disputes of 1644–5 was a squeezing of the parliamentary centre, which led ultimately to the virtual disappearance of the middle-group as a distinct political entity. In any case during the course of 1645 it became increasingly normal to consider politics in terms of what seems at first sight to be two denominational groups, Presbyterians and Independents. This nomenclature in turn reflects a political transformation of first-rate importance to which we must now turn.

PRESBYTERIANS, INDEPENDENTS AND SCOTS, AND THE END OF THE FIRST CIVIL WAR, 1644–6

It will be remembered that the Scots had been brought into the war by Pym and the middle-group, backed strongly by the war-group and equally strongly opposed by D'Ewes, Holles and the other peace-groupers. Yet in the course of 1645–6 these same peace-groupers came to form the nucleus of what became known as the Presbyterian 'party', which was to operate in close cooperation with the Scots, while the latters' former allies of the war and middle-groups – or at least those of the middle-group who did not defect to the Presbyterians – were to form the nucleus of the Independent 'party' which on the whole was sharply critical of the Scots.

Before seeking an explanation for this remarkable political transformation, it would be as well to examine the original religious significance of the distinction between Presbyterians and Independents. In the evolution of a new ecclesiastical settlement in the 1640s there were two main stages. First, there was the hammering out of agreed recommendations in the Westminster Assembly of Divines which had been set up by parliament in 1643, and, second, there was the acceptance, amendment or rejection of these recommendations by parliament. But if the Presbyterian majority in the Assembly of Divines, who had laboured long and unsuccessfully to convince the Independent and Erastian minorities of the error of their ways, expected parliament to accept their recommendations and establish a thoroughgoing Presbyterian ecclesiastical polity, they were courting disappointment. The Presbyterians loathed even the limited toleration recommended by the parliamentary Accommodation Order of September 1644 and favoured by the Independents, and they viewed with the utmost disfavour the Independent emphasis on a loosely organized decentralized church, even though it was only a small minority of Independents who favoured – as their Elizabethan predecessors had done – the complete autonomy of individual congregations.

Although parliament accepted the Presbyterian Directory of Worship early in 1645, it was something very far from a full-blown Presbyterian ecclesiastical polity that it established in the spring of the following year. Indeed if this 'lame erastian Presbytery', as the Scottish divine Robert Baillie disgustedly described it, delighted the hearts of any, these were the Erastians, whose views were much more strongly represented in parliament than in the Assembly of Divines, where they were the tiniest, though not the least vocal, of minorities. Looking to the civil government as the main initiator of godly reform, in the tradition of the English Reformation, they were as opposed to *iure divino* Presbyterianism as they had been to Laudian *iure divino* episcopacy. Nor can there be any doubt that the religious Independents, who had fought a long and losing battle in the Assembly of Divines, derived satisfaction from the settlement in that it set severe limits on the theocratic centralism beloved of high Presbyterians, whose views were outraged by parliament's assumption of the role of supreme authority in spiritual as well as in secular matters. This authority extended even to defining what sins were sufficiently scandalous to merit the sinner's suspension from the Communion, and vesting decision in cases of other sins not in the local presbytery but in commissions responsible to parliament.[16]

Following this brief sketch of the forces which went into the making of the parliamentary religious settlement which assumed its final form in March 1646, we may now return to the nature of the political transformation and the significance of the apparently religious nomenclature of the two new groupings in parliament.[17] At the root of the spectacular reversal of alliances whose product was the emergence of the Presbyterian and Independent groupings in parliament, was the Scottish disillusionment at the meagre fruits of their participation in the war. Now the primary Scottish war aim had been the safeguarding of their kirk and the establishment of Presbyterianism in England. From the Scottish point of view the English parliament's aim of securing its own position and preventing a renewal of the eleven years' tyranny was a relatively minor and purely English concern. In these circumstances it is not altogether surprising that they came round to the view that they might succeed in securing from the king what they had manifestly failed to obtain from the parliament. It was this which gradually brought them increasingly into alignment with the aims of their former opponents, the parliamentary peace-group. To the Scots, peace with the king became a price well worth paying for the establishment of that Presbyterianism *à l'écossaise* which their cooperation with the war- and middle-groups in parliament had manifestly failed to give, although such a view ignored the fact that the king was as unlikely to yield to their wishes in this matter as was parliament. To the peace-groupers, on the other hand, the establishment of Presbyterianism was a price well worth paying for peace with the king. This in essence is how the peace-groupers, some of whom were religious Presbyterians but a large number of whom were Erastians and episcopalians, became the Presbyterian party. The peace-groupers were eventually joined by a number of former middle-groupers, notably Sir Philip Stapleton, Sir John Clotworthy and the recorder of London, John Glyn, who had become alarmed by what they regarded as the increasingly radical direction of events. Other middle-groupers, including the leader, Oliver St John, Sir John Evelyn of Wiltshire, William Pierrepont and John Crewe, became ranged alongside the old war-group, though continuing to exert a more distinct influence than did their former colleagues who had moved in the opposite direction. This new coalition of war-groupers and some defectors from the old middle-group formed the nucleus of the parliamentary Independents, even though many of those so named – for example John Gurdon, Edmund Prideaux and William Purefoy – were thoroughgoing Presbyterians in religion, even if radicals on all else.

The actual transformation was not achieved quite so smoothly as the above account might suggest. At the beginning of 1645, for example, there had been a temporary mending of fences between the Scots and the war-groupers, as the latter threw their influence behind the hard-line Scottish religious terms for a settlement put before the king at the treaty of Uxbridge. This they were the more willing to do because they were confident that the king would reject such terms, thus making it easier for them to push their own radical measures, and notably the Self-Denying and New Model ordinances, through parliament. Even following the renewed deterioration of Scottish relations with the war-groupers (or Independents), there were still some obstacles to be overcome before full support between the parliamentary Presbyterians, as we must now call them, and the Scots was established: most notably Charles's continued support for Montrose, whose spectacular victories over the Covenanters in Scotland were the one bright spot in a disastrous year for royalist arms. Indeed the parliamentary Presbyterians may well have had some cause to doubt the value of their Scottish connection, given the general deterioration of Anglo-Scottish relations due to English resentment at Scottish military inactivity, and Scottish irritation not only at the parliamentary religious settlement, but also at parliament's failure to observe its full obligations in the matter of the payment of the Scottish troops. This in turn led to their exaction of illegal contributions and free quarter from local inhabitants in the north, who also complained bitterly of rapes, murders, torture and pillaging. The Scots' image was more that of a hostile army of occupation than of an allied force, and on 19 May 1646 the House of Commons resolved that England had no further use for the Scottish army, which should be paid off and sent home.

Two weeks earlier Charles had given himself up to the Scots at Southwell near Newark. The military campaigns of the preceding year in England, beginning with the decisive victory of the New Model Army at Naseby on 14 June 1645, had been almost uniformly disastrous for the king. The successes of the New Model Army in the West Country, beginning with the victory at Langport on 10 July 1645 and the fall of Bristol on 10 September and culminating in the capitulation of Exeter on 9 April 1646, meant the spectacular crumbling of royal power in what had, since 1643, been the most powerfully royalist region in England. In Scotland Montrose's run of dazzling successes on the king's behalf ended with his defeat at Philiphaugh on 13 September 1645, while the parliamentarian victory at Rowton Heath on 24 September made it only a matter of time before Chester fell to the Roundheads in the following February.

The succeeding campaigns were little more than prolonged mopping-up operations for the victorious parliamentarians, but, force having failed, Charles now had recourse to intrigue. There can be no doubt that his object in surrendering to the Scots was to sow dissension not only between them and their English allies, but also between the parliamentary Presbyterians and Independents. But although he entertained wild hopes that the Scottish army might now take his side against a divided English parliament, in actual fact he had little to offer to them or anyone else. For, despite the persuasions of the queen in her letters from France and the intrigues of the French ambassador who acted as go-between in communications between king, queen and Scots, Charles would not entertain for a moment the one concession which might conceivably have brought Scottish support for acquiescence in his designs: he would not promise a settlement of the English church on more thoroughgoing Presbyterian lines than the Erastian parliamentary settlement of 1646 which had so disappointed the Scots. In consequence the allies, at variance over so much else for the past year, did not waver over the peace terms which they offered to the virtually captive king at

Newcastle on 13 July 1646. In these the abolition of episcopacy and the taking of the Covenant by the king and his English subjects figured prominently as did the exception of fifty-seven leading royalists from pardon for capital offences, and the vesting of the militia in parliamentary hands for twenty years.[18]

The closing months of 1646 saw a fiercely contested controversy about whether the Scots should have a say in the disposal of the king, who was in their hands even though he was in England. But a combination of his rejection of the Newcastle Propositions and parliament's voting of £400,000 to the Scots in return for their departure induced them to relinquish their trump card and hand Charles over. By the second week of February 1647 they had left both England and the king behind. No one was more relieved at this than their allies, the parliamentary Presbyterians, whose connection with the Scots certainly did not make for their popularity at home. But with the Scots out of the way, they could turn their attention to more congenial matters which would certainly redound to their credit: returning the realm to normal and reducing the size of the armed forces.

PARLIAMENT, THE ARMY AND COUNTER-REVOLUTION, 1647

Although the majority of MPs consisted of persons to whom no 'party' label can be attached, the Presbyterians nevertheless enjoyed a political ascendancy at Westminster at the beginning of 1647. At first the so-called 'recruiter elections' from August 1645 onwards, to fill seats vacated by death or the defection of MPs to the king, seem to have favoured the parliamentary Independents rather than the Presbyterians, but from the autumn of 1646 there had been an effective Presbyterian counter-attack.[19] Even more important was the support which the Presbyterians probably gained from a majority of non-aligned MPs by identifying themselves with the increasingly vocal forces in the country which were yearning for a return to normal now that the war was over. Of this mood the desire sharply to diminish the size and cost of the military establishment was only the most conspicuous manifestation.

Even during the war such discontents had been prominent, finding their main political expression in the doubts and waverings of the peace party at Westminster and their most strident and violent manifestation in the armed neutralism of the so-called clubmen in the southwest, the west Midlands and Sussex.[20] To many other people during the war parliament had seemed to be displaying an alarming readiness to slip into the sort of illegalities and tyrannical action which it had condemned in the personal royal government of the 1630s. Their continuation after the war raised the question of how far they betokened a threat to establish a permanent despotism as distinct from being temporary emergency expedients. Such were the interrogatories and oaths, similar to those formerly administered by Star Chamber and High Commission but now employed extensively by parliamentary committees, by means of which individuals were forced to provide evidence against themselves; and the billeting, martial law, forced loans and arbitrary imprisonment condemned by the Petition of Right of 1628, but now very much part of the Roundhead stock-in-trade. Similarly, royal centralizing pressures on local government agencies, which had been a factor inducing many moderate and conservative gentlemen to take up arms for parliament in 1642, were succeeded by far more powerful, and hence even more resented, parliamentarian centralizing pressures. Some of the most bitter complaints against the allegedly arbitrary rule of parliament were directed against its agencies in the localities: against excise men, sequestration committees and, above all, against the new county committees. Quite apart from the alleged oppressions of these committees and the way they replaced in many cases, and overshadowed in others, the traditional local government mechanism of the Commission of the Peace, they antagonized conservative gentlemen on account of the opportunities, varying from county to county, which they afforded to mean men of exercising authority over their neighbours.[21]

The social composition of the county committees varied from one county to another, as did that of the reconstituted Commissions of the Peace after the end of the war. Broadly speaking, as is demonstrated by the examples of the committees of Lincolnshire and Somerset, the degree of responsiveness of a county committee to directives from central government seems to have been directly proportionate to the degree of social dilution to which membership had been subject, that is to the extent to which the committees were manned not simply by parochial, as distinct from élite county, gentry but even by persons from outside the gentry altogether. Conversely, the higher the proportion of committeemen drawn from those traditionally regarded as the natural rulers of the county, the more likely a committee was to display independence *vis-à-vis* Westminster in matters such as local control and fiscal decentralization. However, these observations are a rough guide rather than a universally applicable rule, and most country gentlemen probably viewed their county committees as far too subservient to the demands of central government. On the other hand, in the view of the government at Westminster far too many county committees appeared to be too heavily tarred with the localist brush to be capable of acting as efficient organs of central control in the counties. This criticism has a very familiar ring to students of the relations of Caroline personal government to local government, and it was partly to combat such strong centrifugal forces that parliament had created the wartime regional associations of eastern, southeastern and west Midland counties.[22] The most successful of these, however, soon developed its own super-localist aspirations. These had found their most striking expression at a meeting of the committee of the Eastern Association at Bury St Edmunds on 30 January 1645, which expressed unconcern for the proposition that the proposed New Model Army was likely to contribute powerfully to the safety of the kingdom, on the grounds that 'that was not our work, being there met as committees for the Association'.

There can be no doubt that in associating themselves with the widespread hostility to county committees, both parliamentary Presbyterians such as Denzil Holles and local Presbyterian politicians such as Colonel King in Lincolnshire were aligning themselves with powerful, if also to some extent counter-revolutionary, currents of opinion. An even more momentous aspect of this conservatively orientated policy was the attempt to cut the army, the pre-eminent cause of high taxation and now arguably redundant following the conclusion of hostilities in 1646, down to size. At the beginning of 1647 there were more men under arms in the provincial forces than in the New Model Army, even though parliament had already conducted extensive disbanding operations among the former during the previous year. The widespread mutinies concerning the arrears of pay in the provincial armies, together with violence against local civil authorities in a number of counties, including Devon, Dorset, Leicestershire and Cheshire,[23] should have given the parliamentary Presbyterians cause for serious reflection before turning their attention to the incomparably better disciplined, and also far more formidable, New Model Army, once the Scots had departed. In attempting to disband that army with totally inadequate arrears of pay and only the unpopular alternative of serving in Ireland under new commanders, the Presbyterians were taking a great risk. They may indeed have estimated correctly the prevailing mood of the taxpaying public, which boggled at the sums of about £2½ million estimated as due to the New Model Army alone, but they totally misjudged the mood and likely reaction of the soldiers. In a very few weeks this was transformed from the moderately worded requests in a soldiers' petition in March, asking for the redress of purely military grievances and notably the payment of their arrears and their indemnity from prosecution for acts against persons and property during the war, to the formulation of a fully-fledged political programme in June. The consequence of the attempts of Holles and his colleagues to rid the nation of the greater part of the burden of the army and of their rash and extreme response to the soldiers' circulating their petition complaining of the manifestly unjust terms on which disbandment was to be put into effect was indeed momentous. It was nothing less than the politicization of the New Model Army, which was hereafter to be a distinct political force and the prime instrument which brought about the revolution of 1648–9.

But for the time being it was counter-revolution that loomed largest on the political scene. The proposed expeditionary force for Ireland was seen by the army and its Independent allies in parliament as a Presbyterian device to crush the New Model and initiate such a counter-revolution. In addition, a Scottish supporting invasion to seize the king's person at Holdenby House in Northamptonshire was thought to be imminent, while the Scots' Presbyterian allies in the City of London were engaged both in encouraging deserters from the New Model and in recruiting 'reformadoes', disbanded soldiers from other forces who had no love for this élite corps. This is the background to the preemptive strike of Cornet Joyce and his troop on 4 June, abducting the king from Holdenby and carrying him off to the army, if not on the orders of the army commanders, at least with their ultimate approval.

The Solemn Engagement of the Army, the product of a mass rendezvous of the army on Newmarket Heath on the following day, asserted the soldiers' determination not to disband until their grievances had been redressed. And by now these grievances were extending from matters of indemnity and arrears to positive political demands which were to be formulated by a General Council of the Army containing elected representatives of both officers and other ranks. This programme, put forward in a declaration of 14 June, included a demand for the purge from parliament and impeachment of eleven Presbyterian MPs, including Holles and Stapleton, who were held responsible both for the parliamentary declaration of 30 March against petitioning in the army and for the allegedly counter-revolutionary preparations in London and elsewhere. It also demanded a dissolution of the current parliament and the election of a new parliament with strictly limited life, some measure of electoral reform, a generous measure of religious toleration, and curtailing of the powers both of the lieutenancy and county committees.

In the initial politicization of the army too much stress is often laid on the influence of Leveller politicians finding a power base in the army via the election of radical 'agitators' or representatives, and the deliberate formulation of a Leveller political programme out of grievances which were originally purely military.[24] For there is nothing of Leveller radicalism about the army's political programme of 14 June. However, as the army became increasingly alarmed at the mounting counter-revolutionary preparations in London, the insistent, but unconnected, advocacy by both army agitators and radical London Levellers of the occupation of London by the army made more and more sense. But despite provocation from the Presbyterian-dominated City and parliament, the more conservative army commanders resisted such pressures, and their restraint appeared to be justified when, on 23 July, following a move of the army in the direction of London, parliament took control of the city militia out of the hands of the city Presbyterian supporters of Holles and put it into those of the Independent allies of the army. However, the army was soon given a perfect excuse for intervention, when, on 26 July, parliament was invaded by a counter-revolutionary mob which demanded and obtained a repeal of the ordinance of 23 July, the restoration of the eleven members whom the army had sought to impeach, and a parliamentary resolution inviting the king to London to treat. This counter-revolutionary violence precipitated the flight to the army of the Speakers of both houses and a large number of Independent MPs. The army responded by occupying London on 4 August in the interests of public order, the restoration of the integrity of parliament and of the fugitive MPs to their seats, and the exclusion once more of the eleven offending Presbyterian MPs. It was to remain at the centre of the political scene for the remainder of the period covered by this book.

DIVERGENT WAR AIMS, AUGUST 1647-JANUARY 1648

To see the army's successive coups between June and August as a blow to a peaceful settlement of the kingdom and a victory for radicalism and republicanism would be to read back attitudes prevalent in the second half of 1648 into the middle of 1647. The soldiers had taken possession of the king not, as in December 1648, to bring him to justice and establish a republic, but to exploit him as a weapon against the parliamentary Presbyterians and to further their own plans and those of their Independent allies in parliament for a settlement of the kingdom. These found expression in the constitutional programme known as the Heads of the Proposals, which was presented to the king at the beginning of August, and which opted unequivocally for a monarchical constitution with a bicameral legislature. It differed from the Presbyterian position in that it envisaged the dissolution of the present parliament (which, of course, by the terms of the statute of 1641, could not be dissolved without its own consent), and the election of parliaments biennially on a wider, though in no sense democratic, franchise. There was to be a reorganization of electoral districts with the number of parliamentary seats in each 'proportionate to the respective rates they bear in the common charges and burdens of the kingdom'. Parliament should both nominate royal ministers and retain control of the militia for ten years. As an indication of how far the army had come since March, only the final clause of its proposals related to the original soldierly grievances which had sparked off the dispute with parliament.[25]

Although the parliamentary Presbyterians who – along with the Scots – still stood by the terms of the Newcastle Propositions of 1646, did their best to blacken the army grandees and their Independent allies as anti-monarchical, it ought not to be assumed that at this stage the king leaned any more strongly towards the Presbyterians than towards his army captors, from whom he had down to this time received rather more considerate treatment. Indeed it was almost certainly Charles's intention to play off one group against the other. It was in pursuit of this tortuous strategy that he rejected the Heads of the Proposals, which in turn had the effect of causing some of the more radical parliamentary Independents, and notably Henry Marten, to urge an end to all negotiations with the king, thus anticipating the Vote of No Addresses of the following January. Another source of opposition to persisting with the Heads of the Proposals were the Levellers, who since 1646 had been very prominent in London, and from the middle of 1647 had gained numerous adherents in the army, not only among the elected agitators and rank and file but also among some high-ranking officers, of whom the most prominent was Colonel Thomas Rainsborough. The Levellers' radical constitutional programme contained in a document called *The Agreement of the People* was to be the subject of fierce and strenuous debate in the army council at Putney at the end of October and beginning of November.[26]

Just how radical these proposals were has become a matter of controversy among historians. Taking issue with what had previously been the generally held view, Professor C. B. Macpherson has argued that the Levellers, while desiring a much wider franchise than that favoured by army grandees such as Cromwell and Henry Ireton, stopped well short of manhood suffrage, and would exclude wage-earners and almsmen from the franchise. To this end he lays particular stress on the views of the Leveller spokesman Maximilian Petty. However, other historians have stressed that there were almost as many Leveller views on the franchise as there were Levellers, since they were, as one of them admitted, 'a heterogenial body'. Some of them like Colonel Rainsborough and John Wildman believed that 'every man that is to be under a government must first by his own consent put himself under that government', while others, like Petty, took a more restrictive view of the franchise, though not so restrictive as that taken by Cromwell and Ireton. The latter in particular put forward at Putney the sort of arguments which were later to be heard in the early nineteenth century about the need for the franchise to be restricted to those with a real property (viz. landed) stake in the country, for political levelling would surely lead to social levelling. Mr Christopher Thompson has recently argued that Petty's views were developed in the course of debate at Putney as some sort of compromise between his original view of manhood suffrage and the very restrictive franchise favoured by Ireton and other more conservative spokesmen. To those willing to go some way in this direction the final decision of the army council in favour of a franchise excluding beggars and wage-earners might still be represented as a notable advance on the conservative views to which Ireton had given such eloquent and cogently argued support. But it is difficult to see how it could have been anything but a profound disappointment to those Levellers who, like Wildman, Sexby and Rainsborough, and unlike Petty, give no indication of modifying their views in the course of the debate. That it was no less disappointing to multitudes of soldiers is clear from the celebrated confrontation which took place at Corkbush Field near Ware in Hertfordshire on 14 November, at which Oliver Cromwell's nerve and courage when faced by mutinous troops with Leveller slogans in their hats restored order at the price of the execution of one of their ringleaders. For the time being at least the Levellers had been quelled.[27]

The other great issue which had been hotly debated at Putney related to the place (if any) of the monarchy and the House of Lords in the constitution. On this matter, as on the franchise, Cromwell, Ireton and the grandees had taken up a conservative position. To both the Levellers at Putney and the more radical wing of the Independents in parliament and the country, Cromwell and Ireton had become the objects of the deepest suspicion as a result of their continued negotiation with the king even after he had rejected the

Heads of the Proposals. It was this futile and ungodly attempt to heal Babylon or to wash a blackamoor white, argued Sexby, which accounted for the current disunity and confusion of the army, which had triumphed over and over again before departing from the paths of righteousness. Oliver was not so confident of the precise direction indicated by the Almighty and counselled extreme caution in adopting such fundamental changes in the constitution, which would surely require a divine directive or dispensation.

Arguably the first such indication was the king's abscondence from Hampton Court to the Isle of Wight only ten days after Cromwell and Ireton had defended at Putney the need to come to terms with him. Hereafter, no more is heard about the Heads of the Proposals, and it was parliament not the army which reoccupied the forefront of the stage in the matter of peace terms which were presented to Charles on Christmas Eve in the form of four bills for his signature on a take-it-or-leave-it basis, allowing of no negotiation. Since the bills contained far stiffer terms than those of the Heads of the Proposals, it is not at all surprising that the king rejected them. They included parliamentary control of the militia for twenty years with no guarantee of its return to the crown thereafter; the permanent abolition of episcopacy; the banning of the use of the Book of Common Prayer even by the royal household; and the revocation of all royal wartime declarations against the parliament and of all titles of honour granted since 20 May 1642.

But there is another reason why Charles I felt able to refuse to sign the four bills and make them law. Two days before he rejected them he had concluded a secret Engagement with the representatives of the more moderate party in Scotland, those led by Hamilton as distinct from Argyll and the high Covenanters, on astonishingly favourable terms. There was to be an interim establishment of a high Presbyterian church in England, but for three years only and with no prejudice to the nature of the ultimate settlement thereafter. The king and his household were to be free to worship as they pleased even during the three years, and the Covenant was not to be compulsorily taken by all. Finally, and most significantly, in the likely event of the English parliament refusing to accede to the demand that the king be allowed to come to London for peace negotiations with parliament and the Scottish commissioners, the Engagement promised a Scottish invasion of England on Charles's behalf. Unaware though English MPs might be of the terms of the Engagement, Charles's flight to the Isle of Wight and his outright rejection of the four bills were enough to harden the hearts of many of them towards the king, and to get a parliamentary majority for the momentous Vote of No Addresses in January. This was a resolution that parliament should settle the kingdom without approaching the king, though there was nothing to stipulate that such a settlement should be a republican one. For many of those who had not yet abandoned hope of a monarchical solution, the later revelations about the terms of the Engagement and the renewal of civil war in 1648 were to be the ultimate 'dispensation' indicating God's republican purpose.[28]

THE SECOND CIVIL WAR AND ITS AFTERMATH, 1648

In 1648 most of the counter-revolutionary dangers which had dominated men's minds during the previous year came to full fruition. There were localist revolts in several parts of England, and most notably in South Wales (where there had been disturbances in 1647), Kent, Essex and the north, the latter in conjunction with the Engagers' invasion from Scotland. In addition, there was the revolt of part of the fleet, which went over to the prince of Wales. But the one counter-revolutionary coup which had actually occurred in 1647, the events of the later July days in London, was not repeated in 1648. By keeping its hands clean this time, the City was able to exert influence in favour of renewed negotiations with the king once hostilities were over.

Fortunately for the English parliament there was little coordination between the insurgents. As a result the parliamentary forces had little difficulty in defeating the South Welsh insurgents at St Fagan's on 8 May and Pembroke on 11 July; those of Kent at Maidstone on 1 June; the revolt led by the duke of Buckingham and the earls of Holland and Peterborough at St Neots on 10 July; and the invading Scottish army at Preston on 17 August. Colchester was surrendered by the Essex and the remainder of the Kentish rebels on 27 August. One crucial factor was the Scottish delay consequent on the difficulties experienced by the Engagers in overcoming the unrelenting opposition of Argyll and the high Covenanting party. Similarly the government's fears of coordination between local risings were not borne out by events. Yet the demands of the insurgents in different regions had much in common with one another. Almost all called for a personal treaty with the king; for the country to be ruled by known laws; for the excesses of county committees to be curbed; and for the army to be disbanded and the burden of taxation reduced.

The insurgents were a very mixed bunch: conservative county gentlemen who had once supported parliament against what they regarded as royal centralizing innovations and now took up arms for the king for similar reasons; and extremist elements including wild ex-Cavaliers – 'dammee Blades' – who flocked to the disaffected areas; and – as in 1647 – reformadoes chafing at what they regarded as the preferential treatment accorded to New Model soldiers in the matter of terms of disbandment and payment of arrears. That military grievances might issue in counter-revolutionary as well as revolutionary action is further demonstrated by the circumstances of the revolt in South Wales. Colonel John Poyer and Major-General Rowland Laugharne had both served parliament in the first Civil War, but the former was alienated at the prospect of having to disgorge some of his wartime gains and the latter infuriated at being superseded in his command. Along with Colonel Rice Powell they exploited the quite different grievances of their countrymen and opted for the king and the prince of Wales in pursuit of these personal ends.

There were other minor outbreaks elsewhere – for instance in Suffolk, Norfolk and Cornwall – but they came to nothing. Apart from the link between the northern insurgents and the Scottish invaders, the main danger of a junction of insurgent forces was presented by the connection established between the Kentish insurgents and the revolted ships of the fleet. The latter also excited alarm on account of the possibility that the ships might link up with the Scottish invasion, or bring over foreign troops, or rescue the king from the Isle of Wight. The sailors had been deeply offended by the replacement of the Presbyterian Vice-Admiral Batten in October 1647 by – of all persons – the ex-Leveller Colonel Rainsborough, which they saw as the probable prelude to a new-modelling of the navy. Rainsborough was unceremoniously dumped on shore in June by the officers of the revolted ships, who then established contact with the Kentish insurgents and enthusiastically adopted their political programme. The insurgent fleet continued to give a good deal of trouble to the parliament long after other revolts had been put down.

Indeed the extent of active support for the insurgents turned out to be a good deal less than the government had feared. How far the City of London's quiescence was forced on it and how far it was willingly adopted is an open question: but a number of significant concessions had been made to it earlier in 1648, including putting the Tower under an officer acceptable to the City and dropping the charges against the aldermen who had allegedly been implicated in the counter-revolutionary disturbances of the previous July. Similarly the charges against the survivors of the eleven Presbyterian MPs – Stapleton had died in exile – were dropped, and they were allowed to resume their seats, to the horror of the more fire-eating radical Independents. No less to the latters' horror was parliament's suspension of the Vote of No Addresses on 24 August, thus allowing the resumption of negotiations with the king. For, they argued, such negotiations had been a principal demand of the defeated insurgents, to concede which was surely to throw away the fruits of victory. But it was precisely the ideas of radical politicians as to what constituted the fruits of victory that made the hurrying forward of negotiations a matter of vital urgency not only to conservative Presbyterians like Holles and D'Ewes, but also to former middle-group Independents like Samuel Browne and William Pierrepont. For the outbreak of the Second Civil War had stiffened the resolution of many radical Independents, as well as of former monarchists such as Ireton, to bring Charles Stuart, that man of blood, to account. Here was a prospect which horrified former middle-group Independents no less than it did Presbyterians, in which circumstances it is not surprising to find five such Independents (Saye and Sele, Pierrepont, Browne, John Crewe and John Bulkeley) nominated – along with nine Presbyterians – to serve as parliamentary commissioners negotiating with the king in the Isle of Wight. The presence of the radical Independent Sir Henry Vane on the same commission suggests that not all even of the radicals were yet prepared to go the whole way of settling the realm without the king.

THE LAST CHANCE OF SETTLEMENT ABORTED, 1648

At Newport in the Isle of Wight during the dismal, wet autumn of 1648, Charles I made many more concessions than he had done in any of the negotiations in which he had engaged since the outbreak of the First Civil War. He agreed to rescind all his wartime declarations against the parliament and revoke the titles of honour which he had granted since May 1642. He accepted parliamentary control of the public debt, Ireland and the militia – this last one of the great issues about which war had been originally waged – and the abolition of wardship in return for the obviously inadequate compensation of £100,000 per annum. But on a number of issues, notably the delinquency of some of his principal adherents, and above all on religion, he stuck fast.

He refused to yield to a Presbyterian-type church settlement for more than an interim period of three years, and to the permanent abolition of episcopacy, as distinct from that of archbishops, archdeacons, deans and chapters, prebendaries and episcopal chancellors. Moreover, he correctly insisted that to forbid the queen and her household to worship according to Catholic rites would be to violate the terms of the marriage treaty with France. In so far as those desiring a settlement were religious Presbyterians, they could not help but share the view – on this, if on nothing else – of those radical parliamentary Independents who were also religious Presbyterians, that the king's replies were a wholly inadequate basis for a settlement. But while a matter for bitter regret for the former, this rejoiced the hearts and confirmed the presuppositions of the latter.

However, both the army leaders and their radical Independent allies in parliament behaved as if they believed that the negotiations with the king were on the verge of succeeding, and that this success would enable Charles to exploit the undoubted desire of taxpayers to get rid of the army, the only obstacle in their view to the successful achievement of thorough-going counter-revolution. This is the context in which the idea of the precipitate dissolution of parliament and the election of another on a new franchise, favoured by Ireton, seems to have been replaced by that of a purge of parliament. The radical Independent MP Edmund Ludlow appears to have convinced Ireton that such an election, even on a Heads of the Proposals franchise, might well have the untoward effect of producing a counter-revolutionary majority in parliament.

On 20 November the army council presented an enormous Remonstrance to the House of Commons, demanding, amongst other things, the trial of the king and the establishment of a republic. This radical programme helped Ireton to win the somewhat reluctant support of the Levellers, even though they suspected – rightly as it turned out – that in the minds of the army grandees, the trial of the king and the establishment of a republic represented the limits, not the beginnings, of reform. The army's Remonstrance and the terms which parliament presented to the king at Newport thus represented two opposed but equally practicable solutions to the problem of settlement. In rejecting the latter Charles was increasing the likelihood of the former being adopted, though the army would probably have taken affairs into its own hands even if the king had accepted parliament's terms in full. The prelude to Colonel Pride's purge of parliament was the Commons' prolonged delay in considering, and their ultimate rejection of, the army's Remonstrance on 30 November by the substantial majority of sixty-eight votes, and the vote of 5 December that the king's last answer to parliament's terms was, though unsatisfactory, at least 'a Ground to proceed upon for the settlement of the Peace of the Kingdom'. It was this which precipitated and provided the grounds for Pride's Purge on the following day, whereby 231 MPs were secluded from parliament and forty-five of them imprisoned for a time.

Who exactly were the victims of Pride's Purge? The formerly held view that it was simply a purge of Presbyterians by Independent MPs has been as discredited by the work of Professor Underdown as has the view which equates these two political groupings with religious denominations.[29] Certainly all of the parliamentary Presbyterians were secluded, and some of them imprisoned into the bargain. But so were many Independent MPs and notably former middle-groupers such as Nathaniel Fiennes and John Bulkeley, who had broken with the radical wing of the Independents over the propriety of negotiating with the king. Indeed of those former middle-groupers who had gone over to the Independents during the political transformation of 1645–6, more than twice as many were victims as were supporters of the purge. This outrageously illegal act had made revolution possible; what sort of a revolution remains to be seen.

REVOLUTION?

In the sense that to bring the king, who had been withdrawn by the army from the Isle of Wight five days before Pride's Purge, to public trial and execution is a revolutionary occurrence, Pride's Purge was beyond doubt the prelude to revolution. But it would be wrong to see these things as inevitable even after the purge. Ireton and the propounders of the army's Remonstrance of the previous month might now be completely convinced of the need to bring matters to this extreme conclusion, in order to placate the Levellers and other radicals in this, if in nothing else. So might longer-standing republicans such as Edmund Ludlow, Henry Marten and Thomas Chaloner, while radical sectaries like Thomas Harrison and John Carew saw the regicide not as the end of revolution but as heralding the millennium and the rule of the Saints on earth. But not all of those who remained in parliament after the purge were even now convinced of the necessity of proceeding to extreme measures. Among the doubters would seem to be Oliver Cromwell, who had been away on a military campaign in the north during the stirring events of the late autumn and early winter of 1648. Recognizing the doubts of Cromwell and the unlikelihood of Lord General Fairfax supporting the trial of the king, there were still royalists who hoped that the army's seizure of the king was, like its earlier move in June 1647, no more than a move in the battle for political supremacy at Westminster. While they were sorely mistaken, Cromwell does certainly seem to have been prepared to have one more attempt at negotiations in the form of a mission of the earl of Denbigh to the king in late December. It was only with Charles's rejection of its terms that he finally determined on the extreme solution: the setting up of a high court of justice to try Charles, his execution on 30 January 1649, and the subsequent establishment of a republic.

That these were revolutionary occurrences is not in any doubt. But some historians have sought to see beyond the removal of the king, with its profound implications for every form of power and authority whether political, parental, institutional or economic, and have seen these events as involving far more than this. They see them as consummating the triumph of one class over another and final replacement of a 'feudal' by a 'bourgeois' regime which was not to be reversed even with the restoration of monarchy in 1660. Since a consideration of these views must involve an examination not only of the significance of the events of the reign of Charles I, but also of the nature of the republican regime which succeeded that reign, and indeed of the Restoration of 1660, it will be convenient to postpone it until the end of the final chapter of this book.

Appendix to Chapter 9

MAPS ILLUSTRATING THE CHANGING TERRITORIAL STRENGTH OF ROYALISTS AND PARLIAMENTARIANS IN THE FIRST CIVIL WAR

Map I England and Wales, 1 May 1643
Map II England and Wales, 25 September 1643
Map III England and Wales, 23 November 1644
Map IV England and Wales, 5 November 1645

Maps I and II illustrate strikingly the extent of royalist gains in the summer of 1643. A comparison with Map III shows parliamentary gains in 1644, and especially following the parliamentarian victory at Marston Moor on 2 July 1644. A comparison with Map IV shows the shrinkage of royalist territory by November 1645, especially following the defeats at Naseby (13 June 1645), Langport (10 July) and elsewhere in the south-west, and Rowton Heath (24 September).

The maps have been taken from S. R. Gardiner *History of the Great Civil War 1642–1649*, vols. I & II (1893).

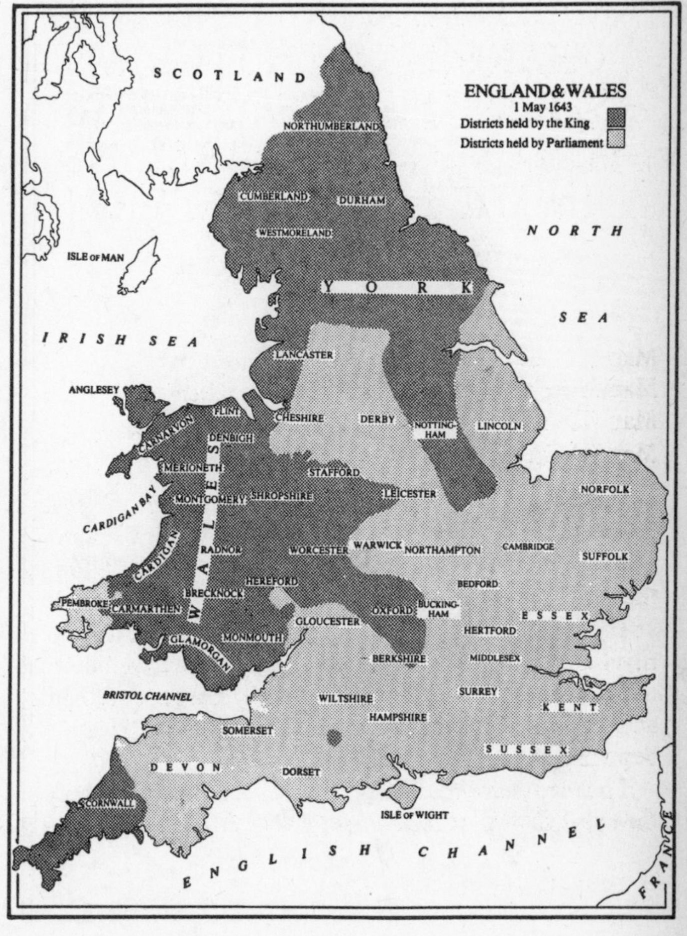
ENGLAND & WALES
1 May 1643
Districts held by the King
Districts held by Parliament
SCOTLAND
NORTHUMBERLAND
CUMBERLAND
DURHAM
WESTMORELAND
NORTH
SEA
ISLE OF MAN
YORK
IRISH SEA
LANCASTER
ANGLESEY
FLINT
CARNARVON
DENBIGH
CHESHIRE
DERBY
NOTTINGHAM
LINCOLN
MERIONETH
STAFFORD
WALES
MONTGOMERY
SHROPSHIRE
LEICESTER
NORFOLK
CARDIGAN BAY
CARDIGAN
RADNOR
WORCESTER
WARWICK
NORTHAMPTON
CAMBRIDGE
SUFFOLK
HEREFORD
BEDFORD
PEMBROKE
CARMARTHEN
BRECKNOCK
OXFORD
BUCKINGHAM
ESSEX
GLOUCESTER
HERTFORD
GLAMORGAN
MONMOUTH
BERKSHIRE
MIDDLESEX
BRISTOL CHANNEL
WILTSHIRE
SURREY
KENT
HAMPSHIRE
SOMERSET
SUSSEX
DEVON
DORSET
CORNWALL
ISLE OF WIGHT
ENGLISH CHANNEL
FRANCE

ENGLAND & WALES
25 Sept 1643
Districts held by the King
Districts held by Parliament
SCOTLAND
NORTHUMBERLAND
CUMBERLAND
DURHAM
WESTMORELAND
ISLE OF MAN
NORTH SEA
YORK
IRISH SEA
LANCASTER
ANGLESEY
FLINT
CHESHIRE
DERBY
NOTTINGHAM
LINCOLN
CARNARVON
DENBIGH
MERIONETH
STAFFORD
CARDIGAN BAY
MONTGOMERY
SHROPSHIRE
LEICESTER
NORFOLK
WALES
CARDIGAN
RADNOR
WORCESTER
WARWICK
NORTHAMPTON
CAMBRIDGE
SUFFOLK
HEREFORD
BEDFORD
PEMBROKE
CARMARTHEN
BRECKNOCK
OXFORD
BUCKINGHAM
ESSEX
GLOUCESTER
HERTFORD
GLAMORGAN
MONMOUTH
BERKSHIRE
MIDDLESEX
BRISTOL CHANNEL
SURREY
WILTSHIRE
KENT
HAMPSHIRE
SOMERSET
SUSSEX
DEVON
DORSET
CORNWALL
ISLE OF WIGHT
ENGLISH CHANNEL
FRANCE

ENGLAND & WALES
23 Nov 1644
Districts held by the King
Districts held by Parliament
SCOTLAND
NORTHUMBERLAND
CUMBERLAND
DURHAM
WESTMORELAND
NORTH SEA
ISLE OF MAN
YORK
IRISH SEA
LANCASTER
ANGLESEY
FLINT
CHESHIRE
DERBY
NOTTINGHAM
LINCOLN
CARNARVON
DENBIGH
MERIONETH
STAFFORD
NORFOLK
MONTGOMERY
SHROPSHIRE
LEICESTER
CARDIGAN BAY
CARDIGAN
RADNOR
WALES
WORCESTER
WARWICK
NORTHAMPTON
CAMBRIDGE
SUFFOLK
HEREFORD
BEDFORD
BRECKNOCK
PEMBROKE
CARMARTHEN
GLOUCESTER
OXFORD
BUCKINGHAM
ESSEX
HERTFORD
GLAMORGAN
MONMOUTH
BERKSHIRE
MIDDLESEX
BRISTOL CHANNEL
WILTSHIRE
SURREY
KENT
HAMPSHIRE
SOMERSET
SUSSEX
DEVON
DORSET
CORNWALL
ISLE OF WIGHT
ENGLISH CHANNEL
FRANCE

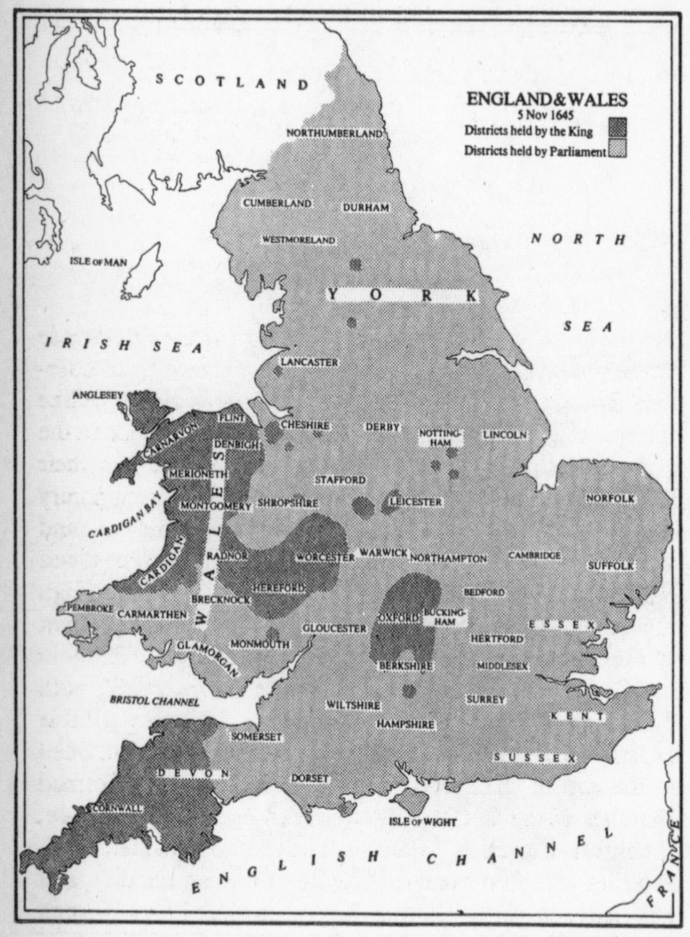
ENGLAND & WALES
5 Nov 1645
Districts held by the King
Districts held by Parliament
SCOTLAND
NORTHUMBERLAND
CUMBERLAND
DURHAM
WESTMORELAND
NORTH
SEA
ISLE OF MAN
YORK
IRISH SEA
LANCASTER
ANGLESEY
FLINT
CARNARVON
DENBIGH
CHESHIRE
DERBY
NOTTING-HAM
LINCOLN
MERIONETH
STAFFORD
MONTGOMERY
SHROPSHIRE
LEICESTER
NORFOLK
CARDIGAN BAY
WALES
RADNOR
WORCESTER
WARWICK
NORTHAMPTON
CAMBRIDGE
SUFFOLK
CARDIGAN
HEREFORD
BEDFORD
BRECKNOCK
PEMBROKE
CARMARTHEN
OXFORD
BUCKING-HAM
ESSEX
GLOUCESTER
MONMOUTH
HERTFORD
GLAMORGAN
BERKSHIRE
MIDDLESEX
BRISTOL CHANNEL
SURREY
WILTSHIRE
KENT
HAMPSHIRE
SOMERSET
SUSSEX
DEVON
DORSET
CORNWALL
ISLE OF WIGHT
ENGLISH CHANNEL
FRANCE

Chapter Ten

WIDER PERSPECTIVES: ENGLAND AND THE WORLD, *c.* 1600–50

POINTS OF CONTACT

Immediately before the opening and during the last decade of the period covered by this book there were two considerable effluxes of Englishmen to continental Europe. Unlike the epic migrations of Englishmen across the Atlantic in the early seventeenth century, these were temporary in their nature but exerted, through the medium of the temporary exiles' experience, a considerable effect on English life and institutions. The earlier and more significant movement was the exodus and subsequent return of Protestants in the reign of Mary, and the second that of some of the most important and influential royalists following the Roundhead victory in the Civil War. The first provided Protestant exiles, both divines and laymen, with the invaluable and unforgettable experience of religious life in what most of them continued to the end of their days to think of as the best reformed churches of the world in centres such as Strasburg, Basle, Frankfurt, Zürich and Geneva. The second provided royalist exiles with first-hand experience of foreign regimes, and especially, in so far as they settled in Spanish or French dominions rather than in the Dutch United Provinces, of that royal absolutism which was to impress many of them as the form of government which pointed the way of true political progress.

Of the two groups of exiles the foreign experiences of the earlier group almost certainly had a greater impact on the course of English history. They profoundly influenced the character of a significant proportion of the original Elizabethan episcopate and the direction and temper of English Protestantism. Certainly they have no subsequent parallel in this period, so far as English divines are concerned. Later Puritan divines, while continuing to talk in terms of the need to follow the example of the best reformed churches abroad, went on thinking of these practices in terms of what the Marian Protestant exiles had brought back with them, ideas and practices which, long before the end of Elizabeth's reign, had become part of the English radical Protestant tradition. With a few exceptions most of the successors of these Marian exiles were far more insular than their predecessors, however strongly they might be moved by foreign developments: by the expulsion of James I's daughter and son-in-law from Bohemia and the Palatinate; by the menace to international Protestantism presented by imperialist victories in the Thirty Years War; or by the spectacular, if all too temporary, triumphs of Protestant arms under the Swedish king Gustavus Adolphus until his death at Lützen in 1632.

While these two migrations were in fact exceptional, it must also be remembered that throughout our period Englishmen with direct experience of foreign countries were themselves decidedly exceptional, even though it is true that foreign travel became more common in the seventeenth than it had been in the sixteenth century.[1] The first and perhaps the most obvious example of persons with such experience were government ambassadors or envoys, whether on a semi-permanent basis, like Sir Ralph Winwood and his successor Sir Dudley Carleton at The Hague, or Sir Henry Wotton at Venice, or greater personages such as Viscounts Doncaster (the later earl of Carlisle) and Kensington (the later earl of Holland), who acted as occasional or extraordinary envoys charged with the conduct of particular negotiations such as the Anglo-French treaty for the marriage of the prince of Wales to Henrietta Maria in 1624. One of the permanent embassies, that of the English ambassador at Constantinople, was maintained at the expense not of the crown but of the Levant Company, though Charles I's appointment of what the company regarded as totally unsuitable men such as Sir Sackville Crow and Sir Peter Wyche occasioned serious friction between the crown and the company. In general the absence of a regular English consular service was to some extent made up for in important centres of English overseas trade such as Middelburg, Rotterdam, Hamburg, Danzig (modern Gdansk) and Elbing by the great chartered companies – in the above cases by the Merchant Adventurers and the Eastland Company. These bodies exercised some at least of the functions which today are performed by the consular service, even if they were unable to do much to rectify such mercantile grievances as the Dutch exaction of 'tare' (compulsory deductions for allegedly faulty cloths) and impositions such as the so-called 'consumption money'. One of the arguments put forward in vain during the reign of James I by those favouring the establishment of a Spanish Company related to the protection which such a body might be able to afford to its members against rapacious Spanish customs officials or overzealous Catholic inquisitors.

It is difficult to speak with certainty about the impact of extensive foreign experience on English merchants or sailors. For most of the former, residing in small and tightly self-contained communities normally close to the English 'factories' (depots), such experience may well have served to confirm and strengthen already existing national and religious prejudices, a reinforcement of Protestant xenophobia. Most of them probably kept very much to themselves, confining their dealings with foreigners to what was necessary in the pursuit of their business operations. Like alien residents in England, they enjoyed a pretty free hand in the matter of religious observance, which tended to be of a more radically Protestant character than that which normally prevailed in English parish churches; though this freedom was menaced by the Laudian drive for conformity, which created resentment both from alien residents in

England and from English merchants – and especially the Merchant Adventurers – abroad.

In contrast to the merchants, to whom travel abroad – whether to Europe, Asia Minor, across the Atlantic or, following the foundation of the East India Company in 1601, to the Far East – was simply a necessary aspect of earning a living, were those high-born travellers who were in a real sense the originators of the so-called 'Grand Tour' which was later to become an essential feature of the education of a nobleman. While there were certainly some merchants who acquired a more than nodding acquaintance with the culture and civilization of the lands where they resided, this was the very *raison d'être* of the journeys of such aristocratic travellers, whether it took the form of taking lessons in courtly accomplishments such as fencing, dancing or riding the great horse in France, collecting antiquities and *objets d'art* in Italy, or even taking the waters at a spa in the Spanish Netherlands. While the English merchant overseas was to be found in centres of commerce such as Middelburg, Hamburg, Elbing, Aleppo or Livorno, the aristocratic traveller favoured centres of fashion and tourism such as Paris, Rome and Venice, to mention only three of the cities most visited.

Of course, it was not only the cultivation of refined and courtly accomplishments which took well-born Englishmen abroad on tour. Among them were Catholics, some of whom never returned, and of these a few even took holy orders in the old church. While the majority of well-born Protestant tourists, duly impressed by the culture and artefacts of baroque and Counter-Reformation Europe, were probably also repelled by the religious ceremonies and other aspects of Catholic observance which they could hardly avoid encountering, there were some young men whose quest for foreign culture led them ultimately to capitulate to the Roman Antichrist.

An important and neglected group of travellers were those who went abroad to serve in foreign armies; not the raw levies who were pressed to serve in Mansfeld's disorderly legions in the 1620s, and who died like flies on board ship or in miserable coastal transit camps, but those to whom the pursuit of a professional military career was often coupled with a deep sense of ideological commitment which was, if anything, increased by their service experience – whether, if Protestant, with the Dutch, or the kings of Denmark or Sweden; or if Catholic, under the Spanish crown. The former were to be found in plenty on both sides, and the latter in the king's service as well as in the ranks of the Irish confederate rebels, during the English Civil War.

Just as English merchant residents abroad tended to keep themselves to themselves, so did foreign immigrants into England. The most important single category of such immigrants was the Flemish and Walloon cloth producers who had fled to England from Spanish religious persecution in the reign of Elizabeth I and who were especially responsible for the introduction of the so-called new draperies, which, as will be shown shortly, contributed not only to the transformation of much of the textile production of East Anglian, Essex and Kentish towns and villages, such as Norwich, Colchester, Halstead, Maidstone and Canterbury, but also to a vitally important reorientation of English overseas trade in the direction of Mediterranean Europe. For all their impeccable religious credentials as Protestant refugees, these immigrants and their descendants were not exempt, especially in times of economic depression, from periodic outbursts of xenophobia, which were accentuated by their tendency to cling tenaciously to the technical manufacturing secrets which they had brought with them from the Low Countries. As with immigrants and their descendants today, some voices were raised in favour of their compulsory repatriation and against their un-English life-style and allegedly dirty and insanitary habits. The last of these grounds for complaint seems, however, to be practically confined to the very large numbers of aliens dwelling in the metropolis, where they included Catholics as well as Protestants, and took in a much wider range of occupations – among them sugar-refiners, silk workers, furniture and clock makers, jewellers and domestic servants.

Vitally important as the contribution of aliens was to the diversification of English economic life, their immediate impact on the quality and character of indigenous civilization and culture does not seem to have been any greater than that of the English, and especially East Anglian, refugees from Laudian religious intolerance who settled in Dutch towns, and especially in Leiden, in even greater numbers than those who crossed the Atlantic to set up a new life in the wilderness. The one notable exception to this rule were the foreign musicians such as Lanier and Ferrabosco and, more especially, the painters such as Mytens and Van Dyck, who enormously enriched the cultural life and profoundly influenced the style and character of the late Jacobean, and especially the Caroline, court.

PEACE AND ECONOMIC REORIENTATION

The peace which was concluded with Spain in the treaty of London in 1604 has already been noted in the context of the significant change which it helped to bring about in the fortunes of the English Catholic community (see above, pp. 217–18). But the treaty marked the abandonment not only of English Catholic extremists by Spain but of Dutch Protestants by England. To many English Protestants it was a shabby compromise with Antichrist, made at the expense of allies who continued to fight on alone and to view their betrayal by the English in much the same way as the latter were to regard the French capitulation to Nazi Germany in 1940. On a more materialist level the peace also meant an end to joint-stock privateering expeditions, though these had become a good deal less attractive and profitable since the Spanish Main and the Spanish treasure fleets had become more efficiently policed and guarded.

Considered from an economic view, however, the peace was an unmitigated benefit to England, and not least to the crown, since the war involved financial burdens which were beyond the capacity of the royal finances to bear, still less the willingness of parliament to provide for adequately. Indeed the mind boggles at the notion of the enormous extraordinary charges of war being added to the excessive ordinary expenditure resulting from Jacobean courtly and royal extravagance. But the crown was certainly not the only beneficiary of peace, the main economic effect of which was the reopening of economic intercourse between England, Spain and the Spanish Netherlands. The decade following 1604 was an Indian summer of economic expansion and prosperity in which the expansion of economic opportunity consequent upon peace played an important part.

The reopening of the Spanish market was a factor of first-rate importance in the southward reorientation of much of English overseas trade, as English exporters sought to exploit new markets and English woollen cloth producers went in for a measure of what a modern economist might describe as product diversification in response both to the market situation and to the increased availability of less fine and longer-stapled wool which was one of the products of widespread enclosure for pasture. As Professor F. J. Fisher has demonstrated, by the outbreak of the Civil War almost as many new draperies as the former staple product of short-stapled fine broadcloth were being exported from London.[2] Of course, it would be wrong to seek to explain the growing importance of the new draperies, whose introduction by Flemish and Walloon refugees was mentioned in the preceding section, solely in terms of peace and trade with Spain, just as it would be wrong to explain the spectacular growth of English trade with southern Europe solely in terms of the new draperies. For one thing these products, though especially suited to warmer Mediterranean climates, also found buyers in northern Europe; for another, in the south they helped to displace the products of native industry in Italy at least as much as they did in Spain. Moreover, the growing importance of English trade with Constantinople and the eastern Mediterranean conducted by the English Levant Company was, in so far as it was concerned with cloth exports, a trade in traditional textile products which are normally associated with English trade to traditional markets in the Low Countries, Germany and the Baltic.

In the years immediately following the foundation of the Levant Company in 1581, the main English exports to the eastern Mediterranean had been lead, tin and the lighter (as compared with broadcloth, though not with the new draperies) and lower-grade woollen fabrics known as kerseys. But from the late 1590s onwards the eastern Mediterranean demand for kerseys yielded to a demand for the dyed Suffolk broadcloths, which had formerly – and especially during the disastrous English harvests of 1594-7 – found their main market in the Baltic lands, where effective demand was temporarily stimulated by the export of rye to the west, but was to decline thereafter. For a time the displaced kerseys found a market in the Balkans and Hungary, tapped through the ports of Ragusa (modern Dubrovnik) and Spalato (modern Split), but this development lasted for no more than a couple of decades. Moreover, in the eastern Mediterranean market even the Suffolk dyed broadcloths were, from the 1620s onwards, being increasingly replaced by similar products from the West Country, and more especially from Wiltshire, Gloucestershire and Worcestershire. As a result many of the Suffolk villages which had formerly specialized in producing coloured (especially blue) broadcloth now increasingly followed the lead of those which had once produced undyed cloth and went over to the production of new draperies of one sort or another. The free port of Livorno (Leghorn) in Tuscany – designed by the Medici to be a sort of Mediterranean Antwerp as well as to be a centre of the Mediterranean trade in Muslim slaves – was an increasingly important port through which these were channelled, as well as an entrepôt taking Suffolk (and later West Country) broadcloths for re-export to the Levant in competition with those exported directly by the English Levant Company.

In all this highly significant southwards reorientation of much of English overseas trade – as in the important growth of the English carrying trade in the Mediterranean – a crucial factor making for English success was the speed, manoeuvrability and defensibility of English vessels. In the north European trade, cargo-space took precedence over such considerations, and the celebrated Dutch fluytschip, constructed to cope with conditions in which the value of cargoes was relatively low in relation to their density, was carrying all before it. But even though many, if by no means all, southern cargoes were of similar density, the main factor which differentiated Mediterranean from north European conditions was the prevalence of Saracen piracy – not, as in the case of the depredations of the Dunkirk privateers in the 1620s, a danger chiefly evidenced in wartime, but a perennial menace to which the bulky Italian argosies and Spanish and Portuguese carracks were especially vulnerable. For the corsairs of Algiers and other places along the southern Mediterranean littoral had profited greatly from the defection to their ranks of French, English, Dutch and other privateering renegades, for whom the making of peace with Spain in 1599 (by France), 1604 (by England) and 1609 (by the Dutch) had removed the opportunities of semi-official and very profitable service as privateers, but who did not disdain the opportunity of service with the infidel. In the face of such modern naval expertise, which the Muslim sailors were quick to learn for themselves, Italian and other north Mediterranean merchantmen offered sitting targets. Even if the English were no better equipped than the Dutch to defend themselves adequately, they at least operated at a distinct advantage as compared with north Mediterranean sailors and certainly not at the sort of disadvantage *vis-à-vis* the Dutch which obtained in the northern, and especially the Baltic, trade. Accordingly English vessels increasingly came to carry not only English cargoes but the goods of Mediterranean countries also.

The reopening of trade with the Iberian peninsula after 1604 was, therefore, by no means the only cause of what amounts to a vital reorientation of English commerce, important though the traditional north European markets for broadcloths and other traditional fabrics remained. Nor was it only cloth producers and cloth exporters who benefited from the revival of trade with Spain. Peace proved to be at least as great a boon to the West Country merchants and fishermen involved in the rapidly expanding export of cod from the Newfoundland fisheries to Spain and to other south European countries. Similar advantages, as has been shown elsewhere,* flowed to the merchants and landowners of the West Country who throve on the export of grain to Spain and Portugal. All such interests were firmly opposed to the proposed revival of a chartered company with strictly limited membership for trade with Spain, which they saw as a totally inappropriate organ for coping with a basically expansionist situation.

PEACE AND TRANSOCEANIC ENTERPRISE[3]

While the coming of peace opened up the opportunity for the revival of trade with old Spain, the Spaniards remained determined to treat their transatlantic empire as an exclusive preserve, and what applied to commerce was, needless to say, applicable *a fortiori* to attempts by non-Spaniards to establish their own transatlantic colonies. However, different views prevailed in England, and it seems to have been held even by the pacific and timorous James I that Spain's inviolable empire extended no further than areas which she effectively occupied and controlled. Effective control of the whole of such an enormous landmass was out of the question, and the greatest opportunities for English colonizing enterprise obviously lay in North, rather than in Central or South, America, though here too there were some chinks in Spain's colonial armour. Such an area, which had been picked out by Sir Walter Raleigh as ripe for exploitation, was the region called Guiana, a term covering the whole of

*See above, p. 211, and accompanying references.

the Orinoco basin and part of the northern basin of the Amazon. Here, it was rumoured, lay the fabulous El Dorado, the land which took its name from its ruler's practice of ritually covering himself with gold dust. The legend appealed to the gold-rush mentality, which, as mentioned in an earlier chapter (see above, pp. 139–40), both stimulated interest in colonization and inhibited so many adventurers from engaging in the painstaking but unspectacular activities which were the real preconditions of long-term success. Even James I's appetite was sufficiently whetted for him to consent to the release of Raleigh from the Tower in 1616 in order to undertake such an expedition.

Raleigh had made earlier exploratory expeditions in the region in the 1580s and 1590s, after the last of which he had published in 1596 his treatise *The Discovery of the Large Rich and Beautiful Empire of Guiana*. Between this and his last fatal voyage in 1617, there had been an attempt to settle Guiana in 1609 under Robert and Michael Harcourt, remnants of which may have survived the abandonment of the intended colony by the bulk of the settlers three years later. Raleigh's failure on two counts – to discover precious metals and to avoid armed clashes with the Spaniards – resulted in his execution in 1618 under the suspended sentence of 1603. Francis Cottington, the English government's agent in Spain, was instructed to inform the Spaniards that James I 'to give them content hath not spared him, when, by preserving him, he might have given great satisfaction to his Subjects, and had at command . . . as useful a man as served any Prince in Christendom'. In other words, Raleigh was viewed by James I as a suitable sacrificial victim of a policy of appeasement. Thus the rumoured atheist, and former courtly concessionaire who, at the beginning of the century, had perhaps been the most unpopular person in England, became one of the great hero-figures of the militantly Protestant tradition.

Raleigh's other two great Elizabethan colonizing ventures had been in Ireland and in the unsuccessful Roanoke colony off the coast of modern North Carolina, part of what his contemporaries termed Virginia. The reign of James I saw momentous development in Ulster, the effects of which are still in our own times tearing that unhappy province apart. A notable feature of the colonization of Ulster was the Londonderry Plantation organized by the City of London at the king's command in 1608–9, a venture which, in the next reign, was to become a major source of dispute between crown and City (see above, p. 290).[4] As described in two distinct and separate colonizing schemes of 1606, Virginia covered most of the eastern seaboard of the modern United States south of Canada to a little to the north of what is now Georgia. A group of West Country adventurers based on Plymouth and including Sir Ferdinando Gorges, the governor of that port, and Lord Chief Justice Popham obtained a charter to colonize what was described as North Virginia, while another group, based mainly on London but with strong support in Bristol, obtained a similar grant further south.

The West Country group's settlement in what is now Maine in 1607 was in a real sense in the tradition of the Norumbega schemes of the great Elizabethan explorer Sir Humphrey Gilbert (see above, p. 138); appropriately, since two of his sons were associated with the enterprise. But the colony did not survive 1608, and the permanent colonization of New England had to wait until the epic Puritan migrations of the 1620s and 1630s. The southern venture, organized by what became known as the Virginia Company, was more successful. Its product was in fact modern Virginia, as distinct from Raleigh's abandoned Roanoke colony. But for a long time its future lay in the balance, and when Lord De La Warr, the newly appointed governor in whom governmental power was vested by a new charter in 1609 in place of the council which had hitherto controlled the colony, arrived in 1610, he had great difficulty in dissuading the sixty emaciated survivors of the previous dreadful winter from abandoning the settlement completely, as had been done by the settlers in Maine two years earlier. In the meantime part of an advance party which had been sent out to relieve the settlers had been wrecked on what is now Bermuda but then became known as the Somers Isles, taking that name from one of the leaders of the expedition, Sir George Somers. The islands were granted to the Virginia Company in 1612, but were soon to become the preserve of a distinct body, the Somers Islands Company, with a membership which overlapped to a considerable extent with that of the Virginia Company.

Some of the difficulties and setbacks experienced by the early settlers in Virginia related to their own inadequacies for the truly formidable task confronting them.[5] To the familiar obsession with the quest for precious metals should be added a not unnatural fear of venturing outside the original settlement at Fort James (the origins of what later became Jamestown), a lack of adaptability, and an unwillingness, and sometimes inability, to improvise resourcefully. These defects were no doubt accentuated for many colonists by totally false visions of the New World as an economic Eden, a paradise in which such hard work as needed to be done could be carried out by following the Spanish example and setting the Indians to work. Early hopes, not only of discovering precious metals but also of exploiting the natural resources of the region as a source of dyewoods or alternative supply of naval stores, were not realized, and attempts to set up the production of glass and other materials came to grief. But from 1612 onwards the planting of tobacco provided a staple crop with – despite James I's prophetic fulminations against the weed – an expanding market. Nevertheless, this limited though welcome success carried with it the very real danger that the new colony would become virtually a monoculture, producing insufficient food and other necessities of life, and therefore dangerously vulnerable on account of its dependence on the sale of one commodity of which it was by no means the exclusive producer.

Like both the earlier privateering ventures and the great chartered companies engaged in long-distance trade such as the Muscovy and East India companies (but not the Levant

Company, which had reverted from a joint-stock to a regulated basis after its first years of operation), both the Virginia and the Somers Islands companies were organized on a joint-stock basis. While this form of company organization was obviously appropriate for ventures where risks were relatively high and there was a relatively long period between investment and return, its adoption has, as Professor T. K. Rabb has pointed out, a further significance in this context in that it gave to non-mercantile investors the opportunity to invest in the overseas expansion of England.[6] For it was especially in joint-stock enterprises associated with colonization that such gentry and aristocratic investors made their mark. In joint-stock enterprises as a whole mercantile investors naturally predominated, but their predominance was much less marked in colonizing ventures than in chartered companies such as the East India Company, which had no connection with colonization. While, as Professor Rabb demonstrates, merchant investors in the Virginia Company outnumbered non-mercantile investors by about two to one in 1609 when profit expectations were apparently high, over the three following years, when such expectations were sorely disappointed, the proportions were reversed. Clearly, either such non-mercantile investors were over-sanguine in their expectations, or their motives in investing were by no means exclusively – and probably not primarily – related to considerations of economic yield. The numbers and proportion of such non-mercantile investors may well have increased during the last five years of the Virginia Company's life after 1619, when the great London merchant-prince, Sir Thomas Smythe, and his associates were ousted from control by a group of aristocratic and gentry investors led by Sir Edwin Sandys and the earl of Southampton, supported by some of Smythe's business rivals in the City; a protest – if their complaints against the control of the company by merchants who 'affected nothing but their own immoderate gain' are to be believed – against the sacrifice of the long-term interests of the colony to considerations of quick profit.[7]

Most of these investors, whether landowners or merchants, were not, of course, themselves migrants, but stayed at home, however much interest in colonization transcended considerations of immediate profitability for at least some of them. Indeed conditions in Virginia, as in all the later Chesapeake colonies, were not a very attractive prospect, and one wonders whether, if the true conditions had been known, any free settlers would have gone at all. Risk of death at the hands of the Indians was coupled with a very high incidence of disease. During the first two decades of the Virginia settlement annual mortality fluctuated between four and thirty per cent, and was at its worst in the densest concentration of population around Jamestown, where typhoid, dysentery and salt poisoning were rife. There was, however, a sharp improvement in mortality in the decade following 1624, mainly due to the movement of population on to higher land away from the estuary, and into the fresh water zone. But even then New England was to be a far healthier place to live in than was Virginia.[8]

From 1616 the Virginia Company had improved the incentive to emigrate by offering to anyone subscribing £12 10s. of its stock fifty acres of land for every such investment, subject only to a nominal rent. Two years later each independent settler was allowed fifty acres by 'headright', on account both of himself and of every dependant whom he took with him, which probably boosted the incentive to emigrate from land-hungry England. The hazards and hardships of life in Virginia were concealed from the would-be emigrant, and its delights and opportunities widely advertised in sermons, pamphlets and other forms of (often misleading) propaganda. Even more dubious means were employed, some of them barely distinguishable from kidnapping, to recruit humbler people. For the advantages of 'headright' meant little to the majority of the emigrants to Virginia, who were indentured bond-servants, bound for periods varying between three and seven years to work off the debts incurred in passage money for a voyage which many of them must later have bitterly regretted undertaking. Similarly onerous conditions applied to the numerous orphans and vagrant children who were shipped out compulsorily by municipal corporations, and notably by the City of London. They were indentured until attaining their majority, when, like the former bond-servants who had served their time, they were free to set up on their own, at least if they possessed the wherewithal to do so.[9] Between 1618 and 1621 the Virginia Company transported some 3,750 persons to the colony, free emigrants as well as bond-servants and vagrant children, including, among both free and bond, some 200 women.

JAMES I AS *REX PACIFICUS*

It will be recalled that one of the considerations which had made Sir Walter Raleigh a suspect figure in the eyes of James I on that king's accession was his firm opposition to the conclusion of peace with Spain which was sought both by the king and by his chief minister Cecil, formerly Raleigh's ally against Essex but by now his implacable enemy. To Raleigh, as to a number of others, the conclusion of a separate peace with Spain, which of course came about in 1604, would be a shameful betrayal of the Dutch. The king, however, viewed the Dutch with a similar sort of ambivalence to that which his predecessor had entertained towards them. On the one hand he deplored the challenge which their revolt had posed to legitimate monarchical authority, while on the other, as one who aspired to Protestant leadership in Europe, he could not be unmindful of the dangerous consequences for the Protestant cause of a Spanish victory in the Netherlands. Thus in 1608, the year before the Dutch concluded their twelve-year truce with Spain, James offered them a guarantee of assistance in the event of a future Spanish violation of any truce that might be made, while not being prepared to approve the sort of terms which the Dutch, not without reason, felt necessary to their future security. Moreover, the Dutch had already secured a similar and less qualified guarantee from the formerly Protestant, but now Catholic, king of France Henry IV. Indeed it is arguable that James's jealousy of Henry caused him to miss a golden opportunity of strengthening the cause of peace by a joint guarantee to the Dutch from England and France, instead of unnecessarily prolonging negotiations with the Dutch by quibbling over petty details. There may, in fact, be more than a grain of truth in the profession which Sir Charles Cornwallis, the English ambassador to Spain, was urged by Salisbury to make to the Spaniards: namely that James had brought a good deal of pressure to bear on the Dutch to accede to terms acceptable to Spain. In reality, whatever part he played in the concluding of the twelve years' truce of 1609 was secondary to that of the French king. The same, moreover, may be said about the settlement of the crisis arising out of the disputed succession to the Rhineland duchies of Julich, Cleves and Berg, when the claims of two Protestant princes precipitated a threat to occupy the duchies by the Catholic Emperor Rudolph II. What might have been an anticipation of the Thirty Years' War eight years before it actually broke out was averted by firm joint action on behalf of the German Protestants by the English, Dutch and French, with the French playing the most prominent part.[10]

At this point it might seem that the greatest champion of European Protestantism was not the Protestant king of England and Scotland but the Catholic king of France. But this was changed overnight by the assassination of Henry IV on 14 May 1610, before the Julich-Cleves crisis had been fully resolved, and when he was preparing to lead an army to combat the Habsburg threat to the duchies. Hereafter James's ambition to play the not altogether compatible roles of arbiter of Christendom and champion of the Protestant cause could be pursued without exciting either the rivalry or the ridicule of the monarch who had earlier played the latter part and was also far better fitted than James for the former.

James's marriage of his daughter Elizabeth to the Protestant Elector Palatine in 1613, preceded by a defensive alliance with the princes of the German Protestant Union, looked like a significant step in the direction of strengthening international Protestantism, as did his effective mediation in the dispute between the Danes and the Dutch. But in James's view his role as arbiter should extend far beyond the patching up of differences between Protestant powers. The marriage of his daughter to a Protestant prince was, for instance, designed not simply to strengthen international Protestantism, but also to be part of a wider scheme for international and inter-confessional pacification. It was to be counterbalanced by a Catholic marriage for the prince of Wales – first Prince Henry, who, however, protested that two religions should never sleep in his bed, and, after his death in 1612, Prince Charles. These dynastic marriages were part of James's scheme to become the arbiter of Christendom, and his need to complement the Protestant match of 1613 by a Catholic match for the prince of Wales was one of the most important factors helping to throw him into the arms of the pro-Spanish faction at court led by the Howards, and especially, until his death in 1614, by Henry Howard, earl of Northampton. It ultimately brought him under the influence of the Spanish ambassador, Don Diego Sarmiento de Acuna, the later Count Gondomar, who was appointed ambassador to the court of St James in 1613. The release of Raleigh from the Tower in 1616 was an attempt by the Protestant faction on the Privy Council to score at the expense of the Howards and to exacerbate Anglo-Spanish relations; Raleigh's execution in 1618 was in fact a product of the king's growing dependence on Spain.

ENGLAND AND THE THIRTY YEARS' WAR

The offer to and acceptance by Frederick, Elector Palatine and James I's son-in-law, of the elective crown of Bohemia in August 1619 precipitated international conflict which was to result in his expulsion not only from his new kingdom but also from his hereditary dominion of the Rhine Palatinate. The major policy goal of the remainder of the reign of

James I was to have the Palatinate restored: at first through a treaty with Spain which was to be cemented by the marriage of the prince of Wales with the Infanta Maria, and later – following the failure of Charles's and Buckingham's ill-advised dash to Madrid in 1623 to clinch the deal – by war against Spain, on which unhappy note the reign of James the Peacemaker ended. In truth the Spanish marriage terms, which included complete freedom of worship for English Catholics, would have been unacceptable to parliament, even though it had no official right to have any say in the matter. Moreover, the idea that the Spanish Habsburgs would be either willing or able to bring effective pressure to bear on their kinsmen in Vienna to secure the restitution of the Palatinate was sanguine in the extreme. As was shown in an earlier chapter on domestic politics (see above, p. 242), the prince and duke returned from Spain eager for war. For a new ally, they turned to France, now under the rule of the anti-Habsburg Richelieu, who was to pursue the traditional French foreign policy of endeavouring to break out of what he saw as Habsburg encirclement and secure the key Alpine valley of the Valtelline. But the removal of Habsburg armies from the Palatinate occupied a much lower place in Richelieu's list of foreign policy objectives.

The marriage alliance with France, which was delayed by the death of James I but came about at the beginning of the new reign, carried with it a far lower dowry than would have been the case if Charles had married the Spanish Infanta. No less, and perhaps more, important, it contained conditions relating to the treatment of English Catholic recusants which were hardly less onerous and unwelcome than those attaching to the Spanish match. It was on this alliance of mutually divergent interests and on the somewhat firmer base of an offer of 6,000 English troops to aid the Dutch against Spain, and an agreement of February 1625 with Christian IV of Denmark that the English king would undertake payment of 7,000 Danish troops who would invade Germany, that the now fading hopes of restoring the Palatinate to Frederick rested at the end of the old reign and the beginning of the new.

The accord with the Danes and the Dutch was confirmed in the treaty of The Hague in December 1625, but the idea of an anti-Habsburg alliance founded upon an Anglo-French entente was to come to nothing. For by 1627 England was at war not only with Spain but also with France: a consequence both of the alleged English failure to live up to the terms of the marriage treaty by neglecting to relax the penal laws against the English Catholics and by dismissing Henrietta Maria's French attendants; and of the withdrawal of the English ships lent to the French king when the seamen refused to use them against the beleaguered Protestants at La Rochelle. In 1627, as has been shown elsewhere,* Buckingham led his unsuccessful expedition against the Isle of Rhé with the idea of relieving the pressure of the French king's troops on La Rochelle.

In the meantime other attempts to force the hands of the Habsburgs to bring about the restitution of the Palatinate had failed dismally. 1625 had seen the disastrous English naval expedition to Cadiz, while the invasion of north Germany by Christian IV in accordance with the terms of the Anglo-Danish treaty, but with totally inadequate assistance from England, resulted in his crushing defeat at Lutter in 1626 and his being forced to make a separate peace in 1629. The same year was to see the end of the English war with France and the following year the conclusion of peace with Spain. During Charles's Personal Rule in the 1630s, England was to be no more than a passive spectator of events on the Continent.

THE PURITANS AND TRANSATLANTIC COLONIZATION

The Virginia Company was dissolved in 1624, following the scandals associated with the names of Sir Edwin Sandys and his associates, who had obtained control of both this and the

*For all these events, see above, pp. 253–4, 257–8.

Somers Islands Company by forcing out James I's man, Sir Thomas Smythe. By that time attention had already shifted northwards to New England. Henceforth Virginia was to be administered as a colony with a colonial governor responsible to the crown, though Bermuda would continue to be controlled by the Somers Islands Company, of which Smythe and his associates regained control before the end of James I's reign. It is perhaps a useful corrective to be reminded that while the estimated population of English mainland North America in 1629 amounted to only about 3,200, of which Virginia took up some 2,500, the population of Bermuda alone amounted to about 3,000 and that of the West Indian islands of Barbados, St Christopher and Nevis together have been estimated at as high as 4,500, though the last two of these were to be devastated by attacks from the French and the Spaniards in the same year. By 1642 the West Indian colonies may have contained as many as 28,000 inhabitants, and from the mid-1630s the importation of black slaves from Africa to these islands had already begun, though in a very modest way compared with what it would become in the late seventeenth and eighteenth centuries. Virginia was to contain over 5,000 immigrant inhabitants by 1634 and about 8,000 by 1642, while the Catholic Lord Baltimore's adjacent colony of Maryland, founded in 1633, had about a thousand immigrant inhabitants by the latter date. More than three-quarters of the immigrant population of both colonies consisted of indentured bond-servants.[11]

This was not true of New England, which was to hold the forefront of English attention in the reign of Charles I. The high proportion of bond-servants and the relatively few females – and indeed families as a whole – who went to the Chesapeake and West Indian colonies made for an important difference in character between them and the New England settlements. These began in the early 1620s, though in a very small way. On 16 September 1620 a small group of 102 emigrants, at least thirty-five of whom were radical separatist congregationalist Puritans who had previously settled in Leiden in Holland, set sail in the *Mayflower* from Plymouth, and were to give the name of that Devonshire seaport to the first permanent English settlement in New England, in what is now called Massachusetts. These were the Pilgrim Fathers, whom modern Americans still revere as the founders of their country, but who, as we have already seen, had been preceded by nearly a decade and a half by the settlers in Virginia. What makes them dear to American national legend is the fact that, unlike the Virginia settlers, most of them were not feckless, downtrodden and dependent bond-servants, but free men and women, many of whom sailed not as individuals but as families, to found a new society far from the persecutions of the Old World. In the words of Professor Bridenbaugh: 'It was the transfer of Puritan families, whole and intact, that explains the uniqueness of New England'.

The nature of the society which emerged from the new stage of transatlantic emigration will be touched on later. First, however, it is important to realize that the Pilgrim Fathers' venture was an isolated instance and that the great age of the colonization of New England was not the 1620s but the 1630s. The main agency of this later development was an organization which we have already had occasion to notice in a different context (see above, p. 284), the Massachusetts Bay Company. This had been founded in 1628 – though originally under a different name – and its settlement was in the vicinity of Boston, forty miles to the northwest of that of the original Plymouth colonists. The leading members of the company, which included merchants, lawyers and country gentlemen, as well as the noblemen Lords Saye and Sele, Brooke and Warwick, all held similar radical Puritan – though, unlike the Plymouth settlers, not separatist – beliefs, and a consequent antipathy to the increasingly Arminian tendencies in the English church. In the Suffolk gentleman and former attorney of the Court of Wards, John Winthrop, who was appointed by the company as the first governor of the projected

Massachusetts Bay colony in October 1629, the colony obtained the service of a pious, dedicated and enormously resourceful leader.

In 1630 alone seventeen ships sailed carrying emigrants from Old to New England, and over the whole decade some 20,000 found their way there. The religious motives for emigration were almost certainly intensified from 1633, following the elevation of Laud to Canterbury and the increasing pressure to high-church conformity which this would inevitably entail. In April 1634 Charles I issued a proclamation establishing the so-called Lords Commissioners for Plantations, an attempt, amongst other things, to ensure the religious conformity of intending emigrants. But the exodus continued virtually unabated, for there were powerful interests – not least shipowners and merchants, among whom the Londoner Maurice Thompson and his associates are the best known – who had far too much to gain from the continued flow of emigrants and supplies to acquiesce in the proposed restrictions. Their nice blend of religious idealism and private profit, no doubt aided by judiciously administered bribes to royal officials whose duty it was to see to the implementation of the restrictions, seems to have been successful in bringing about their circumvention on a massive scale. In the later 1630s, such interests prospered from the growth of a regular triangular trade, carrying emigrants from Old to New England, then sailing on to Newfoundland to take on fish for sale either in Spain or the Canaries, and using the proceeds to purchase goods, and especially wine, for sale on their return to England.

If Laud's elevation to Canterbury had precipitated an increased flow of Puritan emigrants, the events following 1640 produced a flow in the reverse direction and even a net decrease in the number of emigrants, as hopes of establishing the New Jerusalem in Old England were revived. But the scale of this depletion was not great enough to threaten the existence of the New England colonies, where, in any case, the healthy living conditions, as compared with those of the Chesapeake colonies such as Virginia, assured a steady natural increase of those who remained in New England. It has been argued that the colonial population doubled itself every two decades from the 1630s, and, given our knowledge of the unhealthy conditions in the Chesapeake and Caribbean colonies, there can be no doubt that it was especially New England which contributed to the spectacular demographic growth.

Thus far a very strong stress has been laid on the religious factors to which traditional American historiography of the colonial period attaches primacy as motives for the emigrants. This view is well summarized in Professor Bridenbaugh's opinion that 'the massive religious concern of the English people, and of the Puritans in particular, impelled these emigrants to abandon England to save their souls: only secondarily did economic or social considerations figure in their decisions'. However, not all historians would feel quite so confident about confirming this popular view of the origins of the American nation. Bridenbaugh is, of course, referring to New England, and it is interesting to note that his view seems to have been shared by at least one notable contemporary, for John Winthrop himself was quick to ascribe the relative failure of the less enlightened and less godly Chesapeake colonies to the fact that 'their main end was Carnal and not Religious'. All the same, it needs to be asked how far the traditional view of the motives of early New England colonists is based on those of a vocal minority – including Winthrop – of their number, and whether the silent majority may have had more complex and decidedly more mixed motives inducing them to take the decision to leave their homeland and establish themselves thousands of miles across an unknown and turbulent ocean. It may be granted that to take such a decision needed unusual resources of character, which would undoubtedly be steeled and reinforced by a passionately held religious faith. But, as two American historians have observed, the problem of the causes of the emigration has been bedevilled by the tendency of too many historians to consider religion and material motives as if they were mutually exclusive.

Disputing this commonly held view, Professors Breen and Foster point, for example, to 'a marked congruence between disgruntled tradesmen and disgruntled Puritans: people falling into one category would frequently fall into the other, and there is no way to distinguish between them'.[12]

Another student of the motives of migration has emphasized the 'need to look closely at who the emigrants were before attempting to assess why they left'. Dr A. Salerno's examination of 110 emigrants from Wiltshire to Massachusetts Bay in the 1630s finds that a majority of them were aged between sixteen and thirty, male and single, though there were some married couples with children. There was also a significant number of servants among them. The analysis made by Breen and Foster of passenger lists from Great Yarmouth and Sandwich in 1637, a year in which the evidence affords an unusual amount of information about the ages, occupations and places of origin of the passengers, shows no such majority of single males among the emigrants, most of whom group into families consisting of two parents and children, sometimes with one or more servants travelling with them. Of the twenty-five passengers from Great Yarmouth whose ages are given, more than half were in their thirties. This sample, which admittedly comprises only 273 emigrants out of a total of more than 15,000 leaving for New England over the twelve-year period from 1628, comes nearer, for what it is worth, to the traditional stereotype of the character of the early New England colonists themselves than does Dr Salerno's sample from Wiltshire. Both samples, not surprisingly, show the bulk of the emigrants as originating from regions relatively close to their ports of embarkation.

Most of the Wiltshire sample of emigrants came from the rural wood-pasture rather than the open-field area or the towns, and only ten per cent of those whose occupation is listed were textile workers (the proportion for a similar sample in the 1650s was fourteen per cent), despite the fact that this area was the most highly developed sector of the English woollen industry. Dr Salerno sees demographic pressure on local resources as the prime force behind such emigration. The emigrants of Breen's and Foster's sample from Great Yarmouth and Sandwich in 1637 were decidedly more urban in their origins and mostly artisans and their families. The number of textile workers among them was high, more especially when one considers the subsequent failure of attempts to establish a viable textile industry in early Massachusetts. In these circumstances it is not altogether surprising that the number of emigrants, the bulk of whom were artisans, leaving from Great Yarmouth for Holland in 1637 was 414, as opposed to 193 bound for New England. It would appear that English residents across the North Sea were sufficiently numerous and the prospect of industrial employment so much better than in New England for these advantages to more than offset the difficulties of adjustment to living in a foreign country.

Thus a variety of motives supplemented religion as a force making for large-scale emigration. What sort of a society did the emigrants – or, at least, those of them who were able and who wished to exercise an influence on such matters – seek to establish in the wilderness? Was New England seen as a *tabula rasa*, a place to build the New Jerusalem from scratch with the minimum reference to the institutions of the Old World? Or was it to be Old England transplanted to New, or rather Old England as the emigrants would have liked it to be? It is clear that, in proportion as the historian stresses 'pull' factors, whether in the form of aspirations to set up New Jerusalem in New England or of the ecstatic and misleading descriptions of the natural fertility of the colonies, so will he incline to the traditional view, dear to American patriots, that the emigrants sought a new world in every sense of that term and were determined to cut themselves adrift from the old. But the more weight that is attached to 'push' factors – whether in the form of demographic, economic or religious pressures – the greater the possibility that the model of colonizing intention was an Old England, real or imagined, from which these unwelcome pressures were excluded. The slowing down of emigration for a time after 1640 and the return of some emigrants to the mother country suggests that there may be a great deal more in this latter version of events than traditional transatlantic historiography was prepared to admit. In recent decades American historians of the colonial period have shown a much greater inclination than used to be the case to explain both the problems of colonization and the aspirations of the colonists in terms of their English experience.[13] It is, for example, fairly obvious that the character of the Chesapeake colonies reflects, much more nearly than those of New England, the deferential society and the dominance of great landowners which characterized so much of life in England. What is less obvious, perhaps, is the connection, emphasized by Professor Morgan, between the nature of labour organization in the old country and the Virginia colonists' lack of adaptability to the requirements of the new and unfamiliar environment, in particular their concentration on specialist activities and their inability and unwillingness to develop multiple skills, or to learn new ones.[14] Similarly, Breen and Foster and Salerno have seen the willingness of many migrants to New England to move from one colonial settlement to another as an extension of their migratory behaviour in England itself.

It is not simply the skills and aptitudes – or lack of them – but also the aspirations of the settlers which need to be understood in terms of their experience in the Old World. It is not for nothing that New England is littered with familiar place-names such as Dedham, Hingham, Dorchester, Cambridge and Boston. Such names are redolent not of a repudiation of the Old World, but of a mingled nostalgia for familiar and loved places at home and a determination to create the sort of community which Laudian pressures and royal centralization threatened to destroy for ever. Better than that, in John Winthrop's phrase, conscious that 'the eyes of all men are upon us', they would build a 'City upon a Hill', which would serve as a new model for a corrupt and degenerate Old World. It was precisely because many of the long-cherished traditional institutions of Old England were under threat that those who left their homeland were determined to recreate and improve them far from the interference of central government and church. Indeed whenever the magistrates in New England appeared to be threatening the autonomy of local communities, as in the attempt to foist military experts (analogous to the Low Country sergeants and muster-masters in England) on the local militia or to prevent popular nomination of militia officers, they encountered – as Winthrop discovered to his cost – resistance no less determined than that which had confronted Charles I's attempts to establish the perfect militia back at home. The concern for local autonomy and resistance to centralizing pressure was not an indigenous transatlantic, but a transplanted English phenomenon.[15]

Nowhere does this apply more than to the religious organization of the various New England settlements. The church set up by the Pilgrims at Plymouth, Massachusetts, in the early 1620s, and which, it will be remembered, numbered a minority of the original settlers, was organized on a basis of the independent and separatist congregation by settlers now free from the constraints they had experienced, not only in England but also in Holland. The church, like that of their Elizabethan separatist predecessors, was an exclusive body of the faithful, in that those who had demonstrated their unworthiness, either by scandalous behaviour or failure to understand or observe what was regarded as orthodox doctrine and practices, were excluded from membership. By the late 1660s, and perhaps earlier, these qualifications for admission seem also to have included a further requirement to make a confession of the applicant's possession of saving faith which was acceptable to the elders of the church. As Professor Morgan puts it, 'a test has been devised to make the church a company of people, each of whom, in his own opinion and in the opinion of the church was destined for salvation'.[16]

It seems that this formidable additional criterion of worthiness for church membership, which, as was later admitted, distinguished the Plymouth separatists from their counterparts at Leiden in Holland, was not something of their own devising. It was in fact taken over by them from the larger and more successful non-separatist congregationalists of the later Massachusetts Bay colony. Like the Plymouth separatists, these Massachusetts Bay congregationalists elected their own ministers and elders and admitted their own members, but, unlike them – at least at first – they had by the mid-1630s devised a crucially important additional test of admission to the church: the candidate's demonstration, to the satisfaction of the elders, of his possessing that saving faith which was the essential condition of salvation. It is important to realize that this did not mean that the church and the elect of God – the visible and the invisible church – were one and the same. The possibility of mistakes in the identification of saints – those possessed of saving faith – was readily admitted. What the addition of the test of saving faith clearly implied, however, was that the visible church was to be made as close to the congregation of God's elect as was humanly possible to achieve.

'By 1640,' Professor Morgan tells us, 'eighteen new churches had been founded in the Massachusetts Bay colony, two in New Haven colony, three in Connecticut colony, and six in Plymouth colony.' The practice of admission tests in New Haven was, if anything, more stringent than in Massachusetts Bay, but Connecticut, where Thomas Hooker led his congregation from Massachusetts to found a new colony and church in 1636, seems to have been less demanding. Hooker explicitly declared his disapprobation of 'such curious inquisitions and niceties, which the pride or wantonness of men's spirits hath brought into the Church, to disturb the peace thereof'. The opposite extreme to his practice is perhaps that of the separatist churches on Rhode Island, founded by the refugee Roger Williams, who had been expelled from Salem, Massachusetts, in 1636 on account of his views. Another dissident group in Rhode Island were the followers of Mrs Anne Hutchinson, who were unique in claiming a complete identity between church membership and divine election: a staggering claim to complete infallibility in divining the existence of saving grace in applicants for church membership.

THE FRANCHISE AND THE POLITICAL NATION IN NEW AND OLD ENGLAND

The question of church membership has implications which reach over into the political field. Freemanship, that is the right to vote and to hold civil office, was connected with church membership from 1631 in the Bay colony. The only exceptions were those original settlers who had demanded the franchise in October 1630 and received it in May 1631. But henceforward all freemen must be communicating churchmen, though, since freemanship carried burdens as well as rights, not all churchmen chose to be freemen. In 1636 the General Court at Boston which governed the Bay colony, in which the younger Sir Henry Vane had replaced John Winthrop as governor, further narrowed access to the freemanship by insisting that it be restricted to those who had passed the new and more rigorous tests (relating to saving grace) for church membership. None of these provisions linking freemanship with church membership, however, applied to the new colony of Connecticut formed by Hooker and his fellow dissidents in 1634, nor to Maine and New Hampshire, which were incorporated into the Bay colony between 1639 and 1658. But where they did apply, their implications were clearly restrictive.

So far as town, as distinct from provincial, elections were concerned, it has been claimed that the restriction of the franchise to freemen was widely ignored in the Bay colony, but that the General Court at Boston was simply recognizing a *fait accompli* when it passed an act in 1647 making it legal for all adult males to vote. Against this, it has been argued that this act was far more restrictive in practice in that it laid down careful qualifications for the exercise of political rights by non-freemen; moreover, that it subjected these rights to the approval of the town freemen, not once only, but on each successive occasion on which they were exercised. This last qualification was not removed until 1658, when a qualification in terms of good behaviour and ownership of property worth £20 and upwards was substituted for the requirement for freemen to approve the exercise of the vote or the holding of office by non-freemen.[17]

In accordance with his already noted inclination to emphasize Old English experience in explaining the character of New England institutions, Professor T. H. Breen has suggested that what he sees as the restrictiveness of the urban franchise in Massachusetts probably owed more to the colonists' English experience than it did to Puritan notions about church membership. However, since he made this assertion in 1970, Dr Derek Hirst's remarkable study of the English electorate has appeared, indicating both that the franchise in England was far more extensive than had hitherto been assumed and that the electorate varied too much from one constituency to another to provide any sort of clear or uniform electoral model for the colonists. So far as English county constituencies are concerned, an earlier seminal article by Professor J. H. Plumb had suggested that an unlooked-for consequence of later Tudor and early Stuart inflation had been to erode the economic significance of the forty-shilling freehold franchise and effectively to enfranchise increasingly humbler strata of the English rural population. Indeed, the significance of this development is widened by Dr Hirst, who points out that the idea of 'freehold' for franchise purposes extended beyond nominal freeholders to what may be described as 'virtual' freeholders; to tenants such as copyholders of inheritance holding their land in perpetuity.[18]

But it was especially in the boroughs, whose extravagantly increased parliamentary representation under the Tudors was not to be reversed until 1653, and then only temporarily (see below, pp. 404–5), that the most spectacular examples of the extension of the English franchise are to be found. Here the main agency of expansion was less impersonal than the inflation which was transforming the character of the county electorate. It was to be found especially in the encouragement given by interested parties – whether disaffected or competing urban oligarchs or interested outside landowners – to people seeking enfranchisement and prepared to give electoral support to those who were instrumental in obtaining it for them. Dr Hirst's study demonstrates clearly how boroughs where there were franchise disputes or franchise extension were usually also those where there was strong rivalry and friction between rival oligarchic groups.

Moreover, quite apart from the expansion of the electorate, the number of votes cast in parliamentary elections was often much higher than the number of those who were formally entitled to vote. It was probably only in a small minority of contested elections that formal polling took place, as distinct from the issue being decided on the basis of the 'cry' or the 'view'; and, as Dr Hirst has rightly observed, 'when a faceless crowd gave vent to its feelings by roaring the names of the rival candidates or divided into partisan groups to be checked for size, it was obviously nearly impossible to verify credentials'.

These disclosures about the nature and extent of political participation in England before the Civil War have profound implications for the student of the period and of the Civil War and Interregnum. First and foremost, they challenge the familiar view which sees the political activity of Englishmen below the level of respectable men of property with a substantial material stake in the country as a sporadic and exceptional phenomenon which, down to very modern times, surfaces only in occasional incidents such as food and anti-enclosure riots. This traditional view which sees the electorate as very limited, deferential, doing what its betters told it to do and totally quiescent between elections, will hardly stand up to the findings of Dr Hirst's research. Another important received opinion which disappears is the Whiggish identification of anti-court with franchise-extending tendencies. Candidates for election to parliament, whether for or against the ruling group at court, were up to a point quite indifferent as to whether the constituencies for which they stood had a wide or narrow franchise. Indeed newly enfranchised electors – as seems to have been the case, for example, at Maidstone, Northampton and Higham Ferrers – far from owing their enfranchisement to anti-court elements, were sometimes prepared to pledge their support to court candidates, when the corporations whose electoral stranglehold they desired to loosen were opposed to the ruling clique at court. Historians have in general been too ready to read back the fear of extending the franchise, which beset the propertied classes in the later seventeenth century and after, as a more or less permanent feature of the English historical scene, whereas in actual fact it is primarily a post-Civil War phenomenon which owes its origins especially to the political and social upheavals of that time. Before the 1640s, respectable gentlemen, while certainly not unconscious of the dangers of popular disturbance and revolt, were at least equally conscious of the dangers to the liberties and privileges of their order from a centralizing and increasingly authoritarian monarchy. The alliance of crown, squire and parson and their positive phobia about franchise extension is largely a post-Civil War and, especially a post-Restoration, phenomenon.

A salient feature of a good deal, though by no means all, of recent historiographical revision of the period has been to play down the sudden and revolutionary character of change and to stress continuity instead. While this cannot be said to characterize the work of the best-known of the historical revisionists, Professor Conrad Russell, who emphasizes the danger of finding the issues of the Civil War in Jacobean and early Caroline parliamentary history, Dr Hirst's findings about the character of the electorate do point in this direction. More particularly, they suggest the need to modify the view that popular participation in politics was entirely a product of the hothouse conditions provided by the Civil War, and not least by membership of the New Model Army. This is not, of course, to deny completely the importance of such conditions. Popular participation in politics was certainly enhanced by the Civil War and the politicization of the army which was dealt with in the last chapter. But it emphatically did not begin with these developments, in which circumstances the widening of the early Stuart electorate takes on the character of a long and expanding political apprenticeship which came to full fruition in the later 1640s.

These facts make the phenomenon of the emergence of radical political groups such as the Levellers the more easily comprehensible by putting it into a longer historical perspective. Leveller ideas about the franchise are indeed robbed of a good deal of what is normally seen as their startling novelty when it is realized that something akin to the franchise which even the most radical of the Levellers favoured had long been in operation in some parliamentary constituencies. Indeed, if the First Agreement of the People of 1647 had been put into effect, one astonishing consequence would have been actually to restrict and not to extend the franchise in some constituencies. The point which was made earlier about the unlikelihood of the bewilderingly varied English franchise arrangements offering any clear model for the settlers in New England is given additional force by the failure even of informed Englishmen at home to appreciate the significance of this variety. The most striking instance of this is the failure of those grandees such as Henry Ireton, who opposed the extension of the franchise to the propertyless in the debate at Putney on 29 October 1647, to appreciate that something very like these conditions already obtained in boroughs such as Bedford and St Albans. No less striking is the Levellers' failure to cite such cases in favour of the argument that propertyless persons could exercise the vote without any of the untoward effects which were feared by the grandees at Putney, and which were to become a common feature of political arguments after the Restoration, and indeed, as the final chapter of this book will reveal, during the 1650s also.

Chapter Eleven

THE FAILURE OF REPUBLICANISM AND THE RETURN TO MONARCHY, 1649–60

THE COMMONWEALTH AND DISAPPOINTED EXPECTATIONS, 1649–53

While there were some who saw the events of January and February 1649 as enormously rich in revolutionary promise, these events, in the words of a recent historian of the Commonwealth, 'proved to be the end not the beginning of the Long Parliament's revolutionary measures.'[1] To begin with, only fourteen of the twenty MPs nominated to the executive Council of State by parliament, to which the Council was responsible, could reasonably be described as 'revolutionaries', using the term to denote active participation in and approval of the execution of the king and the establishment of a republic; while, of the seven councillors who were not MPs, only John Bradshaw, who had presided at the king's trial and was to be president of the Council, falls into this category.[2] Similar considerations apply to the Rump itself. Of the 470 or so MPs qualified to sit in the lower house, Pride's Purge had directly or indirectly removed about 370, of whom some 110 had been forcibly prevented from entering the House on 6 December 1648, and the remainder had stayed away. However, of these last at least a hundred returned to the House from late February 1649 onwards, and parliament did its best to attract more, with the idea of broadening the basis of the new regime in the interests of stability. But stability and revolution are uncomfortable bedfellows, and the process of readmission, despite the accompaniment of political tests, was a prime factor in blunting the revolutionary edge of the regime. Indeed, as both Professor Underdown and Dr Worden have argued, even the bare, unaugmented Rump of December 1648 cannot be described as a homogeneously revolutionary body, and even among the regicides themselves there were those, like Henry Ireton, who saw the execution of the king and the establishment of the Commonwealth not as the beginning, but as the end, of a process of revolution.

The political tests employed for sifting the potential supporters of the regime from the irreconcilables in this process of re-admitting MPs were not very onerous; at first, no more than to register their dissent at the vote of 5 December 1648 that the king's replies to parliament's propositions in the Newport treaty gave grounds for prolonging negotiations. Since such dissent in no way implied approval of regicide, it was the more readily given. It was not until October 1649 that MPs were required to take the same Oath of Engagement which was already administered to members of the Council of State: that they would be 'true and faithful to the Commonwealth of England, as it is now established without a King or House of Lords'. At the beginning of 1650, when a Scottish invasion on behalf of the so-called King of the Scots was feared, this oath was extended to all males of the age of eighteen and over.[3] But by that time the republican regime had lost some of its worst terrors for moderate and conservative people.

The Rump was inhibited from radical measures both by the increasingly conservative character of its readmitted members and by the logic of its own exposed political position, and to this extent it was the easier for distinctly unradical Englishmen to adhere to the terms of the Engagement oath. Indeed there were not wanting Presbyterians such as Francis Rous and John Dury, and even former royalists such as the several times renegade Marchamont Nedham, who went into print to argue that resistance was against the interests of all; except possibly of royalists 'by necessity' as Nedham called them (distinguishing them from royalists 'by humour', who, having compounded for their delinquency and repossessed their ancestral lands, had everything to lose from further involvement in what was now a hopelessly lost cause). Nedham indeed carefully goes through each political group from Levellers to royalists 'by humour', demonstrating that their interests lay, if not in active support for the regime, then at the very least in acquiescence. For the minority of dedicated republicans, on the other hand, there were the works of John Milton, whose *Tenure of Kings and Magistrates* (1649) sought to provide a reasoned justification of regicidal republicanism, not as a *pis aller* but as the best possible regime in the best of all possible political worlds.[4]

The Commonwealth which Milton extolled is often characterized as a thoroughly corrupt regime, in which unscrupulous men such as Cornelius Holland and Sir Arthur Hesilrige made sizeable fortunes out of their connection with government. But, as Dr Worden pertinently observes, the Rump's reputation for corruption is to no small extent a product of 'its failure to do what radicals, who are mainly responsible for the legend of corruption, wanted it to do'. The regime, he points out, was neither more nor less corrupt than any other recent government, all of which, in the absence of adequate amounts of ready cash, had to employ perquisites in kind as rewards for the services of their officials.[5]

Among the radicals who were free with such charges against the regime were the Levellers, who regarded themselves, not without justification, as having been the victims of a political confidence trick when they had agreed to the army's march on London and to Pride's Purge before getting their model constitution, the new Agreement of the People, approved by the army council. Ultimately a drastically amended version was reluctantly presented to parliament by the officers on 20 January 1649, and, despite these amendments, was rejected by the Rump. The Levellers' protest was not long in coming and was heralded by two abrasive pamphlets which appeared in March, John Lilburne's *England's New Chains Discovered* and Richard Overton's *The Hunting of the Foxes*. The latter contained, among other things, a graphic account of the humiliating punishment of five Leveller soldiers who, using some of Lilburne's arguments, had protested to Lord General Fairfax and the Council of Officers not only about military grievances but also against the composition and powers of the new Council of State and the alleged political backsliding of the officers from the principles of the Solemn Engagement of the Army on Newmarket Heath in June 1647.

In the spring and early summer of 1649 the government was facing a formidable series of radical threats: soldiers' agitation about arrears of pay; the dangers of a Leveller-encouraged campaign of civil disobedience; a number of Leveller mutinies in the army; and, though probably least menacing of all, the unsuccessful attempt of the so-called Diggers or True Levellers to establish a cooperative agrarian community on St George's Hill in Surrey. But long before the end of the summer the government had weathered the radical storm. A combination of stern measures for army mutineers, culminating in the quelling of the Leveller soldiers at Burford by Fairfax and Cromwell, as they had done at Corkbush Field in 1647; rises in soldiers' pay and generous arrangements for payments of arrears; and the provision of adequate clothing and stores for the troops bound for Ireland, where Cromwell was shortly to lead them to overwhelming and sanguinary victories over the Catholic rebels, all contributed to putting an end to the danger. But the fright which it had given the government was almost certainly another important influence inclining it towards moderate policies.[6]

The new chains riveted on England by its new masters probably came as no surprise to the Levellers, following their disillusioning experiences in 1647–8. No less disgusted at the response of the new regime to their demands were the assorted bands of sectarian extremists who, for all their bewildering differences, had in common the rejection of conventional institutionalized religion and repudiation of the idea of a professional clergy. The large numbers of religious Presbyterians and more conservative Independents in parliament were a formidable obstacle to the realization of such sectarian ambitions. Indeed the greater the excesses of the wilder sorts of sectaries, such as the Ranters, the stronger the conservative backlash was likely to be. In face of what they regarded as Antichristian persecutors the sects might call for religious toleration, but in the unlikely event of their ever attaining power, most though not all of them would have been no less ready than the Presbyterians to impose their own conception of godly rule on the ungodly.[7]

Striking examples of parliamentary legislation designed to appeal to conservative opinion in matters of personal conduct and morality are the Rump's celebrated measures of 1650, providing for strict enforcement of the Sabbath, penalizing swearers and blasphemers, and, most notorious of all, imposing the death penalty in cases of adultery. The latter were, however, defined as cases involving married women; intercourse between married men and single women, like that between two single persons, fell under the heading of fornication, which carried a penalty of three months' imprisonment. In addition, brothel keepers were to be whipped, pilloried, branded and jailed for three years, and second offences were to carry the death penalty. These savage laws, which to the modern mind suggest comparisons with those promulgated by fundamentalist Islamic regimes, need to be seen in the context not only of the Puritan emphasis on the sanctity of the marriage bond and the need to protect legitimate heirs from the possible intrusion of bastards, but also of the Rump's need to conciliate conservative, and especially Presbyterian, opinion in the face of the sexual excesses associated with some of the wilder antinomian sects such as the Ranters. It is a relief to learn that strict enforcement proved very difficult.[8]

Emphasis on such savage and illiberal measures should not be allowed to obscure positive reforms of a quite different sort. Although the Council of State had initially, somewhat surprisingly, included the abolition of tithes in a list of desirable reforms, this would have been bitterly opposed by Presbyterians and other conservatives as the likely prelude to the disestablishment of the church and an inadmissible concession to sectarian and radical Leveller demands. However, some provision was made for improved maintenance of parsons. In addition, a dramatic boost was given to Puritan proselytizing in 'the dark corners of the land' by the bill of 1650 establishing the Committee for the Propagation of the Gospel in Wales, and there were similar bills for the north, Ireland and New England. Finally, and rather surprisingly in the circumstances, there was a modest extension of the sphere of religious toleration, despite horrified and unavailing Presbyterian attempts to frustrate the bill of 1650 removing the obligation of compulsory attendance at parish church services.

Just as the sectarian Saints, whose great day was to come after the dissolution of the Rump, were sadly disappointed in their millennial hopes for godly reform, so were the Levellers in their demands for the reform of the legal system, which they justified as the destruction of the relics of Norman oppression. The return to the imagined freedoms of Anglo-Saxon times would involve a new codification and drastic simplification of the law: the use of English as the only language in the courts; the restriction of capital punishment to a very few crimes; reforming and extending the power of the jury system; and a strong measure of legal decentralization. But the desire for legal reform was by no means confined to the Levellers, even though other would-be reformers were far less radical in their demands. As Miss Mary Cotterell has reminded us, a great deal of misunderstanding has arisen from the way in which one of the greatest authorities on English legal history, the late Sir William Holdsworth, characterized the Interregnum movement for law reform as an essentially lay and anti-professional protest. This has led many historians to overstress the influence of self-interested lawyers in parliament and other high places in frustrating reform. Probably more significant are the influences which impelled the regime away from radical reform in general, the need to conciliate those who associated thoroughgoing law reform with radical and Leveller politics and pressure from the army, especially after Cromwell's defeat of the invading Scots and Charles II at Worcester in September 1651. Moreover, the opposition of moderate lawyers to Leveller schemes should not be taken to denote an opposition to reform of any kind. A number of reforming lawyers, of whom Matthew Hale was the most eminent, formed an important pressure group for reform, and in December 1651 the Rump set up a commission headed by Hale and charged with making recommendations to its own parliamentary committee on law reform, which had thus far accomplished nothing. The Hale Commission was hardly a body to turn the legal world upside-down, containing among its twenty-six members only five who by any stretch of the imagination could be described as political radicals. Nevertheless, its recommendations were by no means innocuous milk-and-water proposals dressed up as significant changes. They included the establishment of county courts (though not the elective ones favoured by the Levellers) and small claims courts; new procedures for poor litigants; the abolition of imprisonment for debt; and – like the Levellers – a notable reduction in the number of capital offences. But, apart from one measure, the establishment of a probate court, none of the commission's recommendations became law during the Commonwealth, though in fairness it should be added that the Rump was on the point of considering them when it was dissolved. The matter of legal reform was thus left for its successor, in which a very different temper was to prevail.[9]

The new regime's attitude to social policy has been subject to as many misconceptions as its attitude to legal reform. The economic depression of its opening years and the chronically bad harvests of 1648 and 1649, resulting in steeply rising prices of carbohydrate foodstuffs gave rise to the danger of widespread social disturbance, in itself no doubt a contributory factor to the growth of social radicalism at this time. But the government did not conform to the Marxist stereotype of the new bourgeois regime which joyfully jettisons traditional paternalistic policies and relies on the unfettered operation of the forces of the market. On the contrary, these years see an application of the customary curbs on the activities of middlemen, and measures to keep prices in check. The view which sees the Interregnum as marking the beginnings of a new, more individualistic and harsher attitude to poverty and economic distress in contrast to the paternalistic policies of the 1630s[10] does not rest on a firm foundation of fact. In the first place, Caroline social policy had been neither so unequivocally paternalistic nor so efficient as it is sometimes made out to be (see above, pp. 277–8). Second, while there was undoubtedly some shift from central to local initiative in such matters after 1649, this ought not to be taken to signify that the administration of relief either collapsed or was carried out on radically different principles; that efficient and relatively compassionate policies were replaced by the harsh and callous administration of gradgrind Puritan magistrates. This may have been true in some cases, but recent studies of poor-relief in London and Warwickshire have shown that the reverse is true in others.[11]

Nor should too much stress be laid on the Rump's failure to pass new poor-relief legislation. Its bill of 1653 might prove abortive, but the great Elizabethan code still remained on the statute book, and, as the case of Warwickshire demonstrates, was in places implemented more energetically than ever before. In addition there was a number of far-sighted proposals for the poor. A parliamentary committee of February 1651 is chiefly remembered for its proposal that cathedrals should be demolished and the proceeds of the sale of the stone used to relieve the poor, but it also recommended that the administration of poor-relief funds ought to be investigated by the commissioners for charitable uses. There were also the ingenious schemes of the Czech reformer Samuel Hartlib for a nationally endowed workhouse system and for a so-called Office of

Addresses 'for the relief of human necessities', including in its facilities a sort of rudimentary labour exchange. Another reformer, the economic pamphleteer Henry Robinson, claimed to have set up such a labour exchange, quaintly entitled the Office of Addresses and Encounters, in Threadneedle Street in the City of London, while another, Peter Chamberlain, proposed to turn the poor from a national liability into a national asset by using confiscated royalist property as a source of capital to erect a joint-stock company to employ them. All such schemes, most of which were admittedly abortive, had their repressive side – so, in any case, had the Elizabethan poor law – but they were certainly not based on dehumanized *laissez-faire* assumptions or on the notion that the poor were naturally endowed with over-generous doses of original sin.

It is usually argued with some justice that in no area did the Rump disappoint reforming expectations more than in the sphere of electoral and parliamentary reform.[12] On this matter it was subjected to two quite opposite forms of pressure: from the army and from the readmitted MPs. The army was enthusiastic for reform, and for so long as the danger of internal revolt and external aggression remained, the government could not risk disbanding the soldiers; indeed their numbers increased from about 47,000 in March 1649 to about 70,000 in 1653. Thus the crucial problem of soldiers' pay and arrears remained with the government, though less acutely than in 1647–8, since with the aid of increased revenue from the monthly assessment, the Excise and the sale of confiscated lands, it was even able to raise army pay during the Leveller crisis in 1649.

The widespread resentment of many readmitted MPs at the number and cost of the soldiers was reinforced by their indifference or hostility to the reforms favoured by the army. In general the greater the numbers of readmitted MPs, the greater the pressure against yielding to the army over reform. Indeed it could be argued that in pressing for reform the army was acting against its own best interests, for there was a strong likelihood that a redrafting of the constituency map in favour of the counties would produce a parliamentary majority for the very people against whom the army and the parliamentary radicals had struggled in 1647–8: diehard Presbyterians and crypto-royalists. Nevertheless, the army continued to press for reform, and after the military victory over the Scots and royalists at Worcester in September 1651 this pressure was greatly increased, culminating in the situation which brought about the end of the Rump, in which context it will be most convenient to treat it.

COMMERCIAL AND FOREIGN POLICIES OF THE COMMONWEALTH

Just as the Levellers were the most vociferous and thoroughgoing advocates of parliamentary and legal reform, so were they also the most determined critics of the hold of monopolistic chartered companies on so many branches of English overseas trade. In this, as in the other spheres, they were joined by radical Independents such as Henry Marten and Thomas Chaloner. Since the 1590s economic depressions had been prolific of attacks on the chartered companies, and there was therefore nothing new about the popular identification of their restrictive practices with the economic difficulties which coincided with the establishment of the Commonwealth. It has been argued that both the anti-company agitation and the aggressive economic nationalism which found expression in an Ordinance of 1650 against the trade of foreigners with English colonies in royalist hands (soon extended to all colonies) and in the more famous Navigation Ordinance of the following year were results of the change in the distribution of political power within the government of the City of London. Like the Common Council elections of December 1641, those of seven years later had resulted in an overwhelming radical victory. And just as an ultimate product of the 1641 elections had been the replacement of the royalist Lord Mayor Sir Richard Gurney by the radical Independent Isaac Penington, so had those of 1648 resulted in the replacement of the conservative crypto-royalist Lord Mayor Abraham Reynardson by the radical Independent Owen Rowe. The Common Council was now dominated not by the old-fashioned 'mere merchants' of the great chartered companies but, on the one hand, by merchants whose interests lay in domestic rather than in overseas trade, and on the other by a quite different breed of overseas traders such as Maurice Thompson and William Pennoyer – what has been described as a 'colonial-interloping' complex with strong interests in transoceanic enterprise, especially, though not exclusively, with America.

It is to such interests that both the animus against the chartered companies and the economic nationalism finding expression especially in the Navigation Ordinance has been ascribed. Certainly both this measure and the Ordinance of 1650 dealing with colonial trade by foreigners harmonize well enough with the re-exporting and colonial interests of the colonial-interloping group. The Navigation Ordinance stipulated that all foreign imports should be brought to England either in English ships or in ships of the country of origin of the goods, and that imports from Africa and Asia should be carried only by English ships. It was directed in particular at Dutch shipping and the Dutch dominance of the carrying trade, and was intended to be complemented by the establishment of free ports with bonded warehouses for imported goods awaiting re-export. But while there is no doubt that the anti-chartered company interests exercised more influence under the Commonwealth than at any previous time, there is no conclusive evidence either that the Council of State or the Council of Trade were dominated by such interests, or that there was any diminution of government support for the companies' control of their traditional sphere of operations. Moreover, the view that the anti-Dutch policies of the parliament and government ran counter to the interests of the great chartered companies is not altogether convincing. After all, since the later years of James I these companies had urged on reluctant governments the need for strong measures against the Dutch.[13]

Our consideration of the Navigation Ordinance and the commercial policy of the Commonwealth has taken us close to the matter of its foreign relations. A common feature of most revolutionary regimes is their propensity to indulge in grandiloquent gestures of defiance to a disapproving world, and the English revolution is no exception. 'Monarchy must down the world over,' roared the radical Independent preacher Hugh Peter, '. . . not only here but in France and other kingdoms round about.' Such outbursts were hardly designed to win friends for England among foreign rulers, and, as in the matter of the internal policies of the Commonwealth, revolutionary militancy quickly gave way to the search for international respectability, with the object of isolating the exiled Stuarts from foreign support. Spain was, rather surprisingly, the first to accord *de iure* recognition, and initially it was from the Scots and the Dutch that the exiled Stuarts obtained the most active support, the French going no further than a refusal to accord recognition to the Commonwealth government.

As to the Scots, one serious obstacle to an understanding between Charles Stuart and the Covenanters was removed when the irrepressible Montrose, who had returned to Scotland and again raised the royal standard in 1650, was captured and executed. This event, along with Cromwell's crushing of the Irish Catholics and royalists, which put an end to the possibility of using Ireland as a back door for royalist invasion, were important factors in Charles's convenient abandonment of militant Cavalierism and his move to establish an understanding with the Scottish Covenanters. However Cromwell, who had succeeded Fairfax as lord general following the latter's refusal to take the Engagement Oath, put paid to the danger for the time being when he crushed the Scottish supporters of King and Kirk at Dunbar in September 1650. A year later he had to face a Scottish invasion under Charles, whom he defeated at Worcester on the first anniversary of his victory at Dunbar. Henceforth Scotland was kept under with a heavy hand, culminating in the formal union of the two realms – James

I's great unrealized dream – though not until 1654, after the end of the Commonwealth. This short-lived anticipation of the union of 1707 was not to survive the Restoration of 1660.

Initially the close family ties between the Stuarts and the Dutch Stadholder, the prince of Orange, offered a formidable obstacle to friendly Anglo-Dutch relations. Some relief came with the Stadholder's death in November 1650 and the accession to power of the strongly republican anti-Orangist party. Determined to exploit this apparently more promising situation, the Commonwealth dispatched an extraordinary embassy under Oliver St John and Walter Strickland to The Hague in March 1651, with the twin objects of negotiating an alliance and creating some sort of political union between England and the Netherlands. But these negotiations quickly got bogged down in side-issues and seem to have encouraged Anglo-Dutch antagonism rather than amity. Indeed, one result of the Stadholder's death had been to reduce the anti-Orangist party's need for friendship with the English republican government, and to allow full scope for its members' dislike of the Independents and sectaries who figured so prominently in English governing circles. The Dutch authorities gave an icy reception to the English envoys and certainly did nothing to discourage widespread popular hostility to their mission. Relations deteriorated further with the passing of the Navigation Ordinance, the English insistence that Dutch ships should acknowledge English sovereignty in the Channel and English coastal waters by striking sail to English naval vessels, and English searching of Dutch ships for contraband bound for the royalist navy. The two republics ultimately drifted into war in May 1652. English jealousy of Dutch economic pre-eminence and dislike of the economic aggressiveness which had contributed so powerfully to Dutch supremacy in the Baltic and East Indies as well as in the fishing and carrying trades finally triumphed over ideological affinities with the Dutch and admiration for their long and heroic struggle against Spain.

Cromwell's victories over the Scots and Robert Blake's naval successes in the first Dutch war were to work wonders for English prestige abroad. The latter in particular reversed the humiliations experienced at Dutch hands under the monarchy. It is interesting to find radical republicans such as Henry Marten, Thomas Chaloner and Henry Neville enthusiastically supporting the Dutch war, though the no less radical Sir Henry Vane, who had been one of the most prominent advocates of the abortive Anglo-Dutch union of 1651, refused to succumb to the wave of anti-Dutch sentiment. Oliver Cromwell was certainly against the war in the later days of the Commonwealth and was finally to bring it to an end in 1654 during the Protectorate in the interests of his ideal of Protestant international unity. On the other hand, numerous religious extremists, sectaries of one sort or another, especially in the army, supported war against the 'presbyterian Dutch'. Prominent among the Fifth Monarchists who supported the war were London cloth-finishers, who since before Cockayne's project of 1614–5 had seen their own economic interests as conflicting with those of the Dutch. Similar views were held by London and provincial pinmakers whom the war freed from the competition of Dutch imported pins. No less hostile to the Dutch were those Merchant Adventurers who exported their cloth not to the Netherlands but to Germany, where they met with Dutch competition. But for all these numerous anti-Dutch interests, and despite Blake's naval triumphs – though not all of the eight great naval battles of the war were lost by the Dutch – the war became increasingly unpopular at home with those who had to foot the bill; and with the army, which resented the rival claims of naval expenditure on increasingly short financial resources.[14]

THE END OF THE RUMP, 1653

As Oliver Cromwell's reputation waxed as a result of his victories over Scots and royalists at Dunbar in 1650 and Worcester in 1651 and his successes in Ireland, where countless others had failed before him, so did that of the Rump wane. Increasingly, and especially after Worcester, Cromwell appeared as the mouthpiece of the army's demands for reforms which the Rump seemed reluctant to pursue, though like the Rump itself, he also experienced agonizing ambivalence, moved on the one hand by genuine zeal for reform and on the other, by the search for political respectability and conservative support.[15] It used to be argued, until the appearance of Dr Worden's study of the Rump Parliament in 1974, that Cromwell dissolved the Rump, first because of its failure to bring about social, legal, religious and electoral reform, and secondly, because of its bill for a new representative in April 1653. The text of the bill has unfortunately not survived, but it was seen as being designed to substitute 'recruiter' elections (ie, byelections) in currently unrepresented constituencies for the long-promised dissolution of parliament followed by a general election on a reformed franchise. Dr Worden, on the other hand, contends that the bill for a new representative which came before and precipitated the dissolution of parliament on 20 April, far from providing only for 'recruiter' elections, made provision for a full-scale general election on a reformed electoral franchise. This may seem strange in view of the fact that the Rump had protested again and again since 1649 that the time was not ripe for a dissolution and that a general election without safeguards would be likely to result in a parliament dominated by Presbyterians and crypto-royalists. It may be questioned whether this was any the less true of 1653 than of 1649 or 1651, and indeed this helps to explain the otherwise eccentric provision for the adjournment rather than dissolution of parliament, a provision which might otherwise seem incompatible with proceeding to a general, as distinct from a 'recruiter', election. For this constitutionally curious, and indeed, unique, arrangement would afford to the Rumpers, in Dr Worden's words, 'an insurance policy in case the elections proved disastrous', though what they and what Cromwell and the army would regard as disastrous were two very different things.

In the absence of the text of the bill for a new representative, Dr Worden's argument cannot be proved. However, while there are some difficulties about the curious notion of a parliament not being dissolved before the election of its successor, it is a point in favour of his argument that adjournment (as distinct from dissolution) and subsequent re-assembly – perhaps to enable MPs to scrutinize the credentials of their successors – had been a feature of all the Rump's abortive bills for a new representative since November 1651. Had the Rump in fact called Cromwell's bluff by adopting the very course of action for which he had himself been pressing for so long? Its acting with what Cromwell described as 'preposterous haste' concentrated his mind wonderfully about the dangers posed by its action to the survival of the Good Old Cause. Might this not be safer in the hands of a carefully selected assembly of the godly which would be far more likely to bring to fruition the social, legal and religious reforms which the Rump had so conspicuously neglected? Preferring what seemed to be the certainties of godly rule to the uncertain and possibly radical verdict of a fickle electorate, Oliver now embarked on a new and radical experiment.

BAREBONE'S PARLIAMENT AND THE RULE OF THE SAINTS, 1653

Following the dissolution of the Rump and of the Commonwealth Council of State two alternative courses of action were canvassed on the council of army officers which for the time being was the only institution with which *de facto* executive authority rested. The first was that favoured by the able and down-to-earth Major-General John Lambert, who in many ways succeeded to the role of constitution-monger formerly played by Cromwell's son-in-law, Henry Ireton, who had died in November 1651; and the second that of the fire-eating sectarian visionary, the Fifth Monarchist, Major-General Thomas Harrison. Lambert proposed that executive power should be vested in a new Council of State of about ten men, whose precise relationship with a newly constituted parliament elected on a new franchise and a revised constituency basis should be embodied in a written constitution, such as was eventually to be adopted in the so-called Instrument of Government. In the meantime the Council of State should govern until affairs were sufficiently settled to allow of the election of the new representative body.

Harrison's proposals were very different. Representative institutions of this sort figured nowhere in the calculations of fundamentalist millenarians such as the Fifth Monarchists. For them Christ's second coming was imminent and it should be the pre-eminent aim of any godly government to prepare the way for that glorious day. Power should be vested in an assembly of about seventy godly men, a body much smaller than a parliament and, in fact, modelled on the biblical Jewish sanhedrin. It was of small moment that the members of such an assembly would not represent electoral constituencies as these were normally understood either by parliamentarians or by electoral reformers such as Lambert. If the assembly was to be elected by anyone it should be by the Saints, the so-called 'gathered churches' of the elect, whose function would be to impose the way of righteousness on the community of the realm.

The fact that Lambert's proposals were not accepted does not mean that Harrison's were adopted in their entirety. The work of Professor A. H. Woolrych has clearly demonstrated that the 144 members (including five from Scotland and six from Ireland) of the new nominated assembly which has become known to history by the name of one of its members, the godly London leather-seller and Fifth Monarchy man Praise-God Barebone, were nominated directly by the Council of Officers of the army. They were not, as used to be thought, chosen by the officers from pre-existing lists of nominees sent up by the gathered churches, even though eight such (almost certainly unsolicited) lists have survived. Moreover, two-thirds of the assembly which convened on 4 July and dissolved itself on 12 December 1653, far from being the low-born sectaries of popular legend, were landed gentlemen, even if many of them were probably of a somewhat lower social standing than had been normal for MPs.[16] How then do we account for the traditional picture of the assembly as a body dominated by low-born mechanic saints?

Barebone's Parliament is, as H. R. Trevor-Roper puts it, 'a classic example of an unpolitical assembly colonized from within by a well-organized minority'. While the number of sectarian extremists probably did not exceed about forty, of whom twelve were Fifth Monarchy men,[17] the irregular attendance of the more moderate members – only once between the end of July and the middle of November did the attendance reach ninety – and the consequent ease with which the regularly-attending extremists dominated crucial parliamentary committees, was enough for the wild men to achieve a considerable degree of success for the radical causes they favoured; certainly, enough success to frighten some of the moderates ultimately into the resolute, if surreptitious action which brought the assembly to an end on 12 December. For in the hands of a radical minority, Barebone's Parliament for a brief spell reversed the process of conservative reconstruction and attempted reconciliation which had to some extent characterized the Rump and would, to a far greater extent, characterize the Protectorate. What were the policies which so alarmed its moderate members, and, not least, Oliver Cromwell himself?

It ought perhaps first to be emphasized that not all of the reforms proposed in Barebone's Parliament were of this alarming kind. Some of them – for instance measures of fiscal and educational reform, the proposed union with Scotland, and, perhaps surprisingly, the institution of civil marriage – were later to be confirmed by the more conservative Protectorate regime. On the other hand there were other proposals for reform which made moderate and conservative flesh creep. When dealing with the Commonwealth, it was remarked that law reform was an issue which drew support from moderates as well as radicals, and from professional lawyers as well as laymen. But some of the legal reforms hotly canvassed in Barebone's Parliament were of a very different order: the abolition of the Court of Chancery; the simplification of the common law to the extent that it might all be contained 'within the bigness of a pocket book'; even the substitution of Mosaic for secular law, in the words of the horrified Marchamont Nedham, 'a Catalogue of old dreaming Rabbis to jostle out *Coke* and Littleton'. Hardly less alarming was the proposed abolition of tithes, not only because it meant an end to compulsory maintenance of ministers of the established church and its replacement by the voluntary contributions of members of gathered churches, which was the natural sectarian solution of the problem, but also because an attack on tithes was in a real sense an attack on private property, since a high proportion of tithes were impropriated in the hands of laymen. No less fraught with radical social implications was the purge of local government. Not all of the new magistrates on the reformed commissions of the peace in counties such as Buckinghamshire, where Rumpers like Thomas Scot and his associates were excluded, were in fact low-born sectaries. Some indeed were socially respectable gentry whose main qualification for office was their dislike of the Rump. But for all that, there were enough low-born sectarian fanatics on the new commissions of the peace to give their social superiors serious cause for alarm.

It has already been emphasized how Cromwell, in whom the sectarian extremists had formerly placed such hopes as the Moses who would lead them into the promised land, but whom they came to execrate as 'the man of sin, the old dragon and many other scripture ill names', had taken alarm at the threat to property and stable government implicit in such extreme proposals. He was indeed profoundly disillusioned as a result of his total misreading of the aspirations of the godly men in whom he had placed such hope, as well as being irritated by their opposition to his wish to bring the Dutch war to an end. Yet for all that he does not seem to have been directly responsible for the end of the Barebone's episode on 12 December 1653. On that day a large group of moderate members of the assembly came early to the parliament house, and, before the arrival of the extremists, resigned their powers into the hands of Cromwell, who, in the words of one of the outraged Saints, 'took the crown from off the head of Christ, and put it upon his own'.

THE PROTECTORATE: (I) HEALING AND SETTLEMENT, 1653–5

Just as the Barebone's assembly, the most radical episode since the execution of the king, had marked the temporary ascendancy of Harrison and the Saints over the mind of Oliver Cromwell, so did the successor regime, the Protectorate, mark a significant step towards more traditional forms of government. It is true that the idea of a written constitution, the so-called Instrument of Government, which owed much to Lambert's notions set aside by Cromwell earlier in the year and to earlier constitutional proposals emanating from the army, and notably the Heads of the Proposals of 1647, was a distinctly un-English innovation.[18] It is also true that the new parliament was to continue to consist of one single chamber. But against this should be set the fact that the rule of a single person, so deplored in all the constitutional pronouncements of the new republican dawn in 1649, was in effect re-established, even if that person was Lord Protector Cromwell rather than King Charles II.

Under the new constitution parliament did not have to be called for nine months, a necessary interval in view of the drastic redistribution of constituencies and alteration of the franchise. The new franchise was vested in all adult males (other than Roman Catholics or those who had fought against parliament in the Civil Wars) with landed or personal property worth £200 or more, a solid property-owning franchise replacing the bewildering variety of franchises which had hitherto obtained.[19] The 509 seats in the complete Long Parliament – the Rump, of course, had had very many fewer sitting members – were now reduced to 400, to include, following the political union with Scotland in 1654, thirty members apiece from Scotland and Ireland. Constituency redistribution was on a scale not to be seen again until the Great Reform Bill of 1832, though in 1653 redistribution was in the direction of the growth of county at the expense of the borough representation which had expanded so spectacularly under the Tudors. This has been seen as severely restricting the scope for the exercise of government patronage in the election of its own supporters,[20] though it needs to be remembered that patrons of boroughs had not invariably been inclined to use their influence on the government's behalf; indeed, the reverse had often been true.

All shades of radical opinion, Rumper Commonwealthsmen, Levellers and religious radicals were highly suspicious of and hostile to the new regime, which smacked strongly of Oliver's own declared preference for a constitution 'with somewhat of monarchical power in it'. In the words of the republican Commonwealthsman Edmund Ludlow it was 'a re-establishment of that which we had all engaged against, and had with a great expense of blood and treasure abolished'. This opposition might not matter much if the regime could find support elsewhere. The one policy measure which, above all else, would have been overwhelmingly popular in the country would have been a notable reduction in the size of the standing army, or better, its disbandment and replacement by a locally officered militia. But given the fact that so many people, from out-and-out Commonwealthsmen such as Ludlow and Henry Marten to those who secretly longed for their king to come into his own again, were implacably opposed to Cromwell's rule and his new constitution, he was necessarily dependent on army support to a degree that was entirely incompatible with his objective of moderate conciliatory rule.

Whatever the objections of conservative country gentlemen, whom Oliver dearly wished to associate with the regime in the role of magistrates,[21] to the rule of what they continued to see as a regicide government, the regime was at least preferable to the rule of the Rump or the Saints. Consequently the arguments which had been advanced by Marchamont Nedham in favour of cooperation with the Commonwealth government applied *a fortiori* to the Protectorate. But such conservative elements from crypto-royalists to Presbyterians looked with disfavour on the religious toleration which characterized the religious policy of the government and which they saw as necessarily associated with social and political subversion, whatever the conservative inclinations of the government in other respects might be. While 'such as under the profession of Christ hold forth and practise licentiousness' – an obvious reference to the outrageous Ranters – were specifically exempted from the benefits of the toleration clause in the Instrument of Government, the net was nevertheless drawn far too loosely for the liking of some of the Presbyterians and indeed for many other people also. As to the other pole of religious opinion, although Catholics and episcopalians were also exempted from the benefits of toleration, life was in practice far easier for both groups under the Protectorate than at any time since 1649, so long as they kept their heads down and steered clear of political sedition.[22] In 1656 Cromwell even brought back the Jews who had been excluded from England since 1290.[23]

Conservative opinion may also have viewed with disfavour the alleged threat to the free exercise of advowsons and rights of patronage presented by the commissioners or 'tryers' set up in March 1654 to examine the suitability of parsons presented by patrons to benefices. Despite government protests to the contrary it was later complained that these 'tryers', a mixture of laymen and clerics of varying denominations ranging from Presbyterians to Baptists, had done even more than the Laudian bishops 'to take away men's advowsons'. On the other hand, they and their counterparts, the 'ejectors', who were county commissioners the great majority of whom were laymen, offered some safeguard against the ordination of illiterate mechanic preachers, at least in the established church. But the church was very far from a centralized body imposing uniform discipline, jurisdiction and organization throughout the country as desired by orthodox Presbyterians. There was, even within the established church, let alone among the numerous tolerated sects on its fringes, room for a wide variety of practices and modes of discipline: full Presbyterian 'classical' organization in some districts, such as London and parts of Lancashire, but nothing of this sort in others; fully fledged lay elders assisting the minister in some parishes, but the minister acting alone elsewhere.

During the nine months before the constitution required the first Protectorate parliament to be summoned, as well as during the intervals between parliaments, the government was allowed to legislate by ordinances, which had, however, to be confirmed when parliament met if they were to continue in force. As Professor Roots points out in his study of these ordinances,[24] they represent another significant backward step, since they bear some resemblance to royal proclamations while carrying the additional sanction of being able to create new law. During the whole of the Protectorate over eighty such ordinances were promulgated, covering a wide variety of issues: among them the union with Scotland; taxation; legal reform, including making Chancery, which Barebone's Parliament had wanted to abolish, more accessible to suitors; religion; control of food supply; poor relief; and public order.

The first Protectorate parliament met on 3 September 1654, Cromwell's lucky day, the fourth anniversary of Dunbar and the third of Worcester. Some diehard Rumpers, such as Ludlow, Hesilrige and Scot, had been elected, and at the other extreme some crypto-royalists. Although some former members of Barebone's Parliament were elected, these were mostly moderate men like Francis Rous and Ashley Cooper, and there was no more than a handful of the fire-eating Saints whose activities in that assembly had occasioned such alarm among moderate and conservative Englishmen. A number of former Levellers, among them

John Wildman, were excluded by the Council of State after being elected, though experienced Commonwealthsmen MPs were successful in their questioning of the council's exclusion of other elected candidates. They also made a nuisance of themselves, from the government's point of view, in a variety of other ways and notably by challenging the rule of the 'single person', which on 12 September led the Protector to demand the signatures of MPs to the so-called 'Recognition' of such rule. In the end about 100 Commonwealthsmen MPs withdrew from parliament rather than submit.

But this cutting off of republican noses to spite republican faces did not end the government's difficulties with parliament. It still had to face critics on the other side of the House, and notably Presbyterians such as Arthur Onslow and Colonel John Birch, who, having formerly been excluded from the Long Parliament by Pride's Purge in 1648, had no love for the republican dissenters, but were no more inclined than they to become the Protector's compliant supporters. Indeed they displayed an inclination to treat parliament almost as if it were a constituent, as distinct from a legislative, assembly, by devising piecemeal over the remainder of its duration their own challenging alternative to the Instrument of Government, which would have materially increased the power of parliament *vis-à-vis* that of the Council of State and the Lord Protector.[25] As far as the latter was concerned, the last straw came on 20 January 1655 in the proposal to settle the militia on Protector and Parliament, as distinct from Protector and Council as stipulated by clause four of the Instrument of Government. Two days later Cromwell dissolved the parliament.

Parliament had also been strongly critical of many of the government's ordinances, and the fact that the government continued after the dissolution to enforce ordinances which had gone unconfirmed by parliament speaks volumes about its own willingness to disregard the constitution when it suited its purpose to do so. The next two years were to see many further ordinances, some of them far more contentious and unpopular than anything which had gone before.

In considering the background to these developments we move into the second, more authoritarian and despotic phase in the history of the Protectorate.

THE PROTECTORATE: (II) MILITARY DESPOTISM, 1655–6

The background to these changes is the defeat in March 1655 of the royalist Penruddock's Revolt, begun in Wiltshire and culminating in the surrender of a few pathetic remnants in Devon and the execution of the chief conspirators.[26] In view of the feebleness of this insurrection and the ease with which it was suppressed, some historians have seen it as the excuse for, rather than the occasion of, Cromwell's shift from conciliation to oppression via his division of England into ten regions each governed by a major-general. But this is to miss the point of the rising as the emergent tip of a royalist conspiratorial iceberg, the only element to come to fruition of a plan for coordinated insurrections in many parts of the country. This in itself was the outcome of the Stuart pretender's abandonment of the policy of attempting to square the religious circle by seeking accommodation with both Presbyterians and Catholics, which was urged on him, as it had been urged on his father, by Henrietta Maria. Influenced no doubt by the defeat of king and Scots at Worcester in September 1651 and certainly by the advice of tried and experienced counsellers such as Edward Hyde and the marquis of Ormond, Charles had increasingly concentrated on appealing to the loyalties of good Church-and-King Englishmen who would not be attracted by the idea of a Covenanting king.

This change of royal emphasis had contributed to the growth of Cavalier enthusiasm at home and the foundation of a clandestine royalist council with the splendidly conspiratorial title of the Sealed Knot. It was this body which had coordinated plans for a general uprising which would also make use of manifold discontents among elements with whom the Cavaliers would not deign to associate as allies, and who would no doubt be dealt with in their turn once the king had come into his own: republicans furious at Oliver's treatment of the first Protectorate parliament; high radical army officers such as Colonels Okey, Alured and Saunders, who were similarly offended and had petitioned for a free parliament; sailors in the fleet who had proffered similar petitions; and, not least, Presbyterians who deplored what they regarded as the undue permissiveness and religious toleration of the regime.

The commissioning of the first of Cromwell's major-generals, John Desborough, to put down the Wiltshire revolt and establish a new force of militia to keep the southwest under constant surveillance was to become the model for the military despotism which, between August and October 1655, was extended piecemeal to the rest of the country, under nine other major-generals. The new militias which they raised, officered not by local gentlemen of dubious loyalty but by men whom the regime could trust whatever their social status, were to be financed by a decimation tax, amounting to one-tenth of the income of known ex-royalists with landed property worth at least £100 per annum or personal property valued at £1,500 and upwards. The idea was clearly that the militia should be a charge 'upon those who are the occasion of it'. But in actual fact the militia cost £80,000 a year, a sum by no means provided by the new tax, which nevertheless fell heavily on ex-royalists, many of whom had probably not harboured the least intention of actively participating in the overthrow of the regime, but were now irreconcilably alienated from it. The tax and the role of the major-generals were in fact a serious setback to the healing and conciliation which had hitherto been a feature of the policies of the Protectorate.

Nor was it simply ex-royalists who were alienated. If English county gentry and magistrates had complained about the whips of Stuart and parliamentarian centralization over the three previous decades, they now had to endure chastisement with scorpions. It is true that in some respects the local commissioners appointed to assist the major-generals were sometimes more lax than their predecessors on the county committees during the previous decade, but the major-generals did their utmost to keep them up to the mark. Needless to say, public order and security loomed very large indeed in the regime's activities, and the strictly enforced ordinances against cock-fighting and race meetings were probably more closely connected with this need than with puritanical kill-joy zeal. Nevertheless the latter was certainly not absent.

It was not so much the enforcement of policies basically similar to those which had been pressed on the county magistracy by the lieutenancy in the 1620s and 1630s, such as licensing of alehouses, control of food supplies, administration of poor relief and punishment of malefactors, which made the rule of the major-generals particularly obnoxious. What stamped – somewhat unfairly – a repressive and inquisitorial image on the whole of the Cromwellian regime which has become a matter of national legend was their unceasing scrutiny of private morals and behaviour. The Protector's approval of their role in respect of the 'reformation of manners' again brings to the fore the Puritan, authoritarian, regenerative side of his character, the determination to bring about the New Jerusalem by force, which had previously been evident in his initial support for the Barebone's experiment. There can be little doubt that the inquisitorial aspects of the major generals' rule, their interference with local magistrates and ruthless disregard of local custom, and not least the fact that these things were done by men of lowly social origins, were potent factors contributing to the alienation of far larger sections of the population than the royalist conspirators against whom they were principally directed.[27]

THE PROTECTORATE: (III) THE SECOND PROTECTORATE PARLIAMENT AND THE HUMBLE PETITION AND ADVICE, 1656–8

Although the Instrument of Government did not require a parliament to be called until three years had elapsed since the dissolution of its predecessor, there were in the late summer of 1656 pressing financial reasons for summoning a parliament, for England was now at war with Spain and a costly Caribbean campaign was under way. But parliamentary cooperation was only to be had at a price, the removal of the hated major-generals who, partly because of the constituency redistribution of 1653 favouring county at the expense of borough representation, were unable to exercise as much influence over parliamentary elections as might otherwise have been the case. Cries of 'No Swordsmen: No Decimators' were heard at many election gatherings, and there were some distinctly odd electoral alliances between conservatives and royalists on the one hand and anti-Protectorate republicans on the other. A number of opponents of the regime, such as the Commonwealthsmen Hesilrige and Scot and the crypto-royalist Major-General Richard Browne, the former counter-revolutionary white hope of 1647–8, were elected. However, the council, as in 1654, excluded some successful candidates as not being 'persons of known integrity, fearing God and of good conversation', while others made a point of staying away.

In the event then, although the Protector offered a spirited defence of the actions of his major-generals, there was overwhelming opposition to the prolongation of the post-Penruddock emergency and therefore of their power. Oliver's reward for his reluctant sacrifice of them was a parliamentary vote of £400,000 towards the war, made on the day following the rescinding of the decimation tax. These events mark the resumption of the protectoral emphasis on moderation and the pursuit of conservative and conciliatory policies. The Protector seems increasingly to have hearkened to the counsels of ex-royalists such as Lord Fauconberg, who was to marry one of his daughters, and Lord Broghil, the son of the earl of Cork. Moreover, some Presbyterians, such as Sir John Clotworthy, who had been excluded at Pride's Purge, increasingly gave their support to the regime, though there were others, such as Sir William Waller, the old parliamentary general and, like Clotworthy, one of the eleven Presbyterian members attacked by the army in 1647, who became intransigent royalists. With the major-generals removed, the way was open for the traditional local governors to begin to come into their own again and to exercise that control over local government which they regarded as their natural right. The names of such élite county families begin to reappear in the commissions of the peace and the assessment commissions.[28] Such pillars of respectability were to be further encouraged by the new and more conservative constitutional changes introduced in 1657.

One reason why this process of reconciliation was less than completely successful, quite apart from unhappy memories of the major-generals' regime, was Cromwell's policy of religious toleration, even though this underwent some modification during the last two years of his life. The uncomfortable fact which has to be faced by every student of the Interregnum is that the greater the personal power of the Protector, the greater the scope for religious liberty, while, conversely, the greater the power of parliament, the stronger were the curbs on that liberty and the pressure towards uniformity from the horrified and not very silent majority who were terror-stricken at sectarian excesses. Pursuing the idea of a respectable broad-church establishment, Cromwell was hardly less alarmed by these things, though much less eager to curtail religious freedom and to proceed to savage punitive action.

The case of the Quaker James Nayler was symptomatic of these fears and frustrations. It needs to be emphasized that the Quakers of the 1650s were not the harmless quietistic reformers of later decades, but a violent revolutionary sect determined to wage ferociously the Lamb's war against the forces of Antichrist. To respectable gentlemen they seemed to present an amalgam of the sort of threats to which they had been subjected by religious extremists like the Ranters and the Anabaptists and political extremists like the Levellers and the Diggers: indeed erstwhile adherents of all these groups were to be found amongst them. Another reason for respectable society's disapprobation was the presence of women in their ranks, as had also been true of the Leveller movement. The Quaker belief in an inner light shining within all individuals may have offered to many women an earnest of emancipation from a male-dominated world. It also stimulated some suppressed females to indulge in acts of hysterical ecstasy, of which the most notorious is their strewing of palm leaves in the path of James Nayler and shouting Alleluia as he entered Bristol riding on an ass; admittedly not on Palm Sunday, but on an October day in 1656.

Hardly less hysterical was parliament's response to what MPs not surprisingly regarded as a blasphemous outrage. As in the case of the Catholic Floyd thirty-five years earlier (see above, p. 238), MPs vied with one another in devising suitably barbaric punishments for the unfortunate Nayler, despite the objections of some MPs that the House of Commons, unlike the now abolished House of Lords, was not a court of law and that there was in any case no specific crime at common law for which Nayler could be punished. Punished he was nevertheless, being branded, bored through the tongue and flogged twice by order of the House of Commons. The reaction of flouted and frightened orthodoxy was as savage as that associated in our own times with the theocratic regimes in Iran and Pakistan, and the Protector, needing parliamentary support for the Spanish war, was helpless to do anything about it. However, the fact that parliament's action was constitutionally improper pinpointed the anomalies of the existing constitution and was to contribute powerfully to the constitutional changes of 1657, and, more particularly, to the reintroduction of a second chamber, as well as to the much stricter drawing of the limits of toleration in the new constitution of May 1657, the so-called Humble Petition and Advice.[29]

Of course, the new constitution was a great deal more than a response to the constitutional and religious anomalies created by Nayler's case. It was above all a notable landmark in the Cromwellian policy of reconciliation, and –

seen with the advantages of hindsight – the movement back in the direction of the ancient constitution. Here at last, as Professor A. H. Woolrych has remarked,[30] was a truly parliamentary constitution as distinct from one imposed by a military junta. Prominent among its movers were what has been described as a new courtly party, including Lord Broghil and other members for Irish constituencies which, since 1653, had been virtually pocket boroughs at the disposal of the regime. Among the other Protectorate 'courtiers' were John Ashe, the great West Country clothier, and the Presbyterian Sir Richard Onslow, both of whom had been excluded from parliament by Pride's Purge; Lord Fauconberg, the Protector's son-in-law; Edward Montagu, later to be the post-Restoration earl of Sandwich; Bulstrode Whitelock, who had contrived to serve every parliamentarian regime since 1642; and George Downing, who was to earn his passage after the Restoration by hunting down fugitive regicides. Such were the people who were also responsible for the offer of the crown to Cromwell in March 1657, to create the keystone of the new and more distinctively monarchical constitution. Oliver ultimately refused the crown while obtaining the right to nominate his successor as Protector, thus at least putting an end to the danger of a disputed succession after his death, though not, as will be shown, to that of chronic political instability. A crown for the house of Cromwell might have served better, but while it might have helped further in securing the support of part at least of the traditional ruling class, it would have aroused implacable opposition elsewhere: from Commonwealthsmen, Levellers and sectarian fanatics who would have no king but Jesus; and, above all, from those army officers and grandees who gave their guarded support for the new constitution while refusing to swallow the unacceptable pill of monarchy, even when vested in their old commander.

Oliver may well have felt that he had obtained the substance of his long-desired ideal of a constitution 'with somewhat of the monarchical in it' as a result of sacrificing the form. For many of the powers conferred upon him by the new constitution were certainly quasi-monarchical in character. He was to nominate not only his successor as Protector, but also the members of the Council of State (now significantly described as the Privy Council), though the latter were technically subject to ratification by the parliament and the existing council. But if the Humble Petition and Advice was a significant step back along the road to monarchy, it was none the less a parliamentary constitution. For instance, MPs were to be excluded from serving only by the house of parliament in which they were to serve, and not by the council, as under clause 21 of the Instrument of Government. Moreover, all additional taxes over and above the £1,300,000 settled by parliament on the government, of which £1,000,000 was to go on the army and navy, must be voted by parliament, to which an account must also be given of the precise appropriation of the measures which it had voted for the armed forces.

As to membership of the new upper (or 'other' house), sixty-three writs were issued before parliament reassembled in January 1658. Among those summoned were a few peers and sons of peers, some senior army officers, though not the enraged Lambert, to whom the Instrument of Government was more or less holy writ, and some who had formerly acted as government spokesmen in the lower house. The elevation of Cromwellians made it easier for Hesilrige and other Commonwealthsmen to influence the proceedings of the Commons when parliament reassembled. The Commonwealthsmen's disruptive tactics and refusal to vote additional supplies for the war, along with the Protector's desire to forestall a petition to parliament from City radicals and Baptists complaining of the new constitution and religious settlement and of civilian control of the army, provoked him into dissolving parliament on 4 February only a fortnight after it had reassembled. Shortly afterwards Cromwell dismissed Major William Packer, the commander of the Protector's own regiment of horse, and five other Baptist officers. But more was to be heard both of the dismissed officers and the aborted radical petition during the short reign of Oliver's successor.

Although in the context of the events of the last year of Oliver's life – he died on 3 September 1658, the anniversary of his great triumphs at Dunbar and Worcester – the opposition to his rule seemed to come mainly from republicans and radicals, it is none the less true that his attempted conciliation of the traditional ruling classes was at best only partially successful. To royalists he was, after all, the regicide of 1649; to Presbyterians not only the regicide but the beneficiary of Pride's Purge and the propounder of the horrifying Barebone's experiment of 1653 and the further tyrannical rule of the sects, which reappeared in another form under the hated major-generals in 1655–6. Memories did not have to be very long to preserve at worst a profound mistrust of the Protector, and at best an extremely cautious attitude towards him, for all his apparent conversion to moderate counsels and his expressed desire to heal and conciliate. Perhaps his successor, to whom at least none of these disadvantages by association applied, would be more successful.

THE PROTECTORATE: (IV) ECONOMIC AND FOREIGN POLICY, 1653–9

The economic policies of the Protectorate do not afford convincing backing for the view which sees Interregnum governments as enthusiastic believers in freedom of economic enterprise. However, this should not be taken to mean that in the sphere of foreign trade the chartered companies had things all their own way, though they were on the whole more favoured than under the Commonwealth. The government made determined, but unsuccessful, attempts to secure the restitution of the privileges of the Russia Company, members of which had been expelled by an outraged Tsar who wanted no truck with the subjects of a regicidal state. During the Commonwealth the East India Company had been made to admit its former interloping critics into a now united joint-stock, and for the first three years of the Protectorate the trade was virtually open to all comers, though the company finally obtained its long-sought-after new charter and the right to launch a new seven years' joint-stock in 1657. The delays were probably attributable to the influence exerted over the Protector by the former East India interloper Maurice Thompson, with whom he was also to work closely in the matter of transatlantic trade and his so-called Western Design. Despite the Levant Company's defiance of the government's insistence on the replacement of the royalist-sympathizing ambassador at Constantinople, Sir Thomas Bendyshe – as it had defied Charles I over his predecessor, Sir Sackville Crow – the company was confirmed in its privileges and benefited greatly from Robert Blake's successful naval expeditions against the Barbary pirates of Tunis and Algiers. In the forefront of those who offered the crown to Oliver in 1657 was Sir Christopher Packe, governor of the Merchant Adventurers Company. Although the Protector had confirmed that company's exclusive privileges by proclamation in May 1656, these had been suspended a few months later. It was not until 1658 that the company's privileges were finally confirmed, for in the previous year the Committee of Trade had proposed a bill for free trade to the Low Countries and northwest Germany which, however, never materialized. As to the Eastland Company, its privileges had been in virtual abeyance during the Commonwealth, and although it was given every ground for hoping for the grant of a new charter, with admittedly less restriction on membership, it had to wait until the Restoration before achieving this.[31]

The government's attitude to internal economic regulation was less equivocal. Wage, price and apprenticeship regulations remained in force, and forestallers, engrossers, regrators and other violators of the traditional code of economic behaviour continued to be punished. Moreover, as Dr G. D. Ramsay stresses in an important article, there was no deliberate relaxation of restraints on industrial activity. In so far as the newer enterprises like the manufacture of the new draperies and cotton fabrics were operating largely outside close government control, this was a development which had been going on over most of the previous century, and is in no way symptomatic of any deliberate reorientation of industrial policy in the direction of freedom from economic restraint.[32]

Cromwellian foreign policy has been castigated as backward-looking and inappropriately latter-day Elizabethan in character. It has been argued that the Protector was too obsessed with the need for a pan-Protestant anti-Spanish foreign policy to squeeze the sort of economic concessions out of the Dutch which were merited by English naval victories in the war which he had long opposed and brought to an end in 1654. Yet the terms of the Anglo-Dutch treaty, even though not all of them were fully put into effect, were quite favourable to English interests, with provision for full compensation for losses to English merchant shipping during the late war, and to the East India Company for damage done by the Dutch since the early 1620s; not to speak of the Dutch having to agree to salute English naval vessels in the Channel. Of far more practical advantage was the provision, negotiated separately with the most powerful of the Dutch provinces, the States of Holland, that the office of Stadholder should not be occupied by a member of the house of Orange, allied as it was by marriage with the exiled Stuarts.

In the same year as the Anglo-Dutch treaty came other treaties with Denmark, Sweden and Portugal, all of which brought valuable commercial privileges, and more especially those of direct trade with Portuguese colonial possessions, and paying the same preferential duties for the passage of English ships through the Sound into the Baltic as the Danes had accorded to their Dutch allies. That these were important commercial concessions does not, of course, mean that religion was not also an important element in the Protector's foreign policy. It was, for example, religious considerations, and notably dislike of the French persecution of the Protestant Vaudois of Savoy and Oliver's refusal to relinquish his claim to be the protector of the French Huguenots, which help to account for the delay in concluding an Anglo-French alliance against Spain. It is also true that Cromwell mistook the territorial ambitions of Charles X of Sweden – whom he described in a speech to parliament in January 1658 as having 'ventured all for Protestantism' – for a revival of the Protestant crusade of his predecessor, the great Gustavus Adolphus. But he was not the only statesman in contemporary Europe to be taken in by the Swedish king.

Indeed Cromwell's Baltic policies have received the unstinted approbation of a pre-eminent authority in Swedish history, Professor Michael Roberts.[33] One good reason why the Protector, for all his misplaced admiration for Charles X, could never seriously contemplate affording him assistance against the Danes and their Dutch allies was that it would put in jeopardy the valuable Danish concessions of 1654 in the matter of the Sound duties. No less important admittedly was the fact that he certainly could neither afford a war on two fronts once he had begun war with Spain at the beginning of 1655, nor risk being cut off from sources of Baltic naval stores (above all hemp, but also pitch, tar, iron for nails and ordnance and even timber), as had occurred during the late war with the Dutch. What Cromwell did contemplate was for Swedes, Dutch and Danes to join in a pan-Protestant alliance against the Habsburgs along with those honorary Protestants the French; an admittedly rather unrealistic aim in view of the mutual antipathy between Swedes and Danes which was shortly to issue in war.

It is, however, probably in the matter of his anti-Spanish policies that strictures against Cromwell for neglecting the real interests of the realm in the pursuit of grandiose, backward-looking aims can be made to stick most firmly. Merchants trading to Old Spain, especially in new draperies and Newfoundland cod, were to suffer seriously from the embargo on English goods imposed by Philip IV in September 1655 in response to English aggression in the West Indies. Mrs Prestwich has emphasized how it is in fact a travesty to see England as gaining from the aggressively conceived 'Western Design' for territorial acquisitions in the West Indies more than what she lost by the disruption of trade with Old Spain. The main fruit of the Western Design was the annexation of Jamaica in 1655, and this was very much a *pis aller* after the failure to take Hispaniola, which at the time seemed a far greater prize. Similarly, the Anglo-French alliance of 1657, which committed England to a costly campaign against the Spanish Netherlands, was also unpopular in the City. Indeed the chief gainers from it appeared to be the Dutch, who characteristically filled the vacuum left by the Spanish prohibition of English imports and supplied Spain not only with woollens and fish, but even with munitions of war which could be used against the English. The Anglo-French victory over the Spaniards at the battle of the Dunes in June 1658 was not greeted with enthusiasm in the City, which was more conscious of the cost of the campaign than of the victory for allied arms or even the cession of Dunkirk (a possible centre for a new cloth staple) to England.

It took another decade and the restoration of the Stuarts to make Englishmen recall with pride the respect and awe in which Cromwell's England had been held by foreign powers. To his contemporaries the Protector's policies were highly suspect even in achieving the most basic of short-term aims, the isolation of the Stuarts from active foreign assistance. Sure enough, James, duke of York, was to be found fighting alongside the Spanish enemy (and the French rebel Condé) at the battle of the Dunes, though it has recently been ingeniously argued that the Machiavellian Cromwell was very conscious of the positive advantages of the association of the Stuarts' fortunes with those of Antichrist.[34] More damaging is the notion that he was led astray by his obsession with the need for a crusade against Catholic Spain into policies which were against the long-term interests of England; that in supporting the great rising power of France against Spain, whose hegemony was now passing away, he was helping to establish the very French ascendancy in Europe against which England, from the time of Louis XIV to that of Napoleon I, was to pour out prodigious quantities of lives and treasure. The thesis undoubtedly has some truth in it, though it is largely based on hindsight. But even if Cromwell is found lacking in far-sightedness in this matter, the view which sees him as a backward-looking latter-day Elizabethan in his Western Design neglects the fact that the Elizabethan vision of the bright land to the west was still an authentic vision of the future even in the 1650s. Cromwell would have regarded it as a great compliment to be placed in the same line as Martin Frobisher, Sir Humphrey Gilbert and, above all, Sir Walter Raleigh, the visionary of transatlantic empire and the most spectacular victim of Stuart appeasement of Spain. The century which followed 1658 was to see that vision come to full fruition.

THE END OF THE PROTECTORATE, 1658–9[35]

Although it is no longer fashionable to explain great events in terms of individual character and personality, there can be no doubt that while Oliver Cromwell was one of the truly dynamic personal forces in English history, his son Richard, his chosen successor as Lord Protector, was in no sense a mighty figure cast in his father's heroic mould. Indeed, in some ways he seemed a less suitable candidate for the highest office than his brother Henry, who commanded the army in Ireland. But these very deficiencies might work to his advantage. His modest, frank and open manner made an initial good impression, and he was greeted by a spate of loyal addresses, subscribed by many members of the traditional ruling class of upper gentry, who had not been altogether convinced, in view of the twists and turns of policy since 1653, of the sincerity of Oliver's oft declared desire for healing and conciliation.

The new Protector's position *vis-à-vis* the army proved to be of crucial importance. It will be remembered that Oliver had removed some of the most militantly republican – that is to say, anti-Protectorate and pro-Rump – senior officers, but there still remained others such as Colonels Richard Ashfield and Robert Lilburne who were potential enemies of the regime. The Protector, however, quickly succeeded in winning the enthusiastic support of a number of senior officers, and notably Goffe, Ingoldsby and Montagu, the first two of whom were, significantly, regicides. Less favourably disposed was the so-called Wallingford House group, which took its name from the house of Richard's brother-in-law Fleetwood, and whose other main figures were Desborough, Sydenham, Kelsey and Berry, all of them Oliverian major-generals of the unhappy days of 1655–6, and who, according to the Commonwealthsman Edmund Ludlow, 'had advanced Mr Richard Cromwell in expectation of governing all they pleased'. Since these expectations were not realized, even though Richard promoted Fleetwood to lieutenant-general, the group was far less steadfast and reliable in its support for the new Protector than was his own carefully cultivated faction in the army.

It was this situation which made Richard more dependent on the support of the conservative elements who had been especially responsible for the constitutional changes of 1657 and who were a powerful influence in directing his policies towards what more radical politicians saw as backsliding from 'the Good Old Cause'. One such policy was the move towards re-establishing the old gentry-controlled county militias, which both senior and junior army officers were quick to regard as a threat to their very existence. Another important consideration was the fact that, unlike his father, Richard had no great love for religious freedom and extensive toleration, and indeed seemed to display an increasing and alarming preference for Presbyterian divines. Religious sectarian dissent, always a factor to be reckoned with in the army, became allied with militantly republican sentiments, especially, though not exclusively, among the junior officers. This was the more dangerous because of the possible linkage with civilian Commonwealthsmen like Hesilrige and Scot and with formerly dismissed republican officers such as Okey, Alured, Saunders and Packer. Added to these dangers were the suspicions of the Wallingford House group, culminating in Desborough's accusations in December 1658 that Fauconberg, Montagu and Ingoldsby were planning to imprison him and Fleetwood in Windsor Castle.

In the previous month, writs had been issued for the election of a new House of Commons which, along with the new upper house, was to form the third and last Protectorate parliament. The lower house was to be constituted on a pre-Instrument of Government basis, except for the retention of the new Scottish and Irish seats. Thus the old preponderance of borough over county seats was restored, and with it increased opportunities for the exercise of electoral patronage. The new House of Commons contained MPs of almost every shade of political opinion. There were numerous young and inexperienced members whom the Commonwealthsmen, and especially Hesilrige, were to make a determined and not very successful attempt to convince of the righteousness of the Good Old Cause. But whatever the efficacy of such tactics, there can be no doubt that the Commonwealthsmen dominated the parliament which opened on 7 January 1659, for in the manipulation and exploitation of parliamentary procedures they had no equals, even if they were totally lacking in constructive ideas beyond their desire for an end to the Protectorate and the return of the Rump. 'Yesterday's men,' as Professor Roots describes them in a happy phrase, 'they would stop the clock in fumbling to set it back'.[36] To them the Rump, pitiful remnant of the Long Parliament though it was, was the only legal representative assembly, and its dissolution by Oliver in 1653 had been an outrageous violation of the statute of 1641 according to which the parliament could not be dissolved without its own consent. Their prolonged intrigues and wrangling, their refusal to vote for the bill confirming Richard's title on the ground that it was part of a package deal involving recognition of the Humble Petition and Advice, and their negative and delaying tactics in general were to bring about Richard's dissolution of the parliament on 22 April; the prelude to the restoration, in the short run, of the Rump, but, within hardly more than a year, of the monarchy itself.

But this is to anticipate. Frustrated at the failure of their attempts to win an unquestioned ascendancy in parliament, the Commonwealthsmen had sought to bring pressure to bear via the time-worn device of encouraging popular petitioning. Following the revival of the radical City petition against the new constitution of 1657, which had influenced Oliver's decision to dissolve the second Protectorate parliament before it reached it, there was a further petition on 2 April 1659 from the army officers demanding sterner measures against ex-Cavaliers and the redress of the inevitable and (since 1647) recurrent grievances relating to arrears of pay and lack of adequate indemnity for acts done during the Civil War. Neither petition got anywhere with parliament. On 18 April, deeply resentful of what it saw as outrageous external pressure upon it, parliament passed two resolutions which infuriated the soldiers: that there should be no future meetings of the Council of Officers without protectoral and parliamentary sanction, and that military commanders should undertake specifically not to interrupt parliament's proceedings. But the effect of these resolutions was the reverse of that desired. The army council continued to meet without permission, while, following a number of moves and countermoves, protectoral calling of rendezvous and grandees' calling of counter-rendezvous, Richard was persuaded by the army chiefs to dissolve parliament on 22 April in return for being allowed to retain office, though no more than a pawn in the army's hands.

Only the previous February the Wallingford House grandees had come to an understanding with Richard and had undertaken to cease attempting to pressurize parliament. It must then have seemed to the Commonwealthsmen MPs that their attempt to link military with republican discontents had failed dismally. Yet two months later the grandees proved willing to play the republican game and brought down the third Protectorate parliament. Why should the soldiers who had dissolved the Commonwealthsmen's beloved Rump in 1653 now join forces with them? Their dislike of the strongly civilian and anti-military character of Richard's regime was presumably no greater in April than it had been two months earlier, though the parliamentary resolutions of 18 April may have acted as the last straw. But at least as important was pressure from below – from junior officers convinced by the propaganda of the Commonwealthsmen against the 'backsliding' of politicians and of generals such as Fleetwood, the objects of extreme suspicion to the rank and file, who saw them as damned by their continuing Cromwellian associations.

Of great assistance in fanning these republican flames in the army were assiduously fostered rumours that the crown was shortly to be offered to Richard, who would do no more than keep the throne warm for the Stuart pretender. Nor was this all. No less inflammatory were the parliamentary moves in the direction of stricter enforcement of religious orthodoxy and a more tightly Presbyterian form of church government, and the increasingly voiced opinions of crypto-royalists and political Presbyterians in favour of the disbandment or, at the very least, severe reduction, of the army and the re-creation of an old-fashioned militia officered by local gentlemen. The Commonwealthsmen thus played skilfully on the fears of radical junior officers, while the latter found allies among formerly dismissed republican senior officers and even in Lambert, that deviser of the Instrument of Government but bitter opponent of the Humble Petition and Advice, who may also have been chagrined by his failure to succeed Oliver as Protector. Faced by the alarming coalition of such diverse elements as Lambert and Packer – not to speak of the junior officers and the Rumper politicians – the Wallingford House grandees were compelled to demonstrate their own republican probity. They chose in April 1659, as their predecessors had done twelve years earlier, to put themselves at the head of the agitation as a means of keeping it under control, for otherwise they were in danger of being swept away by it.

In the event, however, Fleetwood and his associates were unable even to keep their undertaking to maintain Richard as Protector in return for his dissolution of parliament. Their subordinates and the civilian Commonwealthsmen were now riding on a floodtide which was to sweep away the Protector and bring back the Rump at the end of May. These forces – army malcontents, civilian Commonwealthsmen and sectarian visionaries – were, as the history of the previous decade amply demonstrates, by no means natural allies. But the events following the establishment of the Protectorate at the end of 1653, and especially following the new constitution of 1657, had brought them closer together in opposition to the regime. There were, after all, affinities between the notion of the rule of the Saints, 'the faithful remnant', and the exercise of power by an allegedly virtuous minority such as the Rump of 1649; what John Milton described as 'the sound and uncontaminated part' of the Long Parliament, absurd though the analogy might seem when one considers that the virtuous included unbelievers like Thomas Chaloner and Henry Neville, sexual profligates like Henry Marten and Gregory Clement and economic racketeers like Cornelius Holland. But the virtues of the Rump tended to become more apparent as its heyday receded in time. England was now controlled by a hastily put together and uneasy coalition of Commonwealthsmen and army grandees, with some sectarian enthusiasts in both categories and some in neither, but all rejoicing at the demise of what they took to be a conservative, persecuting and intolerant government. It remains to be seen what they made of their victory.

CHAOS AND RESTORATION, 1659–60

For a short time at least, the return of the Rump meant not only the triumph of the Commonwealthsmen and what they deemed to be the pure milk of English republicanism, but also the subordination of the military to the civil authorities. This is reflected in the composition of the new executive

Council of State on which the army grandees, Lambert, Desborough and Berry, received places, but twenty-one of whose thirty-one members were Rumper MPs.[37] In addition, as was to be expected, there was an accompanying purge of the county magistracy. In Somerset, for example, as Professor Underdown has shown, John Pyne and his adherents, who had been in eclipse since 1653, were again prominent on the commission of the peace and the militia commission.[38] Thus for the traditional county élites who might have lent their support, however grudgingly, to Richard's Protectorate, the return of the Rump was a significant stage towards realizing that nothing but restoration of the Stuarts would guarantee the restoration of their own traditional hegemony in local affairs.

Whatever the personal wishes of the Rumpers, they at least recognized that they could not go on sitting in perpetuity and voted that the parliament should not continue in being beyond 7 May 1660, which, as it turned out, was to be the day before its successor, the Convention Parliament, proclaimed Charles Stuart king. The Rump's main problem in fact was how to secure that its successor should be dominated by like-minded people. Accordingly a number of possible safeguards and constitutional schemes to ensure the perpetuation of the Good Old Cause following the dissolution of the Rump were canvassed both in and out of parliament. None of them was to come to fruition.[39]

But it was not only the Rump's inability to provide an adequate constitutional foundation for its successor which brought about the demise of English republicanism, which had struck no very deep roots in the country. At least as important was the total failure of its supporters to learn from their experience, so that it needed no militant royalist revolt to sweep it away. The nearest thing to such a revolt was Sir George Booth's rising in south Lancashire and Cheshire in the summer of 1659, and the main supporters of Booth were Presbyterians, of both the religious and the political variety, rather than royalists. However, unlike the pitiful handful of royalists who had followed Penruddock five years earlier, more than 3,000 malcontents flocked to Booth, whose forces for a time controlled virtually the whole of Cheshire and south Lancashire and kept the military garrison cooped up in Chester castle. Nevertheless, the insurgents were easily crushed by the army under Lambert at Winnington Bridge on 19 August. As had been the case with Penruddock's Revolt, the Cheshire and Lancashire rising was to have been part of a general rising of conservative and royalist forces, none of the rest of which, involving amongst other things the seizure of Bristol and King's Lynn as ports of entry for a royalist invasion, got off the ground. Indeed, after the Restoration many Cavaliers went out of their way to denigrate Booth's rising as being unconcerned with the restoration of the monarchy, and it is true that none of Booth's pronouncements mentioned the subject. Like Monck after him, Booth was well aware that many Englishmen feared, not without reason, that a restoration achieved by force of arms would have as its inevitable product a white terror and royalist reign of blood, with wholesale retribution against very wide sectors of the population. Thus, again like Monck after him, he took his stand on a call for a 'free parliament'.[40]

Nothing better illustrates the failure of the republican politicians to learn from the experience of the past decade than the way in which they alienated the army, which had put them into power as well as saving their regime at Winnington Bridge. The ways in which this was done were many: their determination to keep the army under strict civilian control with officers commissioned by the Speaker and not by the commander-in-chief, Fleetwood; their insinuations that senior officers were encouraging agitation against the regime; their threats to institute a militia more obedient to parliament; and their failure to respond to the grandees' desire for a Senate or upper house, in which the generals would be strongly represented and perhaps dominant. In addition there was the failure to redress the familiar recurring grievances which had bedevilled relations between army and parliament since 1647: glaring loopholes in the bill of indemnity for acts done by soldiers during the war, and the Rump's unwillingness to appropriate adequate taxes to meet arrears of pay and to give assurance of prompt payment in the future. What made these last points especially significant, in 1659 as in 1647, was that they helped to reunite senior and junior officers, and contributed to snapping the links between the latter and the Rumper politicians.

In September 1659, officers of the army which had quelled Booth's rising drew up the so-called Derby Petition. Among other things this demanded severe punishment of the rebels, a purge of malignants and neuters from the magistracy and commissions in the armed forces; and, above all, a constitutional settlement acceptable to the army, presumably including the desired Senate or second chamber. The petition circulated among the soldiers much in the manner of 1647, with the exception of those in Scotland, whose commander, General Monck, refused to have anything to do with it. On 23 September parliament ordered the petition to be suppressed – shades of 1647 again! – and the army replied with a new and even more peremptory petition on 5 October, whose import was to demand, as Professor J. R. Jones puts it, 'recognition by the Rump of the army and its council of officers as an equal partner in government'. Hesilrige and his Commonwealthsmen allies, with a few exceptions such as Sir Henry Vane, who was aware of the importance of maintaining good relations with the army, now launched a violent counter-attack. This involved, among other things, the humiliating demotion of Fleetwood, whose command was put into a commission of seven (of whom he was admittedly one), and the arrest of Lambert. Again learning nothing from experience, Hesilrige and his colleagues had palpably overstepped the mark, and on 13 October Lambert destroyed the Rump, using the time-dishonoured expedient of refusing MPs access to the chamber.

A fortnight passed before the leading officers erected the so-called Committee of Safety, which was, in Professor Woolrych's phrase, 'a fig-leaf of respectability' covering otherwise naked military rule. This inadequate constitutional vesture consisted of twenty-three members, including the grandees, Lambert, Fleetwood, Desborough, Sydenham, Hewson and Berry. Among the civilians were Bulstrode Whitelock, the time-server *par excellence*, who for once made a crucial miscalculation; Walter Strickland who, like Whitelock, had liberal views on religious freedom, and had been horrified by the savage treatment of Nayler, but whose main achievements and experience had been in foreign diplomacy rather than internal politics; Sir Henry Vane, once an outstandingly important figure but now discredited; Johnston of Wariston, the Scottish fanatic; and the radical London aldermen Robert Tichborne and John Ireton, who certainly cannot be said to represent the dominant faction in the City. No acceptable constitutional settlement emerged, though several schemes were canvassed. One ominous cloud on the horizon, however, was General Monck's declaration of 20 October from Scotland, denouncing the army coup and demanding the recall of the Rump; though Monck was also significantly taking the opportunity of getting rid of three officers who had been forced on him by the Rump and reinstating those whom it had compelled him to remove.

Even before Monck crossed the Tweed on 1 January 1660, the former Lord General Fairfax had declared his support for whatever course he chose to adopt, and had taken possession of York. In addition, the fleet in the Downs and the army garrison at Portsmouth had declared for a parliament, and the troops sent to suppress the latter had instead joined forces with them. In face of these disasters Fleetwood had lost his never very strong nerve and allowed the Rump to meet once again on 26 December 1659. But its last triumph was short-lived, for the shouts for a free parliament echoing around England were emphatically not for the Rump. Following his arrival in London on 3 February Monck felt his way cautiously forward, and his intentions were – and to some extent still are – clouded in mystery. Of all the political groupings the Presbyterians, so badly mauled in Booth's rising, probably had the highest hopes. Although Monck was silent on the subject, they sensed that a restoration was likely, and had every reason to hope that it would be a restoration on their terms; on something like the terms of the parliamentary propositions at that last treaty with Charles I in the Isle of Wight in the autumn of 1648, which had been so rudely interrupted by Pride's Purge.

Their expectations would surely have been increased when the parliamentary conditions which had favoured that treaty were restored by Monck's allowing the MPs who had been secluded at Pride's Purge to take their places again. Before doing so, he had obtained from them an undertaking that they would vote for the dissolution of the now reconstituted Long Parliament – which, of course, by the terms of the act of 1641, could not be done without its own consent – and also for the calling of a new Convention Parliament. And so on 16 March 1660 the Long Parliament at last dissolved itself. Before doing so, it had voted to adopt the Presbyterian Westminster Confession of Faith and to replace the ecclesiastical system of 'tryers' by a more thoroughgoing Presbyterian system based on central commissioners. The Presbyterians were doing their utmost to preempt the sort of ecclesiastical polity to be set up by the new regime, which few doubted would be a monarchical one.

That they were to be sadly disappointed is amply demonstrated by a study of the ecclesiastical settlement as it is described in the succeeding volume in this series. The first omens in the elections to the Convention Parliament were not propitious either for the old Commonwealthsmen or for the Presbyterians, neither of whose aspirations accorded with the mood of England in 1660. In the Middlesex and Surrey elections there were ominous shouts of 'No Rumpers, no presbyterians that will put bad conditions on the king'. Only sixteen of the Rumpers of 1659 were elected, all for borough seats. Less expected perhaps was the bad showing of the Presbyterians, or at least of the so-called 'strict' Presbyterian, as distinct from the more amenable 'reconcilers'. The chances of imposing a treaty of Newport sort of settlement on the nation were now rather slim.

On 1 May the carefully penned royal Declaration of Breda was presented to the Convention, a bicameral body whose upper house contained not only the parliamentarian peers of 1648 but royalist peers too. By giving indemnity to all save those whom parliament itself might except, the Declaration offered reassurance that the Restoration would not be succeeded by a Cavalier terror, and that a few regicides and extremists would serve, in the barbaric retribution which they suffered, to act the role of scapegoats for the sins of the Interregnum. Parliament responded to the Declaration by proclaiming Charles Stuart as king on 8 May, and he landed at Dover on 25 May amidst widespread rejoicing.[41]

Charles II was restored not through the force of Cavalier endeavour but through the dissensions of the forces which had temporarily triumphed in the overthrow of the Protectorate in April 1659. In retrospect their attitude seems suicidal, and indeed since the Restoration was brought about with the general approval of the country, including those who had found Richard's Protectorate tolerable enough, it is arguable that Scot, Hesilrige and the other Commonwealthsmen and army grandees had been impossibly near-sighted in bringing down the Protectorate and alienating the sources of moderate and conservative support on which it had seemed increasingly to be drawing. Short-sighted doctrinaire republicans they may have been, but the view which sees them as obsessed by a sort of death-wish which made them prefer Restoration to the prolongation of the Protectorate is surely an exercise in hindsight on the part of those who are aware of the ultimate outcome of 1660. Looked at from the perspective of April 1659, it might well have appeared that Richard's regime was taking a path which in itself would surely lead to Stuart restoration. With the advantages of hindsight it is easy for us to see that it was the circumstances in which the Protectorate was brought down, the nature of the regimes which succeeded it, the fears of anarchy and social disorder – of Quakers, Fifth Monarchy men and other religious and social subversives poised to go on the rampage – which allowed the king to come into his own again. Such fears had been further accentuated when Lambert, in his desperate and unavailing attempt to resist Monck's coup, had rallied every available political force around him, including a fearsome array of religious extremists, the very thought of whom was enough to set the teeth of moderate and conservative men on edge. In these circumstances there was no need for internal revolt, or for the external invasion which the peace concluded between France and Spain in the treaty of the Pyrenees of 1659 had made possible, just as a similar peace had done a century earlier. Internal revolt had anyway failed ignominiously, while the most likely outcome of a royalist invasion supported by the army of a foreign power would probably have been to rally support for the Rump or the army and to set back royalist hopes, perhaps for another decade, perhaps for ever. Charles II was restored not through the efforts of diehard Cavaliers but through the political nation's fear of chaos and craving for order expressed through a freely elected parliament.

Herein lay the paradox; as John Milton might have put it, this sort of freedom was freedom to embrace bondage. It was all done by a properly elected parliament, for the restoration of the monarchy was to be the restoration of parliament too, as well as of the traditional apparatus and mechanism of local government. The one thing that Interregnum regimes had never been able to countenance was a 'free and full parliament', a limit which had applied no less to the Protectorate government's exclusion of some elected republicans and monarchists than to the Rump's refusal to admit secluded members. It was not absolute monarchy but the mixed monarchy of the royal answer to the Nineteen Propositions of June 1642 that was restored in 1660.

RESTORATION AND REVOLUTION

When contemporaries referred to the Restoration of Charles II as completing a revolution, they meant something quite different from what that term connotes to the modern reader; in fact they used the term literally, as of a wheel that had come full circle. Few historians today, however, would argue that 1660 saw a return to the conditions prevailing before 1640, and even those who see the Interregnum as no more than 'an untidy interruption' in the flow of English history[42] would argue that it was the threads of 1641, following the reforms of the first session of the Long Parliament, not those of Charles I's Personal Rule, which were taken up again in 1660. To the more thoroughgoing Marxist historians, on the other hand, the Civil War was the irreversible process whereby power was transferred from one ruling class to another by the medium of force, 'the midwife', in Marx's vivid phrase, 'of every old society pregnant with a new one'. While the Restoration was something of a setback to what they regard as the historically progressive forces of emergent capitalism, not all of the gains of the two previous decades were reversed in 1660. Certainly there was no return to the 'feudal' regime of the days before 1640, and what survived 1660 was a good deal more than the legislative achievements of 1640–1.

The thesis that the Interregnum was the crucial stage in the transition from feudal to capitalist society presents some difficulty to historians who are conscious of the fact that a search for predial labour rents or seigneurial personal dues in England before 1640 is unlikely to yield more than a few anachronistic survivals. On the other hand, if one employs the somewhat looser Marxist idea of feudalism as comprising a society in which a landowning aristocracy claims rent from a dependent peasantry, then one is faced with a description which is as applicable to society after 1660 (perhaps even after 1832) as before 1640.[43] To raise such objections is not to deny all truth in the accompanying notion that the Civil War was – for all Charles I's vigorous assertions that through his defence of his own property he was acting as the defender of property in general – a revolt against a regime which threatened the freedom of property-owners to make what use they would of their 'own'; which is not, of course, to say that all the property-owners who were irritated by monopolies, economic controls, wardships, anti-depopulation commissions and unparliamentary taxation were Roundheads rather than Cavaliers.

The nature of the Restoration settlement is a subject which falls within the purview of the succeeding volume in this series. Nevertheless, it is pertinent here to note that the work of Dr Joan Thirsk and others has cast serious doubt on the view that the Interregnum saw a large-scale transfer of lands from backward royalist landowners to new and more efficient men.[44] Not only does accumulating research into early Stuart estate management cast serious doubts on the easy identification of royalism with economic backwardness, but it appears, in addition, that many of the apparent purchasers of royalist lands in the Interregnum were in fact acting on behalf of the original owners. But, it might be claimed, these revelations are not so damaging to the basic Marxist interpretation as might appear at first sight. For even if a higher proportion than used to be conceived of the royalists' lands remained in the hands of – or after 1660 were restored to – the original landowners, these were now under great pressure to adopt more efficient methods of land management not simply through the increasing competition of more businesslike competitors but also – in the 1650s at least – through the need to pay off debts, including delinquency fines, and through differential taxation on ex-Cavaliers.

However, a recent essay by the most distinguished of English Marxist historians of the period argues that the most significant thing about both the pre- and post-Restoration periods was not the transfer of authority from one class to another, which he admits is difficult to demonstrate conclusively, but the greater sensitivity of government to the needs of capitalism than had ever been the case under the early Stuarts.[45] The outcome of the revolution was, Dr Hill argues:

> a state in which the administrative organs that most impeded capitalist development had been abolished: Star Chamber, High Commission, Court of Wards and feudal tenures; in which the executive was subordinated to the men of property, deprived of control of the judiciary, and yet strengthened in external relations by a powerful navy and the Navigation Act; in which local government was safely and cheaply in the hands of the natural rulers, and discipline was imposed on the lower orders by a Church safely subordinated to Parliament. The Church was as different from the Church which Archbishop Laud had wished to see as the state of William III was from the state of Charles I and Strafford . . .

With a good deal of this one can readily agree, though with some important reservations. Does Dr Hill, for instance, perhaps lay too much stress on the purely negative factor of the abolition of much of the traditional apparatus of economic control and the failure to restore it after 1660? Similarly, while it is possible to see the Commonwealth regime of the early 1650s, with its anti-Dutch policies and Navigation Ordinance, as wedded to economic nationalism, in sharp contrast to the government of Charles I, one needs to remember not only that this policy was reversed under Oliver's Protectorate, but also that although there was a Navigation Act and two further Dutch wars after the Restoration, the government's anti-Dutch policies were inspired by motives very different from those of its republican predecessor. Nor, as was observed earlier, were industrial controls less evident under Cromwell than they had been under Charles I.

Similarly the post-Restoration church was far less different from the Laudian church than Dr Hill would have us believe. It is perfectly true that the shared experience of hardship of both deprived Anglican clergy and royalist gentry during the long Cromwellian night had softened the mutual antagonism between squire and Laudian parson which had been a frequent product of the overweening pretensions of the Laudian church. The result was to be the formation of that alliance between squire and parson which was such a characteristic feature of the post-Restoration scene. But in all else the post-Restoration church was far less different from its Laudian predecessor than is sometimes supposed or than Charles II, who favoured a policy of comprehension with regard for tender consciences, would himself have preferred. As Dr Richard Beddard puts it, 'lay intolerance, the joint product of experience and indoctrination, was the decisive factor in restoring the Church of England to its old form and its old ascendancy'.[46]

Since intolerant Anglicanism and divine-right monarchy are historically connected, there is also reason to question Dr Hill's assumption that the mid-seventeenth-century crisis put an end once and for all to the Stuart aspirations towards absolute monarchy on the continental model. Indeed, while it may be doubted whether Charles I had ever entertained such aspirations, the same cannot be said of either of his sons, despite the fact that parliament had been restored with the crown in 1660. The English world was ultimately made safe for constitutional monarchy and indeed for the progress of capitalism, not by the restoration of Charles II in 1660 but by the dethronement of his brother in 1688. Amongst other things, the Glorious Revolution made possible, and the subsequent French wars made necessary, that financial revolution which was to help to lay the basis of the economic achievements of the Georgian age and to mark the beginnings of the modern world.

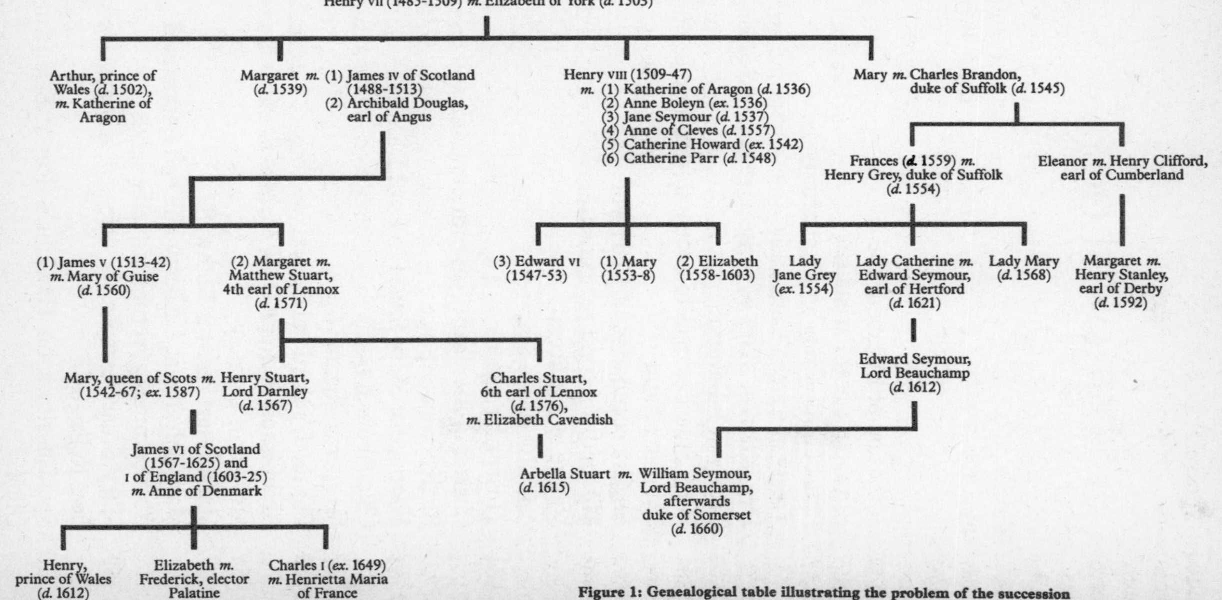

Figure 1: Genealogical table illustrating the problem of the succession

CHRONOLOGY

1558	Accession of Elizabeth I
1559	Elizabeth's first Parliament
	Acts of Supremacy and Uniformity
	Treaty of Cateau-Cambrésis
	Deposition of Mary of Guise as regent of Scotland
1560	Treaty of Edinburgh
1561	Mary Stuart returns to Scotland from France
	Coinage reform
1562	English occupation of Le Havre
1563	Elizabeth's second parliament
	Statute of Artificers
	Anti-Enclosure Statute
1564	Treaty of Troyes
	Charter of Merchant Adventurers Company
	Birth of Shakespeare
1565	Marriage of Mary Stuart to Lord Darnley
	Chaseabout Raid
	Murder of Rizzio
1566	Elizabeth's third parliament
	Archbishop Parker's *Book of Advertisements* issued
1567	Murder of Darnley
	Mary Stuart marries Bothwell
	Mary defeated at Carberry Hill and imprisoned
	Alva becomes governor of Netherlands
1568	Mary Stuart escapes, is defeated at Langside and flees to England
	Spanish attack on Hawkins's fleet at San Juan de Ulloa

1569 Revolt of the northern earls
1570 Excommunication of Elizabeth I
1571 Elizabeth's fourth parliament
Statute effectively allowing interest at maximum of ten per cent
Ridolfi Plot discovered
1572 Revolt of Netherlands begins
Treaty of Blois
Elizabeth's fifth parliament
First Puritan Admonition to Parliament
Second Puritan Admonition to Parliament
Statute for punishment of vagrants and relief of poor
Execution of duke of Norfolk
Massacre of St Bartholomew's Day in Paris
Lord Burghley becomes lord treasurer
1573 Capture of Edinburgh Castle by English
Requesens succeeds Alva as governor of Netherlands
1574 Death of Charles IX of France and accession of Henry III
1575 Elizabeth I closes English harbours to Dutch rebels
Grindal succeeds Parker as Primate
1576 Elizabeth's sixth parliament
Statute for setting poor on work
Death of Requesens
Don John of Austria becomes governor of Netherlands
'Spanish Fury' in Antwerp
1577 Suspension of Archbishop Grindal
Perpetual Edict
Spanish Company founded
Drake sets out on voyage of circumnavigation
1578 Parma defeats Dutch rebels at Gembloux
Fall of Regent Morton
Death of Don John
Parma becomes governor of Netherlands
1579 Eastland Company founded

1580 Drake's circumnavigation completed
Philip II succeeds to throne of Portugal
1581 Levant Company founded
Elizabeth's seventh parliament
1582 Ruthven Raid
1583 Whitgift becomes Primate
1584 Assassination of William the Silent
Elizabeth's eighth parliament meets
'The Bill and the Book' introduced
Treaty of Joinville
1585 End of Elizabeth's eighth parliament
Roanoke colony established
Treaty of Nonsuch
Leicester's army departs for Netherlands
1586 Battle of Zutphen: death of Sir Philip Sidney
Roanoke colonists repatriated
Cavendish's circumnavigation voyage begins
Treaty of Berwick
Babington Plot
Elizabeth's ninth parliament meets
1587 'The Bill and the Book' again
Elizabeth's ninth parliament ends
Execution of Mary Stuart
Raleigh's second Roanoke colony established
Drake raids Cadiz
1588 Cavendish's circumnavigation completed
Defeat of Spanish Armada
1589 Elizabeth's tenth parliament
Sack of Corunna
Assassination of Henry III and accession of Henry IV
1591 Spanish naval victory at Flores
1593 Elizabeth's eleventh parliament
Anti-enclosure legislation repealed
Statutes against Catholic recusants and Protestant sectaries
1595 Last expedition of Drake and Hawkins
1596 Spaniards take Calais
English sack Cadiz

1597 Elizabeth's twelfth parliament meets
Statutes against enclosure and depopulation
Statutes for relief of poor and punishment of vagrants
Islands Voyage
1598 Elizabeth's twelfth parliament ends
Victory of Irish rebels on the Blackwater
Death of Lord Burghley: Lord Buckhurst becomes lord treasurer
1599 Essex assumes command in Ireland, makes peace with Tyrone and returns to England
East India Company founded
1600 Queen refuses to renew Essex's patents
1601 Revolt and execution of earl of Essex
Elizabeth's last parliament
Statute consolidating Elizabethan poor law
Debate on monopolies
1603 Death of Elizabeth I and accession of James I
Millenary Petition
Bye and Main plots
1604 Hampton Court Conference
Bancroft succeeds Whitgift as Primate
James's first parliament meets
Free Trade debate
New canons for church issued
Treaty of London makes peace with Spain
1605 Gunpowder Plot
1606 Oath of Allegiance introduced
First Charter of Virginia Company
Bate's Case in the Court of Exchequer
Second session of James's first parliament
1607 Settlers land in Virginia
1608 Death of Dorset (Buckhurst): Salisbury becomes lord treasurer
1609 Twelve Years Truce between Spain and Dutch
New charter of Virginia Company
French Company founded
Jülich-Cleves succession crisis

1610 Third session of James's first parliament
Debate on Impositions
Failure of Great Contract
Plantation of Ulster begins
Assassination of Henry IV and accession of Louis XIII
1611 Dissolution of James's first parliament
Abbot succeeds Bancroft as Primate
1612 Death of Salisbury: Treasury put in commission
1613 Marriage of Princess Elizabeth to Elector Palatine
Essex divorce and Overbury murder
1614 Addled Parliament
Alderman Cockayne's Project
Suffolk becomes lord treasurer
1615 Fall of Somerset and rise of Villiers
Death of Shakespeare
1616 Raleigh released from Tower
Dismissal of Lord Chief Justice Coke
1617 King visits Scotland
Raleigh's last voyage
1618 Suffolk dismissed as lord treasurer: Treasury in commission
Execution of Raleigh
1619 Elector Palatine accepts crown of Bohemia
1620 Invasion of Palatinate
Battle of White Mountain: Elector driven from Bohemia
Voyage of *Mayflower* to New England
Mandeville becomes lord treasurer
1621 James's third parliament meets
Attack on monopolies and chartered companies
Impeachment of Mompesson and Bacon
Cranfield becomes lord treasurer
1623 Prince Charles and Buckingham visit Spain
Massacre of Amboina
1624 James's last parliament
Dissolution of marriage treaty with Spain

1624 (cont)	Impeachment and fall of Middlesex (Cranfield)
	Statute of Monopolies
	Dissolution of Virginia Company
1625	Death of James I and accession of Charles I
	Charles I marries Henrietta Maria
	Charles's first parliament
	Parliament attacks Buckingham and fails to grant tonnage and poundage
	War with Spain: unsuccessful attack on Cadiz
	Act of Revocation in Scotland
	Treaty of The Hague
1626	Charles's second parliament
	Impeachment of Buckingham
	Christian IV defeated at Lutter
1627	Buckingham's expedition to Isle of Rhé
	Case of the Five Knights
1628	First session of Charles's third parliament
	Petition of Right
	Assassination of Buckingham
	Weston succeeds Marlborough as lord treasurer
	Massachusetts Bay Company founded
1629	Dissolution of Charles's third parliament
	Treaty of Susa ends war with France
1630	Peace concluded with Spain
1632	Wentworth appointed lord deputy of Ireland
	Battle of Lützen: death of Gustavus Adolphus
	Death of Sir John Eliot in Tower
1633	King visits Scotland
	Laud succeeds Abbot as Primate
	Founding of Maryland
1634	First ship money writ issued
1635	Death of Lord Treasurer Portland (Weston): Treasury in commission
	Second ship money writ issued
1637	Prynne, Burton and Bastwick punished
	Hampden's case in Exchequer Chamber
1638	Londonderry forfeited by City of London
	Scottish National Covenant

1639 First Bishops' War
Treaty of Berwick
1640 Short Parliament
Convocation issues new canons
Second Bishops' War
Treaty of Ripon
Long Parliament opens
Root and Branch Petition
1641 Triennial Act
Act 'for a perpetual parliament'
Execution of Strafford
Ten Propositions
King visits Scotland
Second session of Long Parliament begins
Revolt in Ireland
Grand Remonstrance
1642 Attempted arrest of five members
Militia Ordinance and Commissions of Array
Nineteen Propositions
Civil War breaks out
Battle of Edgehill
Royalists fail to take London
1643 Treaty of Oxford
Royalist victories at Stratton, Adwalton Moor, Lansdowne and Roundway Down
Bristol falls to royalists
Solemn League and Covenant
First battle of Newbury
Death of Pym
1644 Royalists defeated at Marston Moor
Montrose's victories at Tippermuir and Aberdeen
Parliamentary army surrenders at Lostwithiel
Second battle of Newbury
Milton publishes *Areopagitica*
1645 Presbyterian Directory of Worship established
Execution of Archbishop Laud
Treaty of Uxbridge

1645 (cont) Montrose's victories at Inverlochy, Auldearn and Alford
New Model Ordinance
Self-Denying Ordinance
Royalists defeated at Naseby, Langport and Rowton Heath
Montrose defeated at Philiphaugh

1646 King gives himself up to Scots
End of First Civil War
Newcastle Propositions

1647 Scots hand over king and leave England
Parliamentary declaration against army
Army seize king at Holdenby
Solemn Engagement of the Army
Army impeach eleven members
Counter-revolutionary disturbances in London
Heads of the Proposals
Agreement of the People
Debates in Council of Army at Putney
King absconds to Isle of Wight
Four Bills presented to king
Royal Engagement with Scots

1648 Vote of No Addresses
Second Civil War
Treaty of Newport
Remonstrance of Army
Pride's Purge
Peace of Westphalia: end of Thirty Years' War

1649 Second Agreement of the People rejected by Rump
Execution of king and establishment of Commonwealth
Levellers crushed at Burford
Cromwell leads expedition to Ireland, storms Drogheda and Wexford
Milton publishes *Of the Tenure of Kings and Magistrates*

1650 Montrose executed
Battle of Dunbar

1650 (cont) Legislation against adultery and other forms of personal immorality
Committees for Propagation of Gospel in Wales and elsewhere established

1651 St John's and Strickland's embassy to The Hague
Battle of Worcester
Navigation Ordinance
Hale Commission established

1652 First Dutch War begins
Battle of Dungeness

1653 Battle of Portland
Dissolution of the Rump
Barebone's Assembly
Battle of the Texel
Instrument of Government and establishment of Protectorate

1654 End of First Dutch War
Treaties with Portugal, Denmark and Sweden
First Protectorate parliament
Union of England and Scotland
Expedition to West Indies

1655 First Protectorate parliament dissolved
War with Spain
Penruddock's Revolt
Major-generals' regime established
Conquest of Jamaica

1656 Naval operations against Spain
End of Major-generals' regime
Second Protectorate parliament meets
James Nayler's case

1657 Humble Petition and Advice
Anglo-French alliance
New charter for East India Company

1658 Second session and dissolution of second Protectorate parliament
Battle of the Dunes
Death of Oliver: Richard becomes Protector

1659 Third Protectorate parliament
Restoration of the Rump and end of the Protectorate
Booth's Revolt
Derby petition
Dissolution and recall of the Rump

1660 Monck restores secluded members of Long Parliament
Dissolution of Long Parliament
Convention parliament meets
Declaration of Breda
Restoration of Charles II

FURTHER READING

The number of books and articles on the period covered by this volume is enormous, and this makes it impossible to do more than to suggest a few of the more important titles. The student should consult the sections relating to the period in G. R. Elton (ed.), *Modern Historians on British History, 1485–1945* (1970). An extremely useful general political history which covers the whole of the period and more is C. Russell, *The Crisis of Parliaments: English History 1509–1660* (1971). Good general studies of the Tudor period offering contrasting approaches are G. R. Elton, *England under the Tudors* (2nd edn 1974), and P. Williams, *The Tudor Regime* (Oxford 1979, pb. 1981). A good brief study of Elizabeth's reign is J. Hurstfield, *Elizabeth I and the Unity of England* (1960). More detailed are W. T. MacCaffrey, *The Shaping of the Elizabethan Regime* (1969) and *Queen Elizabeth and the Making of Policy* (Princeton, NJ, 1981). The seventeenth century is not so well served in general studies, but contrasted approaches are provided in two textbooks: C. Hill, *The Century of Revolution* (1961) and G. E. Aylmer, *The Struggle for the Constitution* (2nd edn 1968).

Much of the most interesting work on the period is being done in the sphere of local and regional history. Good examples are A. Hassell Smith, *County and Court: Government and Politics in Norfolk 1558–1603* (Oxford 1974): W. T. MacCaffrey, *Exeter 1540–1640* (1958 and 1975 pb.); M. James, *Family, Lineage and Civil Society. A Study of Society, Politics and Mentality in the Durham Region 1500–1640* (Oxford 1974); A. Fletcher, *A County Community in Peace and War: Sussex 1600–1660* (1975); S. J. Watts, *From Border to Middle Shire: Northumberland 1586–1625* (Leicester 1975). Of shorter coverage, but historiographically important as the beginning of this modern school of county history, is A. Everitt, *The Community of Kent and the Great Rebellion 1640–60* (Leicester 1966) and *The Local Community and the Great Rebellion* (Hist. Ass. pamphlet 1969).

The Macmillan *Problems in Focus* series contains useful collections of essays by a variety of scholars. Volumes covering this period are A. G. R. Smith (ed.), *The Reign of James VI and I* (1973); C. Russell (ed.), *The Origins of the English Civil War* (1980 edn); J. S. Morrill (ed.), *Reactions to the Civil War* (1982) and G. E. Aylmer (ed.), *The Interregnum: The Quest for Settlement 1646–1660* (1972). To some extent the Elizabethan gap is filled by two Festschriften for distinguished Elizabethan scholars, J. E. Neale and J. Hurstfield: the first is S. T. Bindoff, J. Hurstfield and C. H. Williams (eds), *Elizabethan Government and Society* (1961); and the second, P. Clark, A. G. R. Smith and N. Tyacke (eds), *The English Commonwealth 1547–1640* (Leicester 1979).

Biographies abound, and here it is possible only to mention the best of those of the heads of state. The classic biography of Elizabeth I is J. E. Neale, *Queen Elizabeth I* (repr. 1971); for her successors see D. H. Willson, *King James VI and I* (1962 edn), P. Gregg, *King Charles I* (1981) and C. Carlton, *Charles I. The Personal Monarch* (1983). There is a host of biographies of Oliver Cromwell, of which one of the most interesting is C. Hill, *God's Englishman: Oliver Cromwell and the English Revolution* (1970). Important political biographies are the studies of Burghley and Walsingham by Conyers Read: *Mr. Secretary Cecil and Queen Elizabeth* (pb. 1965); *Lord Burghley and Queen Elizabeth* (pb. 1965); and *Mr. Secretary Walsingham and the Policy of Queen Elizabeth* (3 vols, Oxford 1925). Outstanding Stuart political biographies are R. Lockyer, *Buckingham* (1981), and Linda Levy Peck, *Northampton: Patronage and Policy at the Court of James I* (1982).

The best short account of the economic history of this and the preceding and succeeding periods is D. C. Coleman, *The Economy of England 1450–1750* (OUP Opus ser. no. 81, 1977). For detailed reading on economic history see the bibliography in Coleman's book. Also useful is B. A. Holderness, *Pre-Industrial England. Economy and Society 1500–1750* (1976). Useful collections of essays are the Festschriften written for two of the outstanding economic historians of the period, R. H. Tawney and F. J. Fisher: respectively F. J. Fisher (ed), *Essays in the Economic and Social History of Tudor and Stuart England* (Cambridge 1961), and D. C. Coleman and A. H. John (eds), *Trade, Government and Economy in Pre-Industrial England* (1976). On agriculture and farming regions see J. Thirsk (ed.), *The Agrarian History of England and Wales*, iv, *1500–1640* (Cambridge 1967). On industry in general, D. C. Coleman, *Industry in Tudor and Stuart England* (Economic History Society, Studies in Economic and Social History, 1975), and on overseas trade R. Davis, *English Overseas Trade 1500–1700* (1973). A useful survey of urban history is P. Clark and P. Slack, *English Towns in Transition* (OUP Opus ser. no. 78, 1976) and the volume of essays edited by Clark and Slack, *Crisis and Order in English Towns 1500–1700* (1972). On inflation see R. B. Outhwaite, *Inflation in Tudor and Early Stuart England* (Studies in Economic History, 1969) and P. H. Ramsey (ed.), *The Price Revolution in Sixteenth Century England* (1971). Much of the most significant work on this branch of history, and indeed on others too, is to be found in articles in learned journals, some of the most important of which are cited in the footnotes.

On the area where government finance, politics and business meet, see F. C. Dietz, *English Public Finance 1558–1641* (2nd edn. 1964), an indigestible and rather inchoate study, but the only full treatment of the problem; R. H. Tawney (ed.), *A Discourse upon Usury (1572) by Thomas Wilson* (1962 ed.) with a long and valuable historical introduction by the author; R. de Roover, *Gresham on*

Foreign Exchange (1949); L. Stone, *An Elizabethan: Sir Horatio Palavicino* (Oxford 1956); R. H. Tawney, *Business and Politics under James I* (Cambridge 1958); M. Prestwich, *Cranfield, Politics and Profits under the Early Stuarts* (Oxford 1966); A. F. Upton, *Sir Arthur Ingram c. 1565–1642* (1961); R. Ashton, *The Crown and the Money Market 1603–1640* (Oxford 1960) and his *The City and the Court 1603–1643* (Cambridge 1979).

The most important source of information on the nobility and social stratification and order is L. Stone, *The Crisis of Aristocracy 1558–1641* (Oxford 1965). For long review articles by D. C. Coleman and R. Ashton dealing with this important book see *History* L (1966), and *Econ. Hist. Rev.* 2nd ser. xxii (1969). For the gentry controversy, see R. H. Tawney, 'The Rise of the Gentry 1560–1640', in *Econ. Hist. Rev.* xi (1941); H. R. Trevor-Roper, *The Gentry 1540–1640* (*Econ. Hist. Rev.* supplement no. 1, no date) and J. H. Hexter, 'Storm over the Gentry' in his *Reappraisals in History* (1963 edn), pp. 117–62.

On paternalism and patriarchalism and social order see G. J. Schochet, *Patriarchalism in Political Thought* (Oxford 1975) and P. Laslett, *The World We Have Lost* (2nd edn 1971), a stimulating book, some of whose conclusions, however, should be treated with caution. On kingship and the constitution, order and resistance see the collection of documents and editorial introductions in G. R. Elton (ed.), *The Tudor Constitution* (Cambridge 1975 edn); C. Morris, *Political Thought in England from Tyndale to Hooker* (1953); W. H. Greenleaf, *Order, Empiricism and Politics 1500–1700* (1964); and M. A. Judson, *The Crisis of the Constitution* (New York 1971 edn). On revolts see A. Fletcher, *Tudor Rebellions* (pb. 2nd edn. 1973), and B. Sharp, *In Contempt of All Authority* (1980). On the Civil War itself, only a tiny selection from the enormous volume of books can be given here. Among studies displaying a variety of different approaches are L. Stone, *The Causes of the English Revolution, 1529–1642* (1972); I. Roots, *The Great Rebellion 1642–1660* (1972 edn.), A. Fletcher, *The Outbreak of the English Civil*

War (1981); R. H. Parry (ed.), *The English Civil War and After, 1642–1658* (1970); B. Manning, *The English People and the English Revolution* (pb. 1978); R. Ashton, *The English Civil War: Conservatism and Revolution 1603–1649* (1979 edn.); and D. Underdown, *Pride's Purge* (Oxford 1971).

On government, patronage and office-holding, see A. G. R. Smith, *The Government of Elizabethan England* (1967); J. E. Neale, 'The Elizabethan Political Scene', in his *The Age of Catherine de Medici* (1963 edn.); G. E. Aylmer, *The King's Servants. The Civil Service of Charles I, 1625–1642* (1961) and *The State's Servants. The Civil Service of the English Republic, 1649–1660* (1973). On the economic condition of the church and the status of churchmen see C. Hill, *Economic Problems of the Church from Archbishop Whitgift to the Long Parliament* (Oxford 1956).

On the religious settlement see Claire Cross (ed.), *The Royal Supremacy in the Elizabethan Church* (1969) and N. L. Jones, *Faith by Statute: Parliament and the Settlement of Religion, 1559* (1982). The best studies of Puritanism and the Church are P. Collinson, *The Elizabethan Puritan Movement* (1967), *Archbishop Grindal 1519–1583* (1979); P. Lake, *Moderate Puritans and the Elizabethan Church* (Cambridge 1982); H. R. Trevor-Roper, *Archbishop Laud 1573–1645* (1963 edn.); C. Hill, *Society and Puritanism in Pre-Revolutionary England* (1964); and W. Haller, *Liberty and Reformation in the Puritan Revolution* (pb. New York 1963). W. M. Lamont, *Godly Rule* (1969 pb.) is also very important. On the Catholics, see J. Bossy, *The English Catholic Community, 1570–1850* (repr. 1976).

On parliamentary history and politics especially see J. E. Neale's trilogy, *The Elizabethan House of Commons* (1961 edn), *Elizabeth I and Her Parliaments 1559–1581* (3rd impression 1958) and *Elizabeth I and Her Parliaments 1584–1601* (1957); K. Sharpe (ed.), *Faction and Parliament. Essays on Early Stuart History* (Oxford 1978); W. Notestein, *The House of Commons 1604–1610* (New Haven 1971); T. L. Moir, *The Addled Parliament of 1614* (Oxford 1958); C.

Russell, *Parliaments and English Politics 1621–1629* (Oxford 1979); D. Brunton and D. H. Pennington, *Members of the Long Parliament* (1954); J. H. Hexter, *The Reign of King Pym* (New Haven 1941); B. Worden, *The Rump Parliament* (Cambridge 1974); A. Woolrych, *From Commonwealth to Protectorate* (1982). On parliamentary constituencies and the electorate see D. Hirst, *The Representative of the People? Voters and Voting under the Early Stuarts* (Cambridge 1975).

On foreign affairs, see R. B. Wernham, *Before the Armada. The Growth of English Foreign Policy 1485–1588* (1966); C. Wilson, *Queen Elizabeth and the Revolt of the Netherlands* (1970); J. R. Jones, *Britain and Europe in the Seventeenth Century* (1966); G. M. D. Howat, *Stuart and Cromwellian Foreign Policy* (pb. 1974). On colonial and transoceanic enterprise, A. L. Rowse, *The Expansion of Elizabethan England* (1955); K. R. Andrews, *Elizabethan Privateering* (Cambridge 1964) and *Drake's Voyages* (1970); D. B. Quinn, *Raleigh and the British Empire* (1947); T. K. Rabb, *Enterprise and Empire* (Cambridge, Mass., 1967); C. Bridenbaugh, *Vexed and Troubled Englishmen 1590–1642* (Oxford 1968).

On the armed forces see L. Boynton, *The Elizabethan Militia 1558–1638* (1967); C. G. Cruickshank, *Elizabeth's Army* (2nd edn 1966); C. H. Firth, *Cromwell's Army* (pb. 1962); M. A. Kishlansky, *The Rise of the New Model Army* (Cambridge 1979); R. Hutton, *The Royalist War Effort* (1981); A. Woolrych, *Battles of the English Civil War* (pb. 1966); P. M. Kennedy, *The Rise and Fall of English Naval Mastery* (1976); G. Mattingly, *The Defeat of the Spanish Armada* (1959 edn); M. Lewis, *The Spanish Armada* (pb. 1960).

On education see Joan Simon, *Education and Society in Tudor England* (Cambridge 1966); W. A. L. Vincent, *The State and School Education in England and Wales 1640–60* (1949); M. Curtis, *Oxford and Cambridge in Transition 1558–1642* (Oxford 1959); H. Kearney, *Scholars and Gentlemen: Universities and Society in Pre-Industrial Britain 1500–1700* (1970); and W. R. Prest, *The Inns of Court under Elizabeth I and the Early Stuarts 1590–1640* (1972).

No other period of English cultural history saw such stupendous achievements as those of the period of Shakespeare and Milton, William Byrd and Inigo Jones. Among the many works on aspects of cultural history are Julia Briggs, *This Stage-Play World: English Literature and its Background 1580–1625* (Oxford, Opus ser. 1983); J. F. Danby, *Elizabethan and Jacobean Poets* (pb. 1965) and J. Buxton, *Sir Philip Sidney and the English Renaissance* (pb. 1965). On the theatre, E. M. W. Tillyard, *Shakespeare's History Plays* (pb. 1962) and (of much wider interest) his *The Elizabethan World Picture* (pb. 1963); L. C. Knights, *Drama and Society in the Age of Jonson* (1957 edn); A. Harbage, *Shakespeare's Audience* (New York 1961 edn), *Shakespeare and the Rival Traditions* (1968 edn), and *Cavalier Drama* (New York 1964); for a different view see A. J. Cook, *The Privileged Playgoers of Shakespeare's London* (Princeton 1981) and M. Heinemann, *Puritanism and Theatre* (Cambridge 1980). Also on theatre see M. C. Bradbrook, *Elizabethan Stage Conditions* (pb. Cambridge 1968). On music, see W. L. Woodfill, *Musicians in English Society from Elizabeth I to Charles I* (Princeton 1953). On art history in general the reader will find parts of vols vii and viii in the Oxford History of English Art useful, viz. E. Mercer (ed.), *English Art 1553–1625* (Oxford 1962), and M. D. Whinney and O. Millar (eds), *English Art 1625–1714* (Oxford 1957); likewise parts of two volumes in the Pelican History of Art, E. K. Waterhouse, *Painting in Britain 1530–1790* (1953) and J. Summerson, *Architecture in Britain 1530–1830* (pb. Harmondsworth 1970), and his *Inigo Jones* (pb. Harmondsworth 1966). Finally on the culture of the Stuart court, see G. Parry, *The Golden Age Restor'd; the Culture of the Stuart Court 1603–42* (Manchester 1981); S. Orgel, *The Jonsonian Masque* (New York 1981 edn); P. Palme, *The Triumph of Peace* (1957); and J. Harris, S. Orgel and R. Strong (eds), *The King's Arcadia: Inigo Jones and the Stuart Court* (1973) and O. Millar (ed.), *The Age of Charles I* (1970) and *Van Dyck in England* (1983). The last three of these are admirable catalogues to exhibitions mounted in London.

NOTES

The following abbreviations are used in the notes:

Agric. Hist. Rev. — *Agricultural History Review*
Amer. Hist. Rev. — *American Historical Review*
BIHR — *Bulletin of the Institute of Historical Research*
Econ. Hist. Rev. — *Economic History Review*
Eng. Hist. Rev. — *English Historical Review*
HJ — *Historical Journal*
JBS — *Journal of British Studies*
JMH — *Journal of Modern History*
TLS — *Times Literary Supplement*
TRHS — *Transactions of the Royal Historical Society*

CHAPTER ONE

1 On geography and farming regions, see J. Thirsk (ed.), *The Agrarian History of England and Wales*, iv, *1500–1640* (Cambridge 1967), 1–199
2 H. R. Trevor-Roper, *Religion, the Reformation and Social Change* (1967) 90–192
3 K. Thomas, *Religion and the Decline of Magic* (1971), 435–583; A. Macfarlane, *Witchcraft in Tudor and Stuart England* (1970).
4 See J. Thirsk, 'Industries in the Countryside', in F. J. Fisher (ed.), *Essays in the Economic and Social History of Tudor and Stuart England* (Cambridge 1961), 70–88: also her *Economic Policy and Projects* (Oxford 1978).
5 See F. J. Fisher, 'The Development of the London Food Market, 1540–1640', *Econ.Hist.Rev.* v. (1935), 46–64; A.

Everitt, 'The Development of Private Marketing', in J. Thirsk (ed.), *The Agrarian History of England and Wales*, iv, *1500–1640* (Cambridge 1967), 466–592.

6 E. Hamilton, 'American Treasure and the Rise of Capitalism, 1500–1700', *Economica* ix (1929), 338–57.

7 J. U. Nef, 'Prices and Industrial Capitalism in France and England, 1540–1640', *Econ.Hist.Rev.* vii (1937), 155–85.

8 See D. C. Coleman, 'Labour in the English Economy of the Seventeenth Century', *Econ.Hist.Rev.* 2nd ser. viii (1956), 280–95.

9 On philanthropic benefactions, see W. K. Jordan, *Philanthropy in England 1480–1660* (1959).

10 Very approximate figures based on the tentative and much criticized figures of Professor J. C. Russell. See G. S. C. Tucker, 'English Pre-Industrial Population Trends', *Econ. Hist.Rev.* 2nd ser. xvi (1963), 210–11. On London's population see R. Finlay, *Population and Metropolis: The Demography of London 1580–1650* (Cambridge 1981).

11 On Worcester, see A. D. Dyer, *The City of Worcester in the Sixteenth Century* (Leicester 1973).

12 F. J. Fisher, 'The Growth of London as a Centre of Conspicuous Consumption in the Sixteenth and Seventeenth Centuries', *TRHS* 4th ser. xxx (1948), 37–50.

13 See W. R. Prest, *The Inns of Court under Elizabeth I and the Early Stuarts 1590–1640* (1972).

14 On Exeter, see the essay by W. G. Hoskins in S. T. Bindoff, J. Hurstfield and C. H. Williams (eds), *Elizabethan Government and Society* (1961), 163–87; also W. T. MacCaffrey, *Exeter 1540–1640* (1975). On Leicester, the essay by Hoskins in J. H. Plumb (ed.), *Studies in Social History* (1955), 32–67.

15 L. Stone, 'Social Mobility in England, 1500–1700', *Past & Present* 33 (1966), 31–2.

16 E. A. Wrigley, 'A Simple Model of London's Importance in Changing English Society and Economy, 1650–1750', *Past & Present* 37 (1967), 44–70.

CHAPTER TWO

1 R. Mousnier, *Social Hierarchies* (1973), 23.

2 [Charles Hotham], 'A true stating the case of a Negative

Voice', British Library, Harleian MSS 7032, fo. 234. I owe this reference to the kindness of Mr Victor Morgan.

3 D. L. Keir, *The Constitutional History of Modern Britain 1485–1937* (4th edn 1950), 117.

4 See R. W. K. Hinton, 'English Constitutional Theories from Sir John Fortescue to Sir John Eliot', and C. C. Weston 'The Theory of Mixed Monarchy under Charles I and After', *Eng.Hist.Rev.* lxxv (1960), 410–43.

5 On the phenomenon of revolt, see R. Mousnier, *Peasant Uprisings in Seventeenth Century France, Russia and China* (1971); M. E. Jones, 'Obedience and Dissent in Henrician England in the Lincolnshire Rebellion 1536', *Past & Present* 48 (1970), 3–78, and 'The Concept of Order and the Northern Rising of 1569', ibid. 60 (1973), 122–34; C. S. L. Davies, 'Peasant Revolt in France and England: A Comparison', *Agric.Hist.Rev.* xxi (1973), 122–34; A. Fletcher, *Tudor Rebellions* (1977).

6 L. Stone, *The Crisis of the Aristocracy 1558–1641* (Oxford 1965). On the inflation of honours, see ch.3.

7 N.B. Harte, 'State Control of Dress and Social Change in Pre-Industrial England', in D. C. Coleman and A. H. John (eds), *Trade, Government and Economy in Pre-Industrial England* (1976), 132–65.

8 C. Hill, *Economic Problems of the Church from Archbishop Whitgift to the Long Parliament* (Oxford 1956), 176–82.

9 R. C. Richardson, *Puritanism in north-west England* (Manchester 1972), 165 and note.

10 G. E. Aylmer, *The King's Servants: the Civil Service of Charles I 1625–1642* (1961).

11 See I. Green, 'Career Prospects and Clerical Conformity in the Early Stuart Church', *Past & Present* 90 (1981), 71–115; also R. O'Day, *The English Clergy: the Emergence and Consolidation of a Profession, 1558–1642* (Leicester 1979). For the more traditional view, see C. Hill, *Economic Problems of the Church*, esp. 199–223; also M. H. Curtis, 'The Alienated Intellectuals of Early Stuart England', *Past & Present* 23 (1962), 25–43.

12 Cited Stone, *The Crisis of the Aristocracy 1558–1641*, 336.

13 See his classic essay 'The Elizabethan Political Scene' in J. E. Neale, *The Age of Catherine de Medici* (1963), 145–70.

14 On patronage and office, see A. G. R. Smith, *The Government of Elizabethan England* (1967), esp. 57–69; and G. E. Aylmer, *The*

King's Servants: the Civil Service of Charles I 1625–1642 (1961), esp. 69–96, and *The State's Servants: the Civil Service of the English Republic 1649–1660* (1973), esp. 58–69.

15 See J. E. Neale, *The Elizabethan House of Commons* (1950), esp. 140–245; V. A. Rowe, 'The Influence of the Earls of Pembroke on Parliamentary Elections, 1625–41', *Eng.Hist.Rev.* l (1935), 242–56; L. Stone, 'The Electoral Influence of the Second Earl of Salisbury, 1614–68', ibid. lxxi (1956), 384–400.

16 Hill, op.cit., 63–5, 211–15, 219–21.

17 R. O'Day, 'The ecclesiastical patronage of the Lord Keeper 1558–1642', *TRHS* 5th ser. xxiii (1973), 89–109.

18 P. Collinson, *The Elizabethan Puritan Movement* (1967).

19 Cited E. Rosenberg, *Leicester, Patron of Letters* (1955), 200.

CHAPTER THREE

1 R. B. Wernham, *Before the Armada* (1966), 237.

2 J. E. Neale, 'The Elizabethan Acts of Supremacy and Uniformity', *Eng.Hist.Rev.* lxv (1950), 304–32; *Elizabeth I and Her Parliaments 1559–1581* (1953), 51–84.

3 N. L. Jones, 'Profiting from Religious Reform: the Land Rush of 1559', *HJ* xxii (1979), 279–94. Dr Jones's important study *Faith by Statute: Parliament and the Settlement of Religion, 1559* (1982) unfortunately appeared too late for use to be made of it here. For a good brief summary of the historiography of the settlement, see P. Collinson, *Archbishop Grindal 1519–1583* (1979), 85–8.

4 See W. T. MacCaffrey, *The Shaping of the Elizabethan Regime* (1969), esp. 105–25.

5 The most thorough account of these developments is G. D. Ramsay, *The City of London in International Politics at the Accession of Elizabeth Tudor* (Manchester 1975).

6 On inflation, see R. B. Outhwaite, *Inflation in Tudor and Early Stuart England (Studies in Economic History,* 1969); P. H. Ramsey (ed.), *The Price Revolution in Sixteenth-Century England* (1971).

7 Table constructed from statistical appendix by P. J. Bowden, in J. Thirsk (ed.), *The Agrarian History of England and Wales,* iv, *1500–1640*, 862. For a summary of the statistical snags relating to these figures, see ibid. 868–70.

8 J. Cornwall, 'English Population in the Early Sixteenth Century', *Econ.Hist.Rev.* 2nd ser. xxiii (1970), 32–44.

9 See his essay in Ramsey (ed.), *The Price Revolution*, 117–46; and his *The Tudor Coinage* (Manchester 1978).
10 See R. B. Outhwaite, 'The Trials of Foreign Borrowing: the English Crown and the Antwerp Money Market in the Mid-Sixteenth Century', *Econ.Hist.Rev.* 2nd ser. xix (1966), 289–305, esp. 290, 296–7.
11 E. Kerridge, 'The Movement of Rent, 1540–1640', *Econ. Hist.Rev.* 2nd ser. vi (1953), 16–34.
12 On this see K. R. Andrews, *Elizabethan Privateering* (Cambridge 1944).
13 F. J. Fisher, 'Commercial Trends and Policy in Sixteenth-Century England', *Econ.Hist.Rev.* x (1940), 95–117.
14 L. Stone, 'State Control in Sixteenth-Century England', *Econ.Hist.Rev.* xvii (1947), 103–20; J. D. Gould, *The Great Debasement* (Oxford 1970), 114–60.
15 This can be read in R. H. Tawney and E. Power (eds), *Tudor Economic Documents* (1924), ii, 45–7.
16 J. Thirsk, *Economic Policy and Projects* (Oxford 1978).
17 See his essay in S. T. Bindoff, J. Hurstfield and C. H. Williams (eds), *Elizabethan Government and Society* (1961), 56–94.

CHAPTER FOUR

1 See R. B. Wernham, *Before the Armada: the Growth of English Foreign Policy 1485–1588* (1966); also his essay in S. T. Bindoff, J. Hurstfield and C.H. Williams (eds), *Elizabethan Government and Society* (1961), 340–68.
2 For an admirable recent account of the Anjou match see W. T. MacCaffrey, 'The Anjou Match and the Making of Elizabethan Foreign Policy' in P. Clark, A. G. R. Smith and N. Tyacke (eds), *The English Commonwealth 1547–1640* (Leicester 1979), 59–75.
3 See A. Hassell Smith, 'Militia Rates and Militia Statutes 1558–1663', in P. Clark, A. G. R. Smith and N. Tyacke (eds), *The English Commonwealth 1547–1640* (Leicester 1979), 93–110.
4 See L. Boynton, *The Elizabethan Militia 1558–1638* (1967), 91; C. G. Cruickshank, *Elizabeth's Army* (2nd edn 1966), 25.
5 M. Lewis, *The Spanish Armada* (1960), *Armada Guns* (1963). For a concise criticism of this view see David Quinn, 'Spaniards at Sea', *TLS* 4107 (18 December 1981), 1473–4.

6 K. R. Andrews, *Elizabethan Privateering* (Cambridge 1964), 224–6.

CHAPTER FIVE

1 J. Bossy, 'The Character of Elizabethan Catholicism', *Past & Present* 21 (1962), 39–59.
2 On all this, see M. E. James, 'The Concept of Order and the Northern Rising of 1569', *Past & Present* 60 (1973), 49–83.
3 C. Haigh, 'From Monopoly to Minority: Catholicism in Early Modern England', *TRHS* 5th ser. xxxi (1981), 129–47.
4 On Grindal's fall see especially P. Collinson, 'The Downfall of Archbishop Grindal and its place in Elizabethan political and ecclesiastical history', in Clark, Smith and Tyacke (eds), op.cit., 39–57. On Grindal in general, see Collinson, *Archbishop Grindal 1519–1583* (1979).
5 For extensive details see P. Collinson, *The Elizabethan Puritan Movement* (1967), 280–1; C. Hill, *Economic Problems of the Church from Archbishop Whitgift to the Long Parliament* (1956), 206–7, *Society and Puritanism in Pre-Revolutionary England* (1964), 52–3, and 'Puritans and "the Dark Corners of the Land"', *TRHS* 5th ser. xiii (1963), 77–102.
6 J. E. Neale, *Elizabeth I and Her Parliaments 1584–1601* (1957), 292–3.
7 R. C. Richardson, *Puritanism in North-West England* (Manchester 1972), 18–19.
8 On modifications in the service by Puritan parsons, see P. Collinson, *The Elizabethan Puritan Movement*, 356–71.
9 See R. A. Marchant, *The Church under the Law* (Cambridge 1969), 4–5.
10 On royal landed revenues see F. C. Dietz, *English Public Finance 1558–1641* (2nd edn 1964), 291–304.
11 On Elizabethan customs yield and practices see Dietz, op.cit., 7, 44, 63, 305–28.
12 See J. D. Gould, 'The Crisis in the Export Trade, 1586–7', *Eng.Hist.Rev.* lxxi (1956), 212–22.

CHAPTER SIX

1 P. Clark, *English Provincial Society from the Reformation to the Revolution* (Hassocks 1977), 250. For the depression in Kent, see ibid., 221–6.

2 See A. B. Appleby, *Famine in Tudor and Stuart England* (Stanford 1978), esp. 109–21, 133–45; see also his 'Disease or Famine? Mortality in Cumberland and Westmorland 1580–1640', *Econ.Hist.Rev.* 2nd ser. xxvi (1973), esp. 414–24.

3 For an example see note p. 173, Chapter 5.

4 See the classic essay by J. E. Neale, 'The Elizabethan Political Scene' (Proceedings of the British Academy, 1948) reprinted in his *The Age of Catherine de Medici* (1963), 45–70.

5 J. Thirsk, *Economic Policy and Projects* (Oxford 1978), esp. 51–77.

6 On the Essexians, see L. Stone, *The Crisis of the Aristocracy 1558–1641*, 482–7.

7 P. Clark, *English Provincial Society*, 260–5; A. Hassell Smith, *County and Court*, 340–1: D. Mathew, *The Celtic Peoples and Renaissance Europe* (reprinted New York 1974), 336–444; H. A. Lloyd, *The Gentry of South-West Wales 1540–1640* (Cardiff 1968), 112–18; A. H. Dodd, *Studies in Stuart Wales* (Cardiff, 1971 edn.) 56–7, 81–2, 183–4, and 'North Wales in the Essex Revolt of 1601', *Eng.Hist.Rev.* lix (1944), 348–70.

8 See J. Hurstfield's essay in S. T. Bindoff, J. Hurstfield and C. H. Williams (eds), *Elizabethan Government and Society* (1961), 369–96; also A. Pritchard, *Catholic Loyalism in Elizabethan England* (1979).

9 On Greville, see R. A. Rebholz, *The Life of Fulke Greville, First Lord Brooke* (Oxford 1971), esp. 124–80. For a valuable and more favourably disposed account of Howard, published after this book had gone to press, see Linda Levy Peck, *Northampton: Patronage and Policy at the Court of James 1* (1982).

10 On the difficulties of expenditure reduction in the largest item on the ordinary account, see P. R. Seddon, 'Household Reforms in the Reign of James I', *BIHR* liii (1980), 44–55.

11 M. Prestwich, *Cranfield. Politics and Profits under the early Stuarts* (Oxford 1966), 22–4.

12 For further details, see R. Ashton, *The Crown and the Money Market 1603–1640* (Oxford 1960), 87–90, 106–7, 193; *The City and the Court, 1603–1643* (Cambridge 1979), 98–100; Linda Levy Peck, *Northampton*, 132–7.

13 See R. H. Tawney, *Business and Politics under James 1* (Cambridge 1958), 109–13.

14 For full details see R. Ashton, 'Deficit Finance in the Reign of James I', *Econ.Hist.Rev.* 2nd ser. x (1957), 15–29.

15 On the Contract, see A. G. R. Smith, 'Crown, Parliament and Finance: the Great Contract of 1610' in P. Clark, A. G. R. Smith and N. Tyacke (eds), *The English Commonwealth* (Leicester 1979), 111–27.

16 See D. Hirst, *The Representative of the People?* (Cambridge 1975).

17 On various forms of composition for purveyance, see G. E. Aylmer 'The Last Years of Purveyance, 1610–1660', *Econ. Hist.Rev.* 2nd ser. x (1957), 81–9.

18 J. Hurstfield (*The Queen's Wards* (1958), 323) argues in favour of this view.

19 See W. Notestein, *The Winning of the Initiative by the House of Commons* (Proceedings of the British Academy, 1925).

20 C. Russell, 'Parliamentary History in Perspective 1604–1629', *History* lvi (1976), 1–27. See also G. R. Elton, 'A High Road to Civil War', in C. H. Carter (ed.), *From the Renaissance to the Counter-Reformation* (1966), 325–47.

21 R. C. Munden, 'The defeat of Sir John Fortescue: Court versus Country at the Hustings', *Eng.Hist.Rev.* xciii (1978), 811–16; see also his essay in K. Sharpe (ed.), *Faction and Parliament* (Oxford 1978), esp. 53–6.

22 There is a good short summary of the proposals for union in D. H. Willson, *James VI and I* (1956), 249–57; also his essay in W. A. Aiken and B. D. Henning (eds), *Conflict in Stuart England* (1960), 41–55. See also T. K. Rabb, 'Sir Edwin Sandys and the Parliament of 1604', *Amer.Hist.Rev.* lxix (1964), 649–54.

23 See P. Croft, 'Free Trade and the House of Commons 1605–6', *Econ.Hist.Rev.* 2nd ser. xxviii (1975), 17–27. For two different interpretations of the aims of free traders in 1604, see T. K. Rabb, *Amer.Hist.Rev.* art. cit, 661–9, and 'Free Trade and the Gentry in the Parliament of 1604', *Past & Present* 40 (1968), 165–73; R. Ashton, 'The Parliamentary Agitation for Free Trade in the Opening Years of the Reign of James I', ibid. 38 (1967), 40–55, and 'Jacobean Free Trade Again', ibid. 43 (1969), 151–7; also R. Ashton, *The City and the Court 1603–1643* (Cambridge 1979), 84–98.

24 M. H. Curtis, 'The Hampton Court Conference and its Aftermath', *History* xlvi (1961), 1–16. There is also an excellent treatment of Puritanism at the beginning of the reign in P. Collinson, *The Elizabethan Puritan Movement*, 448–67.

25 On Hutton, see P. Lake, 'Matthew Hutton – A Puritan Bishop', *History* lxiv (1979), 182–204. On Bancroft see S. B. Babbage, *Puritanism and Richard Bancroft* (1962).

26 On the training of common lawyers, see W. R. Prest, *The Inns of Court under Elizabeth I and the Early Stuarts, 1590–1640* (1972). On the civil lawyers, see B. P. Levack, *The Civil Lawyers in England 1603–1641* (Oxford 1973).

27 On the Catholics see J. Bossy, 'The English Catholic Community 1603–1625', in A. G. R. Smith (ed.), *The Reign of James VI and I* (1973), 91–105.

28 On this see Carol Z. Wiener, 'The Beleaguered Isle. A Study of Elizabethan and early Jacobean Anti-Catholicism', *Past & Present* 51 (1971), 27–62.

CHAPTER SEVEN

1 See Linda Levy Peck, 'Problems in Jacobean Administration: was Henry Howard, Earl of Northampton, a Reformer?', *HJ* xix (1976), 831–58 and *Northampton: Patronage and Policy at the Court of James I* (1982).

2 On the parliament, see T. L. Moir, *The Addled Parliament of 1614* (Oxford 1958).

3 For examples, see M. Prestwich, *Cranfield, Politics and Profits under the Early Stuarts* (Oxford 1966), 139–47.

4 For details see A. F. Upton, *Sir Arthur Ingram, c. 1565–1642* (1961), 107–47.

5 This is the interpretation of B. E. Supple, *Commercial Crisis and Change in England 1600–1642* (Cambridge 1959), 33–51, which, I believe, best fits the facts. For the view that the project was designed to prevent the re-export by the Dutch of English cloth finished in the Netherlands, see A. Friis, *Alderman Cockayne's Project and the Cloth Trade* (1927), 224–381.

6 Abbot's account is printed in R. Ashton (ed.), *James I by His Contemporaries* (1969), 126–9.

7 On Ingram's role, see Upton, *Ingram*, 72–8.

8 For detailed accounts of the reforms of these years, see R. H. Tawney, *Business and Politics*, 152–83; M. Prestwich, *Cranfield*, 199–252, 259–85; F. C. Dietz, *English Public Finance 1558–1641*, 171–85.

9 It is curious that neither Tawney nor Prestwich gives much information about Mandeville as lord treasurer, on which

subject see the rather brief and inconclusive account in Dietz, *English Public Finance*, 182–5.

10 On all the parliaments of the 1620s, see C. Russell, *Parliaments and English Politics, 1621–1629* (Oxford 1979).

11 On the depression see B. E. Supple, *Commercial Crisis and Change*, 52–98; J. D. Gould, 'The Trade Depression of the Early 1620s', *Econ.Hist.Rev.* 2nd ser. vii (1954), 81–8.

12 For a full summary of grievances, see Tawney, *Business and Politics*, 184–5.

13 For full details, see Ashton, *The City and the Court*, 106–9.

14 On parliamentary procedure against monopolists, see the paper by E. R. Foster in W. A. Aiken and B. D. Henning (eds), *Conflict in Stuart England* (1960), 57–85.

15 C. Russell, *Parliaments and English Politics*, 103–4. For a rather different view of the revival of impeachment, see C. Roberts, *The Growth of Responsible Government in Stuart England* (Cambridge 1966), 22–35.

16 On foreign affairs in this and the next parliament see the paper by S. L. Adams in K. Sharpe (ed.), *Faction and Parliament* (Oxford 1978), 139–71.

17 See R. Zaller, *The Parliament of 1621* (Berkeley 1971), 151–3; R. Lockyer, *Buckingham* (1981), 108–11.

18 For detailed accounts of Middlesex's policies, see Tawney, *Business and Politics*, 194–238; Prestwich, *Cranfield*, 330–74.

19 See the paper by K. Sharpe in Sharpe (ed.), *Faction and Parliament*, 209–44; also R. Lockyer, *Buckingham*, 173–80.

20 On Preston see I. Morgan, *Prince Charles's Puritan Chaplain* (1957); C. Hill, *Puritanism and Revolution* (1958), 239–74.

21 On the impeachment, see Tawney, *Business and Politics*, 231–74; Prestwich, *Cranfield*, 423–68; R. E. Ruigh, *The Parliament of 1624* (Cambridge, Mass. 1971), 303–44.

22 For details see Ashton, *The City and the Court*, 109–20.

23 Dr C. Thompson, on the other hand, argues that 'to enforce the penal laws against recusants would cost nothing'. See 'The Origins of the Politics of the Parliamentary Middle Group, 1625–1629', *TRHS* 5th ser. xxii (1972), 78.

24 On the Arminians, see the essay by N. Tyacke in C. Russell (ed.), *The Origins of the English Civil War* (1975 edn), 119–43.

25 The charges and Buckingham's reply are printed in S. R. Gardiner (ed.), *The Constitutional Documents of the Puritan Revolution 1625–1660* (Oxford 1962 edn), 7–44.

26 See the paper by J. N. Ball in K. Sharpe (ed.), *Faction and Parliament,* esp. 186–7; also J. S. Flemion, 'The Dissolution of Parliament in 1626; a Revaluation', *Eng.Hist.Rev.* lxxxvii (1972), 784–90.

27 On the financing of war and borrowing, see Dietz, *English Public Finance,* 214–47; Ashton, *The Crown and the Money Market,* passim.

28 For details see Ashton, *The English Civil War,* 45–7; M. W. Beresford, 'The Common Informer, the Penal Statutes and Economic Regulation', *Econ.Hist.Rev.* 2nd ser. x (1957), esp. 233–4.

29 For details see Ashton, *The English Civil War,* 49–61; L. Boynton, *The Elizabethan Militia 1558–1638* (1967), 209–91; and the paper by A. Hassell Smith in P. Clark, A. G. R. Smith and N. Tyacke (eds), *The English Commonwealth* (Leicester 1979), 93–110.

30 On this see H. Hulme, *The Life of Sir John Eliot 1592 to 1632* (1957), 184–5; the paper by J. N. Ball in K. Sharpe (ed.), *Faction and Parliament,* 194; K. Sharpe, *Sir Robert Cotton 1586–1631* (Oxford 1979), 183.

31 On this, consult J. G. A. Pocock, *The Ancient Constitution and the Feudal Law* (Cambridge 1957), esp. 30–69. See also my paper in J. G. A. Pocock (ed.), *Three British Revolutions, 1641, 1688, 1776* (Princeton 1980), 208–23.

32 The Petition of Right is printed in Gardiner (ed.), *Constitutional Documents of the Puritan Revolution,* 66–70.

33 For details see C. Russell, *Parliaments and English Politics,* 394–5.

34 On the importance of the divided leadership in the Commons, see the paper by C. Thompson in K. Sharpe (ed.), *Faction and Parliament,* 245–84.

35 For full details see Ashton, *The City and the Court,* 121–36.

36 The Protestation and royal declaration are printed in Gardiner (ed.), *Constitutional Documents of the Puritan Revolution,* 82–99.

CHAPTER EIGHT

1 'An Ode upon occasion of His Majesty's Proclamation in the year 1630 Commanding the Gentry to reside upon their estates in the Country'.

2 For biographies of these two important figures, see M. van C. Alexander, *Charles I's Lord Treasurer* (1975) and M. J. Havran, *Caroline Courtier: The Life of Lord Cottington* (1973). On Laud, see H. R. Trevor-Roper, *Archbishop Laud 1573–1645* (2nd edn 1963).

3 See R. M. Smuts, 'The Puritan Followers of Henrietta Maria in the 1630s', *Eng.Hist.Rev.* xciii (1978), 26–45.

4 See Ashton, *The Crown and the Money Market*, 41–4. On the finances of personal rule, see Dietz, *English Public Finance 1558–1641*, 257–88.

5 For full details see Ashton, *The Crown and the Money Market*, 96–104, 108–10, 173–5. On impositions, see Dietz, *English Public Finance*, 268–9, 375–6.

6 On the yield of Ship Money, see M. D. Gordon, 'The Collection of Ship Money in the Reign of Charles I', *TRHS* 3rd ser. iv (1910), 141–59.

7 See G. Hammersley, 'The Revival of the Forest Laws under Charles I', *History* xlv (1960), 85–102.

8 On Juxon's achievement, see Dietz, *English Public Finance*, 276–84. T. Mason of the University of Virginia is engaged on a study of Juxon.

9 For details see Ashton, *The Crown and the Money Market*, 97, 100–5, 109–10.

10 See G. Unwin, *Industrial Organization in the Sixteenth and Seventeenth Centuries* (1957 edn), esp. 126–69; Ashton, *The City and the Court 1603–1643*, 43–82.

11 See J. Thirsk (ed.), *The Agrarian History of England and Wales*, iv, *1500–1640* (Cambridge 1967), 213, 237–8; also the essay by M. W. Beresford in F. J. Fisher (ed.), *Essays in the Economic and Social History of Tudor and Stuart England* (Cambridge 1961), esp. 50–1.

12 See P. Slack, 'Books of Orders: the Making of English Social Policy, 1577–1631', *TRHS* 5th ser. xxx (1980), 1–22; B. W. Quintrell, 'The Making of Charles I's Book of Orders', *Eng.Hist.Rev.* xcv (1980), 553–72.

13 T. G. Barnes, *Somerset 1625–1640* (1961), 172–202; J. S. Morrill, *Cheshire 1630–1660* (1974), 26, 230–1; P. Clark, *English Provincial Society from the Reformation to the Revolution* (Hassocks 1977), 350–3; A. Fletcher, *A County Community in Peace and War. Sussex 1600–1660* (1975), 150–1, 154–5, 157–8, 224–5. As a general account Quintrell is to be preferred to L.

M. Hill's essay in C. Russell (ed.), *Origins of the English Civil War*, 77–83, which follows Barnes uncritically.

14 See H. F. Kearney, *Strafford in Ireland 1633–41* (Manchester 1959).

15 On this and other aspects of the material problems of the church, see C. Hill, *Economic Problems of the Church* (Oxford 1956).

16 See P. Seaver, *The Puritan Lectureships* (Stanford 1970); C. Hill, *Society and Puritanism in Pre-Revolutionary England* (1964), 79–123. Not all lecturers were Puritans, however.

17 See A. P. Newton, *The Colonizing Activity of the English Puritans* (New Haven 1914); J. H. Hexter, *The Reign of King Pym* (Cambridge, Mass., 1941), 77–89; also R. Brenner, 'The Civil War Politics of London's Merchant Community', *Past & Present* 58 (1973), esp. 65–70, 76–80.

18 For a brief account see R. Ashton, *The English Civil War: Conservatism and Revolution 1603–1649* (1978), 54–9. For more detail see L. Boynton, *The Elizabethan Militia 1558–1638* (1967), 244–97; Barnes, *Somerset 1625–1640*, 244–80.

19 On Wales, see P. Williams, *The Council in the Marches of Wales under Elizabeth I* (Cardiff 1958), and 'The Attack on the Council in the Marches, 1603–1642', *Trans.Hon.Soc.Cymmrodorion* (1961), 1–22. On the North see R. R. Reid, *The King's Council in the North* (1921), and F. W. Brooks, *The Council of the North* (1953).

20 For full details about London's disputes with the crown, see Ashton, *The City and the Court*, 136–76, 185–98. For a different view see V. L. Pearl, *London and the Outbreak of the Puritan Revolution* (1961), passim.

21 For a more detailed account see Ashton, *The English Civil War: Conservatism and Revolution*, 21–42; also the essay by P. W. Thomas in C. Russell (ed.), *Origins of the English Civil War*, 168–93; and G. Parry, *The Golden Age Restor'd: The Culture of the Stuart Court, 1603–1642* (Manchester 1981).

22 See M. Heinemann, *Puritanism and Theatre* (Cambridge 1980).

23 See A. Harbage, *Cavalier Drama* (New York 1964). For a recent emphasis on the importance of fashionable clientele for public as well as private playhouses, see A. J. Cook, *The Privileged Playgoers of Shakespeare's London, 1576–1642* (Princeton 1981).

24 See S. Orgel, *The Jonsonian Masque* (New York 1981).

25 For different emphases on this theme, see M. Weber, *The Protestant Ethic and the Spirit of Capitalism* (9th impression 1968); R. H. Tawney, *Religion and the Rise of Capitalism* (1944 edn); C. Hill, *Society and Puritanism in Pre-Revolutionary England* (1964).

26 H. R. Trevor-Roper, 'The Social Origins of the Great Rebellion', *History Today* v (1955), 376–82.

27 M. Walzer, *The Revolution of the Saints* (1966), esp. 187.

28 For detailed accounts of these events, see G. Donaldson, *Scotland, James v to James vii* (1965), esp. 295–329; D. Stevenson, *The Scottish Revolution 1637–1644* (Newton Abbot 1973), esp. 15–247. For a different sort of treatment, see D. Mathew, *Scotland under Charles i* (1955).

29 The Covenant is printed in Gardiner (ed.), *Constitutional Documents of the Puritan Revolution*, 124–34.

CHAPTER NINE

1 On members of the Long Parliament, see M. F. Keeler, *The Long Parliament 1640–1* (Philadelphia 1954), and D. Brunton and D. H. Pennington, *Members of the Long Parliament* (1954).

2 The best account of their efforts is B. H. G. Wormald, *Clarendon* (Cambridge 1964), esp. 1–113.

3 The Grand Remonstrance is printed in Gardiner (ed.), *Constitutional Documents of the Puritan Revolution*, 202–32.

4 For these two conflicting views see Pearl, *London and the Origins of the Puritan Revolution* (1961) and Ashton, *The City and the Court, 1603–1643* (Cambridge 1979).

5 The Nineteen Propositions are printed in Gardiner (ed.), *Constitutional Documents of the Puritan Revolution*, 249–54.

6 See the very important study by J. H. Hexter, *The Reign of King Pym* (Cambridge, Mass., 1941). On Marten, see the essay by C. M. Williams in D. Pennington and K. Thomas (eds), *Puritans and Revolutionaries* (Oxford 1978), 118–38. On Holles, P. Crawford, *Denzil Holles 1598–1680* (1979).

7 For details of such disturbances see B. Manning, *The English People and the English Revolution* (1978 edn), 181–215.

8 The parliamentary terms are printed in Gardiner (ed.), *Constitutional Documents of the Puritan Revolution*, 262–7.

9 On Scotland, see the references in note 28 to Chapter 8; also H.

R. Trevor-Roper, *Religion, the Reformation and Social Change* (1967), 392–444, and L. Kaplan, *Politics and Religion during the English Revolution* (New York 1976), and 'Steps to War: the Scots and Parliament, 1642–3', *JBS* ix (1970), 50–70.

10 The Solemn League and Covenant is printed in Gardiner (ed.), *Constitutional Documents of the Puritan Revolution*, 267–71.

11 See V. Pearl, 'Oliver St John and the "middle-group" in the Long Parliament, August 1643–May 1644', *Eng.Hist.Rev.* lxxxi (1966), 490–519, and 'The "Royal Independents" in the English Civil War', *TRHS* 5th ser. xviii (1968), 69–96. For different views, see J. R. MacCormack, *Revolutionary Politics in the Long Parliament* (Cambridge, Mass., 1973), 1–19; L. Glow, 'Political Affiliations in the House of Commons after Pym's Death', *BIHR* xxxviii (1965), 48–70.

12 The Self-Denying Ordinance is printed in Gardiner (ed.), *Constitutional Documents of the Puritan Revolution*, 287–8. For its significance in connection with the dispute between Cromwell and Manchester, see A. N. B. Cotton, 'Cromwell and the Self-Denying Ordinance', *History* lxii (1977), 211–31.

13 See C. H. Firth, *Cromwell's Army* (1962 edn); M. Kishlansky, *The Rise of the New Model Army* (Cambridge 1979).

14 See C. Holmes, *The Eastern Association in the English Civil War* (Cambridge 1974), 162–205.

15 See Kishlansky, op.cit., passim; also his 'The Emergency of Adversary Politics in the Long Parliament', *JMH* xlix (1977), 617–40.

16 On these developments, see especially W. Haller, *Liberty and Reformation in the Puritan Revolution* (1955 edn), esp. 100–42, 216–37; W. M. Lamont, *Godly Rule* (1969), esp. 106–31.

17 On this see the very different views of J. H. Hexter, *Reappraisals in History* (1963), 163–84; D. Underdown, *Pride's Purge* (Oxford 1971), 45–77, 'The Independents Reconsidered', *JBS* iii (1964) 57–84, 'The Independents Again', ibid. viii (1969), 83–93; G. Yule, *The Independents in the English Civil War* (Cambridge 1958), 35–41, 'Independents and Revolutionaries', *JBS* vii (1968), 11–32; S. Foster, 'The Presbyterian Independents Exorcised. A Ghost Story for Historians', *Past & Present* 44 (1969), 52–75, and the comments of a number of historians on this, in ibid. 47 (1970), 116–46.

18 The Newcastle Propositions and the king's replies are printed

in Gardiner (ed.), *Constitutional Documents of the Puritan Revolution*, 290–316.

19 See Underdown, 'Parliamentary Management in the Recruiter Elections 1645–1648', *Eng.Hist.Rev.* lxxxiii (1968), 235–64.

20 On the clubmen see J. S. Morrill, *The Revolt of the Provinces* (1976), 98–111, 196–200, and D. Underdown, 'The Chalk and the Cheese: Contrasts among the English Clubmen', *Past & Present* 85 (1979), 25–48.

21 On these agencies see Ashton, *The English Civil War*, 254– 87; Morrill, *The Revolt of the Provinces*, passim; and any of the notable county studies and more especially, A. Everitt, *The Community of Kent and the Great Rebellion 1640–1660* (Leicester 1966); *Suffolk and the Great Rebellion 1640–1660*, Suffolk Rec. Soc. iii (1961); A. Fletcher, *A County Community in Peace and War: Sussex 1600–1660* (1975); D. Underdown, *Somerset in the Civil War and Interregnum* (Newton Abbot 1973); J. S. Morrill, *Cheshire 1630–1660* (1974).

22 On the most successful regional association, see C. Holmes, *The Eastern Association in the English Civil War* (Cambridge 1974).

23 See J. S. Morrill, 'Mutiny and Discontent in English Provincial Armies 1645–1647', *Past & Present* 56 (1972), 49–74.

24 On this see M. Kishlansky, *The Rise of the New Model Army*, esp. 179–272, and 'The Army and the Levellers: the Road to Putney', *HJ* xxii (1979), 795–824.

25 The Heads of the Proposals are printed in Gardiner (ed.), *Constitutional Documents of the Puritan Revolution*, 316–26.

26 The Agreement is printed in Gardiner, ibid. 333–5. An edited version of the Putney debates is printed in A. S. P. Woodhouse (ed.), *Puritanism and Liberty* (1966 edn), 1–124.

27 For different views on the Levellers and the franchise, see C. B. Macpherson, *The Political Theory of Possessive Individualism* (1964 edn), 107–59; B. Manning, *The English People and the English Revolution* (1976), 308–13; K. Thomas's essay in G. E. Aylmer (ed.), *The Interregnum* (1972), 57–78; J. C. Davis, 'The Levellers and Democracy', *Past & Present* 40 (1968), 174–80; R. Howell, Jr, and D. E. Brewster, 'Reconsidering the Levellers: the Evidence of *The Moderate*', ibid. 46 (1970), 68–86; C. Thompson, 'Maximilian Petty and the Putney Debate on the Franchise', ibid. 88 (1980), 63–9.

28 The four bills, the king's reply, the Engagement and the Vote

of No Addresses are printed in Gardiner, *Constitutional Documents of the Puritan Revolution*, 335–56.

29 See D. Underdown, *Pride's Purge*, esp. 208–56.

CHAPTER TEN

1 On this subject see J. W. Stoye, *English Travellers Abroad 1604–1667* (1952). For an excellent brief summary of English contacts with the continent, see J. R. Jones, *Britain and Europe in the Seventeenth Century* (1966).

2 F. J. Fisher, 'London's Export Trade in the Early Seventeenth Century', *Econ.Hist.Rev.* 2nd ser. iii (1950), 151–61; D. C. Coleman, 'An Innovation and Its Diffusion: The "New Draperies"', ibid. 2nd ser. xxii (1969), 417–29. On the growing importance of the Mediterranean trade see the essay by Ralph Davis in F. J. Fisher (ed.), *Essays in the Economic and Social History of Tudor and Stuart England* (Cambridge 1961), 117–37. On the character and fluctuations of trade in general see B. E. Supple, *Commercial Crisis and Change in England 1600–1642* (Cambridge 1959).

3 For a useful summary of Jacobean transoceanic enterprise see the essay by Louis B. Wright in A. G. R. Smith (ed.), *The Reign of James VI and I* (1973), 123–39; also C. Bridenbaugh, *Vexed and Troubled Englishmen* 1590–1642 (Oxford 1968).

4 See T. W. Moody, *The Londonderry Plantation 1609–1641* (Belfast 1939); Ashton, *The City and the Court 1603–1643*, 158–60.

5 See Edmund S. Morgan, 'The Labor Problem at Jamestown 1607–18', *Amer.Hist.Rev.* lxxvi (1971), 595–611.

6 T. K. Rabb, *Enterprise and Empire: Merchant and Gentry Investment in the Expansion of England, 1575–1650* (Cambridge 1967).

7 W. F. Craven, *Dissolution of the Virginia Company: the Failure of a Colonial Experiment* (New York 1932), 41.

8 See T. W. Tate and D. L. Ammerman (eds), *The Chesapeake in the Seventeenth Century* (Chapel Hill 1980).

9 See the essay by R. C. Johnson in H. S. Reinmuth (ed.), *Early Stuart Studies* (Minneapolis 1970), 137–51.

10 On these developments see Maurice Lee Jr, *James I and Henry IV: An Essay in English Foreign Policy 1600–1610* (Urbana 1970).

11 Bridenbaugh, *Vexed and Troubled Englishmen*, 409–10, 424–5, 427, 432.

12 See T. H. Breen and S. Foster, 'Moving to the New World: The Character of Early Massachusetts Immigration', *William and Mary Quarterly* 3rd ser. xxx (1973), 189–222. See also A. Salerno, 'The Social Background of Seventeenth Century Emigration to America', *JBS* xix (1979), 31–52.

13 For an emphasis in the reverse direction which criticizes historians' neglect of 'the importance of the New World in restructuring and redefining Puritan ideas', see P. N. Carroll, *Puritanism and the Wilderness: the Intellectual Significance of the New England Frontier, 1629–1700* (New York 1969).

14 Edmund S. Morgan, 'The Labor Problem at Jamestown 1607–18', *Amer.Hist.Rev.* lxxvi (1971), 595–611.

15 See especially T. H. Breen, 'The Case of the Covenanted Militia in Seventeenth-Century Massachusetts', *Past & Present* 57 (1972), 74–96, and 'Persistent Localism: English Local Change and the Shaping of New England Institutions', *William and Mary Quarterly* 3rd ser. xxxii (1975), 3–28.

16 Edmund S. Morgan, *Visible Saints* (Ithaca 1965), 62. This is a brilliant and concise introduction to New England religious history. See also P. Miller, *Orthodoxy in Massachusetts* (Cambridge, Mass., 1933) and *The New England Mind in the Seventeenth Century* (New York 1939).

17 See T. H. Breen, 'Who Governs: The Town Franchise in Seventeenth-Century Massachusetts', *William and Mary Quarterly* 3rd ser. xxvii (1970), 460–74; S. E. Morison, *Builders of the Bay Colony* (Boston 1930), esp. 84–6; B. K. Brown, 'Freemanship in Puritan Massachusetts', *Amer.Hist. Rev.* lix (1954), 865–83; R. Simmons, 'Freemanship in Early Massachusetts: Some Suggestions and a Case Study', *William and Mary Quarterly* 3rd ser. xix (1962), 422–8, and 'Godliness, Property and the Franchise in Puritan Massachusetts: An Interpretation', *J.Amer.Hist.* lv (1968), 495–511; S. Foster, 'The Massachusetts Franchise in the Seventeenth Century', *William and Mary Quarterly* 3rd ser. xxiv (1967), 613–23.

18 D. Hirst, *The Representative of the People? Voters and Voting under the Early Stuarts* (Cambridge 1975); J. H. Plumb, 'The Growth of the Electorate in England from 1600 to 1715', *Past & Present* 45 (1969), 90–116.

CHAPTER ELEVEN

1 B. Worden, *The Rump Parliament* (Cambridge 1974), 40.

2 On the composition and powers of the successive Councils of State, see Worden, *The Rump Parliament*, 177–82, 280–2, 313–14.

3 On the oath and the different categories of persons to whom it was extended, see S. R. Gardiner, *History of the Commonwealth and Protectorate, 1649–1660*, i (1894), 5–8, 196–7, 215–16.

4 On the Engagement controversy see J. Wallace, *Destiny His Choice: the Loyalism of Andrew Marvell* (Cambridge 1968), 43–68; M. Nedham, *The Case of the Commonwealth of England Stated* (1650), ed. P. A. Knachel (Charlottesville 1969), Introduction and passim; and the essay by Q. Skinner in Aylmer (ed.), *The Interregnum: the Quest for Settlement 1646–1660* (1972), 79–98. On Milton see D. M. Wolfe, *Milton in the Puritan Revolution* (New York 1963), and C. Hill, *Milton and the English Revolution* (1979 edn).

5 On this see Worden, *The Rump Parliament*, 93–102; G. E. Aylmer, *The State's Servants* (1973), esp. 125–67.

6 For a lively and detailed account of Leveller agitation, see H. N. Brailsford, *The Levellers and the English Revolution* (1961 edn), esp. 474–522. Lilburne's and Overton's pamphlets are printed in (respectively), W. Haller and G. Davies (eds), *The Leveller Tracts 1647–1653* (Gloucester, Mass., 1964), 156–89; and D. Wolfe (ed.), *Leveller Manifestoes of the Puritan Revolution* (1967), 355–83.

7 The best general account of such groups is C. Hill, *The World Turned Upside Down* (1972). On particular sects see e.g. B. S. Capp, *The Fifth Monarchy Men* (1972) and A. L. Morton, *The World of the Ranters* (1979 edn).

8 See the essay by K. Thomas in D. Pennington and K. Thomas (eds) *Puritans and Revolutionaries* (1978), 257–82.

9 On legal reform see D. Veall, *The Popular Movement for Law Reform 1640–1660* (Oxford 1970), 78–85, 97–126; Worden, *The Rump Parliament*, 105–118, 202–6, 271–3; M. Cotterell, 'Interregnum Law Reform: the Hale Commission of 1652', *Eng.Hist.Rev.* lxxxiii (1968), 689–704.

10 For this view see M. James, *Social Problems and Policy during the Puritan Revolution* (1966 edn).

11 On London, see V. Pearl's essay in D. Pennington and K. Thomas, *Puritans and Revolutionaries*, 206–32. On Warwickshire, see A. L. Beier, 'Poor Relief in Warwickshire 1630–1660', *Past & Present* 35 (1966), 77–100.

12 For full details, see Worden, *The Rump Parliament*, 139–60.

13 See R. Brenner, 'The Civil War Politics of London's Merchant Community', *Past & Present* 58 (1973), esp. 91–107; J. E. Farnell, 'The Navigation Act of 1651, the First Dutch War and the London Merchant Community', *Econ.Hist.Rev.* 2nd ser. xvi (1964), 439–54, and 'The Usurpation of Honest London Householders: Barebone's Parliament', *Eng.Hist.Rev.* lxxii (1967), esp. 24–41. For a critical view of these theses and a useful summary of economic policy in general, see the essay by J. P. Cooper in G. E. Aylmer (ed.), *The Interregnum: the Quest for Settlement*, 121–42.

14 For a good brief account of Anglo-Dutch rivalry see J. R. Jones, *Britain and the World 1649–1815* (1980), 60–70. For a longer account, see C. H. Wilson, *Profit and Power* (1957).

15 On Cromwell's relations with all his parliaments see H. R. Trevor-Roper, *Religion, the Reformation and Social Change*, 345–91. On the mounting agitation for reform, see Worden, *The Rump Parliament*, 265–384.

16 See A. H. Woolrych, 'The Calling of Barebone's Parliament', *Eng.Hist.Rev.* lxxx (1965), 492–513. On the parliament in general see his essay in R. H. Parry (ed.), *The English Civil War and After, 1642–1658* (1970), 59–77; H. R. Trevor-Roper, *Religion, the Reformation and Social Change*, 362–7: I. Roots, *The Great Rebellion* (1966), 163–9. For a not altogether convincing criticism of Woolrych's argument see Tai Liu, 'The Calling of the Barebone's Parliament Reconsidered', *J. Eccles. Hist.* xxii (1971), 223–36. The consummation of Woolrych's work on Barebone's Parliament, *Commonwealth to Protectorate* (Oxford 1982), appeared too late to be used in this book.

17 On the Fifth Monarchists in Barebone's Parliament, see B. Capp, *The Fifth Monarchy Men* (1972), 62–75. On the Baptists, see J. E. Farnell, 'The Usurpation of Honest London Householders: Barebone's Parliament', *Eng.Hist.Rev.* lxxxii (1967), 24–46.

18 The Instrument of Government is printed in Gardiner (ed.), *Constitutional Documents of the Puritan Revolution*, 405–17. On the Heads of the Proposals, see above, p. 334.

19 On the complexities of the old franchise, see D. Hirst, *The Representative of the People?* (Cambridge 1975).

20 H. R. Trevor-Roper, *Religion, the Reformation and Social Change*, 371–5.

21 See the essay by D. Underdown in Aylmer (ed.), *The Interregnum: the Quest for Settlement*, 165–82.

22 See the essay by C. Cross in Aylmer (ed), *The Interregnum: the Quest for Settlement*, 110–15.

23 See D. S. Katz, *Philo-Semitism and the Readmission of the Jews to England 1603–1655* (Oxford 1982).

24 See his essay in Aylmer (ed.), *The Interregnum: the Quest for Settlement*, 143–64.

25 It is a useful exercise to compare the main points of difference between these proposals (printed in Gardiner (ed.), *Constitutional Documents of the Puritan Revolution*, 427–47) and the Instrument of Government (ibid., 405–17).

26 See A. H. Woolrych, *Penruddock's Rising* (Hist. Ass. pamphlet 1955). On royalist conspiracy in general, see D. Underdown, *Royalist Conspiracy in England 1649–1660* (New Haven 1960).

27 On the major-generals, see I. Roots's essay in R. H. Parry (ed.), *The English Civil War and After, 1642–1658* (1970), 78–92; also the essay by A. Fletcher in D. Baker (ed.), *Religious Motivation: Biographical and Sociological Problems of the Church Historian (Studies in Church History* xv (1978), 259–66).

28 See D. Underdown's essay in G. E. Aylmer (ed.), *The Interregnum: the Quest for Settlement*, esp. 176–82.

29 This, together with the Additional Petition and Advice, is printed in Gardiner (ed.), *Constitutional Documents of the Puritan Revolution*, 447–64.

30 On the whole period between the new constitution and the Restoration, see Woolrych's essay in Aylmer (ed.), *The Interregnum: the Quest for Settlement*, 183–204.

31 See M. P. Ashley, *Financial and Commercial Policy under the Cromwellian Protectorate* (1962 edn), esp. 111–13; R. W. K. Hinton, *The Eastland Trade and the Common Weal in the Seventeenth Century* (Cambridge 1959), 122–37.

32 G. D. Ramsay, 'Industrial *Laisser-faire* and the Policy of Cromwell', *Econ.Hist.Rev.* xvi (1946), 93–110.

33 M. Roberts, 'Cromwell and the Baltic', *Eng.Hist.Rev.* lxxii (1961), 402–46. For a far less favourable view of foreign policy

in general, see M. Prestwich, 'Diplomacy and Trade in the Protectorate', *JMH* xxii (1950), 103–21.

34 C. P. Korr, *Cromwell and the New Model Foreign Policy* (Berkeley 1975), 199.

35 For more detailed treatment of these events, see I. Roots, *The Great Rebellion*, 232–41; J. R. Jones, *Country and Court: England 1658–1714* (1978) 113–20; and (more detailed) G. Davies, *The Restoration of Charles II 1658–1660* (1969 edn), 3–100, and A. H. Woolrych, 'The Good Old Cause and the Fall of the Protectorate', *Camb.Hist.J.* xiii (1957), 133–61.

36 See his essay on them in D. Pennington and K. Thomas (eds), *Puritans and Revolutionaries*, 283–309.

37 On the composition and power of the Council of State, see G. Davies, *The Restoration of Charles II, 1658–1660*, 101–3.

38 D. Underdown, *Somerset in the Civil War and Interregnum* (Newton Abbot 1973), 189–90.

39 For a summary of such schemes, see A. H. Woolrych's essay in Aylmer (ed.) *The Interregnum: the Quest for Settlement*, esp. 196–9.

40 On Booth's rising, see D. Underdown, *Royalist Conspiracy in England, 1648–60* (New Haven 1960), 254–86; J. S. Morrill, *Cheshire 1630–1660* (1974), 300–28; J. R. Jones, 'Booth's Rising of 1659', *Bull. of the John Rylands Library* xxxix (1957), 416–43.

41 The Declaration is printed in Gardiner (ed.), *Constitutional Documents of the Puritan Revolution*, 465–7.

42 H. R. Trevor-Roper, 'The Social Origins of the Great Rebellion', *History Today* v (1955), 382.

43 For more detailed criticism along these lines, see R. Ashton, *The English Civil War: Conservatism and Revolution 1603–1649* (1978), 72–97; and Ashton's essay in R. H. Parry (ed.), *The English Civil War and After, 1642–1658* (1970), 93–110.

44 J. Thirsk, 'The Sale of Royalist Land during the Interregnum', *Econ.Hist.Rev.* 2nd ser. v (1952), 188–207, and 'The Restoration Land Settlement', *JMH* xxvi (1954), 315–28; H. J. Habakkuk, 'Landowners and the Civil War', *Econ.Hist.Rev.* 2nd ser. xviii (1965), 130–51.

45 See the essay by C. Hill in J. G. A. Pocock (ed.), *Three British Revolutions, 1641, 1688, 1776* (Princeton 1980), 109–39.

46 See his essay in J. R. Jones (ed.), *The Restored Monarchy 1660–1688* (1979), 155–75.

INDEX

INDEX

INDEX

History in Paladin Books

A five-part Paladin archaeological history series:
Britain before the Conquest c.1500 BC-AD 1066

The Origins of Britain £2.50 ☐
Lloyd and Jennifer Laing
This first volume follows the path of man's occupation of Britain from the scattered pockets of habitation in the earliest Palaeolithic period through to his growing domination of the landscape and his capacity to mould his environment, evident in the late Bronze Age. Illustrated.

Celtic Britain £2.95 ☐
Lloyd Laing
Dr Laing traces the history of the Celts and Celtic culture from the arrival of the first groups of settlers in Britain in the seventh century BC to the development of the kingdoms of medieval Scotland and Wales. Illustrated.

The Coming of Rome £2.50 ☐
John Wacher
The Roman conquest of Britain and the progressive extension of Roman control marked a dramatic transformation of British society. Mr Wacher here looks at the basic features of Roman Britain, the cities and towns, the monuments of an urban culture, and considers the evidence mainly from inscriptions of British society during the first two centuries of Roman rule. Illustrated.

Later Roman Britain £2.50 ☐
Stephen Johnson
Charting the end of Roman rule in Britain, ***Later Roman Britain*** gives an overall impression of the beginning of the so-called 'Dark Ages' of British history, the transitional period which saw the breakdown of Roman administration and the beginnings of Saxon settlement. Illustrated.

Anglo-Saxon England £2.50 ☐
Lloyd and Jennifer Laing
The period from the 5th Century AD to AD 1066 is perhaps the most enigmatic in British history. In these turbulent centuries the post-Roman, native British and Continental influences amalgamated in a manner which is often difficult to unravel. The authors show how the Anglo-Saxons built up a flourishing civilization which has greatly influenced the English-speaking people of the New World. Illustrated.

To order direct from the publisher just tick the titles you want and fill in the order form.

PAL7282

History in Paladin Books

Africa in History £2.95 ☐
Basil Davidson
Revised edition of 'one of the most durable and most literate guides to contemporary knowledge of Africa' ***Tribune***

A Higher Form of Killing £2.50 ☐
Robert Harris and Jeremy Paxman
The escalating nuclear capabilities of the superpowers have been extensively publicized. Less well documented has been the revival of interest in chemical and biological weaponry. Drawing extensively on international sources, this book chronicles for the first time the secret history of chemical and germ warfare. Illustrated.

Decisive Battles of the Western World (Vols 1 & 2) £3.95 ☐ each
J F C Fuller
The most original and influential military thinker Britain has ever produced: his major work.

The Paladin History of England – the first three titles of the series are

The Formation of England £2.95 ☐
H P R Finberg
This volume deals with Britain in the Dark Ages between Roman and Norman conquests.

The Crisis of Imperialism £3.95 ☐
Richard Shannon
England in the realm of Victoria. A time of development, expansion, colonisation, enormous social upheavals and reform.

Peace, Print and Protestantism £3.95 ☐
C S L Davies
C S L Davies' book deals with the period 1450–1558 encompassing the reign of the Tudors and the breakaway from the Church of Rome.